Volksgeist as
Method and Ethic

HISTORY OF ANTHROPOLOGY

Volume 1
Observers Observed
Essays on Ethnographic Fieldwork

Volume 2
Functionalism Historicized
Essays on British Social Anthropology

Volume 3
Objects and Others
Essays on Museums and Material Culture

Volume 4
Malinowski, Rivers, Benedict and Others
Essays on Culture and Personality

Volume 5
Bones, Bodies, Behavior
Essays on Biological Anthropology

Volume 6
Romantic Motives
Essays on Anthropological Sensibility

Volume 7
Colonial Situations
Essays on the Contextualization of Ethnographic Knowledge

Volksgeist as Method and Ethic

ESSAYS ON BOASIAN ETHNOGRAPHY AND THE GERMAN ANTHROPOLOGICAL TRADITION

Edited by

George W. Stocking, Jr.

HISTORY OF ANTHROPOLOGY
Volume 8

THE UNIVERSITY OF WISCONSIN PRESS

The University of Wisconsin Press
2537 Daniels Street
Madison, Wisconsin 53718

3 Henrietta Street
London WC2E 8LU, England

2   4   6   8   10   9   7   5   3

Printed in the United States of America

Library of Congress Cataloging-in-Publication Data
Volksgeist as method and ethic: essays on Boasian ethnography and the
German anthropological tradition / edited by George W. Stocking, Jr.
          358 pp.   cm. — (History of anthropology ; v. 8)
          Includes bibliographical references and index.
          ISBN 0-299-14550-6 (cloth: alk. paper)
          ISBN 0-299-14554-9 (pbk.: alk. paper)
1. Anthropology—Germany—History.   2. Anthropology—Germany—
Philosophy.   3. Boas, Franz, 1858–1942.   4. Anthropology—United
   States—History.   5. Anthropology—United States—Philosophy.
          I. Stocking, George W., 1928–   . II. Series.
                    GN17.V65   1996
                    301—dc20   95-25272

HISTORY OF ANTHROPOLOGY

INFORMATION FOR CONTRIBUTORS

This, the eighth volume in the *History of Anthropology* series, is the last of which George Stocking will be the primary editor. Beginning with Volume 10, that role will be taken on by Richard Handler, Professor of Anthropology at the University of Virginia, and author of several articles in previous volumes in the series. Volume 9, to be jointly edited by Handler and Stocking, will be devoted to a reassessment of the historiography of anthropology as it has developed over the last quarter century, and to a consideration of the role that *History of Anthropology* may appropriately play as anthropology enters the next millennium. In addition to more general historiographical reflections, we hope to include essays on specific historical cases or problems, drawn from the work-in-progress of a range of authors (historians, anthropologists, and others, representing different historiographical or historical-critical perspectives), as exemplars or case studies of alternative approaches to the history of anthropology. Authors who wish to have their work considered for this or subsequent volumes should communicate with

> *Richard Handler (HOA)*
> *Department of Anthropology*
> *Cabell Hall*
> *University of Virginia*
> *Charlottesville, Virginia, 22903 U.S.A.*

All communications relating to standing orders, orders for specific volumes, missing volumes, changes of address, or any other business matters should be addressed to:

> *Customer Service*
> *The University of Wisconsin Press*
> *114 North Murray Street*
> *Madison, Wisconsin 53715*

Contents

Volksgeist as Method and Ethic

BOASIAN ETHNOGRAPHY AND THE GERMAN ANTHROPOLOGICAL TRADITION

This volume of *HOA* has been long in realization. It began with a title, recollected from a colleague's anecdote about a student who had misunderstood a lecturer's reference to the *fin-de-siècle*. Fantasy Echo seemed a title waiting for a volume, and what volume better than one on the emergent modern anthropology of the 1890s, preresonant, perhaps, of issues facing the postmodern anthropology of the 1990s? Unfortunately, however, suitable material did not come to hand in sufficient quantity, and we tried extending the time span to the First World War—thereby rendering unapt that charmingly suggestive student mishearing. As it happened, the "turn-of-the-century" theme proved also problematic, and it was only with the appearance of several essays on Franz Boas and Boasian ethnography that a somewhat more effective thematic focus began to emerge. On the one hand there were essays on German physical anthropology and archeology in the turn-of-the-century decades; on the other, several on the practice of Boasian ethnography in the same period. In between, mediating, if not unifying, were essays on the German *Volksgeist* tradition and Franz Boas' own early enculturative experience. Acknowledging the lacunae inherent in such a circumstantially constituted thematic structure, we offer now a volume entitled *Volksgeist as Method and Ethic: Essays on Boasian Ethnography and the German Anthropological Tradition*. Published in the centennial year of Franz Boas' appointment to the faculty at Columbia University—the establishing moment of Boasian anthropology as the dominant tendency in the United States—the volume may nevertheless have a certain retrospective unity, and perhaps even occasional prospective resonance to the issues facing the discipline at the turn of the millennium.

When Franz Boas died in 1942, his obituarist Ruth Benedict—less conflicted, perhaps by oedipal angst than potential inheritors of his patriarchal role—saw him not simply as father of American anthropology, but as a kind of culture-hero forming it out of a preanthropological muck: "[H]e found an-

3

thropology a collection of wild guesses and a happy hunting ground for the romantic lover of primitive things; he left it a discipline in which theories could be tested and in which he had delimited possibilities from impossibilities" (Benedict 1943:61). By the 1950s, however, a reaction had set in: Boas' contribution to the culture concept was minimized (Kroeber & Kluckhohn 1952); his ethnography was attacked as atheoretical "particularism" (Wax 1956; White 1963); and among some writers there was a reassertion of the evolutionary approaches he and his early students had systematically critiqued (White 1963; Harris 1968). Along with critique came historiographical revisionism. Far from being a formless slime, there was a well-established pre-Boasian American anthropological tradition, both ethnographic and theoretical, in at least one member of which (Frank Hamilton Cushing) one could find a pluralistic, holistic "anthropological" notion of culture—based more on ethnographic experience than intellectual inheritance (Mark 1980). Against this it might be argued that Cushing's marginality to the evolving institutional framework forestalled any influence his cultural thought, however premonitory, might have had on later American cultural anthropology. Even so, it is nevertheless the case that, prior to Boas, there was a more deeply rooted Americanist tradition, the appreciation of which was repressed by the Boasian triumph, and the resonances of which may be found not only in the neo-evolutionism of Leslie White, Marvin Harris, and others, but in certain more pervasive features of American anthropology—notably the focus on cultural psychology and linguistic differentiation—which were also characteristic of Boasian anthropology itself (Hinsley 1981; Bieder 1986).

That said, one must still insist on the formative (or perhaps better, reformative) role of Franz Boas, both intellectually and institutionally. Although he did not develop a systematic theory of culture, his critique of nineteenth-century racial and cultural evolutionary assumptions, both in anthropology and popular thought, not only cleared the way for the emergence of a more "anthropological" (i.e., pluralistic, holistic, non-hierarchical, relativistic, behaviorally determinist) concept of culture, but in the process established some of its essential presuppositions (cf. Stocking 1968, 1974). And although he did not "invent" the modern ethnographic tradition (and in fact pursued a somewhat different ethnographic agenda), it was primarily among students to whom he gave a postgraduate academic training, and who in turn gave similar training to others, that an academically based professional ethnographic tradition emerged in the United States (cf. Stocking 1976). For Boas, the intellectual and the institutional were intimately (and consciously) connected, insofar as intellectual influence depended on institutional power; and in both respects, his underlying orientations were established in the three decades before he emigrated from Germany.

In 1940, when Boas selected for republication the papers he felt best illustrated the various aspects of his anthropological work over the half century of his anthropological career, the volume's last piece was an essay originally published in 1887, shortly after he had settled in New York as geography editor for the journal *Science*. Offered as an indication of "the general attitude underlying my later work" (1940:v), "The Study of Geography" defined two fundamentally different epistemological and methodological approaches to the understanding of the natural and human worlds: that of the physicist and that of the cosmographer (which Boas also called the "historical"). Although he did not pose the matter in these terms, this opposition clearly reflected the distinction, characteristic of the German intellectual tradition, between the *Natur-* and the *Geisteswissenschaften*. In this spirit, Boas set up a series of oppositions: between the "aesthetic" and the "affective" as motivating impulses; between phenomena with an "objective" unity and phenomena with a "subjective" unity; between the "deduction of laws" and the "thorough understanding" of phenomena "for their own sake"; between the resolution of a phenomenon "into its elements" for systematic comparative study and the study of the "whole phenomenon" by a more subjective method which Boas at one point described erotically as a loving penetration (as opposed to a "systematical arrangement"). Although his own career may be interpreted in terms of a never fully resolved tension between the physical and the cosmographical approaches (Stocking 1968), it is clear that in 1887, he was intent on justifying the latter against the former. And it was the cosmographic impulse that motivated both his critique of evolutionary racialism and his emerging conception of culture—insofar as any given human culture, like the geography of a single country, was a totality which had a "merely subjective connection" existing "in the mind of the observer" (or, by extension, in the mind of the self-conscious native enactor). Because a number of the essays in the present volume refer explicitly to or reflect indirectly the argument and the assumptions of "The Study of Geography," we have included it here as a general textual reference point.

From this point of view, the next two chapters in this volume may be seen as exemplifying the cosmographic and physicalist tendencies within the German anthropological tradition, as those tendencies were available to Boas in his formal education and informal enculturation. While the rootedness of Boas' conception of culture in the German intellectual tradition has been insisted on before (e.g., Stocking 1968, 1974, 1992), Bunzl's "Franz Boas and the Humboldtian Tradition: From *Volksgeist* and *Nationalcharakter* to an Anthropological Concept of Culture" represents the first systematic attempt to explore these intellectual connections, along two lines going back to the brothers Wilhelm and Alexander von Humboldt, and beyond them to Herder. Although Boas himself (and his student Robert Lowie, who more than some others maintained a close connection to the German tradition) on various occasions noted Boas' debt, what is most striking here is the frequent close parallelism of argument, extending even to similarities of phrasing, in some cases to sources not yet directly available to Boas. Emphasizing the cosmographical tendency in Boas' thought, Bunzl interprets the more physicalistic aspects of his early anthropology as an intellectual accommodation to his institutional situation, in which he was dependent on evolutionary anthropologists for the support of his ethnographic research.

In contrast to Bunzl's emphasis on the cosmographical cultural tradition, Benoit Massin's "From Virchow to Fischer" focuses on the physicalistic and biologistic tendency in German anthropological thought, and on the growing power of the racial determinism which, like the anthropological idea of culture, can be seen as linked to the Herderian *Volksgeist* tradition. While Boas figures only incidentally in his account, Massin does provide an essential background for understanding Boas' critique of race, which was heavily influenced by Rudolf Virchow, the dominant figure in German physical anthropology throughout the last four decades of the nineteenth century. It is worth noting also that, especially in relation to his work on the plasticity of human headform, Boas continued to be a participant in discussions in German physical anthropology up to the beginning of World War I. More important, however, Massin offers a new and more complex perspective on the development of racism within the German anthropological tradition. Rather than following a straight line from Gobineau's Aryanism to Hitler's Nazism, physical anthropology in Germany was long dominated by what were at the time relatively anti-racist Lamarckian tendencies, and only succumbed to a harsher racial determinism after Virchow's death in 1902. Before then, it could (and did) help to form the anti-racist anthropology of Franz Boas.

With the cosmographical/cultural and physicalist/biological background thus in mind, we turn to "German Culture and German Science in the *Bildung* of Franz Boas," by Julia Liss. Drawing on family and personal papers from Boas' adolescence and early manhood, Liss shows how the intellectual and cultural influences which formed his mature anthropological viewpoint were manifest in his family relationships, his education in the *Gymnasium* and university, his entrance into German science, and his affiliation with the New York German liberal emigré community after his arrival in this country.

The next three essays shift the focus from the German anthropological tradition to the development of a particular aspect of Boasian anthropology in the United States: the ethnographic representation of indigenous American groups. Here, the focus is on certain problematic aspects of the *Volksgeist* tradition, conceived as the study of culture in a cosmographical rather than a physicalist manner, by constituting, for each cultural group, a permanent archive of cultural materials which, free of the contamination of European categories, would be true representations of "the native point of view."

In "The Ethnographic Object and the Object of Ethnology," Ira Jacknis traces a shift in Boas' ethnographic goals, paralleling Bunzl's suggestion of an early accommodation to the dominant natural scientific physicalism of late nineteenth-century anthropology, followed by a reassertion of a more humanistic cosmographical approach. Despite Boas' insistence on cultural meaning as opposed to adaptive function in his 1887 critique of evolutionary museum arrangement, his early ethnographic collecting was very much in the dominant objectivist mode, and it was only with the establishment of a less dependent institutional position that his more meaning-oriented contextual (and textual) mode of ethnography came to the fore.

Much of that ethnographic work was carried on through the intermediation of George Hunt, the son of an English trader and a Tlingit woman who, having been reared among the Kwakiutl, was employed by Boas to collect texts that would represent "The Culture as It Appears to the Indian Himself." In analyzing the actual constitution of these texts as reflected in Hunt's marginal cultural situation, Boas' instructions, the circumstances of their recording, the original manuscripts produced, and the compromises of meaning introduced by their translation from Kwak'wala to English and re-presentation in published form, Judith Berman illuminates some of the paradoxes inherent in the attempt to capture "the native point of view."

Thomas Buckley's "Little History of Pitiful Events" shifts the focus from the methodological to the moral implications of *Volksgeist* ethnography. Examining the early ethnographic work of Alfred Kroeber, first and foremost of "the Boasians," Buckley focuses attention on the devastation of Native American cultures which was the unacknowledged context of Kroeber's attempt to reconstitute ethnographically the variety of pre-contact *Volksgeister* of Californian Indians. Like Jacknis and Berman, however, he ends with an acknowledgment of the value of the Boasian archival project. However problematic the methodological and moral circumstances of its implementation, it did in fact produce a rich body of materials which have been not only the basis for continuing anthropological cultural interpretation, but also a resource for Native American cultural renewal.

The final paper in the volume returns to the German tradition with which the volume began. Although the focus is historic archeology in the European tradition, a field beyond the margins of Boasian anthropology, Suzanne Marchand's "Orientalism as *Kulturpolitik*" complements several of the essays in the volume. Resonant of many of the cultural influences of Boas' *Bildung*, it augments Massin's representation of the institutional, ideological, and political context of German anthropology in the turn-of-the-century period—providing as well a distant counterpoint to the colonial situation of Kroeber's Californian ethnography.

Thus re-presented, we hope that the volume achieves a unity that is more than a juxtaposition of diversely motivated and adventitiously accumulated essays. By an editorial process analogous to Boas' "secondary rationalization," we hope to have brought together borrowed elements in a manner that illuminates the *Volksgeist* of Boasian anthropology by bringing it more closely in relation to the German intellectual and anthropological traditions which were so influential in its formation. Obscured during the early twentieth century by the divergent internal development of the two national traditions, retroactively severed by the Boasian culturalist critique of Nazi racist anthropology, these formative influences are here for the first time seriously investigated.

References Cited

Benedict, R. 1943. Franz Boas. *Science* 97:60–62.

Bieder, R. 1986. *Science encounters the American Indian, 1820–1880: The early years of American ethnology.* Norman, Okla.

Boas, F. 1940. *Race, language and culture.* New York.

Harris, M. 1968. *The rise of anthropological theory.* New York.

Hinsley, C. 1981. *Savages and scientists: The Smithsonian Institution and the development of American anthropology, 1846–1910.* Washington, D.C.

Kroeber, A., & C. Kluckhohn. 1952. *Culture: A critical review of concepts and definitions.* Papers of the Peabody Museum of Archaeology and Ethnology, Harvard University 47. Cambridge, Mass.

Mark, J. 1980. *Four anthropologists: An American science in its early years.* New York.

Stocking, G. W., Jr. 1968. *Race, culture and evolution: Essays in the history of anthropology.* New York.

———. 1974. The basic assumptions of Boasian anthropology. In *The shaping of American anthropology: A Franz Boas reader, 1883–1911,* ed. Stocking, 1–19. New York.

———. 1976. Ideas and institutions in American anthropology: Thoughts toward a history of the interwar years. In 1992:114–77.

———. 1992. *The ethnographer's magic and other essays in the history of anthropology.* Madison.

Wax, M. 1956. The limitations of Boas' anthropology. *Am. Anth.* 58:63–74.

White, L. 1963. *The ethnography and ethnology of Franz Boas.* Texas Memorial Museum Bulletin 6. Austin.

THE STUDY OF GEOGRAPHY

FRANZ BOAS

It is a remarkable fact, that, in the recent literature of geography, researches on the method and limits of that science occupy a prominent place.[1] Almost every distinguished geographer has felt the necessity of expressing his views on its aim and scope, and of defending it from being disintegrated and swallowed up by geology, botany, history, and other sciences treating on subjects similar to or identical with those of geography. If the representatives of a science as young as geography spend a great part of their time in discussions of this kind, though the material for investigations is still unlimited; if they feel compelled to defend their field of research against assaults of their fellow-workers and outsiders—the reason for this fact must be looked for in a deep discrepancy between their fundamental views of science and those of their adversaries.

Formerly, when the greater part of the earth's surface was undiscovered, and European vessels sailed only over their well-known routes from continent to continent, careful not to stray from the old path and fearing the dangers of unknown regions, the mere thought of these vast territories which had never been sighted by a European could fill the mind of geographers with ardent longing for extended knowledge; with the desire of unveiling the secrets of regions enlivened by imagination with figures of unknown animals and peoples. But the more completely the outlines of continents and islands became known, the stronger grew the desire to *understand* the phenomena of the newly discovered regions by comparing them with those of one's own country. Instead of merely extending their study over new areas, scientists began to be absorbed in examining the phenomena more intently, and comparing them with the results of observations already made. Thus Humboldt's admirable works and Karl Ritter's comparative geography arose out of the rapidly extending knowledge of the earth.

1. The text reproduced here, except for minimal adjustments of punctuation, is that of the original publication, in *Science* 9 (#210, 2/11/1887): 137–41. Although there were a few minor editorial changes in the version Boas reprinted in 1940 in *Race, Language and Culture* (pp. 639–47), none were such as to affect the meaning.

The fact that the rapid disclosure of the most remote parts of the globe coincided with the not less rapid development of physical sciences has had great influence upon the development of geography; for while the circle of phenomena became wider every day, the idea became prevalent that a single phenomenon is not of great avail, but that it is the aim of science to deduce laws from phenomena; and the wider their scope, the more valuable they are considered. The descriptive sciences were deemed inferior in value to researches which had hitherto been outside their range. Instead of systematical botany and zoölogy, biology became the favorite study; theoretical philosophy was supplanted by experimental psychology; and, by the same process, geography was disintegrated into geology, meteorology, etc.

Ever since, these sciences have been rapidly developed, but geography itself has for a long time been almost overshadowed by its growing children. However, we do not think they can fill its place, and wish to prove that its neglect cannot be remedied by the attentive cultivation of those sciences separately.

Those accustomed to value a study according to the scope of the laws found by means of it are not content with researches on phenomena such as are the object of geography. They consider them from a physical stand-point, and find them to be physical, meteorological, or ethnological; and, after having explained them by means of physical, physiological, or psychological laws, have finished their work. It is very instructive to consider thoroughly their definition of geography. They declare that the domain of this science comprises neither magnetical and meteorological nor geological phenomena and processes. They generously grant it the study of the distribution of animals and plants, as far as physiologists and evolutionists will permit; but all agree that anthropogeography—the life of man as far as it depends on the country he lives in—is the true domain of geography.

It is not difficult to discover the principle on which this segregation is founded. Physical phenomena are subject to physical laws which are known, or which will assuredly be found by the methods used in discovering those that are known. Physiological, and, to a still higher degree, psychological, laws are not so well known as to allow their being treated in the same way as physical laws. The conditions of the phenomena are generally so complicated, that, even if the most general laws were known, a strict conclusion cannot easily be drawn. But were those auxiliary sciences just as far developed as physics, no doubt the same scientists who at the present time concede them willingly to geography would not hesitate to claim them for physiology and psychology. It is evident that there is no middle way: geography must either be maintained in its full extent or it must be given up altogether.

As soon as we agree that the purpose of every science is accomplished when the laws which govern its phenomena are discovered, we must admit that the subject of geography is distributed among a great number of sciences; if, however, we would maintain its independence, we must prove that there exists another object for science besides the deduction of laws from phenomena. And it is our opinion that there *is* another object—the thorough understanding of phenomena. Thus we find that the contest between geographers and their adversaries is identical with the old controversy between historical and physical methods. One party claims that the ideal aim of science ought to be the discovery of general laws; the other maintains that it is the investigation of phenomena themselves.

It is easily understood, therefore, why in geography the contest between these views is particularly lively. Here naturalists and historians meet in a common field of work. A great number of modern geographers have been educated as historians, and they must try to come to an agreement with the naturalists, who, in turn, must learn to accommodate their views to those of the historians. It is evident that an answer to this fundamental question on the value of historical and physical science can only be found by a methodical investigation of their relation to each other.

All agree that the establishment of facts is the foundation and starting-point of science. The physicist compares a series of similar facts, from which he isolates the general phenomenon which is common to all of them. Henceforth the single facts become less important to him, as he lays stress on the general law alone. On the other hand, the facts are the object which is of importance and interest to the historian. An example will explain our meaning more satisfactorily than a theoretical discussion.

When Newton studied the motion of the planets, the distribution of those celestial bodies in space and time were the means, not the object, of his researches. His problem was the action of two bodies upon each other, and thus he found the law of gravitation. On the other hand, Kant and Laplace, in studying the solar system, asked the question, Why is every one of the bodies constituting the solar system in the place it occupies? They took the law as granted, and applied it to the phenomena from which it had been deduced, in order to study the history of the solar system. Newton's work was at an end as soon as he had found the law of gravitation, which law was the preliminary condition of Kant's work.

Here is another example: according to Buckle's conception, historical facts must be considered as being caused by physiological and psychological laws. Accordingly, he does not describe men and their actions as arising from their own character and the events influencing their life, but calls our attention to the laws governing the history of mankind. The object of the historians is a different one. They are absorbed in the study of the facts, and dwell admiringly on the character of their heroes. They take the most lively interest in the persons and nations they treat of, but are unwilling to consider them as subject to stringent laws.

We believe that the physical conception is nowhere else expressed as clearly as in Comte's system of sciences. Setting aside astronomy, which has been placed rather arbitrarily between mathematics and physics, all his sciences have the one aim, to deduce laws from phenomena. The single phenomenon itself is insignificant: it is only valuable because it is an emanation of a law, and serves to find new laws or to corroborate old ones. To this system of sciences Humboldt's 'Cosmos' is opposed in its principle. Cosmography, as we may call this science, considers every phenomenon as worthy of being studied for its own sake. Its mere existence entitles it to a full share of our attention; and the knowledge of its existence and evolution in space and time fully satisfies the student, without regard to the laws which it corroborates or which may be deduced from it.

Physicists will acknowledge that the study of the history of many phenomena is a work of scientific value. Nobody doubts the importance of Kant's researches on the solar system; nobody derogates from that of investigations upon the evolution of organisms. However, there is another class of phenomena the study of which is not considered of equal value, and among them are the geographical ones. In considering the geography of a country, it seems that the geological, meteorological, and anthropo-geographical phenomena form an incidental conglomerate, having no natural tie or relation to one another, while, for instance, the evolutionist's subject of study forms a natural unity. We may be allowed to say that the naturalist demands an objective connection between the phenomena he studies, which the geographical phenomena seem to lack. Their connection seems to be subjective, originating in the mind of the observer.

Accordingly there are two principal questions which must be answered: first, the one referring to the opposition between physicists and cosmographers, i.e., Is the study of phenomena for their own sake equal in value to the deduction of laws? second, Is the study of a series of phenomena having a merely subjective connection equal in value to researches on the history of those forming an objective unity?

We shall first treat on the difference of opinion between physicists and cosmographers. The two parties are strongly opposed to each other; and it is a hard task to value justly the arguments of opponents whose method of thinking and way of feeling are entirely opposed to one's own. An unbiased judgment cannot be formed without severe mental struggles which destroy convictions that were considered immovable, and had become dear to us. But those struggles lead to the grander conviction that both parties, though in a permanent state of conflict, aspire to the same end—to find the eternal truth.

The origin of every science we find in two different desires of the human mind—its aesthetic wants, and the feelings, which are the sources of the two branches of science. It was an early desire of developing mankind to arrange systematically the phenomena seen by the observer in overwhelming number, and thus to put the confused impressions in order. This desire must be considered an emanation of the aesthetical disposition, which is offended by confusion and want of clearness. When occupied in satisfying this desire, the regularity of the processes and phenomena would attain a far greater importance than the single phenomenon, which is only considered important as being a specimen of the class to which it belongs. The clearer all the phenomena are arranged, the better will the aesthetic desire be satisfied, and, for that reason, the most general laws and ideas are considered the most valuable results of science.

From this point of view, the philosophical ideas of Epicurus are very interesting, as they may be considered the extreme opinion to which this aesthetical desire can lead if the pleasure one enjoys in arranging phenomena in a clear system is the only incentive. He considered any explanation of a phenomenon sufficient, provided it be natural. It does not matter, he taught, if an hypothesis is true, but all probable explanations are of the same value, and the choice between them is quite insignificant. We believe this opinion is called to a new life by a number of modern scientists, i.e., by those who try to construct the evolution of organisms in details which, at the present time at least, can neither be proved nor refuted. If, for instance, Müller describes the history of the evolution of flowers, he gives only a probable way of development, without any better proof than that it seems to be the simplest and therefore the most probable. But this construction of a probable hypothesis as to the origin of these phenomena gives a satisfaction to our aesthetical desire to bring the confusion of forms and species into a system. But it should be borne in mind that a theory must be true, and that its truth is the standard by which its value is measured. Therefore naturalists are always engaged in examining the truth of their theories by applying them to new phenomena, and in these researches those phenomena are the most important which seem to be opposed to the theories. As soon as the question whether the theory is applicable to the class of phenomena is solved, the whole class is of little further interest to the investigator.

While physical science arises from the logical and aesthetical demands of the human mind, cosmography has its source in the personal feeling of man towards the world, towards the phenomena surrounding him. We may call this an 'affective' impulse, in contrast to the aesthetic impulse. Goethe has expressed this idea with admirable clearness: "It seems to me that every phenomenon, every fact, itself is the really interesting object. Whoever explains it, or connects it with other events, usually only amuses himself or makes sport of us, as, for instance, the naturalist or historian. But a single action or event is interesting, not because it is explainable, but because it is true" (*Unterhaltungen deutscher Ausgewanderten*).

The mere occurrence of an event claims the full attention of our mind, because we are affected by it, and it is studied without any regard to its place in a system. This continuous impulse is the important counterbalance against the one-sidedness of a science arisen from merely aesthetic impulses. As the truth of every phenomenon causes us to study it, a true history of its evolution alone can satisfy the investigator's mind, and it is for this reason that Epicurus's probable or possible explanation is not at all satisfactory for science, but that every approach to truth is considered a progress by far superior to the most elaborate system which may give proof of a subtile mind and scrupulous thought, but claims to be only one among many possible systems.

Naturalists will not deny the importance of every phenomenon, but do not consider it worthy of study for its own sake. It is only a proof or a refutation of their laws, systems, and hypotheses (as they are deduced from true phenomena), which they feel obliged to bring as near the truth as possible. The deductions, however, are their main interest; and the reward of the indefatigable student is to review, from the summit of his most general deductions, the vast field of phenomena. Joyfully he sees that every process and every phenomenon which seem[s] to the stranger an irregular and incomprehensible conglomerate is a link of a long chain. Losing sight of the single facts, he sees only the beautiful order of the world.

The cosmographer, on the other hand, holds to the phenomenon which is the object of his study, may it occupy a high or a low rank in the system of physical sciences, and lovingly tries to penetrate into its secrets until every feature is plain and clear. This occupation with the object of his affection affords him a delight not inferior to that which the physicist enjoys in his systematical arrangement of the world.

Our inquiry leads us to the conclusion that it is in vain to search for an answer to the question, Which of the two methods is of a higher value? as each originates in a different desire of the human mind. An answer can only be subjective, being a confession of the answerer as to which is dearer to him— his personal feeling towards the phenomena surrounding him, or his inclination for abstractions; whether he prefers to recognize the individuality in the totality, or the totality in the individuality.

Let us now turn to the discussion of the second point. We have seen that physicists are inclined to acknowledge the value of a certain class of cosmographical studies. It is the characteristic quality of those phenomena that they are the result of the action of incidental causes upon one group of forces, or upon the elements of phenomena. The physicist does not study the whole phenomenon as it represents itself to the human mind, but resolves it into its elements, which he investigates separately. The investigation of the history of these elements of phenomena leads to a systematical arrangement, which gives to the aesthetical desire as much satisfaction as the formulation of laws. The end which evolutional and astronomical researches tend to is the best proof of this fact. A study of groups of phenomena, which seem to be connected only in the mind of the observer, and admit of being resolved into their elements, cannot lead to a similar result, and is therefore considered of inferior value. However, we have tried to prove that the source of cosmographical researches is an affective one. If this be right, we cannot distinguish between complex and simple phenomena, as the physicist tries to do, and neglect their subjective unity—the connection in which they appear to the mind of the observer. The whole phenomenon, and not its elements, is the object of the cosmographer's study. Thus the physiognomy of a country is of no interest to the physicist, while it is important to the cosmographer.

From the stand-point we occupy, a discussion as to the value of these researches is of just as little avail as that on the value of the two branches of science, for the judgment will be founded on the mental disposition of the judge, and be only a confession as to which impulse predominates, the aesthetic or the affective. However, one fact appears from our inquiry: cosmography is closely related to the arts, as the way in which the mind is affected by phenomena forms an important branch of the study. It therefore requires a different treatment from that of the physical sciences.

We will apply these results to the study of geography. Its objects are, the phenomena caused by the distribution of land and water, by the vertical forms of the earth's surface, and by the mutual influence of the earth and its inhabitants upon each other.

What does the physicist do with this object of study? He selects a single element out of phenomena which are observed at a certain point of the earth's surface, and compares it with another one found at another place. He continues in this way searching for similar phenomena, and loses sight altogether of the spot from which he started. Thus he becomes the founder of the sciences into which geography has gradually been resolved, as his studies are either directed to geological phenomena alone, or to meteorological, botanical, or whatever it may be. The most general deductions which can be reached in the pursuit of these studies still have a close connection with the single object, as they cannot be carried farther than to the most general geographical ideas, as mountain ranges, running water, oceans, etc. The most general results of his investigations will therefore be a general history of the earth's surface. If he bring these results into a system, he acts, as it seems to us, against the cosmographical character of the science. For instance, a system of all possible actions of water as forming the earth's surface seems to us of little value, except from a practical stand-point as being useful in studying the geological history of a district or of the earth's surface. Therefore these systems must be considered as important auxiliary sciences, but they are not geography itself. Their value is founded only on their applicability to the study of geography. The invention of geographical systems, so far as they do not serve this purpose, must be considered as useless, and classifications must be made only as far as geographical phenomena of a similar kind must be explained by different causes.

But there is another branch of geography besides this, equal to it in value— the physiognomy of the earth. It cannot afford a satisfactory object of study to the physicist, as its unity is a merely subjective one; and the geographer, in treating these subjects, approaches the domain of art, as the results of his study principally affect the feeling, and therefore must be described in an artistic way in order to satisfy the feeling in which it originated.

Our consideration leads us to the conclusion that geography is part of cosmography, and has its source in the affective impulse, in the desire to understand the phenomena and history of a country or of the whole earth, the home of mankind. It depends upon the inclination of the scientist towards physical or cosmographical method, whether he studies the history of the whole earth, or whether he prefers to learn that of a single country. From our point of view, the discussion whether geology or meteorology belongs to geography is of little importance, and we are willing to call all scientists geographers who study the phenomena of the earth's surface. We give geology no preference over the other branches of science, as many modern scientists are inclined to do. The study of the earth's surface implies geological researches as well as meteorological, ethnological, and others, as none of them cover the scope of geography, to delineate the picture of the earth's surface.

Many are the sciences that must help to reach this end; many are the studies and researches that must be pursued to add new figures to the incomplete picture; but every step that brings us nearer the end gives ampler satisfaction to the impulse which induces us to devote our time and work to this study, gratifying the love for the country we inhabit, and the nature that surrounds us.

FRANZ BOAS AND THE HUMBOLDTIAN TRADITION

From Volksgeist *and* Nationalcharakter *to an Anthropological Concept of Culture*

MATTI BUNZL

In 1887, the year Franz Boas settled permanently in the United States, he published an article on "The Study of Geography." More than fifty years later, he included the essay, along with "The Aims of Ethnology," written in 1888, in the collection *Race, Language and Culture*, because the two pieces indicated "the general attitude underlying my later work" (1940:vi). In "The Study of Geography," Boas contrasted two scientific methodologies: the physical and the historical. For the former "the aim of science [was] to deduce laws from phenomena," and the "single phenomenon itself" was insignificant, but merely served as "an exemplification of a law," as a means "to find new laws or to corroborate old ones." In contrast, the historical method had as its goal "the investigation of phenomena themselves," and was "unwilling to consider them as subject to stringent laws." The two methods had their origin in "two different desires of the human mind." Arising from "its aesthetic wants," the physical method sought to arrange the myriad of phenomena of the world "systematically," so as to "put the confused impressions in order." The historical method, in contrast, grew out of an "affective" impulse; "the mere occurrence of an event" triggered the desire to study its "true history" (1887a:640–44).

Underlying this dichotomy was the traditional German separation between the *Naturwissenschaften* and the *Geisteswissenschaften*, or, in the words of Boas' contemporary Hermann Paul, the eminent historical linguist, the distinction

---

Matti Bunzl is a graduate student in the departments of anthropology and history at the University of Chicago. He is currently undertaking dissertation research on issues of race, class, gender, and sexuality in Late Imperial Vienna, focussing in particular on the members of the literary circle *Jung Wien*.

17

between the *Gesetzeswissenschaften* (the law-giving sciences) and the *Geschichtswissenschaften* (the historical sciences). The former, such as physics and experimental psychology, sought to find the exact laws governing the natural and human realm; the latter recognized the limitations of positive knowledge and focussed on individual phenomena as historical products (Paul 1880:1). That this is what Boas had in mind is evident in his examples: the French sociologist Auguste Comte and the British historian of civilization H. T. Buckle for the physical method, and the German explorer and natural historian Alexander von Humboldt for the historical or—after Humboldt's masterpiece *Kosmos*—"cosmographical" method. While Buckle called our "attention to the laws governing the history of mankind," he failed to "describe men and their actions as arising from their own character and the events influencing their lives." Similarly, Comte's "system of sciences" subordinated individual phenomena to the laws deduced from them. Cosmography, on the other hand, considered "every phenomenon as worthy of being studied for its own sake"; "its mere existence" entitled it to a "full share of our attention" (1887a:642). Illustrating the cosmographical method, Boas quoted Goethe, who had "expressed this idea with admirable clearness: 'It seems to me that every phenomenon, every fact, itself is the really interesting object . . . a single action or event is interesting, not because it is explainable, but because it is true'" (644).

For Boas, it was impossible to privilege one method over the other: every scientist had to choose according to "which is dearer to him—his personal feeling towards the phenomena surrounding him, or his inclination for abstractions; whether he prefers to recognize the individuality in the totality, or the totality in the individuality" (645). But if the affective and aesthetic impulse were both present throughout Boas' career, the search for general laws was always constrained by the cosmographer's desire to describe and understand individual phenomena. While he never completely abandoned the search for the laws of human behavior, he gradually became less confident of ever finding them, and the corpus of his work largely comprised detailed descriptions of particulars rather than attempts at generalization (cf. Stocking 1968:154–55; Kluckhohn & Prufer 1959:24–25).

It is a commonplace that Boasian anthropology was to a certain degree the product of his intellectual socialization in Germany. Yet "The Study of Geography" only begins to reveal the debt of Boas' thinking to German thought of the eighteenth and nineteenth centuries. We know that Boas read and appreciated Herder and Kant, had an affinity for Goethe and Schiller, and approached Humboldt's "admirable works" with "great awe" (1887a:639, 1904:24; Cole 1983:29; Kluckhohn & Prufer 1959:6). But the specific influences of German scholarship have not been systematically explored—especially the influence of the brothers Wilhelm and Alexander von Humboldt, who between them shaped nineteenth-century German scholarship to a remarkable degree. Born in 1767, Wilhelm von Humboldt was both scholar and administrator. As Prussian secretary of education in the first decade of the nineteenth century, he implemented significant school reforms and founded the University of Berlin (Sweet 1980:33–71). As a scholar, he influenced the development of several branches of the *Geisteswissenschaften,* including not only linguistics, but also history and folk psychology. Two years younger than Wilhelm, Alexander von Humboldt was the foremost *Naturwissenschaftler* of his day. An explorer, geographer, and natural historian, his career was a model for generations of natural scientists, including Charles Darwin (cf. Krüger & Buchheim 1959:364). His interest in the relationship between humans and their environment contributed to the development of ethnology as well as geography, one of the academic traditions into which Boas was educated. When Boas abandoned geography for anthropology, he incorporated history, folk psychology, and linguistics into his theoretical framework. Thus, Boas' anthropology may be viewed as uniting the intellectual currents emanating from both Wilhelm and Alexander von Humboldt.

Wilhelm von Humboldt's Plan for a Comparative Anthropology

Wilhelm and Alexander von Humboldt spent their childhood at Potsdam, near Berlin, and were educated by private tutors at home, as was common practice among the nobility. They were introduced early into the circles of the Berlin Enlightenment, attending lectures by the leading scholars and frequenting the households of local luminaries. Wilhelm particularly enjoyed the company of the group that had gathered around Moses Mendelssohn, who even after his death still loomed large as a major intellectual figure (Sweet 1978:3–19). Immersing himself in the works of Mendelssohn, Lessing, and Wolff, he felt the reverberations of the principles of the French Enlightenment: the universality of human reason across space and time, the subjection of an essentially uniform human nature to unchanging natural laws, the steady progress of civilization through history toward an enlightened state of reason, and the possibility of finding the laws that governed this process (cf. Berlin 1980:1–24; Beiser 1987:1–15).

When Wilhelm von Humboldt came under the influence of these ideas, however, their underlying assumptions were already being severely questioned. Off in the Eastern part of Prussia, Immanuel Kant was preparing his *Critiques,* which subverted the naive optimism of the progressive course of Enlightenment by arguing that human reason was bound by certain *a priori* assumptions conditioning the perception of reality (1781:126–127). Even so, Kant maintained a belief in the universal nature of human reason, which could itself overcome its epistemological dilemma through an internal critique of its own

natural laws. Kant's contemporary Johann Georg Hamann, a fellow citizen of
Königsberg, went much further in his critique of Enlightenment doctrines,
rejecting the independent existence of human reason in the abstract. To Hamann, reason was a phenomenon linked to specific historical formations and
therefore could not serve as a universal external standard for the classification
of human experiences. It was Hamann's rejection of universal reason that initiated the German Counter-Enlightenment[1] (Berlin 1980:1–25; cf. Beiser
1987:9).

Hamann's historicist critique of Enlightenment rationalism was developed
further by his pupil Johann Gottfried Herder, who in 1774 published *Auch
eine Philosophie der Geschichte zur Bildung der Menschheit*, a polemical essay directed primarily against Voltaire's philosophy of history. Rejecting as an "arbitrary mechanism" any *raison universelle* that propelled a uniform development of civilization, Herder argued instead for the uniqueness of values
transmitted throughout history (1774:54, 57–58). The comparison of any
given nation or age with the Enlightenment or any other external standard
was therefore unacceptable: each human group could be understood only as a
product of its particular history. Embodying a unique genius, or *Geist*, each
Volk formed an organic whole, the values, beliefs, traditions, and language of
which could only be understood from within by entering into the viewpoint
of the members. History as an observable process occurred not on a universal level, but only among particular social entities (1774:33; cf. Iggers
1968:3–29).

Herder's celebration of cultural individuality as a reflection of the plenitude
of God was combined, however, with a genuine cosmopolitan outlook in the
Humanitätsideal, which reaffirmed the common bond of humanity, but saw it
expressed in the diversity rather than the similarity of human forms. In opposition to the French Enlightenment, which based its universalism on the essential sameness of human beings as rational actors, Herder stressed the individual contribution of each cultural entity to humanity at large. And since
humanity was the totality of its multitudinous elements, each *Volk* must be
studied in its individuality (1774:43). Herder's program was realized in an en-
cyclopedic treatment of history, the *Ideen zur Philosophie der Geschichte der
Menschheit*, the first volume of which was published in 1784 (cf. Iggers 1968:
33–38; Beiser 1987:142–44, 1992:3–8).

Wilhelm von Humboldt was deeply impressed with these criticisms of the
universal reason of the Enlightenment. As a university student at Göttingen
(1788–89), he spent the better part of a year immersed in Kant's *Critique of
Pure Reason*; its argument augmented doubts he had already been harboring

1. Throughout this article, I use Berlin's term "Counter-Enlightenment" to refer to the initial
critiques of the Enlightenment project and the traditions emanating from them.

about the Enlightenment project (Sweet 1978:38). Among his first writings were treatises on the limits of state intervention, which were influenced by Kant's programmatic essay "Was ist Aufklärung?" ("What Is Enlightenment?") (Humboldt I:45–254[2]; cf. Mueller–Vollmer 1987:65). He also developed a deep interest in ancient Greece, and took up philological studies with F. A. Wolf, the foremost Greek scholar of the day. Aside from translations of ancient texts, he produced in 1793 a short treatise "Über das Studium des Altertums und des Griechischen insbesondere" ("On the Study of Antiquity, Especially the Greek") in which, in Herderian fashion, he advocated the intensive study of a particular nation (ancient Greece) in its political, religious, and domestic aspects in order to grasp its national character (I:262–65). None of these early texts, however, was published, and in 1794, Humboldt, who had just married, decided to further his own education by moving to Jena, where Johann Gottlieb Fichte had just arrived to take the chair in philosophy. More importantly for Humboldt, the town was the home of the playwright Friedrich Schiller, with whom in daily sessions he pondered issues in philology, literature, and politics (Sweet 1978:153–57). When Schiller decided to publish an annual literary journal, Die Horen, in order to bring together the "the finest minds in the nation," Humboldt was chosen, along with Fichte, as an associate on the board of editors (in Sweet 1978:156).

Humboldt contributed two essays to the first volume of Die Horen (1795)— "Über den Geschlechtsunterschied und dessen Einfluß auf die organische Natur" and "Über die männliche und weibliche Form"—as a step toward a general theory of Bildung, a prescription for individual human perfection which in Humboldt's view could only be achieved through the assimilation of the highest qualities of male and female (I:345–52; cf. Sweet 1978:167–68). The two essays, however, proved a major disappointment for Humboldt. Rather than being recognized as significant contributions to scholarship, they were dismissed for their obscurity—most devastatingly by Kant, who in a letter to Schiller said he could make little sense of Humboldt's argument (Sweet 1978: 169, 175).

After he had recuperated from the disappointment, Humboldt set to work anew, on two projects that would "break really new ground" (in Sweet 1978: 176). The first was a characterization of life in the eighteenth century in all its aspects, and the second an even loftier plan—a "comparative anthropology." Sometime between 1795 and 1797, he laid out the scope and methodology of this undertaking in a programmatic essay, in which he sought to combine the Herderian Humanitätsideal with his own ideal of Bildung. The "Plan

2. All references to Wilhelm von Humboldt's writings are to the seventeen volumes of the Gesammelte Schriften (1903–36). In the case of Humboldt and other German authors whose work is not translated into English, all renditions are my own.

einer vergleichenden Anthropologie" ("Plan for a Comparative Anthropology") asserted that the common nature of humanity, its *Gattungs-Charakter*,
was expressed through "individual characters," which Humboldt conceived as
national entities (I:377–80). Each individual *Volk* had a *Nationalcharakter*, a
distinct *Volk* character, which was embodied in the totality of its outward
manifestations: traditions, customs, religion, language, and art.[3] These in turn
revealed the degree of *Bildung* attained by a given nation. Since these achievements were based on capacities intrinsic to each national entity, they could
not be compared to an external standard, but deserved an unconditional respect (380–81). However, some nations, including the Germans, English,
French, Italians, and the ancient Greeks, had made the most of their innate
potentialities and reached a higher state of self-realization, serving as models
by which the rest could learn to maximize their own cultural potential. While
Humboldt felt that "comparative anthropology should encompass the entire
human race," he focussed on these leading peoples, studying their historical
trajectories in order to arrive at objective guidelines of national *Bildung*, with
the expectation that the improvement of individual national characters would
enhance humanity at large (394).

The methodology of Humboldt's proposed anthropology merged the "various spirits of the natural scientist, the historian, and the philosopher," achieving a unification of "the transcendental with the empirical" by treating "empirical materials speculatively [and] historical objects philosophically" (I:390,
397). In this, it was an attempt at a "synthesis of Herder and Kant" (Trabant
1990:52). To realize his *Bildungsideal*, Humboldt hoped to derive general principles through philosophical reflections; but, in opposition to Kant's abstract
speculations, his reflections would be based on "empirical observation," since
"high ideals" were "vain" if there were "no means for relating them to reality"
(390). But if Humboldt's anthropology thus mirrored the *Ideen zur Philosophie
der Geschichte der Menschheit*, he felt that Herder, too, had made hasty conclusions in the absence of sound evidence; he intended to proceed much more
rigorously, probing his material like an observer of nature (Sweet 1978:144).
The anthropologist could not, however, adopt the methodology of the natural
scientist, in whose domain one could presuppose the existence of natural laws
(Humboldt I:396). Although finding the regularities underlying the variety of
human existence was the ultimate goal of his anthropology, these could not be
determined deductively in analogy to the laws of the natural world, since all
"historical detail" was "as accidental and arbitrary as the accident and arbi-

3. In Humboldt's usage, the terms *Volk* and *Nation* designated something akin to the present
notion of "individual cultural entities." The term *Kultur*, in contrast, was used in its humanistic
sense, referring to and encompassing the great artistic and literary achievements of individuals
and peoples.

Wilhelm von Humboldt, during the post-retirement period of his most intensive linguistic work, wearing the Iron Cross he was awarded by Friedrich Wilhelm III in gratitude for his diplomatic services at the Prague Conference of 1813. (Drawing by Franz Krüger, 1827; reproduced courtesy of the Bildarchiv preussischer Kulturbesitz, Berlin.)

trariness which produce it." Rather, Humboldt insisted on the inductive approach of the historian, who "asked with complete, objective indifference what happened here, and no more," thus "avoiding all temptation to proceed from causes and laws to phenomena rather than the other way around" (396–97).

> For this is what distinguishes the historian from the natural scientist and the philosopher: he limits his dealings to that which had happened, and regards his

field as neither nature nor will, but fate and accident, for whose individual
quirks, at least in their detail, no one is responsible. (397–98)

Despite the numerous analogies between Humboldt's "plan for a comparative anthropology" and Boas' theoretical articles, it is unlikely that Boas ever
read Humboldt's text. If he did, it was after 1903 when it was published for the
first time in the opening volume of Humboldt's *Gesammelte Schriften*. But like
many of Humboldt's early unpublished projects, the comparative anthropology
was important as an intellectual manifesto, foreshadowing later writings that
were widely influential.

Shortly after 1800, after repeated failures to leave his intellectual mark,
Humboldt abandoned the life of a scholar and embarked on a political career,
which was available to him as a member of the nobility with university training. In 1802 he was made Prussian envoy in Rome, and in 1808 he became
secretary of education in the Prussian government. Seizing the chance to implement his *Bildungsideal* on a national scale, he secured the establishment of
the humanistic *Gymnasium*, which through comprehensive training in mathematics, history, and languages would prepare students to enter university,
where they would join their professors in a communal scholarly enterprise.
Humboldt realized this goal in 1809 when he founded the University of Berlin,
which was dedicated both to *Bildung* and *Wissenschaft* (Sweet 1980:40–71).
In 1810, Humboldt was sent as envoy to Vienna, where he later took part in
the Congress of Vienna, the forum that rearranged the territory of Europe in
the wake of the Napoleonic Wars. His political career, however, came to an
end when he was ousted from government for his liberal politics in 1819.
Upon his retirement from office, Humboldt resumed his scholarly activities
and devoted the rest of his life to his studies (Sweet 1980).

All of Humboldt's mature work, from 1819 until his death in 1835, was an
elaboration of ideas introduced in the "Plan for a Comparative Anthropology." Through these later writings, Humboldt exerted substantial influence on
a number of scholarly disciplines over the course of the nineteenth century. In
1822, he published a short text on historiography, "Über die Aufgabe des Ge-
schichtsschreibers" ("On the Task of the Writer of History"), which became a
cornerstone of the German historical tradition and reverberated through the
works of Leopold von Ranke, Johann Gustav Droysen, and Wilhelm Dilthey.
Humboldt also influenced the discipline of *Völkerpsychologie* ("folk psychology"), whose founders Heymann Steinthal and Moritz Lazarus set out to complete his project of a comparative treatment of national characters. Most importantly, however, Humboldt's monumental treatises on language engendered
a tradition of the comparative study of language along anthropological lines.
All these lines of influence converged in Franz Boas.

By the time Humboldt presented his historiographical treatise to the Royal Academy of Sciences, the cosmopolitan outlook of the late eighteenth century embodied in the *Humanitätsideal* had given way to Romantic nationalism in Germany. While Humboldt retained his liberal humanism, he was not unaffected by the anti-rationalist upsurge that accompanied the new trend (cf. Iggers 1968:40–41; Meinecke 1963:118–48). In two short philosophical sketches, written while still in political office, Humboldt had already abandoned all systematic and philosophical attempts at describing history, including even Kant's critical approach (III:350–66). His paper to the Royal Academy laid down the foundations of an alternative inductive method in the historical sciences.

Rather than the construction of elaborate systems or the presentation of daring conjectures, "the task of the historian is the depiction of what happened" ("die Darstellung des Geschehenen") (IV:35–36). Like the products of the national character in comparative anthropology, the actual events of history were inherently interesting, and were thus a primary object of investigation. However, the simple accumulation of facts was only the starting point of a hermeneutic interpretation. The ultimate goal was the *Verstehen,* or understanding, of the historical facts "as part of a whole" through "the intuitive conjecture of that which is not attainable" through the collection of historical facts (38, 41). In this, the historian closely resembled the poet, who by way of intuition attempted to uncover truths that lay hidden from immediate perception. Rejecting "natural laws" as the driving force of history, Humboldt introduced the notion of multiple "ideas," the internal essences of individual entities governing their historical trajectories (48, 52). Partially the products of history themselves, they were inextricably intertwined with the historical process at large and could not be analytically separated from it. In a radical break with philosophical history, which "distorted the uninhibited view of the peculiar workings of the forces" of history by pressing oftentimes irrational human ideas into a teleological rationalizing scheme, Humboldt insisted that the elucidation of these multiple ideas was the ultimate goal of the historian (37–46).

Humboldt did not deny the applicability of cause and effect to the study of history, for every "occurrence produces another one." But in addition to factors of "mechanistic determination" which operated with the force of natural laws, at least two others had to be taken into account (IV:49). One must consider also physiological factors, which operated on the exterior forms of all living entities, such as individuals, nations, peoples, and the entire human race, with discoverable regularity. However, while these could contribute to historical understanding, they were not the driving forces of history but only forms to which history had to yield. More important were the fundamentally irrational psychological factors, such as "abilities, feelings, dispositions, and desires," which were inherent in the agents of history and completely eluded "discernable laws." Although these could only be grasped through intuitive processes, in the form of individual and national characters, they were the primary object of study; determining individual historical trajectories, they offered insights into the ideas that governed world history (49–52).

Much like Friedrich Schleiermacher, who had codified the hermeneutic method of text criticism, Humboldt saw historical scholarship as an ongoing creative process. As Schleiermacher put it, "The vocabulary and the history of an author's age together form a whole from which his writings must be understood as a part, and vice versa." By continuously moving back and forth between text and context, the interpreter was led to ever deeper levels of understanding (1819:84). Humboldt extended this method to historical scholarship. By crossing the "bridge of understanding" that separated the historian from the course of history, he hoped to make each historical event intelligible in its specific context. Echoing the dialectic of Schleiermacher's "hermeneutic circle," Humboldt argued that this could be achieved "through repeated reciprocal action," through which "clarity as well as certainty emerge" (IV:48).

Although "On the Task of the Writer of History" was Humboldt's last venture into the field of history, its message reverberated throughout the tradition of nineteenth-century German historical scholarship. More than any other publication, it provided a coherent framework for the historicist critique of the Enlightenment project. Humboldt's call for an inductive approach to history was followed by Leopold von Ranke, the most influential historian of his time (cf. Iggers 1968:63–89; Jaeger & Rüsen 1992:34–40). In the theoretical appendix to his first book, in a phrase echoing Humboldt, Ranke defined the task of history as "merely to show what really happened" (in Iggers 1968:67). Sustaining Humboldt's criticism of philosophical history against Hegel, Ranke insisted that what distinguished philosophers and historians was the approach toward understanding. Philosophers approached reality from the perspective of general concepts and attempted to subsume all of life under a unifying framework; historians, in contrast, proceeded from the conditions of existence. Consequently, historians had inherent interest in individual phenomena, which to philosophers only mattered as examples of larger wholes (Iggers 1968:77–78).

While Ranke stressed the recording of historical facts over their interpretation, Humboldt's hermeneutic approach to history was continued by Johann Gustav Droysen, one of the leading historians of the next generation. Writing in the 1850s, Droysen extended Humboldt's critique of teleological schemes of history to the historical positivism of Buckle, who explained historical events by laws patterned after the natural sciences. To distinguish his enterprise from this new trend, Droysen invoked Humboldt, "the Bacon of historical sciences," and his interpretive method. With Droysen, *Verstehen* (understanding) became the central aspect of historical scholarship, denoting both the particular nature and method of the historical sciences. As a technical term, Droysen contrasted *Verstehen* with *Erklären*, the natural scientific mode of cognition which sought to explain individual phenomena according to natural laws. Because history defied explanations based on fictitious laws of history, he advocated the method of "forschendes Verstehen" ("understanding by means of investigation") as the sole tool of historical scholarship, through which it was possible to comprehend the meaning and motivating forces of historical events (in Mueller-Vollmer 1990:121; cf. Mueller-Vollmer 1990:14–24).

Verstehen was also the central concept for Wilhelm Dilthey, who sought to place the Counter-Enlightenment project on sound epistemological footing by subjecting it to a critique of historical reason. In 1883, he published his *Einleitung in die Geisteswissenschaften* ("Introduction to the Humanities"), in which he attempted to establish a philosophical framework for the human sciences independent of the natural sciences and philosophical history. Rejecting such positivist approaches to the human sciences as Comte's and Mill's, Dilthey's central concern was with the possibility of understanding as the source of objective knowledge of the human condition (1883:104; Mueller-Vollmer 1990:24; Bulhof 1980:18). Central to the act of *Verstehen* was the ability to re-experience (*nachempfinden*) the situation of the historical actor through empathy. This was possible because, much like the phenomena investigated in the various human sciences themselves, understanding was rooted in lived experience (Mueller-Vollmer 1990:25–27). These notions pervaded Dilthey's numerous publications, which ranged from intellectual history and the history of science to philosophy and the history and methodology of the human sciences. Widely read in the last decades of the nineteenth century, Dilthey directly influenced Boas, who on several occasions cited his work (cf. Boas 1908: 276, 279).

In addition to history, another discipline in the Humboldtian tradition which influenced Boas during his academic training was *Völkerpsychologie*. As well as from Humboldt, *Völkerpsychologie* derived inspiration from the psychology of Johann Friedrich Herbart, professor of philosophy at Göttingen and Königsberg in the first three decades of the nineteenth century. Opposing the dominant trend of idealist philosophy, Herbart proposed to transform philosophy into an individual psychology based on mechanical and mathematical models. For Herbart, the mind was a unique structure of "presentations," an "apperceptive mass" which was altered by the reception of each new presentation; conversely, the effect of a new presentation depended on the nature of the particular apperceptive mass it encountered. The task of scientific psychology was to discover the laws that governed these processes and secure their practical applications. Like Humboldt, Herbart saw these in the realm of *Bil-*

dung, differing insofar as he sought to perfect them with mathematical precision. To this end, he published numerous highly influential treatises on the implication of his mechanistic psychology for individual cognitive development (Dunkel 1970:11, 48–51).

Völkerpsychologie, developed in the 1850s by Moritz Lazarus, a professor of philosophy at the University of Bern, was an attempt to extend the scope of Herbart's psychological investigations from the individual to larger units. Lazarus explicated its theoretical and methodological foundations in cooperation with Heymann Steinthal, a professor of linguistics in Berlin, in the introduction to the *Zeitschrift für Völkerpsychologie und Sprachwissenschaft* (1859), which became the organ of the new discipline (Belke 1971:xiv–xlii). In addition to Herbart, the two authors specifically referred to Humboldt as their main inspiration, particularly through his writings on language (1859:14). The object of *Völkerpsychologie* was the workings of the *Volksgeist*, the genius of a people, a concept which had its ultimate roots in Herder. In close analogy to Humboldt's *Nationalcharakter*, the *Volksgeist* was the unifying psychological essence shared by all members of a *Volk* and the driving force of its historical trajectory (29, 35). It found its purest expression in the psychological products of a people, foremost its language and mythology, but also its religion and customs, all of which were embodiments of a unique apperception of nature (40–56). The *Volksgeist* was not, however, conceived as a stagnant entity, but changed through historical processes that could best be studied by following the alterations of myths over time (45, 63).

For Lazarus and Steinthal, *Völkerpsychologie* had a two-fold objective. First, it was to describe, in the greatest detail possible, the actual manifestations of various *Volksgeister* over space and time. Based on this data, and by strictly inductive reasoning, *Völkerpsychologie* would then proceed to its second and primary objective, which separated it from all other disciplines, namely, finding the laws that governed the psychological development of a people (19, 23–24). Because the essence of mankind was expressed by its "division into *Völker*" and its development was "tied to the diversity of peoples," the laws of folk psychology would have to emerge slowly out of data collected from many different peoples; by these means, folk psychology would eventually achieve genuine understanding both of the general nature (*Wesen*) of the *Volksgeist* and its individual expressions among particular peoples (5–7, 26). Although adopting in principle Humboldt's plan for a comparative anthropology, Lazarus and Steinthal in fact devoted themselves largely to producing descriptions of languages and myths rather than their psychological analysis. Nevertheless, it was the larger goal of finding the laws governing the development of particular *Volksgeister* that ultimately justified the enterprise. When Boas, in his first theoretical piece on anthropology, spoke of folk psychology as one of "the aims of ethnology," he referred to it as the investigation of the "laws of the lives of peoples" (Boas 1889a:20).

Wilhelm von Humboldt and the
Comparative Study of Languages

In addition to his contribution to the fields of history and folk psychology, Humboldt pioneered the comparative study of non-Indo-European languages. His rich and complex linguistic thinking is best understood in relation to his plan for a comparative anthropology, as another approach to the diversity of humanity in its mental and spiritual manifestations. Linguistics, too, was to be founded on a solid understanding of the full variety of the world's languages as a precondition to more general philosophical conclusions. But, whereas his comparative anthropology had originally been conceived as an inclusive study of all aspects of the human condition, he had since gradually come to the conviction that language was the defining element of human life, and, consequently, that its elucidation would lead to a genuine understanding of humanity in all its aspects. He proposed, in short, a theory of language that would encompass a theory of anthropology (cf. Trabant 1990:34–59; Heeschen 1972:70).

Humboldt's fascination with language developed early in life. Like many men of the upper class, he knew a number of different European tongues, and, in addition to Latin and Greek, he also studied Hebrew. His scholarly interest in the languages outside the Indo-European family was awakened when he discovered the Basque language during a trip through Spain in 1801. Despite the constraints on his intellectual endeavors, he pursued a structural analysis of this language isolate during the years of his political career. In 1817, he published his work in J. C. Adelung's and J. S. Vater's *Mithridates*, the standard work on comparative philology at the time (Sweet 1980:231, 396–97).

After his forced retirement in 1819, Humboldt devoted himself almost entirely to the study of the world's languages—a venture which he pursued "comprehensively, analytically, comparatively, empirically, philosophically" (Sweet 1980:371–72). During the 1820s, he worked primarily on American Indian languages, contributing occasional reports to the Royal Academy of Science in Berlin. Toward the end of the decade, however, he discovered the Kawi, the traditional literary language of the island of Java, and this occupied his attention until his death in 1835. His monumental treatise, the *Kawi-Werk*, published posthumously by his brother Alexander (1836–1839), comprised three volumes of detailed synchronic analyses of the languages of Southeast Asia, Indonesia, and Polynesia, prefaced by a book-length introduction, which has since been called "the first great book on general linguistics" (Bloomfield 1933:18). In the course of the nineteenth century, it was reprinted separately a number of times under the title *Über die Verschiedenheit des menschlichen Sprachbaues und ihren Einfluß auf die geistige Entwicklung des Menschengeschlechts* (Flitner & Giel 1981:487).

Curiously, however, Humboldt's linguistic ideas were not utilized in the way that he intended. His interest in the analytical treatment of languages lay outside the dominant tradition of historical linguistics, which was concerned with the reconstruction and classification of Indo-European languages. Humboldt himself had been in scholarly contact with both Friedrich Schlegel and Franz Bopp, whose works had established beyond a doubt the relation between Sanskrit and the European tongues (Schlegel 1808; Bopp 1816), and thereby laid the basis for the discipline of comparative philology or historical linguistics (Sweet 1978:239; Mueller-Vollmer 1989:184). Humboldt, who was himself greatly interested in Sanskrit, contributed institutionally to the nascent discipline—for example, by using his political influence to secure Bopp's appointment as professor of Indian language and philology at the University of Berlin in 1821 (Sweet 1980:420). But while Humboldt's name was frequently invoked by Indo-Europeanists, they did not pursue his more general plan of comparative investigation (Trabant 1990:60). It was Bopp himself who set the stage for this neglect in his review of the *Kawi-Werk*, where, while praising it, he reappropriated its contents for his own scholarly purposes: the reconstruction of proto-languages (Mueller-Vollmer 1991:115). Lacking an appreciation for the sheer beauty of individual languages, Bopp treated Humboldt's work as a late survival of the tradition of philosophical grammar going back to the *Grammaire générale et raisonnée* of Port Royal (1660) (Mueller-Vollmer 1991: 118–19; Trabant 1990:20). Despite his role in establishing its institutional base, Humboldt's scholarly influence on German historical linguistics was limited (cf. Hymes 1983:374–75; W. Lehman 1992).

Unappreciated as a linguist by the middle of the nineteenth century, Humboldt was later periodically rediscovered by linguists who appropriated particular aspects of his theory, usually taken out of their original context without careful readings of the body of his writings. Humboldt is thus frequently stereotyped as an advocate of typological classification, an image which we owe to August Pott, who, in 1848, used the "Humboldtian" categories of *isolating, inflecting, agglutinative*, and *incorporating* as a means to classify the world's languages (Trabant 1990:63). In fact, however, typological classification occupied a subordinate position within the entire framework of Humboldt's thinking.[4]

In pursuing his linguistics, Humboldt initially oriented himself in relation

---

4. Complicating the reception of his work in the twentieth century, Humboldt has been invoked as an intellectual ancestor of opposing theories. On the one hand, Chomsky saw in Humboldt's thinking an early formulation of his theory of transformational generative grammar (Chomsky 1966). On the other hand, Humboldt is commonly linked to the development of the Sapir-Whorf hypothesis (cf. Koerner 1992). Two seriously flawed English editions of the introduction of the *Kawi-Werk* have not helped the elucidation of Humboldt's linguistic approach (W. Humboldt 1971, 1988).

to two standard works on language, representing two rather distinct approaches. On the one hand, there was A. F. Bernhardi's *Sprachlehre* (1801–3), a treatment of language universals in the tradition of the Port Royal grammars (Sweet 1980:396). While Humboldt affirmed certain universal characteristics of the world's languages, however, he was more interested in linguistic differences, which were most comprehensively treated in the *Mithridates*. However, with the exception of Humboldt's own contribution on Basque, its four volumes consisted for the most part of the compilation of scanty linguistic data (including almost five hundred versions of the Lord's Prayer), which nevertheless served Adelung and Vater as the basis for daring speculations—a practice that Humboldt had already criticized in Herder's work (Sweet 1980:397).

Dissatisfied with the lack of empirical and philosophical rigor displayed in the *Mithridates*, Humboldt developed a comprehensive and analytical treatment of language that could in theory be extended to all the world's languages. The cornerstone of this method was the systematic synchronic analysis of languages according to their distinguishing structural features, clearly foreshadowing the later development of structural linguistics (cf. Sapir 1921:120–46). Humboldt employed a number of different terms to describe his mode of analysis, but it mainly demanded a break with the common practice of analyzing an unknown tongue by using the grammatical categories of European languages, Latin in particular, as a basis for comparison. For Humboldt, "the first rule" of linguistic analysis was the "study [of] each known language in its inner structure" ("inneren Zusammenhange"). This program was intended to yield "monographs" of all languages presented according to their own grammatical rules—a process which must necessarily precede any comparison other than mere guesswork (Humboldt IV:11).

In practice, this program meant a rigorous daily schedule for Humboldt, spent mostly in the preparation of more or less elaborate grammars of the world's languages. While the largest published part of these synchronic analyses dealt with the Kawi and other Southeast Asian languages, Humboldt also prepared a voluminous manuscript corpus of grammars of American languages. Lost for the better part of a century, most of these documents have been uncovered only recently in various libraries in Central Europe, including elaborate grammatical sketches of twenty-four American Indian languages (Mueller-Vollmer 1989:185–86, 1991:12, 1993). Humboldt had collected much of his American data from 1802 to 1808 when, as Prussian envoy in Rome he secured access to the grammars prepared by Jesuit missionaries in the New World—a body of material that strengthened his commitment to use language-specific structures, since the missionary grammars consistently treated the languages analogously to Latin and oftentimes contained little more than "incomplete and accidental collections of words" (Humboldt IV:289, VII:29). A second major source of linguistic material from the American

continent was of course his brother Alexander, who collected data during his
expedition to New Spain, and who asked Wilhelm to contribute an essay on
the languages of America for the accounts of his travels (Sweet 1978:277).
Wilhelm, however, never completed the task, leaving the "Essai sur les langues
du Nouveau Continent" an unfinished fragment.

Following the individual description of each language according to its peculiar structure, Humboldt was willing to advance to the next step of linguistic
studies—the classification of the world's languages according to their genetic
affiliation. However, this goal remained thoroughly subordinated to the structural analysis of languages. He specifically warned of unfounded speculation
that progressed without care from the known to the unknown, and he was well
aware of the potential obfuscation of clear distinctions between languages due
to the historical diffusion of language traits. The fact that smaller peoples displaced, subordinated, and mixed with others "naturally affects their languages"; indeed, the confluence of various vernaculars was one of the main
reasons for the development of individual languages in the first place (IV:5–
12). In light of these factors, Humboldt felt that classification, in the final
analysis, could only reveal the histories of individual languages, but not their
genetic relationships (Trabant 1986:189). Regarding typological classification, supposedly his main contribution to linguistics, he had relatively little to
say, and in fact contended that "various languages" of the same morphological
type "shared nothing with each other," and could be "classified together only
in a very uncertain and undecided way" ("unbestimmte Weise") (VII:274).

Apart from the empirical investigation of individual languages, Humboldt's main concern was the psychological processes associated with them:
the relation between language and *Nationalcharakter* and between language
and thought. Humboldt believed that the national character of a people,
driven by its inner forces, or *Volksgeist*, determined and was manifested in a
variety of its cultural aspects, including its customs and morals. Most important, however, *Nationalcharakter* decisively affected the language of each individual "tribe" (*Völkerstämme*), which was the direct product of its "spiritual
peculiarity" (*Geisteseigenthümlichkeit*) (VII:18): "Language is the external representation of the genius of peoples" ("die äußere Erscheinung des Geistes der
Völker") (VII:42). Since the national character was so thoroughly imprinted
on the language, the two terms became virtually synonymous, so closely related that one could not, at any given moment, determine decisively which
affected which (VII:42, 44). Humboldt viewed their relationship in organis-
mic and dialectic terms: language was in "every moment a changing and passing entity" ("in jedem Augenblicke Vorübergehendes"), it was not *ergon* (the
result of a process) but *energeia* (the process itself) (VII:46–47, 168–69).
Since various languages originated in various *Volksgeister*, Humboldt held that
they each contained the respective truths of the *Geister*, which were revealed

unconsciously to the speaker through the use of language—which explained why each language afforded its speakers a distinct "world view" (*Weltansicht*) (IV:28). Because human consciousness was inseparable from human language, the thinking of an individual depended "to a certain degree" on the particular language (IV:15–16, 22). Nevertheless, the individual had cognitive freedom within the limits of the grammatical and semantic scheme of a language, allowing the individual genius to act upon language and, by implication, on the *Nationalcharakter* as well (IV:28). Thus, the relation between the national character and individuals was an on-going dialectical process, in which they were forever "intertwined with each other" (VII:42).

Although a similar notion of the relation between language and national character had been suggested in speculative terms by Hamann and Herder, Humboldt developed a more systematic approach. Following the guiding principles of his original plan for a comparative anthropology, comparative linguistics would reveal the psychological processes that determined the courses of history of various peoples, based on "the connection of linguistic diversity and the distribution of peoples with the production of human thinking" ("Geisteskraft") (VII:15). Since language was the fundamental external aspect of national character, a thorough investigation of linguistic structures could reveal the true nature of the former. Of all ethnic phenomena, languages were the most authentic and immediate representations of particular *Volksgeister*, affording the researcher a glimpse of their *Weltanschauungen* (VII:172–73). All empirical investigation, then, culminated in the analysis of the relation between language and national character, and in this lay the "destination" of linguistics, achieving its unity with "science and art" (IV:13).

As a result of his investigation into the relation between language and thought, Humboldt came to favor Indo-European inflective languages over other morphological types. While such arguments have since served to justify racial prejudices, Humboldt himself dismissed "race" as a possible explanation for different mental abilities (VI:196–97). He valued inflecting languages because he presumed that they facilitated the thought process, ensuring a smooth interaction between language and thought. This notion was rooted in Humboldt's distinction between "concepts"—the concrete ideas steering the cognitive process—and "grammatical relations," which never occurred independently in thought, but nevertheless modified the concepts. In inflected languages, grammatical relations were symbolically subordinated to concepts, since they appeared as meaningless attachments to words in the form of affixes—thus maintaining on the linguistic level the distinction of concepts and grammatical relations existing on the level of thought (cf. Manchester 1984: 135–36). This was in contrast to isolating languages, where each morpheme was represented by a distinct word, or agglutinative languages, where grammatical relations appeared as separate entities added to the verb stem. In both these cases, the ideal thought process was hindered because meaningful units, which could also serve as concepts, had to fulfil meaningless grammatical relations. This limited the degree of perfection the language could attain, since "the development of ideas (*Ideenentwicklung*) and the enjoyment of formal thinking" could not develop properly in such languages. There was, then, a decisive gap between uninflected languages and the *höchstgebildeten* tongue— Greek, both the most highly developed language and the one that had realized its potential to the maximum degree (IV:293–94).

Despite his emphasis on the diversity of the world's languages, Humboldt had a deep appreciation for the oneness of human language, which he saw expressed in that very diversity itself (VII:51). For Humboldt, language was the unifying element of humanity, originating in a common "need for language" (*Sprachbedürfnis*) and a common "language ability" (*Sprachvermögen*) among all humans, and corroborated by similarities found among all languages (IV:12; cf. V:365). Humboldt's fundamental respect for language as a human phenomenon kept him from condemning any one language; even the languages of "the wildest savages" were too precious to be denied full attention (VII:256; cf. IV:10–11). He regarded all languages as functionally equivalent, capable of expressing any conceivable idea (IV:17). Any great idea could be rendered into isolating and agglutinative languages, even if speakers of such languages could not develop these great ideas independently. But while only the speakers of inflected languages were likely to attain the highest level of thinking, yielding thereby the greatest cultural output, Humboldt was quick to concede that uninflected languages were also capable of reaching high degrees of culture, specifically noting Chinese and ancient Mexican (Nahuatl) (VII:272). Moreover, Humboldt valued the ability of the human mind to acquire different languages, enabling any individual to acquire numerous *Weltanschauungen* by virtue of the different psychological structures inherent in various languages (IV:12). Implicit in this argument was the humanistic notion that any human being, "even the wildest savage," could be brought into civilization through the acquisition of cultured languages.

Regarding many pertinent linguistic questions of the day, Humboldt exercised his typical caution. The origin of language could only be the object of futile speculation—worthy of a metaphysical discussion rather than an historical investigation, since comparative linguistics offered no answers to questions beyond the realm of immediate experience (cf. Trabant 1990:78). In contrast to the assumption that "primitive" American languages were remnants of the process of original language formation, Humboldt explicitly rejected the notion that any known language offered a glimpse into the past. No language had been found that lacked grammar or that was so recent as not to be the product of the activities of many generations of speakers. (IV:115–16; VII:47). In the historicist tradition of Herder, Humboldt also refused to propose a uniform law for the development of languages. Recognizing that the distinction between isolating, inflective, agglutinative, and incorporative languages could be interpreted as the stages of a unilinear development, he was quick to denounce such a scenario, and warned against "constructing a general type of progressive language development according to which all individual phenomena are judged" (IV:285, 299). Skeptical of natural laws as the governing agents of human behavior, he remained committed to the uniqueness of each language and national character.

While the mainstream of nineteenth-century German Indo-European linguistics had little use for Humboldt's comparative approach, his legacy was carried forward in the *Völkerpsychologie* of Lazarus and Steinthal. It was Steinthal, however, who concerned himself primarily with language, conceiving his place in relation to Humboldt as that of "Theophrast next to Aristotle" (in Bumann 1965:15). The Introduction of the *Kawi-Werk* was the basis of his linguistic thought, and his entire opus can be seen as an explication of Humboldt's writings (Trabant 1990:95, 61). As guardian of Humboldt's reputation, Steinthal disputed Pott's misrepresentation of Humboldt's system as a comprehensive typological classification of the world's languages (Trabant 1990:64; cf. Steinthal 1850). In 1883, he published an edition of Humboldt's major writings of language, including the text of the introduction to the *Kawi-Werk*, supplemented with meticulous notes and careful interpretations in which he sought to rectify certain philosophical weaknesses he perceived in them. In his own theorizing, Steinthal attempted to place Humboldt's work on what he felt was firmer (i.e., Hegelian) epistemological ground, drawing also on Herbartian psychology, which had been fundamental to the development of *Völkerpsychologie* (Steinthal 1848; Bumann 1965:27–30).

Apart from these philosophical qualms, Steinthal had nothing but praise for Humboldt as empirical linguist and folk psychologist (Steinthal 1850:23). The emphasis on linguistics within *Völkerpsychologie* was a direct consequence of Steinthal's adoption of the Humboldtian framework of comparative linguistics. It was Steinthal who prevented Humboldt's original program of anthropological linguistics from being forgotten in the middle of the nineteenth century (Trabant 1990:61). Aside from investigations into various *Volksgeister* through their languages, he promulgated Humboldt's interest in non-Indo-European tongues, which he analyzed synchronically in terms of their "inner form"—a term he borrowed directly from Humboldt. As the organizing principle derived from the character of a nation and expressed in the grammatical and lexical structure of each individual language, "inner form" could only be derived by way of synchronic structural analysis rather than by comparison with the grammatical categories of other languages.

Die Mande-Neger-Sprachen (1867), perhaps Steinthal's most ambitious Humboldtian work, involved a structural analysis of four languages of the Niger-Congo region: Mande, Vai, Soso, and Bambara, which he subsumed under the term "Mande-Neger-Sprachen." Intended not just for "researchers of language, but also for psychologists," the book contained the analytical treatment of each language, followed by an investigation into the psychological processes of thought formation in connection with the structural aspects of the languages (Steinthal 1867:v). Discussing kinship terms, for example, Steinthal noted that the Mande languages lacked distinct terms for "son" and "daughter," but contained a generic term for "child," which was modified by a female or male gender marker. At the same time, Mande had obligatory age markers lacking in the majority of the world's languages—suggesting that while gender was not of prominent psychological concern to the Mande, age was (Steinthal 1867:202–3). Recognizing the drastic departure of his treatise from the "usual organizations of our grammars," Steinthal pointed to the unique insights his investigation had yielded (1867:x). In his effort to uncover the unique psychological configuration of a particular language family through synchronic analysis, Steinthal pursued his major comparative investigation, *Charakteristik der hauptsächlichsten Typen des Sprachbaues* (1860), in which his discussions of Mexican and Eskimo were apparently based on some of Humboldt's manuscripts (Mueller-Vollmer 1993).

However, despite Steinthal's Humboldtian break with historical linguistics, there was a continuity with the Indo-European philological tradition. Steinthal had been a student of August Boeckh, the leading text critic of the day, who, following Schleiermacher and Humboldt, attempted to shed light upon ancient Greece by hermeneutic interpretation of its literary monuments. Steinthal approached original Mande texts as he would have ancient Greek documents, seeing them as expressions of linguistic and national genius. In his *Mande-Neger-Sprachen*, he included fifty pages of original texts, closely explicated in the fashion of Indo-European text criticism (1867:267–320). By emphasizing their literary qualities, he extended the traditional field of philology beyond Indo-European peoples. Foreshadowing Boas, this move implied the recognition of all the world's peoples as carriers of culture, whose development could be studied by methods analogous to those of culture history.

Alexander von Humboldt and the Anthropogeography of the Cosmos

While Wilhelm von Humboldt greatly influenced the humanistic disciplines, his brother Alexander was a central figure in the development of the natural sciences in Germany. A wide-ranging intellect whose scholarship encom-

Alexander von Humboldt and Aimé Bonpland in their camp on the Orinoco, 1800, surrounded by botanical and zoological specimens, with a group of Native Americans visible outside beneath the palm tree. (Courtesy of the Bildarchiv preussischer Kulturbesitz, Berlin.)

passed work in anatomy, botany, and chemistry, Humboldt was most renowned for his explorations in the Americas and the subsequent publications of his travel accounts. His contributions to geology, mineralogy, meteorology, and related fields helped to establish geography as a scientific discipline, and his concern with the relations of humans with their immediate environment dominated German geography in the nineteenth century through the works of Karl Ritter and Friedrich Ratzel (cf. Meyer-Abich 1969:186–96; Gärtner 1959:39–48; Dickinson & Howarth 1933:144–53).

Early in life Humboldt developed a deep appreciation for the phenomena of the natural world, which he studied intensively, taking as his example Goethe's research on natural history. After completing his training at the mining academy in Freiburg, then the leading German institution for the study of natural history, he spent several years in various administrative positions overseeing German mining endeavors. All the while, however, he harbored plans for various scientific expeditions, inspired by his personal friendship with Georg Forster, who had voyaged with Captain Cook. After a number of setbacks, Humboldt finally succeeded in mounting an expedition to the Spanish possessions in America. Under royal protection, he embarked on a scientific exploration of South and Central America, which lasted from 1799 to 1804 and produced twenty-nine volumes on American geography, zoology, botany, along with numerous ethnological observations. This work immediately established him as a leading naturalist, and, after declining the opportunity of a political career in Berlin, he spent the years following his return from the New World in Paris—then the center of natural scientific scholarship (Klencke 1852:11–35, 85–105; Beck 1959:25). He did not return to Germany until 1827, when he took up residence in Berlin, living there until his death in 1859. Throughout this time, Humboldt was a public figure, serving as advisor to the Prussian kings and regularly participating in the intellectual life of the city. In the year of his return, he gave a series of sixty-one lectures on the physical description of the natural world. Eminently successful, these formed the basis of Humboldt's masterpiece, which was published in five volumes under the title *Kosmos* (1845–62). There, Humboldt attempted a comprehensive description of the universe, encompassing a wide range of scientific knowledge: the physical geography of the world (I), the history of the investigation and description of the natural world (II), astronomy (III & IV), and volcanic and seismic activity (V) (Klencke 1852:106–58; Beck 1961:80).

The original conception of the *Kosmos*, "whose undefined image" had "floated" around in Humboldt's head "for almost half a century," dated back to the 1790s (1845:vii). Its theoretical orientation and methodology reflected Herder's plan for an empirical investigation of all the world's phenomena, Kant's skepticism concerning deductive classification, and Wilhelm von Humboldt's inductive approach to history. Alexander von Humboldt conceived of nature as "a unity within the diversity of phenomena," which by means of the "animated breath of life" were interrelated in an intricate system of "natural forces" that "made [them] mutually dependent upon each other" (23–24). Although this conception of nature was very much in accord with the Romantic *Naturphilosophie* of Schelling, Fichte, and Hegel, Humboldt violently opposed their speculative and anti-empirical procedures (Bunge 1969:18–19; Beck 1961:79, 81). In place of the "vague and poetic garb" in which "the philosophy of Nature . . . had been enveloped from her origin," Humboldt demanded "induction and reasoning" to eclipse "conjecture and assumption" (1845:24). In a sense, Humboldt attempted to reconcile the speculative adulations of nature so characteristic of Schelling's *Naturphilosophie* with the empirical facts of the natural world. To do so, he demanded the thorough description of the physical reality of nature as the primary object of cosmography. He in fact conceived the *Kosmos* as a full account of "the physical history of the world" and its "physical geography, combined with a description of the regions of space and the bodies occupying them." The term "history" was not accidental; Humboldt drew the analogy between his approach and the German historical sciences, for "the unity . . . in the development of the great phenomena of the universe is analogous to that which historical composition is capable of acquiring" (vii, 49).

Although he was a *Naturwissenschaftler*, Alexander von Humboldt's approach to the phenomena of the world was that of a natural historian rather than a physicist. Along with his brother and other historicist thinkers, Alexander von Humboldt was skeptical of the Enlightenment attempt to reduce the world to abstract principles along Newtonian lines. Echoing Kant's concern, he sought scrupulously to avoid the fallacy of arbitrary and premature classification based on deductive reasoning alone (cf. Nicolson 1987:170–71).

> All points relating to the accidental individualities, and the essential variations
> of the actual, whether in the form and arrangement of natural objects, in the
> struggle of man against the elements, or of nations against nations, do not admit
> of being based only on a *rational foundation*. (1845:49–50)

Any valid classification would have to be achieved by induction based on the data at hand, rather than by superimposing predetermined categories on the world's external reality. Avoiding unwarranted classification, Humboldt's goal in the five volumes of the *Kosmos* was to embrace all individual phenomena in their totality, since as "partial facts" they could "be considered only in relation to the whole" (55). Thus, the object of study was to place each specimen in its "zone of habitation" (61).

Humboldt conceived his cosmography in explicit contrast to positivistic approaches to the natural world such as those of Auguste Comte and John Stuart Mill, which classified phenomena exclusively "with reference to the principles of gradation in their development" (1845:61; cf. Bunge 1969:28). But if it was not the purpose of the *Kosmos* simply to "reduce all sensible phenomena to a small number of abstract principles, based on reason alone," Humboldt did not refuse to investigate the regularities found in the natural world (1845:49). On the contrary, while his emphasis was on the description of individual phenomena in relation to larger units, he recognized the "ultimate object" of science to be the discovery of the laws that governed natural processes (50). Like his classifications, however, these laws would have to be discovered through a process of induction, as they revealed themselves in the available empirical data, apprehended by "a half indistinct and more or less just intuition of the connection existing among natural objects or forces" (74). The natural historian's method essentially duplicated Wilhelm von Humboldt's hermeneutic methodology in his "On the Task of the Writer of History."

In contrast to natural laws, the "empirical laws" Alexander von Humboldt sought explained only the regularities of the phenomena under observation. To move from empirical laws to natural laws, the researcher had to proceed with extraordinary care, and it was by no means certain that universal laws could be found at all. "The empire of certain natural laws grand and simple as nature itself" had so far been glimpsed only in very limited domains (1845:73–74). Thus in the field of astronomy, due to the "high degree of simplicity to the mechanism of the heavens," the "laws of motion alone" sufficed to explain the movement of planets. But in the realm of the "physical sciences of the earth," phenomena were "so complicated" as to resist "the application of rigorous method" that might ensure "the same certainty and simplicity in the exposition of facts and their mutual connection, which characterizes the celestial portion of the Cosmos" (64–65). In the face of these complexities, Humboldt warned that "the time when it [would] be possible for us to reduce, by operation of thought, all that we perceive by the senses, to the unity of a rational principle" was "very far" off. Given "the vast extent of the Cosmos," he doubted that "such a victory could ever be achieved." Humboldt therefore limited the *Kosmos* to "the domain of empirical ideas"—"measurements, experiments, and the investigation of facts" (73, 75).

Alexander von Humboldt was not an anthropologist per se. While the accounts of his travels contained demographic and economic information along with some description of cultural features, his main focus was always on physical geography (cf. Humboldt 1809, 1826). Without pursuing the matter systematically, however, he insisted that the earth's "physical phenomena . . . influence the intellectual advancement of mankind," a notion already proposed in Herder's *Ideen zur Philosophie der Geschichte der Menschheit* (1845:23; Herder 1784:115–29). It was Humboldt's protégé Karl Ritter who, with his approval, undertook a more systematic explanation of the relation between nature and humanity. In the *Kosmos*, Humboldt lauded

> the admirable work . . . in which Karl Ritter so ably delineates the physiognomy of our globe, and shows the influence of its external configuration on the physical phenomena on its surface, on the migrations, laws, and manners of nations, and on all the principal historical events enacted upon the face of the earth. (1845:48)

Ritter was professor of geography in Berlin, a position he had secured with Humboldt's support; his mammoth project, *Erdkunde*, unfinished at his death in 1859 after the publication of nineteen volumes, established him, second only to Humboldt, as among the foremost geographers of his time (Dickinson & Howarth 1933:152). Despite his frequent avowals of admiration for Humboldt's life work, Ritter had relatively little experience as a field geographer, gaining his reputation through the immense erudition he brought to bear on the main object of his investigation—the relation of nature to human history. In his philosophical outlook, Ritter shared the national particularism of Herder:

> It is characteristic of human nature that in every man some peculiarity is lodged, his own alone, through whose unfolding he can become a complete being. This is true of every nation, also. In the perfect development of this peculiarity lies the moral greatness, and indeed all the greatness of man. (Ritter 1863:57)

As a good historicist, Ritter sought to explain the current situation of a people as a product of its particular history, linking the methodology of geography to that of the historical sciences: both "proceed from plain and positive details," and thence "to more hidden relations" that would reveal "the inner laws of nature, as well as moral principles (241–42). However, in contrast to Wilhelm von Humboldt and the folk psychologists, who had viewed the course of history as a result of psychological factors, Ritter looked instead to the environmental situation. In doing so, he was following Herder, who, arguing the inseparability of "natural history" and the "histories of peoples," had suggested that "geography is the basis of history and history is nothing but the geography of times and peoples set in motion" (in Lehmann 1883:4). Ritter went beyond this to derive a straightforward geographical determinism: "The customs of individuals and nations differ in all countries, because man is dependent on the nature of his dwelling-place" (1863:318). To unearth the laws that governed the interrelation of human beings with their natural environment, Ritter proposed an inductive method analogous to Alexander von Humboldt's (86). But although he deemed the discovery of these laws paramount, his *Erdkunde* was largely descriptive; insofar as it went beyond this, it was to systematize rather than to seek causes (Dickinson & Howarth 1933:153). Ritter's "laws"—perhaps better termed "trends"—were rather specific observations of the interactions of certain peoples with their surroundings in the course of their history. Focussing on population movements, he attempted to derive a "law of migrations" that could systematize the movements of peoples in history along geographical features such as mountain ranges and coast lines. Like Herder, and in opposition to Alexander and Wilhelm von Humboldt, Ritter was not altogether disinclined to broader speculations. Assuming population movements had been continuous since prehistoric times, he thought that the nomadic peoples of the day represented the remnants of this ancient period (Kluckhohn & Prufer 1959:14–16).

Some fifteen years after Ritter's death, his ideas were developed in a more systematic way by Friedrich Ratzel, a trained zoologist and one-time follower of Ernst Haeckel, the leading German proponent of social Darwinism. Following a scientific journey to the American continent, Ratzel came under the influence of Moritz Wagner, a student of Ritter and professor of geography, and he abandoned evolutionism to pursue the study of geography along Ritterian lines (Steinmetzler 1956:50–90). From 1875 on, Ratzel investigated the interrelation between humans and their environment, giving a new name to the inquiry with the publication of the first of two volumes of his *Anthropogeographie* (Ratzel 1882; cf. Steinmetzler 1956:16). Acknowledging Ritter's insistence on the "inseparable bond between geography and history," Ratzel conceived the study of geography, and anthropogeography in particular, as an essentially historical investigation (1882:32). Theoretically, Ratzel saw the relationship between humanity and nature as reciprocal, but in practice he only discussed the effect of the natural environment on human behavior. Focussing solely on the discovery of geographical laws, he insisted that an understanding of the geographical situation of a people could be equated with an understanding of history: "the origin of a people can only be imagined and investigated geographically" (172; cf. Steinmetzler 1956:20–39).

In the tradition of Ritter and Alexander von Humboldt, Ratzel argued that the first and foremost obligation of the anthropogeographer was the thorough description of the geographical features of a given region, including detailed documentation of human residential patterns. On this basis, it was possible to investigate the geographical reasons underlying large scale population movements and the distribution of the earth's inhabitants. The final object of investigation was an analysis of the "effect of nature on the body and spirit of individuals and entire peoples" (1882:77–78). Ratzel replaced Ritter's rather diffuse teleological conception of history with a more causal one, rooted solidly in the soil of the earth, as opposed to a divine plan that was revealed through humanity's interaction with nature (Steinmetzler 1956:16, 111). But his debt to Ritter was never in doubt: "[I]n all of Ritter's *Erdkunde*, there was no sentence on the relation of nature and history that we did not approve of" (1882:38).

Following Ritter and Wagner, Ratzel's anthropogeography equated history with the sum of the population movements it embodied (Steinmetzler 1956:97). The more the anthropogeographer probed the depth of history, the more could be learned about the true nature of different peoples, because through a knowledge of their various dwelling places, it was possible to understand both their *Volksgeister* and their history (1882:114). Since motion was inherent to humans, a process akin to population movement occurred even among sedentary peoples, revealing itself in the constant diffusion of various human traits. Hinted at in the first volume of *Anthropogeographie*, the idea of the perpetual diffusion of ethnic traits was elaborated in great detail in Ratzel's three-volume *Völkerkunde* (1885–88) and in the second volume of *Anthropogeographie*, published in 1891 (cf. Buttmann 1977:84). In these texts, Ratzel linked anthropogeography to physical anthropology and ethnology, arguing that "through the application of anthropogeographical methods, it was possible . . . [to] find the historical relations of peoples" by considering "their anthropological features and ethnographic possessions" (1891:578). After having shown the continuous diffusion of physical, linguistic, and ethnographic traits, he argued that studying their geographical distribution would reveal the historical relations of their carriers (78–98). To Ratzel, the occurrence of similar traits in different peoples automatically revealed their historical connection, even in cases where the two features were found in areas separated by great distance and by territories lacking the similar traits (605, 651). Disinclined to entertain the possibility of independent invention, Ratzel assumed that all ethnic phenomena developed in one place and diffused from there to all the other localities in which they were found.

In this approach to the study of human history, Ratzel stood opposed to the thinkers who had dominated his early intellectual upbringing. Although he never abandoned a general belief in the process of biological evolution, he took a decisive stand against Ernst Haeckel and Herbert Spencer and their "crude hypothesis of the survival of the fittest" (in Steinmetzler 1956:87). In a review of *The Principles of Biology*, Ratzel scolded Spencer for making careless use of ethnographic facts to support his theories, claiming he lacked any understanding of their meaning, and rejecting his generalizations as schematic and hasty (Steinmetzler 1956:128–29). Ratzel responded similarly to Auguste Comte, attacking the hierarchical system of sciences because it precluded utilization of the historical method until after the establishment of a positive sociology. In contrast, Ratzel felt that the historical method was the procedure best able to lead to classification and causation. "Comte and his followers were on the wrong track" when they concentrated too narrowly "on the successive steps on which peoples ascended toward higher development" (1882:28–30). The correct goal was to study the histories of all peoples, for "even the population movements of Central Africa" had "their history," and only the knowledge of these particular events could reveal the "history of humanity" at large (87–88).

The Humboldtian Tradition in
German Anthropology

While Ratzel elaborated the Ritterian paradigm with its emphasis on the relationship of geography and history, other thinkers expanded the scope of anthropology by embracing the traditions emanating from both Alexander and Wilhelm von Humboldt. Theodor Waitz and Adolf Bastian were the first to merge these two Humboldtian currents systematically, thereby establishing a historicist Counter-Enlightenment viewpoint in the study of humanity as a whole. Their distinctive intellectual biographies, however, linked them each primarily to a different Humboldt brother: Waitz to Wilhelm, Bastian to Alexander. Waitz was a *Geisteswissenschaftler*, a trained philologist, who published an edition of Aristotle's *Organon* at age twenty-three, thereby winning an appointment as professor of philosophy at Marburg. Developing an interest in pedagogy and in the psychological factors underlying *Bildung*, he explored these cross-culturally through the critical analysis of travel accounts and related materials (Gerland 1896:629–33). Bastian, in contrast, was a *Naturwissenschaftler* trained in medicine and the natural sciences. Inspired by the ex-

ample of Alexander von Humboldt, he sought to document the full diversity
of human life through empirical research and direct observation (Fiedermutz-
Laun 1970:5–7). From their respective vantage points, Waitz and Bastian effectively bridged the gulf between the natural historical and philological traditions, linking the precise description of physical realities with a sensitivity
toward cultural particularities and their individual historical trajectories, thus
paving the way for the embracive approach of Boasian anthropology.

By virtue of his scholarly background, Waitz initially oriented his work to
the efforts of the folk psychologists. However, despite their shared concern
with the psychological characteristics of the world's peoples, Waitz never became a folk psychologist in the sense of Lazarus and Steinthal. Indeed, he
opposed their *Völkerpsychologie* by denying the existence of its object of investigation, the *Volksgeist*, which he considered a mere abstraction (Gerland
1860). Moreover, he regarded as one-sided the folk psychologist's approach to
the study of human history, which focussed exclusively on psychological aspects while neglecting external forces (Waitz 1859:476). On the other hand,
Waitz also opposed Ritter's view that history was exclusively determined by
geographical circumstances (89). In place of such monistic explanations for
the course of the individual histories of peoples, Watiz proposed an embracive
approach reminiscent of Wilhelm von Humboldt's suggestions in his comparative anthropology and "On the Task of the Writer of History." He pursued the
task in the highly influential six-volume *Anthropologie der Naturvölker*, characterized by Robert Lowie as a "forerunner of Boas' *The Mind of Primitive
Man*," which directly referred to Waitz's book and "closely parallels its argument" (Lowie 1937:17).

Waitz conceived the *Anthropologie der Naturvölker* in reaction to the polygenist ideas advanced by mid-nineteenth-century writers opposed to the doctrine of the psychic unity of mankind (cf. Stocking 1987:142). Among others
challenged by Waitz were Louis Agassiz, who had argued for the existence of
up to twelve distinct species resulting from multiple creations, and Gustav
Klemm, who had proposed the separation of humanity into two major races:
one "active," culturally advanced, and masculine; the other "passive," innately
inferior, and feminine, subsuming all non-Indo-European peoples (Waitz
1859:221, 344; cf. Lowie 1937:14). Against the polygenists, Waitz argued that
only a rigorously inductive analysis could settle the question whether various
groups of peoples were distinct species, or lacked certain mental capabilities.
The first volume of his *Anthropologie der Naturvölker* was devoted to these
problems, along with discussions of his theoretical and methodological framework. The first part dealt with the physiological question of the unity of mankind; the second addressed the question of whether or not humans were of one
species in their mental abilities. Waitz insisted that the case for distinct human
species was the result of arbitrary categorization based on "abstract deductions

lacking proper empirical basis" (1859:4). Amassing all the data available on physical traits among all the world's groups, Waitz demonstrated the constant blurring of purported lines of racial demarcation, asserting that this precluded the existence of truly distinct types—an argument that Alexander von Humboldt had previously made in the *Kosmos* (158, 212; cf. Humboldt 1845:356). In regard to psychological traits—which reflected the degree of culture attained along the lines of the German *Bildungsideal*—Waitz found a similar situation. There was no group that lacked culture altogether, and any attempt to classify the actually existing gradations of civilization along psychological lines could only be based on subjective criteria. Echoing a notion Wilhelm von Humboldt had developed in regard to linguistic ability, Waitz also rejected any immediate relation between the physical and psychological features of peoples (cf. Humboldt III:243–44). Waitz argued that "race" was evidently unrelated to cultural achievement, since the members of a single race showed greatly varying degrees of cultivation. While some Caucasian peoples might have achieved the highest form of civilization, the cultural achievement of the great majority of Caucasians was clearly less, for example, than that of the Chinese, whose culture, in turn, was much more advanced than that of the physically related Siberian peoples (1859:297, 337). For Waitz, there was no basis for the equation of physical types with culture other than *a priori* deduction. Developing Alexander von Humboldt's original criticism of the deductive method of such thinkers as Agassiz and Klemm, Waitz stressed that classification of human groups by different criteria produced different results. He particularly warned against physical classification, which, due to the constant diffusion of racial traits by intermarriage, was highly arbitrary. Although a classification along linguistic lines appeared more tenable, even here the influence of historical factors precluded certainty (259, 291).

According to Watiz, four factors determined the historical trajectory of a given people: the "physical organization" of the people; the particular form of its spiritual (*geistigen*) life, which created distinct "views, interests, and emotions" in each individual; its natural environment; and the sum of the social relations of the individuals and larger units within the group (1859:6). While all these factors affected the course of history, some were more important than others. Watiz argued, for example, that climate by itself exerted little force on history, while the degree of culture had a pronounced effect (102). To understand humanity at large, it was necessary for anthropology to investigate the differences between various peoples, for these differences were the most important characteristic of human life. It could not limit itself to the investigation of certain peoples, but must study the histories of all peoples, the summation of which comprised history at large. And along with their history, it must investigate the "anatomy, physiology, and psychology" of peoples, since all of these factors helped shape the individual trajectory of a people (4–11).

The psychic unity of humanity proclaimed by Waitz was thus fundamentally distinct from that of the French Enlightenment, which assumed the uniform working of the human mind over space and time. Following Herder and Wilhelm von Humboldt, Waitz recognized that cognitive processes were diverse, in some respects irrational, and always the result of particular histories. Insisting that the cognitive diversity of humans was the product of historico-psychological processes rather than a reflection of physiological dissimilarities, Waitz rejected any innate racial hierarchy in cultural achievement (1859: 157). But while the basic abilities of humans were alike, every cultural situation was the product of the unique historical processes that had shaped it (475, 478). Citing Wilhelm von Humboldt, Waitz forcefully attacked all attempts at a "philosophy of history" of the kind set out by Condorcet or Comte. Such notions of uniform progression could not account for the "great diversity" or "manifold entwinements of the circumstances causing cultural development among peoples" (278, 475).

In the *Anthropologie der Naturvölker*, Waitz moved a step closer to the cultural relativism implied in the historicist worldview, but never fully realized by its early proponents. Like the young Boas, he used the pivotal term "culture" in the humanistic sense of the accumulation of mental achievements of a people, accepting the distinction between *Naturvolk* and *Kulturvolk*. But he was aware of the arbitrariness of such a classification, insisting that every society had a unique position within humanity and afforded equal satisfaction for its members (1859:484). Confronted with the diversity of cultural life forms, all that one could do was to "refrain from comparing their value and to appreciate them in their totality as a magnificent spectacle, in whose colorful interchange, rich intricacy, and delightful unfolding one relished, participated, and learned" (478). Waitz thus reasserted the unique combination of universalism and particularism exemplified in the anthropology of Herder and Wilhelm von Humboldt; like them, he saw the separation of humanity into distinct peoples as an affirmation of common humanity. Accordingly, Waitz saw no reason for non-European cultures to adopt the standard of "European civilization," especially in the face of the "unimaginable suffering" that had been brought upon the *Naturvölker* when exposed to "our cultural standards" (480, 483).

Waitz's liberal humanism was echoed by Bastian, who voiced similar views throughout his career, although he arrived at them as a natural historian rather than a philologist. Born in 1826 and educated at five different universities, Bastian eventually obtained a doctorate in medicine at Würzburg in 1850. There he met Rudolf Virchow, the great pathologist and physical anthropologist, who became a lifelong friend and collaborator. Following the example of Alexander von Humboldt, Bastian embarked in 1851 on his first voyage around the world, returning in 1859 after visiting Australia, China, South East

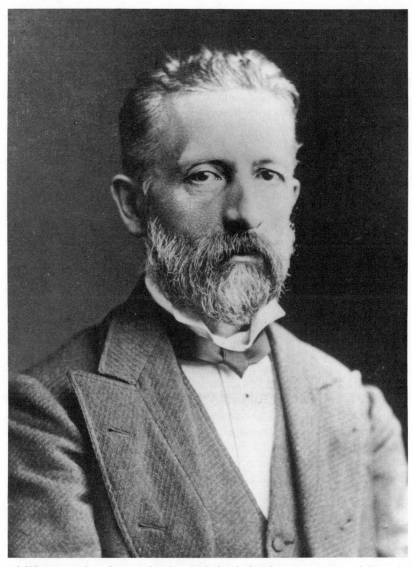

Adolf Bastian, at about the time when Boas worked under him for a year arranging exhibits at the Royal Ethnographic Museum in Berlin. (Courtesy of the Bildarchiv preussischer Kulturbesitz, Berlin.)

Asia, the Americas, and Africa (Fiedermutz-Laun 1970:5–12). He then set to work on his major treatise, the three-volume *Der Mensch in der Geschichte*, which he dedicated to Humboldt, who, in fact read and approved drafts of the text just before his death in 1859 (1860:V). Over the next forty years, Bastian elaborated the theoretical framework presented there, producing a great number of books and articles based on his travels, which took him outside of Germany for a total of more than twenty years (Fiedermutz-Laun 1970:9–10). Although his accounts were widely regarded as "inconceivably crabbed" and virtually impenetrable (Lowie 1937:32), Bastian played a pivotal role in the development of German anthropology, not only as a practitioner, but also as an administrator and teacher. In 1868, he became the president of the Gesellschaft für Erdkunde, the geographical society, which, since its foundation by Ritter, had treated ethnological issues as well as geography. A year later, he joined Virchow in founding the Berliner Gesellschaft für Anthropologie, Ethnologie und Urgeschichte, assuming also the position of docent of *Völkerkunde* at the University of Berlin, where he eventually became full professor. Perhaps even more significantly, however, the artifacts he acquired in the course of his travels provided the foundation of a museum of ethnology—the Königliches Museum für Völkerkunde, where Bastian trained a number of young men who went on to become professional anthropologists, including Franz Boas (Fiedermutz-Laun 1970:5–12; Stocking 1968:151–52).

In all his endeavors, Bastian united Alexander von Humboldt's desire to account for the entirety of the cosmos with an appreciation—echoing Herder and Wilhelm von Humboldt—for each individual *Volk* as a moment in the plenitude of humanity (cf. Bastian 1869:157–62, 1893–94:28). Because the right of existence of each *Volk* was severely threatened by colonial expansion, which was causing the rapid disappearance of indigenous populations, Bastian regarded it as his urgent calling to collect as many ethnic products as possible, whether in the form of artifacts, myths, religious beliefs, grammars, or descriptions of political and economic systems.

> Even now, material perishes in front of our eyes through our inconsiderate neglect; we could have salvaged so much more than we have through our contact with living native societies. Indeed each year, each day, nay each hour, things disappear from this earth; and we look on without moving so much as a little finger. . . . Our guiding principle, therefore, in anthropology, prehistory or ethnology should be to collect everything. (1881:217)

In his museum work and publications, Bastian sought to capture the wealth of diversity that constituted humanity at large for the sake of future generations of ethnologists who might not have the opportunity to appreciate the human cosmos to its full extent (cf. Fiedermutz-Laun 1970:11).

In line with his efforts as a salvage anthropologist, Bastian's theoretical framework was conceived in the spirit of the *Humanitätsideal*, uniting a sense of the universal with an appreciation of the particular aspects of humanity. It rested on two central concepts, the *Elementargedanken* and the *Völkergedanken*. Bastian argued that a limited range of elementary ideas, or elementary patterns of thought permanent through space and time, were common to all of humanity. These elementary ideas, however, never occurred as such, but were always clothed in a unique fashion and expressed as folk ideas, the specific patterns of thought of particular groups. Developing out of the limited number of *Elementargedanken*, the unique pattern of *Völkergedanken* among each people depended primarily on the environment of the group. From this notion sprang the concept of the "geographical province," in which a homogeneous environment, conditioning a relatively uniform cultural setting, produced similar folk ideas (1893–94:170–75; cf. Fiedermutz-Laun 1970:77–88). But while folk ideas were shaped primarily by geographical factors, they were always susceptible to change through historical processes, and were thus in a constant state of flux. Through "transactions with neighbors," a people received "new ideas," which provoked "new activities" (1860:141). The relative simplicity of folk ideas around the world was thus confirmation of the psychic unity of mankind, because it revealed "a monotonous sub-stratum of identical elementary ideas" (1893–94:175). But for Bastian, as for Waitz, this did not imply a uniform historical process, because the various influences exerted on the monotonous *Elementargedanken* produced a multitude of particular *Völkergedanken* among the peoples of the world.

The resemblance of Bastian's *Völkergedanken*, Lazarus's and Steinthal's *Volksgeister* and, by implication, Wilhelm von Humboldt's *Nationalcharakter* was very close. Each designated the particular psychological core of any given people, which ultimately determined cultural production and individual behavior. Consequently, the task of the researcher was the collection and interpretation of specific folk ideas, as they were manifest in the psychological products of various peoples. But in contrast to the folk psychologists, Bastian demanded a more thorough investigation of the geographical component, since, in his view, the development of particular folk ideas was so closely linked to geographical factors, especially among "cultureless" peoples whose behavior was in large part determined by their immediate environment (1871:168). Bastian also rejected the folk psychologists' use of Herbartian psychology, because its epistemological framework was limited to individual cognition. Since he held that communal cognition always preceded and shaped individual thought, Bastian sought to replace Herbart's individualistic psychology with a unique scientific approach emphasizing the thought processes common to entire groups. These could be illuminated by the science of ethnology, which thereby prepared the epistemological ground for scientific psychology (1881:163).

For ethnology itself to become a scientific discipline, Bastian felt that it had to be based exclusively on inductive reasoning. Invoking the authority of

Alexander von Humboldt, the "hero for our age" who had "provided the plat-
form on which to erect the temple of the harmonious cosmos by inductive
research," Bastian adapted Humboldt's cosmographical approach to human
behavior, conceiving each individual *Volk* and each folk idea as particular entities within larger frameworks (1869:158). But as an ardent empiricist, unwilling to engage in deductive speculation, he felt the need for a comprehensive collection of data, encompassing "the social character of man in all its
ethnic manifestations" (1893–94:170). To this end, he eventually proposed
an ambitious documentary project, which he called a *Gedankenstatistik*, a "statistical tabulation of ideas," which would include all folk ideas present in the
world—"all possibilities of thought in space and time" (1893–94:172). Like
the folk psychologists, Bastian had hoped ultimately to find the laws that governed the mental development of the world's peoples (1860:160). But in
1881, he had postponed the realization of such goals to some future generation
on grounds that foreshadow Boas:

> Ethnology, that newly rising star of science, seemed to offer a ray of hope, hope
> that we might finally find a solution to the contemporary situation in which our
> world view is both unsure and fragmented. Ethnology seemed to offer the chance
> to put the Science of Man on the same solid base of actual proof as we find now
> in the natural sciences. . . . This hope entranced and enticed us: we began with
> fresh vigor to pursue ethnological enquiries, and indeed our efforts proceeded
> most smoothly and pleasantly. . . . Yet these daring intentions soon began to
> crumble to dust as we looked into the more intricate depths of the materials so
> copiously accumulated, and as the mountain of publications grew to an awesome
> height.
>   It is my considered opinion, and the situation corroborates this, that we must
> abandon the aim, indeed the very idea, of achieving one comprehensive and
> comprehensible whole from the materials thus far presented to us: such an
> achievement is not for our generation. We must therefore unconditionally as-
> sume the responsibility for preserving and transmitting the basic materials as we
> pass the burden of building ethnology onto the shoulders of the next generation.
> If we fail on that point the whole endeavor will again fade away into that fata
> morgana of philosophical deductionism. (Bastian 1881:216–17).[5]

5. Cf. Boas: The "history of anthropology is but a repetition of that of other sciences. When
the facts begin to array themselves in seeming order, the ultimate goal of inquiry appears to be
near at hand. The fundamental laws which governed the growth of culture and civilization seem
to manifest themselves copiously, and the chaos of beliefs and customs appears to fall into beautiful order. But investigation goes on incessantly. New facts are disclosed, and shake the foundation of theories that seemed firmly established. The beautiful, simple order is broken, and the
student stands aghast before the multitude and complexity of facts that belie the symmetry of the
edifice that he had laboriously erected. . . . Anthropology has reached that point of development
where the careful investigation of facts shakes our firm belief in the far-reaching theories that
have been built up. The complexity of each phenomenon dawns on our minds, and makes us
desirous of proceeding more cautiously" (1898a:107–8).

Given his inductivist empiricism, it is not surprising that Bastian consistently opposed evolutionary anthropology. Throughout the 1870s, Bastian engaged in bitter disputes with Haeckel, attacking his idea of the descent of different human races from different ape species. Pointing to its similarity with myths found among Southern African and East Asian peoples, he regarded even Darwin's own theory of the "descent of man" as little more than an ill-conceived if bold scenario (Fiedermutz-Laun 1970:52, 55). Bastian was also critical of the ethnocentrism characterizing much of the social evolutionism of the day. Despite his reference to the "cultureless," he cautioned against dividing the world into savage and civilized peoples, refusing to place diverse ethnic groups on a hierarchical ladder, or to assume a uniform progression of either particular ethnic groups or of humanity at large. It was therefore impossible to locate the origin of humanity among "savages" or its destination among "civilized" nations (cf. Koepping 1983:17, 52–53). In lines anticipating Boas, he suggested:

> The idea of a process of evolution to higher forms in which mankind progresses to ultimate perfection can be no more than a hypothesis, for we do not know the final goal. It is easy to see why such an idea was acclaimed: people think our own culture has reached a high level, so high indeed that it will envelope the whole earth at some future date. . . . No factual evidence exists for the postulate of an uninterrupted and constant progression in the evolution of culture, a regularly ascending line from lower to higher stages: rather do we find a multitude of astonishing phenomena which remain twisted and knotty enigmas for research. (1871:166–67)[6]

Despite his critical attitude toward social evolutionism, when it came to explaining cultural similarities, Bastian emphasized independent invention rather than cultural diffusion—a position which brought him into conflict with Ratzel. Bastian, the folk psychologist, favored internal causation for the development of cultural forms, while Ratzel, the historical geographer, favored diffusion along anthropogeographical lines, asserting its occurrence even when no historical connection could be demonstrated with any degree of certainty (Bastian 1893–94:173–75; cf. Boas 1904:30). In opposition to Ratzel's diffusionism, Bastian held a more flexible position, allowing for the possibility of diffusion, but assuming independent invention in the absence of actual historical evidence for contact between two widely separate regions. Bastian never raised independent invention to a dogma, however, and consistently

6. Cf. Boas: "It may be recognized that the [evolutionary] hypothesis implies the thought that our modern Western European civilization represents the highest cultural development towards which all other more primitive cultural types tend, and that, therefore, retrospectively, we construct an orthogenetic development towards our own modern civilization. It is clear that if we admit that there may be different ultimate and co-existing types of civilization, the hypothesis of one single general line of development cannot be maintained" (1920:282).

preferred sound historical explanation to psychological conjectures (cf. Koepping 1983:65).

Despite their disagreements on such technical issues, Ratzel and Bastian shared a historicist viewpoint in the human sciences that was embedded in Counter-Enlightenment assumptions. Both opposed Haeckel's evolutionary assumptions, insisting on viewing the plurality of cultural phenomena as the products of complex historical processes rather than eternal natural laws. But while Ratzel's anthropogeography never transcended a rather crude geographical determinism, Bastian, along with Waitz, sought to arrive at a more inclusive understanding of the human condition. In their respective efforts, they merged the ideas of Wilhelm and Alexander von Humboldt, conceiving humans as historical products of both their *geistigen* ("spiritual") world and their physical environment. Waitz did so in his investigation of the possibility of *Bildung* among the world's peoples, Bastian, in his examination of the trajectories of *Völkergedanken* in relation to geographical provinces. By uniting the historical with the psychological and the physiological with the physical, Waitz and Bastian prepared the intellectual ground for Boas' embracive anthropology.

Boasian Anthropology: From Museum Debates to the Cosmographical Critique of the Comparative Method

Boas began developing his wide-ranging interests early on in his educational career. As he noted later in life, his "university studies were a compromise" between his "intensive emotional interest in the phenomena of the world" and his "intellectual interest" in the natural sciences (1938:20). As a student in Heidelberg, Bonn, and Kiel, he studied geography on behalf of the former interest, and mathematics and physics on behalf of the latter, earning his doctorate in 1881 with a dissertation on the color of water (*Beiträge zur Erkenntniss der Farbe des Wassers*) (Kluckhohn & Prufer 1959:7–8). Conceived in the framework of Fechner's psychophysics, Boas' work, however, raised certain epistemological concerns. Acting simultaneously as subject and experimenter in the course of his sensory experiments, he observed that the quantitative results he obtained were in part conditioned by situational factors. Led to the realization that there were "domains of our experience in which the concepts of quantity" were "not applicable," he began to question his materialistic *Weltanschauung*, since it seemed rather doubtful that a general law governed the relationship of stimulus and perception. Influenced by "the writings of philosophers" who "stimulated new lines of thought," his interests shifted to epistemological questions; in particular, he sought to "understand the relations between the objective and the subjective worlds" (Boas 1938:20). In this situation, Boas turned to the study of geography (cf. Stocking 1968:142–44).

While at Bonn and Kiel, Boas had received instruction in geography from Theobald Fischer, an ardent Ritterian historical geographer concerned primarily with the interrelation between humans and their environment (Kluckhohn & Prufer 1959:9). Driven by the "desire to see the world," and searching for a way to investigate the relationship of the external and the internal, the physical and the psychic, Boas decided to undertake a journey into the Arctic. In this relatively uncomplicated geographical context, he hoped to study "the reaction of the human mind to natural environment" by analyzing the knowledge of the external world in relation to the actual topography (Boas 1938: 20; Stocking 1968:143–44). After a year in Baffinland, he wrote up the results of his exploration in a monograph clearly marked by the influence of Ratzel's geographical determinism. *Baffin-Land: Geographische Ergebnisse einer in den Jahren 1883 und 1884 ausgeführten Forschungsreise* was a rather straightforward anthropogeographical investigation combining formal description of the physical geography of the area with an analysis of the relation of its inhabitants to their local surroundings (1885:39, 62). The longest section of the account, presented under the heading "anthropogeography," discussed population movements in relation to seasonal and geographical features, paying particular attention to the interaction of the various peoples of Baffinland and the diffusion of cultural traits (62–88).

In the course of his anthropogeographical work, Boas also returned to some of the epistemological questions raised initially in his psychophysical investigations. He did so in the context of widespread concern in Germany with epistemological issues. In his *Präludien* (1884), Wilhelm Windelband, a leading figure of the Neo-Kantian movement, identified two scientific methods: the "nomothetic" and the "idiographic." Recalling Kant's distinction in the *Critique of Judgment* between the "generalizing" and the "specifying" interests of reason, he argued that the former produced general laws, while the latter was concerned with detailed depictions of individuality. Even though all scientific fields used features of both, on a theoretical level, their division was "absolute." Dilthey asserted the distinction between the generalizing and specifying methods even more forcefully in his *Einleitung in die Geisteswissenschaften* (1883), arguing for the complete epistemological separation of the *Natur-* and *Geisteswissenschaften*, because they were grounded in two different ways of experiencing the world. The human sciences were based upon lived experience which formed a coherent texture of relations and meanings in the mind; the natural sciences, in contrast, produced knowledge through the conversion of sensory experience into abstract laws (Ermath 1978:88–89, 194–97; Ollig 1979:53–55).

Between the detailed topographic descriptions and historical accounts

Franz Boas, posing in Eskimo costume, shortly after returning from his Baffinland expedition of 1883–84. (Courtesy of the American Philosophical Society.)

resulting from his anthropogeographical investigations in Baffinland and the general laws he had sought in psychophysics, Boas clearly felt similar epistemological tensions. In "The Study of Geography," which was apparently written in 1885 upon the completion of his Baffinland monograph, Boas systematically worked through these issues (Stocking 1968:154). Echoing Windelband's distinction between the nomothetic and idiographic methods, Boas gave the dichotomy a distinctly geographical gloss. Was geography the domain of the Humboldtian "cosmographer," concerned with the documentation and "thorough understanding" of individual phenomena as the outcome of specific historical processes; or, was it that of the "physicist," whose goal was the deduction of the laws that governed the physical world, in which case individual phenomena had no intrinsic value and merely served as a means to discover abstract laws? Echoing Kant, whose work he had read intensively in the Arctic so he would "not be so completely uneducated" upon his return (in Cole 1983), he asserted that the cosmographer followed the "affective" impulse of studying an individual phenomenon regardless of "its place in a system." The physicist, in contrast, was guided by the "aesthetic" desire to systematize the seemingly chaotic world. But since the two approaches had their respective origin in a "different desire of the human mind," any choice between them would only reflect the "mental dispositions of the judge, and be only a confession as to which impulse predominates." In general, Boas therefore granted equal value to the affective and the aesthetic desires, recognizing that they selected different paths toward the same end—"to find the eternal truth." The field of geography, however, was ultimately "part of cosmography," because it originated in the affective "desire to understand the phenomena and history of a country or of the whole earth, the home of mankind" (1887a:640–47).

During this period, Boas came under Bastian's immediate influence, serving as assistant at the Royal Ethnographic Museum in Berlin, while waiting to qualify as *Privatdozent* in geography at the University of Berlin—a process prolonged by the opposition of a member of the faculty who felt that Boas' work had strayed too far from physical geography (Stocking 1968:151–52). At the museum, Boas' interests shifted even further toward ethnology. He abandoned the geographical determinism that had dominated his first monograph, whose results he later called a "thorough disappointment," since the "immediate influence" of the environment was "patent" and could not account for the "driving forces that mold behavior" (1938:21). Having concluded from his Arctic study that human behavior was determined not only by geographical circumstances, but also by psychological and historical factors, Boas shifted his interest to the Northwest Coast, where he hoped to study their complex interrelation. Although Bastian rejected a four-year project Boas proposed in early 1886, he was able that fall to travel to Canada largely on personal funds.

Although Boas did in fact qualify as docent of geography, he resigned from the University of Berlin to stay in New York as geographical editor of the journal *Science*. Inhibited by the political and intellectual atmosphere as well as by the anti-Semitic climate in Germany, Boas early in 1887 decided to marry and settle in the United States (Stocking 1968:150–54, 1974b:84; Rohner 1969:310).

At the time of Boas' immigration, American anthropology was dominated by evolutionary thinking. Although Lewis Henry Morgan had died in 1881, his influence was still strong, especially among the government anthropologists under the leadership of John Wesley Powell, the director of the Bureau of Ethnology in Washington. The other major figure, Daniel Garrison Brinton, although institutionally isolated in Philadelphia, was also motivated by the aesthetic desire to arrange the phenomena of the world in lines of hypothetical development and to posit natural laws underlying cultural evolution (cf. Darnell 1969; Hinsley 1981). Apparently unaware at this point of the extent to which evolutionism governed American ethnology, Boas in the spring of 1887 published a letter in *Science* calling into question on epistemological grounds the system of displaying ethnographical specimens at the U.S. National Museum, where he had previously consulted the collection of artifacts from the Northwest Coast (cf. Stocking 1968:155, 1974b:1–15; Jacknis 1985:77). Coming straight from the Ethnographic Museum in Berlin, which was arranged along the lines of Bastian's concept of geographical provinces, Boas was unpleasantly surprised to find the ethnographic objects exhibited according to their presumed typological evolution rather than "according to the tribes to whom they belong" (1887b:61). The curator Otis T. Mason, working within an evolutionary paradigm, had arranged developmental sequences for all classes of artifacts which served the same purpose, regardless of their origin, in an attempt to "classify human inventions and other ethnological phenomena in the light of biological specimens" (61; Jacknis 1985:78). Boas objected to the application of the "rigid abstractions species, genus, and family," which he considered arbitrary *a priori* categories taken from the field of biology and superimposed on the realm of human behavior (62).

According to Boas, Mason's "method of research was founded on the hypothesis that a connection of some kind" existed between ethnological phenomena separated widely in space, based on the presumption that "like causes produce like effects." The hypothesis of the universal working of the human mind made it possible to assume that "under the same stress and resources" the same inventions would arise and that these could be classified in developmental sequences (61). To Boas however, "the disposition of men to act suitably" was a cause "so general" that it could not be the "foundation of a system of inventions." Echoing the Counter-Enlightenment skepticism of positive laws of human behavior, Boas argued that "the elements affecting the human mind are so complicated; and their influence so utterly unknown" that linear causality was necessarily obscured, rendering Mason's system of classification a "vague hypothesis" (62).

Boas countered Mason's evolutionary positivism with the axiomatic, if ill-phrased, historicist notion that even "though like causes have like effects, like effects have not like causes [sic]" (66). Although unidiomatic, this sentence contained the essence of Boas' later more systematic critique of evolutionism (cf. 1896a). Giving "evolution" his own Humboldtian gloss, Boas suggested that its "true meaning" was that the "object of study is the individual, not the abstraction from the individual under observation" (62). The apparent similarity of the artifacts displayed together in developmental sequence was "deceptive," since the "immanent qualities" of phenomena whose "outward appearance" seemed "identical" might be "altogether different," as a result of the different historical processes that had produced them (66). Complaining that "the marked character of the North-west American tribes" was "almost lost, because the objects" were "scattered in different parts of the building," he insisted that "classification is not explanation" and that "in ethnology all is individuality" (62, 66).

> We have to study each ethnological specimen individually in its history and in its medium, and this is the important meaning of the "geographical province" which is so frequently emphasized by A. Bastian. By regarding a single implement outside of its surroundings, outside of other phenomena affecting that people and its productions, we cannot understand its meaning (62).

Meaning, not function, was the goal of ethnological investigation, and it could only be understood in its geographical and historical context.

Invoking his earlier article on "The Study of Geography," Boas asked whether ethnology was a physical science or a form of cosmography, "the former trying to deduce laws from phenomena, the latter having for its aim a description and explanation of phenomena." While Boas had previously maintained that both approaches were of "equal scientific value," the methodology he now suggested for the study of ethnological phenomena was unmistakably cosmographical. Like Waitz and Bastian, he argued that ethnological phenomena needed to be understood in "their historical development and geographical distribution" as well as in "their physiological and psychological foundation." Concretely, this approach had two aspects: first, an investigation into the "surroundings," tracing the "history of the people" through its "migrations" and "contacts"; second, research into the "physical and psychical character of a people." In approaching the latter problem, two methods suggested themselves to the ethnologist. "Professor Mason's method"—the deductive method—was "to compare the phenomena, and to draw conclusions by analogy." The alternative was the "inductive method" which "traces the

full history of the single phenomenon." Like his historicist predecessors, Boas
had little patience with the deductive method, which had been the "foundation of most errors of the human mind" (63–64). While deduction was the
"most effective method of finding problems," it remained futile speculation
unless inductive methods could be applied to "scrutinize the ideas found by
deduction" (65; cf. Stocking 1974b:12). Although he granted that "Professor
Mason's system was a suggestive one," it was "not fit for scientific research,"
since it did not "allow the application of the inductive method" (65). For
this method, "the tribal arrangement" of museum specimens was the only satisfactory one," since it was the only way to "show the single phenomenon
in its peculiar character and surroundings," geographical, ethnological, and
historical (64).

The response of government anthropologists to Boas' letters was very unfa-
vorable. Mason defended his museum display against Boas' "ingenious" suggestions, arguing that his critique would not hold up in light of the axiom that
"like effects spring from like causes," which justified the treatment of ethnological specimens using the "methods and instrumentalities of the biologist"
(1887:534). A few weeks later, Powell replied along similar lines, arguing
that the tribal arrangement Boas proposed was unfeasible because it would
require too much space and would lead to "monotonous and meaningless"
duplications of material. Similarly, while an "arrangement along geographic
districts" was possible, it would be "excessively expensive." The "scientific or
technological classification" was by far the most economical way of presentation. Furthermore, it corroborated the main findings of anthropological inquiry—the "unity of mankind" (1887:613–16). Resoundingly rebutted by
the most powerful single figure on the American anthropological scene, and
without a secure institutional base of his own, Boas retreated. In a final letter
in the same issue of *Science,* he conceded that there was "really no difference
of opinion between Major Powell and myself" (1887c:614).

In this phase of his career, Boas tried to accommodate his theoretical views
to the dominant evolutionary line. His first theoretical paper on anthropology,
written the following year, was a systematic retreat from the cosmographical
position he took in the controversy with Mason and Powell. Presented originally as a lecture to the German Scientific Society of New York, "The Aims of
Ethnology" clearly emphasized the aesthetic law-seeking impulse over the affective desire to understand each individual phenomenon in its historical context. Historical investigation was merely a supplementary tool in the study of
physical traits, language, and culture, since the limited availability of historical
data in the field of ethnology forced one to seek evidence in the present. Invoking the evolutionary axiom of the uniform working of the human mind,
Boas went on to argue that the comparison of ethnic traits could reveal regularities of human behavior. Boas sounded here much like the physicist he was

by academic training, explicitly subordinating the investigation of individual historical phenomena to the search for general laws, which was "the greatest aim of our science" (1889a:27). Indeed, one of these laws was the universal line of development from matrilineal to patrilineal forms, a thesis Johann Bachofen had initially postulated in *Das Mutterrecht* (1861), and which Boas then accepted as a universal law, confirmed by "endless variants" (23).[7]

But while Boas adopted certain evolutionary assumptions in 1888, he articulated them within a pluralistic framework, setting himself sharply off from the ethnocentrism of much of current anthropology. He questioned the concept of the *Naturvolk* as a people living in a pure state of nature, insisting instead on the historicity of all human populations. And despite the universal substratum underlying human behavior, he was still concerned with the particularities developing in the course of historical processes. In fact, scientific ethnology proved that seemingly natural feelings—such as the love of a father for his children—were relative to cultural conditions, under which Boas subsumed such factors as language, customs, migrations, and physical characteristics (1889a:18, 23). It was with this notion of cultural relativism in mind that Boas proposed the elucidation of the general laws of cultural development, a program quite similar to the project of the folk psychologists and their attempts to find the general laws of the development of individual *Volksgeister*. Boas, in fact, referred to the investigation of the laws of the lives of peoples as "the study of folk psychology" (1889a:20).

Boas' aesthetic turn may be viewed in the context of his field investigations on the Northwest Coast over the next few years, which were funded in part by Powell's Bureau and in part by a committee of the British Association for the Advancement of Science chaired by the leading British evolutionist Edward B. Tylor. Charged with providing the ethnic data needed for comparative treatment, Boas' fieldwork had a survey character (Stocking 1974c:84–85, 157). He was particularly influenced by Tylor's paper "On a Method of Investigating the Development of Institutions; Applied to Laws of Marriage and Descent," in which Tylor studied the "adhesions"—the more than chance tendency of various social customs to cluster together—among 350 peoples, in order to establish (or confirm) developmental sequences along evolutionary lines. Boas was already familiar with Bastian's *Gedankenstatistik*, and Tylor's paper apparently resonated with Boas' natural scientific inclinations; for a while he thought that "everything could be solved by methods" implicit in the article (Lowie, in Stocking 1968:207; cf. Stocking 1974c:129). But while Tylor's method became a cornerstone of Boas' early ethnology, it in fact led

---

7. When "The Aims of Ethnology" was reprinted in 1940, these passages were eliminated because they had reflected a "current view" which was no longer "tenable since it is impossible to derive all forms of family organization from a single source" (Boas 1940:635).

him away from the evolutionary approach, paving the way for his historicist critique of anthropology.

The systematic studies of myths and folklore Boas undertook between 1891 and 1896 occupied the central role in this process, linking him to the traditions emanating from both Alexander and Wilhelm von Humboldt. This cosmographical impulse was exemplified in his paper on "The Growth of Indian Mythologies" (1896b), which contained the theoretical results of Boas' surveys of the distribution of folk tales and their elements along lines suggested by Tylor's statistical method. Rather than seeking universal laws, however, Boas followed Ratzel's historical *Völkerkunde*, investigating the diffusion of myths and demonstrating correlations between the geographical locations of peoples and their stories. Physical proximity and frequent interaction of peoples led to the dissemination of entire folk tales, or significant elements; with the help of statistical analysis, these lines of diffusion could be traced over large areas. In opposition to evolutionary assumptions about similarities of myth, Boas asserted that "similarities of culture on our continent are always more likely to be due to diffusion than to independent development" (Boas 1896b:9).

Boas was careful, however, to dissociate himself from any one-sidedly historical interpretation. In contrast to Ratzel, Boas allowed for the possibility of both diffusion and independent invention, demanding rigorous inductive research to elucidate each individual case (1896b:10). Underlying Boas' theoretical approach was Bastian's distinction between *Elementar-* and *Völkergedanken*, which linked a universal substratum of inaccessible elementary ideas to the "forms which these ideas take among primitive people of different parts of the world." Because these folk ideas were the result in part of "the geographical environment," in part of the "peculiar character of the people," and "to a large extent" of their history, it was necessary to treat "the culture of primitive people by strict historical methods" (11). With this commitment to a holistic and historically oriented anthropology, Boas returned to the theoretical stance he had taken in the museum controversy.

While the trait-distribution studies pointed the way to the systematic critique of evolutionism, Boas waited until 1896 to present his position to a wide audience. Again, this may be viewed in relation to his professional situation. His stint at *Science* ended in 1889 because of economic cutbacks, and his docentship in psychology at Clark University lasted only until the faculty revolt of 1892. It was not until 1895 that he received an appointment at the American Museum of Natural History in New York, followed by a lectureship in physical anthropology at Columbia University. His institutional base finally secured, Boas felt free to pursue a general attack on evolutionism (Stocking 1974c:58, 85, 158, 284).

He did so in "The Limitations of the Comparative Method of Anthropol-

ogy," a paper given in 1896 at the annual meeting of the American Association for the Advancement of Science—the most general assembly of American anthropologists, to whom Brinton had given a presidential address a year
earlier on "The Aims of Anthropology," in which he insisted strongly on the
doctrine of independent invention (Brinton 1895; cf. Stocking 1968:209).
Boas acknowledged that anthropology had begun to receive a "liberal share of
public interest" only with the acceptance of the evolutionary theory, which
promised the "discovery" of the "laws" of history, instead of the mere description of "curious customs and beliefs of strange people." But the search for
such laws of human behavior rested on the axiom that "identities or similarities of culture" could be attributed to "the uniform working of the human
mind," which made it "possible to deduce historical sequences from present
phenomena," rather than seeking "actual historical proof" to "explain analogies" (1896a:901). Elaborating his position in the earlier Mason-Powell controversy, Boas offered what could be considered *the* formative statement of
early twentieth-century American anthropology.

> In treating this, the most difficult problem of anthropology, the point of view is
> taken that if an ethnological phenomenon had developed independently in a
> number of places its development·has been the same everywhere; or, expressed
> in a different form, that the same ethnological phenomena are always due to the
> same causes. This leads to the still wider generalization that the sameness of
> ethnological phenomena found in diverse regions is proof that the human mind
> obeys the same laws everywhere. It is obvious that if different historical devel-
> opments could lead to the same results, that then this generalization would not
> be tenable. Their existence would present to us an entirely different problem,
> namely, how it is that the developments of culture so often lead to the same
> results. It must, therefore, be clearly understood that anthropological research
> which compares similar cultural phenomena from various parts of the world, in
> order to discover the uniform history of their development, makes the assump-
> tion that the same ethnological phenomenon has developed everywhere in the
> same manner. Here lies the flaw in the argument of the new method, for no such
> proof can be given. Even the most cursory review shows that the same phe-
> nomena may develop in a multitude of ways. (903)

Boas here tied together the theoretical currents of historicist Counter-
Enlightenment thinking: first, the skepticism of finding natural laws governing
human behavior; second, the rejection of a psychic unity of humanity, operating according to rational principles regardless of space and time; third, the
focus on the individuality and diversity of phenomena as opposed to their
similarity and universality; finally, the emphasis on actual historical development in place of conjectures and speculation, on induction as opposed to deduction. In the face of these reservations, the "construction of a grand system
of the evolution of society" was "of very doubtful value" because it ordered

phenomena along the lines of a pre-determined theory. That method was fundamentally "opposed to the inductive process by which the actual relations of definite phenomena may be derived" (905). Appropriately, Boas exemplified his point by challenging the universal development of familial systems he had postulated in "The Aims of Ethnology." Reconsidering his former acceptance of a universal movement from maternal to paternal forms, he now argued that if the same phenomena have not "everywhere developed from the same causes, we may just as well conclude that paternal families have in some cases arisen from maternal institutions, in other cases in other ways" (904–5).

Having called into question the underlying assumptions of evolutionary anthropology, Boas went on to propose an alternative method of anthropological research that could account for the occurrence of similar phenomena in a much safer way: the "much ridiculed historical method." In order to find the actual "processes" of cultural development, Boas proposed "a detailed study of customs in their relation to the total culture of the tribe practicing them, in connection with an investigation of their geographical distribution." This would reveal the "environmental conditions," the "psychological factors" and the "historical connections" that shaped them. This data, too, was amenable to comparative treatment, but not by the global approach of evolutionary anthropology. Along the lines of Boas' folklore studies, comparison had to be limited to a "well-defined, small geographical territory," where the development of similar ethnic features was more likely to be the product of a common historical development. Comparisons could not exceed "the limits of the cultural area that forms the basis of the study," since only within a given cultural area was the assumption tenable that like effects did in fact spring from like causes (1896a:905–6; cf. Stocking 1968:209–10). In proposing the concept of the culture area as the main analytic tool, Boas' debt to Bastian's "geographical province" was readily apparent (cf. Lowie 1937:37; Stocking 1968:152).

Beyond Bastian, however, there were echoes of Alexander von Humboldt's cosmographical approach to natural history. In proposing a historical inquiry into the totality of the world's ethnic phenomena, Boas was in effect advocating a cosmographical mapping of the human realm. The understanding of individual traits in their immediate surroundings, would in turn reveal the "histories of the cultures of diverse tribes," which were the actual "subject of study." Despite his emphasis on history, Boas did not discard the search for "general laws," which—again echoing Humboldt—he still saw as the "ultimate aim of our science." Following the cautious cosmographer, however, he warned against proceeding "too hastily." Since comparisons could only be undertaken with "the greatest care" and required the establishment of the exact "distribution" of the traits under investigation as well as their historically specific meanings, the discovery of laws receded into an indefinite future. In the meantime, the anthropologist's task was the description of the human cosmos in all its aspects, supplying the "actual history" of the world's individual entities (1896a:906–7).

If such trait-distribution studies reflected the aesthetic side of Boas' scientific persona, as well as the natural history of Alexander von Humboldt, they also contained the kernels of an anthropology oriented along the more systematically humanistic lines of Wilhelm von Humboldt. In the course of his study of American Indian languages, Boas developed his linguistic approach; and when he published *The Handbook of American Indian Languages* in 1911, its theoretical preface reverberated with the central notions of Humboldtian linguistics.

Boasian Linguistics: From Humboldtian Studies of American Indian Languages to the Development of the Culture Concept

Notoriously sparse in his acknowledgment of intellectual debt, Boas mentioned Wilhelm von Humboldt only once in passing, in a little-known article published in Mexico in Spanish (1910:227; cf. Mackert 1993:332). Nevertheless, there can be little doubt that he was intimately familiar with Humboldt's thought, if not in the original, then by way of Humboldt's followers. Aside from Bastian, who consistently based his discussion of language on Humboldt (cf. 1860), Boas became personally acquainted with Steinthal while serving as assistant in the Königliches Museum für Völkerkunde (Stocking 1968:151, 1974a:64). It is tempting to speculate on the content of their meeting, which apparently occurred at a time when Boas was grappling with Eskimo linguistic material. Steinthal was keenly interested in the promulgation of Humboldtian linguistics, having recently published his ambitious edition of Humboldt's writings on language (Steinthal 1883). It does not seem farfetched to assume that Steinthal at that time would have urged Boas to consult the volume which contained many of the results of Humboldt's analyses of American Indian languages, perhaps even in conjunction with Boas' imminent departure on his first field trip to the Pacific Coast (Rohner 1969:310).

When Boas arrived in the United States, the study of American Indian languages was also a prominent concern of the leading anthropologists. Both Powell and Brinton published extensively on linguistic matters, and, despite a number of disagreements, their goals were alike: their rather un-Humboldtian language studies served, on the one hand, to corroborate evolutionary hypotheses and, on the other, to provide useful data in the classification of American peoples. In publications such as the *Introduction to the Study of Indian Languages* (1877), Powell suggested that language developed along evolutionary lines from complexity to simplicity. Therefore the "polysynthetic" languages of the American continent were the lowest forms of a steady

linguistic progress that culminated in English, which Powell placed at the pin-
nacle, on the basis of its lack of unnecessary inflection (cf. Stocking 1974a:
77). Influenced by Indo-European scholarship, Brinton was exasperated by
this assumption, arguing that only "a fully inflected language like Greek or
Latin" deserved this kind of praise; yet he also believed that American tongues
reflected earlier stages of human mental development. Brinton placed them on
the bottom of the evolutionary ladder because, lacking the essential grammatical feature of inflection, they assembled all linguistic elements in unsys-
tematic fashion. In an article revealingly titled "The Language of Paleolithic
Man," he took this idea further, asserting that the "judicious study of the existing languages" of America offered the researcher a glimpse into the "earliest
tongues spoken by man." Linguistics allowed the penetration into "the secret
and hidden mysteries of aboriginal man," who was on occasion reminiscent of
the "lower animals" (1890:311–13, 322, 340–43, 392).[8]

Both Powell and Brinton also used the study of native languages to classify
the peoples of the American continent—although, again, the two disagreed
on fundamental points when they published their respective results in partial
competition with each other in 1891. Powell's classification of the "Indian
Linguistic Families of America North of Mexico" was based on lexical material, partly because he held it to be the most stable aspect of language, and
partly because his lack of philological training did not allow him to move significantly beyond comparing word lists (Powell 1891:83–218; cf. Darnell
1988:115–16). Brinton, in contrast, favored classification along morphological lines, which offered evidence for his prior assumption of the sameness of all American peoples. In *The American Race*, he argued that all American Indian languages were "incorporative" and therefore "strikingly alike"
(1891:56).

Using Boas' categories, it seems evident that the study of American Indian
languages had been guided by the "aesthetic impulse" that sought to order the
seeming chaos of the human cosmos. Dominated by the same scholars who
dominated ethnology, its debates and issues provided the context of Boas' early
work in linguistics, which closely paralleled his ethnological endeavors. De-

8. Somewhat ironically, Brinton consistently invoked Wilhelm von Humboldt in support of
his "rather extreme racial determinism and evolutionary dogmatism" (Stocking 1974a:87). Like
Steinthal, Brinton saw himself as the legitimate heir of the Humboldtian tradition, which he
sought to further in America by his publications, among them a translation of an early treatise of
Humboldt on "The American Verb" (Brinton 1885). However, Brinton's interpretation of Humboldt, based in part on what seem to be clear misreadings, forced Humboldt into an evolutionary
framework, neglecting his central concern for the unique contributions of individual languages
and national characters to humanity at large. Instead, Brinton misconstrued Humboldt's theory
as a teleological development of language caused by the uniform working of the human mind (cf.
Bunzl 1993:97–102).

spite a lack of formal training in linguistics upon his arrival in the United States, Boas was quick to challenge some of the prevalent assumptions of evolutionary linguistics. In 1888, he wrote a short article, in the spirit of the museum debate with Mason and Powell, attacking some of Brinton's ideas about paleolithic speech. That year at the American Philosophical Society, Brinton had discussed the phenomenon of "alternating sounds," the apparent fluctuation of pronunciation in American Indian languages, and attributed them to a low developmental stage (Stocking 1968:158–59). Apparently already familiar with Brinton's argument, Boas countered that alternating sounds did not in reality exist, but were simply "alternating apperceptions of one and the same sound," conditioned by the "phonetic system" of the researcher. He had himself experienced the phenomenon when he had recorded the same words differently on different occasions in the course of his fieldwork in Baffinland and the Northwest Coast. This led Boas to hypothesize that speakers of languages with seemingly alternating sounds would in turn perceive the sounds of English as alternating, which indeed he found to be the case. Undermining Brinton's underlying assumptions and foreshadowing much of his later critique of evolutionism, Boas implied that from any given linguistic vantage point, any other language could be considered primitive (1889b:76–77; cf. Stocking 1974a:78–79). In another sense, the article also implied a call for what Boas later termed the "purely analytical" study of language, in which grammatical features of American Indian languages were investigated from the point of view of their inner systematicity rather than from an external position susceptible to "wrong apperception" (1889b:76; cf. 1905a:178).

While "On Alternating Sounds" should be interpreted in conjunction with Boas' "affective" critique in the Mason-Powell controversy, much of his linguistic work in the early 1890s can be seen as an outgrowth of the "aesthetic" position he took in "The Aims of Ethnology." Financed in his linguistic work in part by the Bureau of American Ethnology, Boas operated largely within a "Powellian framework" of regional surveys, vocabulary lists, grammatical "notes," and issues of linguistic classification (Stocking 1974a:66). These efforts culminated in 1894 in a paper on the "Classification of the Languages of the North Pacific Coast," which Boas subsumed under four groups largely on the basis of the "comparison of vocabularies" of seven languages (1894:159). But if Boas pursued Powell's scientific objectives, the article already contained a promissory note of a linguistic approach along Humboldtian lines. In the article's concluding paragraph, Boas questioned linguistic classification based on "a meager list of vocabularies." To avoid sinking "to the level of mere guessing," he demanded "closer" studies that could reveal the "structure" of languages (165–66).

Even though in character Boas' first linguistic fieldwork had been a survey, he had early on expressed interest in conducting intensive research on Salish.

When he encountered Chinook in 1890, he became intrigued by the intricacy of the language for its own sake, and turned to the "elucidation" of its structure (in Stocking 1974a:66–67). As in the case of his ethnology, it was around 1896 that his institutional affiliations allowed Boas to pursue this independent research agenda. And, like his ethnology, Boas' linguistics became a primarily historicist endeavor, valuing particular languages as unique entities. While Boas' approach implied the existence of a universal substratum of language as a human phenomenon, he subordinated comparison and classification to the analysis of individual languages. Like Wilhelm von Humboldt seventy-five years before, Boas began to relish the diversity of American Indian languages for its own sake (cf. Stocking 1974b:7).

Fascinated by the linguistic data he was able to obtain from the New World, Humboldt's plan of investigation had been three-fold: firstly, the synchronic analyses of the structures of individual American Indian languages; secondly, an investigation into their genetic relations; and thirdly, the elucidation of their psychological influence and dependence on the respective national characters (V:4). But if Humboldt's comprehensive treatment of American Indian languages never materialized, Boas' *Handbook of American Indian Languages* may be seen as the realization of Humboldt's original project. Growing out of a similar understanding of the task of linguistics, Boas' plan—as stated in the preface of the first volume of the *Handbook*—echoed Humboldt's very closely. The project was to "emphasize" the "analytical study of grammar," revealing the "psychological foundation" of the "structure" of American Indian languages. As a promissory note for future volumes, Boas also proposed systematic comparison which would reveal "the essential psychological characteristics of American languages" and shed light on "the probable historical development of grammatical forms" of various "linguistic stocks" (1911a:v).[9]

In its conception, the *Handbook* dated back to the late 1890s, when Boas had begun to consider the prospects of revising Powell's *Introduction to the Study of Indian Languages*, which was by then out of print, and which he felt had begun "to prove inadequate." Plans became concrete in 1901, when Boas approached the Bureau of American Ethnology with his proposal. By that time, Boas felt that he had trained enough scholars who could contribute

---

9. In an interesting parallel between Humboldt's and Boas' projects, it may be noted that neither arrived at the originally proposed genetic classification. Boas relegated it "to a later time," when upon "a thorough analysis and comparison of all the dialects of each linguistic stock," a "comparative discussion of all the languages" would be possible (1911a:82). However, the fourth volume of the *Handbook*, which was projected to contain comparative analyses and classifications, never appeared. Just as the possibility of finding laws of human behavior receded "behind the horizon of mounting empirical data of American cultures," the possibility of linguistic classification began to recede "behind the empirical complexity of American Indian languages (Stocking 1974a:87). Similarly, Humboldt never undertook a classification, largely because, in the absence of clear linguistic boundaries, he was not willing to engage in unfounded speculations (V:5).

grammatical sketches to the *Handbook*, and he sent out invitations to prospective collaborators. It was not until the end of 1903, however, that revised and more detailed plans were approved (Stocking 19874a:67–68).

Boas exercised tight control during the editorial process, and he frequently reminded the contributors to adhere to the methodological principles he set forth. As a model, Boas offered the "Sketch of the Kwakiutl Language" he had published in 1900, in which he attempted to present "the fundamental traits of the language," correcting a grammar that had been published in 1889 by Rev. Alfred J. Hall, who had "not succeeded in elucidating its structural peculiarities" (1900:167). Boas consistently found flaws in the treatises on American Indian languages, especially those prepared by missionaries, who had no knowledge of scientific philology and, along with other late nineteenth-century students of American Indian languages, constructed their grammars along the Indo-European categories of noun, pronoun, verb, adverb, adjective, preposition, conjunction, and interjection (Stocking 1974a:69, 76). In contrast, Boas insisted that the grammars for the *Handbook* were to be "purely analytical," by which he meant that the "grammatical categories" were to be derived internally, keeping out the "point of view of Indo-European languages as thoroughly as possible." The "essential traits of the grammar" were to be presented "as they would naturally develop" if a native speaker, "without any knowledge of any other language, should present the essential notions of his own grammar" (1905a:178; in Stocking 1974a:81).

Echoing Humboldt's complaint about the tendency of missionary grammars to "assimilate everything to Latin" (V:355), Boas noted in the Introduction of the *Handbook* that in the present treatise "no attempt had been made to compare the forms of the Indian grammars" with English or Latin. Like Humboldt, who had coined the term, and Steinthal, who had made it the cornerstone of his linguistic project, Boas sought to base his analyses entirely upon the "inner form" of each language (1911a:81). But not only its analytical premises suggested the position of *The Handbook of American Indian Languages* in the Humboldtian tradition; Boas himself noted the immediate connection. In a letter to Robert Lowie, he remarked that his main achievement in the field of linguistics was the "presentation of languages on Steinthal's principles, i.e., from their own, not an outsider's point of view" (Lowie 1943:184). And in the short article published in Mexico, Boas pointed even more specifically to Steinthal's descriptions of Mexican and Eskimo (1860) as models for his analyses of American Indian languages (Boas 1910:227; cf. Mackert 1993:332).

Beyond his Humboldtian presentation of American Indian grammars, linguistics was also a central component in the development of Boas' culture concept as it progressed from a modified version of the humanistic sense of "Culture" toward the relativized notion which defined American cultural anthropology for most of the twentieth century (Stocking 1968:196, 203). In

line with the German dichotomy of *Natur-* and *Kulturvölker,* Boas' initial notion of culture was much like that of Herder and Humboldt, viewing cultural
achievement—in the forms of knowledge, art, literature, and science—as
equivalent to the liberation from the control by nature (cf. Stocking 1968:
150, 201). But while this notion of culture was commonly invoked in arguments for hierarchical orders of the world's peoples—as in some of the classic
formulations of evolutionary anthropology—Boas sought to relativize the
nature/culture distinction by uncovering the potential if not the actual presence of culture among all human groups. Consequently, one of the main concerns of Boas' early ethnography was to find the roots of humanist culture
among the peoples of the Northwest Coast (cf. Stocking 1968:223).

Boas located the germs of culture in myths and folklore, which he treated
along philological lines. Extending Steinthal's principles of text criticism of
non-Indo-European literary materials to Native American texts, Boas in effect
demonstrated their equivalence to the classical object of the philological
enterprise. In analogy to the ancient documents of Indo-European peoples,
whose hermeneutic interpretation could reveal their cultural context and
historical meaning, the myths and folklore of American tribes reflected the
"peculiar character of the people" who produced them, as well as, their "history" (1896b:11; cf. Stocking, 1977:4–5). But while ancient European texts
were readily available, the situation on the American continent was complicated by the absence of written documents. These had to be recovered as part
of a general anthropological project which Boas outlined in a paper read at a
joint meeting of the American Anthropological Association, the Philological
Association, and the Archaeological Institute (1906:183–88). There he repeated an argument he had made a few months earlier in a letter written to
promote the publication of a large body of original texts by the Bureau of
American Ethnology:

> I do not think that anyone would advocate the study of antique civilizations or,
> let me say, of the Turks or the Russians, without a thorough knowledge of their
> languages and of the literary documents in these languages; and contributions
> not based on such material would not be considered as adequate. In regard to our
> American Indians we are in the position that practically no such literary mate-
> rial is available for study, and it appears to me as one of the essential things that
> we have to do, to make such material accessible. My own published work shows,
> that I let this kind of work take precedence over practically everything else,
> knowing it is the foundation of all future researches. Without it a control of our
> results and deeper studies based on material collected by us will be all but impos-
> sible. Besides this we must furnish in this way the indispensable material for
> future linguistic studies. (1905b:122–23)

In the *Handbook of American Indian Languages,* such philological issues were
still a prominent concern. Discussing the rationale for emphasizing the study
of native languages as part of the anthropological endeavor, Boas compared

the task of the ethnologist to that of the "investigator of cultures of the Old World." Just as "nobody" expected "authoritative accounts of the civilization of China or Japan" from a person who did not "speak the languages readily" or who had not "mastered their literatures," an ethnologist could not be expected to "elucidate the innermost thoughts and feelings of a people without so much as a smattering of knowledge of their language" (1911a:60). Boas' conviction that these thoughts and feelings could be discovered through the philological treatment of native texts was evident in the grammars themselves. Duplicating the structure of Steinthal's *Mande-Neger-Sprachen*, all ten sketches published in the first volume of the *Handbook of American Indian Languages* closed with a few pages of original text explicated like ancient Indo-European documents.

Linguistic investigations not only helped Boas to demonstrate the presence of humanist culture among American peoples, it also pointed the way toward a more anthropological view of culture as the locus of the historical transmission of ethnic traits. While his thought on the culture concept was by no means systematic, it grew out of his interest in the process of acculturation. He had observed the phenomenon initially in his trait-distribution studies, which revealed the continuous dissemination of entire folk tales, as well as the distribution of their individual elements. In the face of this constant diffusion, Boas noted that individual myths were not just the products of "organic growth," but largely the consequence of the "accretion of foreign material," which was in turn "borrowed," "adapted," and "changed" by the individual "genius of a people" (1896b:5). While Boas' work in the 1890s concentrated on the historical processes of diffusion—the most potent argument in the critique of evolutionism—after 1900, his interest shifted gradually toward the retrospectively rationalizing and imperfectly synthesizing process by which the "genius of a people" assimilated the elements brought together in a similar culture by historical accident (cf. Stocking 1974b:6–7).

Much like myths, languages were also the products of complementary historical processes, modifying organic growth by outside intervention. Even though somewhat ambiguous, Boas' notion of the inner development of language was linked to the psychological investigations he had proposed as early as 1898 when he noted that "forms of thought" were expressed most clearly in the "forms of language" (1898b:624). Following Steinthal, who—according to Boas—had elucidated the "intimate ties between language and ethnic psychology" most clearly, Boas sought the pertinent "psychological groupings" in "inner forms" of languages in a manner consistent with Humboldt's original formulations (1904:28, 1911a:81).

In one respect, every language was the product of an ethnically idiosyncratic point of view. Each individual language classified the "infinitely varied" range of personal experience into separate units, which differed so greatly from language to language that they could be considered arbitrary from any given linguistic vantage point (1911a:24, 67). This categorization—Boas illustrated his point with the great variety of terms designating the concept of "water" in English and the many forms of "snow" in Eskimo—was determined by the "chief interest of a people" (25–26). This explained, for example, the absence of abstract concepts in many native American languages. Boas argued that there was simply no need for such terminology because the interests of the people centered "around the occupations" of "daily life." However, if the "mode of life" required it, abstract forms would "develop just as soon as needed" (64–66). By implication, the interests of a people also affected the morphology of languages. Different languages encoded different grammatical categories. While most Indo-European languages classified nouns according to gender, number, and case, American Indian languages tended to treat nouns differently, modifying them in terms of such categories as animation, location, or possession (36–43).

But if individual languages reflected the particular characteristics of a people, they also had a potentially creative component. Supplying evidence from Native American groups, Boas noted that metaphorical terms of poetry and kin terminology became the basis of rituals and social relations. Echoing the Humboldtian dialectic of language and national character, Boas concluded that "linguistic expression" could be considered a "secondary reflex of the customs of the people," but that the reverse was also possible, suggesting that "the customs of the people" might have "developed from the unconsciously developed terminology" (1911a:73).

The historical processes of language development, however, extended beyond the mere interaction between a language's "inner form" and the "chief interests of a people." Through the dissemination of linguistic traits, any given tongue was likely to be modified by elements originating in different languages. Boas emphasized these historical processes, noting that they could occur along several linguistic dimensions. In particular, he documented how languages absorbed phonetic, grammatical, and lexical influences by integrating them into their own structures (1911a:47–50). Ultimately, if only by implication, this process of linguistic acculturation was identical to the assimilation of folk tales through the "genius of a people;" and it was this "analogy of ethnology and language" which made the latter "one of the most instructive fields of inquiry in an investigation of the formation of the fundamental ethnic ideas"—the process of culture (70).

Each language integrated according to its own inherent principles the various elements brought together in the course of its history. But while these principles organized the assimilation of historically transmitted material through the "grouping-together of a considerable number of activities under the form of a single idea," these ideas and processes themselves were never perceived consciously by the speakers (1911a:70). Although a historical product, language was also *a priori* in the sense that—through its acquisition in the process of socialization—it determined the linguistic behavior of its speakers by providing a set of unconscious grammatical categories that had to be expressed for communication to occur.

By implication, culture—in the anthropological sense—operated in much the same way. A product of accidental historical processes integrated into unique configurations, it developed "at present in each individual and in the whole people entirely sub-consciously." "Impressed vigorously upon the child while it is still young," the unconsciously transmitted and oftentimes irrational ethnic phenomena that made up culture were nevertheless "most potent in the formation of our opinions and actions" (1911a:68). However, in most ethnic phenomena, the unconscious transmission of ideas from generation to generation eventually became the object of conscious reasoning. Table manners, for example, even though ultimately irrational historical products, were rationalized through the process of secondary explanation.

> It is not customary to bring the knife to the mouth, and very readily the feeling arises, that the knife is not used in this manner because in eating thus one would easily cut the lips. The lateness of the invention of the fork, and the fact that in many countries dull knives are used and that a similar danger exists of pricking the tongue or the lips with the sharp-pointed steel fork which is commonly used in Europe, show readily that this explanation is only a secondary rationalistic attempt to explain a custom that otherwise would remain unexplained (69).

Such secondary explanations were central to the integration of accidentally accumulated material into cultural entities, providing the conscious underpinnings of cultural practices. Nevertheless, by distorting the actual historical processes that gave rise to their existence, secondary explanations obscured the development and integration of cultural traits. The only ethnic phenomenon which never became the object of conscious reflections was language; and "because linguistic classifications never rise into consciousness," no secondary reinterpretation of their historical origins occurred (67). For the anthropologist, limited to data available in the present, languages thus provided an untainted record of acculturation processes, showing how unconsciously transmitted elements determined behavior at any moment in time. While secondary reasoning about other ethnic phenomena clouded the historical, irrational, and unconscious dimensions of cultural integration, language offered a virtually unobstructed view into the workings of culture (cf. Aberle 1960; Stocking 1968, 1974b).

From *Volksgeist* and *Nationalcharakter* to an Anthropological Concept of Culture

As Boas himself might have predicted, the "aesthetic" impulse has never disappeared from anthropology. In the spirit of Mason and Powell, latter-day evo-

lutionists and others dedicated to a generalizing anthropological project have
at various points attacked "Boasian particularism" as an inadequate or misguided approach to the study of human variety in space and time (e.g. Harris
1968; White 1963). Parallel to this methodological and theoretical critique,
there has been a current of historiography emphasizing the American as opposed to the Germanic roots of American cultural anthropology. Thus it has
been argued that the culture concept was developed prior to and independent
of Boas in the work of Frank Hamilton Cushing, as a response (which Boas
might have called "affective") to Cushing's extended first-hand experience of
Zuñi culture in the early 1880s. Cushing's use of the plural "cultures" in a
paper written in 1888 and published two years later has been a key piece of
evidence for the assertion that the central concept of American cultural anthropology had its origin in fieldwork among Native Americans rather than in
any external intellectual tradition (Mark 1980:1, 109–12; Cushing 1890).

    Since it seems quite likely, as Boas himself might have argued, that an an-
thropological idea of culture could have arisen out of different historical traditions, there is no need to deny Cushing's contribution, or the generative role
of fieldwork experience as well as intellectual influences—or, more generally,
the enduring institutional and intellectual influences of anthropologists in the
American national tradition: Powell, Brinton, Putnam, Morgan, and, before
them, Schoolcraft, Gallatin, and Jefferson (cf. Hinsley 1981; Bieder 1986). But
it would be historiographically perverse to minimize the contribution of Franz
Boas, for better or worse, both intellectually and institutionally. Especially in
relation to Cushing, the latter aspect deserves particular emphasis. Affiliated
with Powell's Bureau of Ethnology—an organization which employed but did
not reproduce anthropologists—Cushing produced no cohorts of student followers. His eccentric personal and ethnographic style left him an isolated and
idiosyncratic oddity, even within the Bureau (Kroeber 1931:657). In contrast,
Boas—with Bastian and Virchow as models—realized early in his career that
the dissemination of his anthropological orientation was dependent on the
establishment of a solid institutional base (Stocking 1968:280; cf. Boas 1902:
37–38). When Boas received his appointments at the American Museum of
Natural History and at Columbia University, he set out to create a "well-
organized school of anthropology" which would provide students with comprehensive training not available anywhere else in the world. In order to
establish "a definite systematic basis" for anthropology, he attempted to con-
centrate in his own hands "a considerable part of the ethnological work that
is being done on our continent," until such time as students trained by him
might take up the burden (1901:286–89).

    In the successful development of his school of anthropology, Boas was care-
ful to delimit its position from that of the previously dominant institutional
locus, the Bureau of Ethnology. But his anthropological standpoint had other

(and more deeply rooted) bases than institutional pragmatism, or his own eth-nographic experience in the Arctic and the Pacific Northwest—though these surely contributed to it. What ethnographic experience enhanced and insti-tutional pragmatism established was an orientation that was grounded in a German anthropological tradition extending back through Bastian and Ritter, through Steinthal and Waitz, to the brothers Alexander and Wilhelm von Humboldt. It is in that tradition that one finds the roots of Boas' critique of evolutionism and its racialist concomitants, as well as of his linguistic relativ-ism and his cultural historicism. By this route, one may trace the later Ameri-can anthropological idea of culture back through Bastian's *Völkergedanken* and the folk psychologist's *Volksgeister* to Wilhelm von Humboldt's *Nationalchar-akter*—and behind that, although not without a paradoxical and portentous residue of conceptual and ideological ambiguity, to the Herderian ideal of *Volksgeist*.[10]

Acknowledgments

For their generous critical comments on various drafts, I wish to thank Joseph Green-berg, Dell Hymes, Richard Mitten, Kurt Mueller-Vollmer, Billy Vaughn, and Arthur Wolf. For his trenchant comments and tireless encouragement, my deepest gratitude goes to George Stocking, who first suggested the project. In grateful recognition of his unfailing support, I dedicate this article to my father, John Bunzl.

References Cited

Aberle, D. 1960. The influence of linguistics on early culture and personality theory. In *Essays in the science of culture in honor of Leslie A. White*, ed. G. Dole & R. Car-neiro, 1–29. New York.
Bachofen, J. 1861. *Das Mutterrecht*. Stuttgart.
Bastian, A. 1860. *Der Mensch in der Geschichte*. Vol. 1. Leipzig.
———. 1869. Alexander von Humboldt. Festrede. Translated in Koepping 1983: 145–62.
———. 1871. Die Cultur und ihre Entwicklung auf ethnologischer Grundlage. Ex-cerpted and translated in Koepping 1983:164–69.

10. The double potential (racial as well as cultural) of the Herderian *Volksgeist* is evident in the appeal made to Herder by later racist writers. Thus Alfred Rosenberg, chief ideologist of the Nazi party, after quoting a passage from Herder "which is relevant to our own age and our joyful message: '*Each nation has its centre of happiness within itself . . .*'" went on to suggest that "the most complete unfolding of self stems from experiencing 'the centre of happiness,' and in the language of this book this means: *from the experienced Mythus of the Nordic racial soul serve the honour of the Volk in love*" (Rosenberg 1938:89).

————. 1881. *Die heilige Sage der Polynesier*. Excerpted and translated in Koepping 1983:215–19.

————. 1893–94. *Controversen in der Ethnologie*. Excerpted and translated in Koepping 1983:170–78.

Beck, H. 1959. *Alexander von Humboldt*. Vol. 1. Wiesbaden.

————. 1961. *Alexander von Humboldt*. Vol. 2. Wiesbaden.

Beiser F. C. 1987. *The fate of reason: German philosophy from Kant to Fichte*. Cambridge, Mass.

————. 1992. *Enlightenment, revolution, and romanticism*. Cambridge, Mass.

Belke, I., ed. 1971. *Moritz Lazarus and Heymann Steinthal. Die Begründer der Völkerpsychologie in ihren Briefen*. Tübingen.

Berlin, I. 1980. *Against the current*. New York.

Bernhardi, A. F. 1801–3. *Sprachlehre*. Berlin.

Bieder, R. 1986. *Science encounters the Indians 1820–1860: The early years of American ethnology*. Norman, Okla.

Bloomfield, L. 1933. *Language*. New York.

Boas, F. 1885. *Baffin-Land: Geographische Ergebnisse einer in den Jahren 1883 und 1884 ausgeführten Forschungsreise*. Ergänzungsband Nr. 80, *Petermanns Mitteilungen*. Gotha.

————. 1887a. The study of geography. In Boas 1940:639–47.

————. 1887b. The occurrence of similar inventions in areas widely apart, [and] Museums of ethnology and their classification. In Stocking 1974c:61–67.

————. 1887c. Letter to *Science*. *Science* 9:614.

————. 1889a. *Die Ziele der Ethnologie*. New York. (cf. "The Aims of Ethnology," in Boas 1940:626–38).

————. 1889b. On alternating sounds. In Stocking 1974c:72–77.

————. 1894. Classification of the languages of the North Pacific Coast. In Stocking 1974c:159–66.

————. 1896a. The limitations of the comparative method in anthropology. *Science* 4:901–8.

————. 1896b. The growth of Indian mythologies. *J. Am. Folklore* 9:1–11.

————. 1898a. The Jesup North Pacific Expedition. In Stocking 1974c:107–16.

————. 1898b. Advances in methods of teaching. In Boas 1940:621–25.

————. 1900. Sketch of the Kwakiutl language. In Stocking 1974c:167–77.

————. 1901. Letter to Z. Nuttall 5/16/01. Published as "The Boas plan for American anthropology." In Stocking 1974c:286–89.

————. 1902. Rudolf Virchow's anthropological work. In Stocking 1974c:36–41.

————. 1904. The history of anthropology. In Stocking 1974c:23–36.

————. 1905a. Letter to W. Thalbitzer 2/15/05. Published as "A purely analytical study of language." In Stocking 1974c:178–79.

————. 1905b. Letter to W. Holmes 7/24/05. Published as "The documentary function of the text." In Stocking 1974c:122–23.

————. 1906. Some philological aspects of anthropological research. In Stocking 1974c:183–88.

————. 1908. Anthropology: Lecture delivered at Columbia University 12/18/07. In Stocking 1974c:267–81.

———. 1910. Publicaciones nuevas sobre la lingüística americana. In *Reseña de la Segunda sesión del XVII Congreso Internacional de Americanistas, La Ciudad de México 1910*, 225–32. Mexico City.

———, ed. 1911a. *Handbook of American Indian languages*. Vol. 1. Bulletin of American Ethnology Bureau 40. Washington, D.C.

———. 1911b. *The mind of primitive man*. New York.

———. 1920. The methods of ethnology. In Boas 1940:281–89.

———. 1932. The aims of anthropological research. In Boas 1940:243–59.

———. 1938. An anthropologist's credo. In Fadiman 1939:19–29.

———. 1940. *Race, language and culture*. New York.

Bopp, F. 1816. *Über das Conjugationssystem der Sanskritsprache in Vergleichung mit jenem der griechischen, lateinischen, persischen und germanischen Sprache*. Frankfurt am Main.

Brinton, D. G. 1885. The philosophic grammar of American languages as set forth by Wilhelm von Humboldt: With a translation of an unpublished memoir by him on the American verb. *Proceedings of the American Philosophical Society 22*: 306–54.

———. 1890. *Essays of an Americanist*. Philadelphia.

———. 1891. *The American race: A linguistic classification and ethnographic description of the native tribes of North and South America*. Philadelphia.

———. 1895. The aims of anthropology. *Proceedings of the American Association for the Advancement of Sciences 44*:1–17.

Bulhof, I. N. 1980. *Wilhelm Dilthey: A hermeneutic approach to the study of history and culture*. The Hague.

Bumann, W. 1965. *Die Sprachtheorie Heymann Steinthals*. Meisenheim am Glan.

Bunge, M. 1969. Alexander von Humboldt und die Philosophie. In Pfeiffer 1969: 17–31.

Bunzl, M. 1993. From historicism to historical particularism: Franz Boas and the tradition of nineteenth century German anthropology and linguistics. M.A. thesis, Stanford University.

Buttmann, G. 1977. *Friedrich Ratzel*. Stuttgart.

Chomsky, N. 1966. *Cartesian linguistics*. New York.

Cole, D. 1983. "The value of a person lies in his *Herzensbildung*": Franz Boas' Baffin Island letter-diary, 1883–1884. *HOA* 1:13–52.

Cushing, F. H. 1890. Preliminary notes on the origin, working hypothesis, and primary researches of the Hemenway Southwestern Archaeological Expedition. In *7th congrès international des americanistes*, pp. 151–94. Berlin.

Darnell, R. 1969. The development of American anthropology 1879–1920: From the Bureau of American Ethnology to Franz Boas. Doct. diss., University of Pennsylvania.

———. 1988. *Daniel Garrison Brinton*. Philadelphia.

Dickinson, R. E., & O. J. R. Howarth. 1933. *The making of geography*. Oxford.

Dilthey, W. 1883. *Einleitung in die Gesiteswissenschaften*. In *Wilhelm Diltheys Gesammelte Schriften*. Vol. 1. Leipzig (1922).

Dunkel, H. B. 1970. *Herbart and Herbartianism: An educational ghost story*. Chicago.

Ermarth, M. 1978. *Wilhelm Dilthey: Critique of historical reason*. Chicago.

Fadiman, C., ed. 1939. *I believe*. New York.

Fiedermutz-Laun, A. 1970. *Der kulturhistorische Gedanke bei Adolf Bastian.* Wiesbaden.

Flitner, A., & K. Giel. 1981. Kommentare und Anmerkungen zu Band I–IV. In Wilhelm von Humboldt, *Werke.* Vol. 5:285–700.

Gärtner, I. 1959. Alexander von Humboldt (1769–1859): Eine biographische Übersicht. In Harig 1959:39–48.

Gerland, G. 1860. Psychologische Anthropologie. *Zeitschrift für Völkerpsychologie und Sprachwissenschaft* 1:387–412.

———. 1896. Theodor Waitz. *Allgemeine Deutsche Biographie* 40:629–33.

Goldschmidt, W., ed. 1959. *The anthropology of Franz Boas: Essays on the centennial of his birth.* San Francisco.

Harig, G., ed. 1959. *Alexander von Humboldt.* Leipzig.

Harris, M., 1968. *The rise of anthropological theory.* New York.

Heeschen, V. 1972. *Die Sprachphilosophie Wilhelm von Humboldts.* Bochum.

Herder, J. G. 1774. *Auch eine Philosophie der Geschichte zur Bildung der Menschheit.* In *Werke in 2 Bänden.* Vol. 2. Munich (1953).

———. 1784. *Ideen zur Philosophie der Geschichte der Menschheit.* In excerpts in *Werke in 2 Bänden.* Vol. 2. Munich (1953).

Hinsley, C. M. 1981. *Savages and scientists: The Smithsonian Institution and the development of American anthropology, 1846–1910.* Washington, D.C.

Humboldt, A. von. 1809. *Cuba-Werk.* In *Alexander von Humboldt: Studienausgabe.* 7 vols., ed. Hanno Beck. Darmstadt (1992).

———. 1826. *Mexico-Werk.* In *Alexander von Humboldt: Studienausgabe.* 7 vols., ed. Hanno Beck. Darmstadt (1991).

———. 1845. *Cosmos.* Vol. 1. Trans. E. C. Otté. New York (1864).

Humboldt, W. von. 1836. *Linguistic variability and intellectual development.* Trans. G. C. Buck & F. A. Raven. Miami (1971).

———. 1836. *On language: The diversity of human language structures and its influence on the mental development of mankind.* Trans. P. Heath. Cambridge (1988).

———. 1903–36 *Wilhelm von Humboldts Gesammelte Schriften.* 17 vols., ed. Albert Leitzmann. Berlin.

Hymes, D. 1983. *Essays in the history of linguistic anthropology.* Amsterdam.

Iggers, G. 1968. *The German conception of history.* Middletown.

Jacknis, I. 1985. Franz Boas and exhibits: On the limitations of the museum method in anthropology. *HOA* 3:75–111.

Jaeger F., & J. Rüsen. 1992. *Geschichte des Historismus.* Munich.

Kant, I. 1781. *Critique of pure reason.* Trans. N. K. Smith. New York (1965).

Klencke, H. 1852. *Lives of the brothers Humboldt.* London.

Kluckhohn, C., & O. Prufer. 1959. Influences during the formative years. In Goldschmidt 1959:4–28.

Koepping, K.-P. 1983. *Adolf Bastian and the psychic unity of mankind.* St. Lucia.

Koerner, K. 1992. The Sapir-Whorf hypothesis: A preliminary history and a bibliographical essay. *J. Ling. Anth.* 2:173–98.

Kroeber, A. L. 1931. Frank Hamilton Cushing. *Encyclopedia of the Social Sciences*, IV: 657.

Krüger, G., & G. Buchheim. 1959. Zeitgenossen über Alexander von Humboldt. In Harig 1959:351–368.

Lazarus, M., & H. Steinthal. 1859. Einleitende Gedanken über Völkerpsychologie. Zeitschrift für Völkerpsychologie und Sprachwissenschaft 1:1–73.

Lehmann, P. 1883. Herder in seiner Bedeutung für die Geographie. Berlin.

Lehmann, W. 1992. Historical linguistics. London.

Lowie, R. 1937. The history of ethnological theory. New York.

———. 1943. The progress of science: Franz Boas, anthropologist. Scientific Monthly 56:184.

Mackert, M. 1993. Franz Boas' view of linguistic categories. Historiographia Linguistica 20(2/3):331–51.

Manchester, M. 1985. The philosophical foundations of Humboldt's linguistic doctrines. Amsterdam.

Mark, J. 1980. Four anthropologists: An American science in its early years. New York.

Mason, O. 1887. The occurrence of similar inventions in areas widely apart. Science 9: 534–35.

Meinecke, F. 1963. Cosmopolitanism and the national state. Trans. R. Kimber. Princeton (1970).

Meyer-Abich, A. 1969. Alexander von Humboldt as a biologist. In Pfeiffer 1969: 179–96.

Mueller-Vollmer, K. 1987. Humboldts Bildungspolitik und die Französische Revolution. Diskursanalysen 2:63–81.

———. 1989. Wilhelm von Humboldts sprachwissenschaftlicher Nachlaß: Probleme seiner Erschließung. In Scharf 1989:181–204.

———, ed. 1990. The hermeneutics reader. New York.

———. 1991. Mutter Sanskrit und die Nacktheit der Südseesprachen. Athenäum 1: 109–33.

———, ed. 1993. Wilhelm von Humboldts Sprachwissenschaft: Ein kommentiertes Verzeichnis des sprachwissenschaftlichen Nachlasses. Munich.

Nicolson, M. 1987. Humboldtian science and the origins of the study of vegetation. History of Science 25:165–85.

Ollig, H.-L. 1979. Der Neukantianismus. Stuttgart.

Paul, H. 1880. Principien der Sprachgeschichte. Tübingen (1970).

Pfeiffer, H., ed. 1969. Alexander von Humboldt: Werk und Weltgeltung. Munich.

Powell, J. W. 1877. Introduction to the study of Indian languages. Washington, D.C.

———. 1887. Museums of ethnology and their classification. Science 9:612–14.

———. 1891. Indian linguistic families of America north of Mexico. Lincoln (1966).

Ratzel, F. 1882. Anthropogeographie. Vol. 1. Stuttgart (1899).

———. 1885–88. Völkerkunde. 3 vols. Leipzig.

———. 1891. Anthropogeographie. Vol. 2. Stuttgart.

Ritter, K. 1863. Geographical studies. Trans. W. L. Gage. Boston.

Rohner, R., ed. 1969. The ethnography of Franz Boas. Chicago.

Rosenberg, A. 1938. Der Mythus des 20. Jahrhunderts, as excerpted in Race and race history, ed. R. Pois. New York (1970).

Sapir, E. 1921. *Language*. San Diego.

Scharf, H.-W., ed. 1989. *Wilhelm von Humboldts Sprachdenken*. Essen.

Schlegel, F. 1808. *Ueber die Sprache und Weisheit der Indier*. Heidelberg.

Schleiermacher, F. D. E. 1819. *Compendium of 1819*. Trans. J. Duke & J. Forstman. In Mueller-Vollmer 1990:73–97.

Steinmetzler, J. 1956. *Die Anthropogeographie Friedrich Ratzels und ihre ideengeschicht-lichen Wurzeln*. Bonn.

Steinthal, H. 1848. *Die Sprachwissenschaft Wilh. v. Humboldt's und Die Hegelsche Philo-sophie*. Hildesheim (1971).

———. 1850. *Die Classification der Sprachen dargestellt als die Entwicklung der Sprachidee*. Frankfurt am Main (1976).

———. 1860. *Charakteristik der hauptsächlichsten Typen des Sprachbaues*. Berlin.

———. 1867. *Die Mande-Neger-Sprachen*. Berlin.

———, ed. 1883. *Die sprachphilosophischen Werke Wilhelm's von Humboldt*. Berlin.

Stocking, G. W., Jr. 1968. *Race, culture, and evolution: Essays in the history of anthropol-ogy*. New York.

———. 1974a. The Boas plan for the study of American Indian languages. In Stocking 1992:60–91.

———. 1974b. The basic assumptions of Boasian anthropology. In Stocking 1974c: 1–20.

———, ed. 1974c. *The shaping of American anthropology 1883–1911: A Franz Boas reader*. New York.

———. 1977. The aims of Boasian ethnography: Creating the materials for tradi-tional humanistic scholarship. *Hist. Anth. Newsl*. 4(2): 4–5.

———, ed. 1983. *Observers observed: Essays on ethnographic fieldwork*. HOA 1. Madison.

———, ed. 1985. *Objects and others: Essays on museums and material culture*. HOA 3. Madison.

———. 1987. *Victorian anthropology*. New York.

———. 1992. *The ethnographer's magic and other essays in the history of anthropology*. Madison.

Sweet, P. 1978. *Wilhelm von Humboldt: A biography*. Vol. I. Columbus.

———. 1980. *Wilhelm von Humboldt: A biography*. Vol. II. Columbus.

Trabant, J. 1886. *Apeliotes oder der Sinn der Sprache: Wilhelm von Humboldt's Sprachbild*. Munich.

———. 1990. *Traditionen Humboldts*. Frankfurt am Main.

Waitz, T. 1859. *Anthropologie der Naturvölker*. Vol. 1. Leipzig.

White, L. 1963. *The ethnography and ethnology of Franz Boas*. Texas Memorial Museum Bulletin 6. Austin.

Windelband, W. 1884. *Präludien: Aufsätze und Reden zur Einleitung in die Philosophie*. Freiburg.

FROM VIRCHOW TO FISCHER

Physical Anthropology and "Modern Race Theories" in Wilhelmine Germany

BENOIT MASSIN

In 1900, Houston Stewart Chamberlain, the most famous racist writer of his time, complained bitterly that at a recent German anthropological congress, "under the pontificate of Virchow and the curacy of Kollmann"—two leading German craniologists who preached "the dogma [that] 'all men are equally gifted'"—science had "gone obviously insane." By "extolling hotchpotch of bloods as the panacea of mankind," Virchow and his school had over the last forty years "wreaked a lot of havoc" in Germany's "practical and political life" (1900:32).[1]

Chamberlain's lament introduces a somewhat jarring note into the chorus of the historiography of German racism. Looking backward from the Nazi Holocaust, one current of that literature emphasizes the continuity of racial thinking, if not "from Luther to Hitler," then at least from Herder and the Romantics in "the Holy Land of racial fantasies in Europe" (Poliakov 1987: 270). In contrast, the present study suggests that, in the highly salient discipline of physical anthropology, there is no such clear-cut ideological continu-

---

Benoit Massin is finishing a doctorate at the École des Hautes Études en Sciences Sociales in Paris, on the history of German physical anthropology and the relations between science and politics. He is the author of numerous articles on the history of the biomedical sciences and "scientific racism" in Germany, and has edited a volume on the history of German "race hygiene."

1. In its present form, this essay is less than half its original length, and the bibliography has been reduced in about the same proportion—with the result that many details of argument and documentation are not included here, and will no doubt appear in future essays by the author. Editor's note.

ity. A second historiographical tendency, emphasizing the role of "scientific racism," locates the origin of the "Aryan myth" of the Nazis in the laboratories of nineteenth-century craniology (Stölting 1987). In contrast, the present study suggests that, if such a "national style" of science did exist (Harwood 1992), German physical anthropology, in contrast to the dominant French and American schools of the 1860–90 period, could, in regard to the issues of Aryanism and anti-Semitism, in fact be described as "anti-racist." A third body of literature, stressing social and economic factors, treats the "science of race" and "race hygiene" as "pseudosciences" forced upon the universities by the Nazi regime (Kater 1989). In contrast, the present study shows that the teaching of racial anthropology began in the later nineteenth century, while race hygiene (a distinct discipline) began to be taught in the first decade of the twentieth. Both were at the time regarded as legitimate scientific endeavors, and cannot simply be equated with racism, anti-Semitism, and bourgeois conservatism (Merten, 1983; Müller-Hill 1989). On the other hand, it is the case that, in response to "external" political agendas, there was a break in the liberal-humanitarian tradition of German anthropology at the turn of the century, and that this influenced the "internal" development of the discipline, reorienting research programs, methodology, paradigmatic postulates, and disciplinary ethics. A fourth historiographic tendency would find the "scientific origins of National Socialism" specifically in German Social Darwinism, emphasizing the role of Ernst Haeckel (Gasman 1971). Here, again, the relationship is complex. Aryanism was not a product of German biology, but of linguistics and archeology, and German physical anthropology, long resistant to Haeckel's Darwinism, only converted to Darwinism after the mid-1890s. The critical link between racial politics and biological science came after 1900, in the debate between neo-Lamarckians and neo-Darwinians, when "good politics" became linked with "bad science" (and vice versa)—two fatal alliances which were to have far-reaching influence on the consolidation of a racial political line within the German bio-medical community.

As Chamberlain's lament suggests, late nineteenth-century German physical anthropology—in which Franz Boas had received a brief early training under Virchow—was, in contemporary terms, quite "liberal" on matters of race. Indeed, a survey of German anthropological literature during the 1850–90 period indicates nothing to predestine the later intimate collaboration of German anthropology with the Nazi regime. Among all Western countries, Germany was the one where the first comprehensive statement of the Aryan myth—the famous *Essai sur l'inégalité des races humaines* (1853–55), by the French diplomat, amateur orientalist, and writer Arthur de Gobineau—initially met the most critical reception (Schemann 1910:61–71, 186–87). Prior to Gobineau's death in 1880, the number of copies of the *Essai* circulating in Germany was no more than several dozen (Lémonon 1971:I, 386). The few German scholars who had read Gobineau, whether naturalists like the old explorer Alexander von Humboldt, linguists like August Pott, or physical anthropologists like Hermann Schaffhausen, opposed his Aryan epic on both scientific and moral grounds (Lémonon 1971:I, 126–328; Honigmann 1990). Dismissing Gobineau's arguments for the permanent inferiority of Blacks and the immutability of types, Schaffhausen concluded in 1857: "[J]ust as Christianity teaches the equality of all men, science must recognize that in spite of the diversity of levels of civilization, all human stocks have the same natural base and each race has the right to live and the ability to develop" (in Lémonon 1971:I, 323–24).

By the time Chamberlain penned his complaint, however, changes were already under way in the surrounding popular and scientific racial discourse that were also to affect German anthropology. From the 1880s on there was a rising stream of speculation by linguists and archeologists on Aryan origins. Eugenic ideas found their first German advocates in the next decade: in 1891, Wilhelm Schallmayer published *Über die drohende körperliche Entartung der Culturmenschheit* ("On the Impending Physical Degeneration of Civilized Humanity"); and in 1895, Alfred Ploetz, the main organizer of the "Race hygiene" movement in Germany, published *Die Tüchtigkeit unserer Rasse und der Schutz der Schwachen* ("The Fitness of Our Race and the Protection of the Weak"). In 1894, Ludwig Schemann, Gobineau's apostle in Germany, founded a "Gobineau Society"; in 1899, Chamberlain brought out the first edition of his bestselling *Die Grundlagen des neunzehnten Jahrhunderts* ("The Foundations of the Nineteenth Century"). The major books of the German "anthroposociological" school by Otto Ammon, Ludwig Woltmann, and Ludwig Wilser appeared between 1893 and 1907 (Massin 1992). In the first years of the century, three new reviews were created, each one dedicated to the dissemination of one of those currents of thought: 1902 saw the first number of *Der Hammer*, edited by the crudely racial anti-Semite Theodor Fritsch, as well as the founding of Woltmann's *Politisch-Anthropologische Revue* as organ of the anthroposociological school; in 1904, Ploetz's *Archiv für Rassen- und Gesellschaftsbiologie* was established as an outlet for the eugenic movement. Little discussed a few years before, these "modern race theories" (Hertz 1904) became the focus of nation-wide debates at the turn of the century, when nationalistic political organizations such as the Pan-German League provided a public forum (Chickering 1984:245). The new ideas were immediately translated into political programs: in 1905, the Austrian Josef Reimer published *Ein pangermanisches Deutschland: Versuch über die Konsequenzen der gegenwärtigen wissenschaftlichen Rassenbetrachtung für unsere politischen und religiösen Probleme*, in which he visualized the future Third Reich as a "racial democracy" uniting all Teutonic countries from Scandinavia to Austria, controlling Western Europe and colonizing Eastern Europe.

Faced with this ideological landslide, how did German physical anthropology react? Had Chamberlain lived until 1933, he would have seen a radical transformation: German biological anthropologists, most of them members of the Nazi party, were among the most zealous scientific supporters of the Nazi regime, with one of the lowest emigration and persecution rates of all the sciences (Proctor 1988a, 1988b; Weingart, Kroll, & Bayertz 1988; Müller-Hill 1989; Weindling 1989; Massin 1993a). The question, then, which this essay addresses is: What happened to the liberal German anthropology that Chamberlain lamented in 1900?

Rudolf Virchow and the Institutionalization of German Physical Anthropology, 1869–1902

Physical anthropology in Germany was formed at the cross-road of a number of scientific traditions: medical and comparative anatomy, craniology, and anthropometry; geography, ethnology, and linguistics; archeology and history; and geology and paleontology.[2] It was only in the 1860s that it began to be established as a discipline claiming scientific autonomy and endowed with a specific methodology, and, although medical men took the leadership (Querner 1969), the institutions established in that decade were quite mixed in character.

After several preliminary initiatives, it was Rudolf Virchow who in 1869 led in the founding of the first German anthropological society, the Berliner Gesellschaft für Anthropologie, Ethnologie und Urgeschichte (Andree 1969), and who played a leading role also in the formation of the similarly named German national society the following year. The most famous cellular pathologist of his day, Virchow was Professor of Pathological Anatomy at the University of Berlin, where he also served as Rector. A scholar of wide-ranging scientific interests, he pursued a variety of anthropological researches, including work in prehistory, craniology, and large-scale anthropometric surveys. As scientist, he was a staunch empiricist, to the point of regarding Darwinian

2. In the Anglo-Saxon tradition, the unmodified form "anthropology" has, since the 1870s, generally been used to refer to a more embracive inquiry including what in the United States have come to be called "the four fields"—one of which is "cultural anthropology" or (in an earlier usage) "ethnology." "Ethnology" itself has a complex history, and before its usage as an equivalent to cultural anthropology it referred (in both the Anglo-Saxon and French traditions) to "the science of race." In Germany (and in France as well) the term *Anthropologie* has (with a few exceptions) been used to refer to what in Anglo-Saxon countries came to be called "physical anthropology," whereas "cultural anthropology" or "ethnology" (in the more recent Anglo-Saxon sense) has been referred to by *Ethnologie, Ethnographie,* or *Völkerkunde.* Following Virchow, who once said that "anthropology" has "by itself nothing to do with culture" (*VhB* 1894:504), in this essay "anthropology" will refer to physical anthropology.

biological evolution as an unproven hypothesis. In politics, he was an out-spoken left-liberal, a leader of the anti-Bismarckian Progressive Party and a member of the Reichstag from 1880 to 1893. And he continued to play a pivotal role in the institutionalization of German anthropology: according to Franz Boas, who in 1885 had worked under Virchow and the ethnologist Adolf Bastian at the Berliner Museum für Völkerkunde, Virchow's "far-reaching in-fluence" depended largely on his "leading part in the organization of anthro-pological work in Germany" (1902:47). For more than thirty years before his death in 1902, Virchow was in fact the dominant force in German physical anthropology—intellectually, ideologically, and institutionally (Ackerknecht 1953; Andree 1976).

Following the formation of the Berlin and national societies, the next quar-ter century saw the founding of twenty-five local and regional anthropological societies, including those at Munich and Leipzig. The *Archiv für Anthropologie* became the organ of the national society, which also published a monthly ab-stract of its proceedings, the *Correspondenz-Blatt*; the *Zeitschrift für Ethnologie*, founded by Adolf Bastian in 1869, became the official organ of the Berlin society. The Munich society, presided over by Virchow's second-in-command, Johannes Ranke, published its own organ, as did a number of local societies. By 1896 there was also an international bibliographic review of anthropologi-cal literature, Buschan's *Centralblatt*, which grew at a rapid pace. For the year 1894 alone, Ranke counted 365 anthropological publications in Germany (*CoB*: 1896:88). Three years later, the Strasbourg anatomist Gustav Schwalbe began publishing the *Zeitschrift für Morphologie und Anthropologie* as a journal "exclusively dedicated to physical anthropology."

During the turn-of-the-century period, German physical anthropology played a leading role in the European scientific world. Its sphere of influence did not stop at the territorial boundaries of Bismarck's Reich but included German-speaking Switzerland, Austria, Hungary, Bohemia, Poland, and the Baltic countries, as well as parts of the Netherlands, the Balkans, and Scandi-navia. Students, academicians, and scientific meetings circulated continuously between the German Reich, the Austrian double monarchy and German-speaking Switzerland, forming in effect one "scientific nation." Attracted by the prestige and power of German science, students and scientists from much of continental Europe outside the French sphere came to study and work at German universities and museums. In turn, a great number of German anthro-pologists spent some time in the course of their career studying or teaching in universities in Switzerland or Austria. Central European anthropologists often published their work in German, in German anthropological reviews or through German publishing houses. Outside Europe, the German anthropo-logical community was linked to a German-speaking diaspora, with people such as Franz Boas in New York, Erwin von Bälz in Tokyo, and Paul Adolf

Lehmann-Nitzsche in Buenos Aires, all of whom participated actively in
German scientific discussions and made occasional trips to Germany.

Despite the prestige and influence of German physical anthropology, however, the level of anthropological professionalization and institutionalization
was still low. Although there was a considerable degree of what might be called
"internal" disciplinary institutionalization (in terms of organizations and publications), "external" institutionalization (in terms of academic and government recognition) was quite limited, both relatively and absolutely.

Assuming, on the basis of the 2350 persons known to have belonged to the
German Anthropological Society in 1884 (Zängl-Kumpf 1990:96), that there
were at least 2500 members at the turn of the century, and (somewhat arbitrarily) that one-third of these had a primary interest in physical anthropology,
only about 1 percent (i.e., fewer than ten) were practicing physical anthropology as a full-time academic profession on the territory of the Reich (Ranke
1903). Although the number of academics in German universities grew almost
fourfold between 1864 and 1910 (Ringer 1988:94), physical anthropology did
not profit much from this tremendous expansion. There was not a single chair
until 1886, and for the twenty years following, from 1886 to 1906, the only
anthropological institute (and full professorship) among twenty-one German
universities was that of Ranke at Munich. It was only in 1907 that a second
institute, directed and largely funded by the anatomist Hermann Klaatsch, was
established at the University of Breslau. In Berlin, Virchow was professor of
pathology in the faculty of medicine, and had to store the ten thousand skulls
and skeletons he had collected either at the Pathological Institute or in his
home (Hiltner 1970:51). It was not until 1900 that an extraordinary professorship was established in Berlin for Felix von Luschan, an Austrian physician
who had studied with Paul Broca, the leading figure in French physical anthropology, and who had served as docent at the Berlin Museum since 1885. And
while Luschan's chair became a full professorship in 1909, he never succeeded
in founding an anthropological institute (Kiffner 1961; Schott 1961). Although he was by this time director of the prestigious Oceania-Africa section
of the museum (most prestigious because it included the German overseas
colonies), Luschan had to be content with a rather dark "miserable room in
the basement" to store and measure his thousands of skulls (Rusch 1985:442;
Grimm 1986:423).

Since Virchow's institutional policy was to separate physical anthropology
both from philosophy and from non-medical natural sciences like zoology and
geology, most of the well-known anthropologists were professors of medicine
who treated anthropology as *Nebenfach*, a side interest, or an unremunerated
hobby. These included Klaatsch at Heidelberg (until 1907), Gustav Schwalbe
at Strasbourg, and Gustav Fritsch, Wilhelm Krause, and Wilhelm von Waldeyer at Berlin. The very few who held academic positions as anthropologists,
such as Emil Schmidt at Leipzig or Georg Thilenius at Breslau, were only hon-

Rudolf Virchow, the leader of German physical anthropology in the last third of the nineteenth century, surrounded by human skeletal material, in the Institute for Pathology of the University of Berlin, c. 1900. (Courtesy of the Bildarchiv preussischer Kulturbesitz, Berlin.)

orary professors, extraordinary professors (i.e., without chairs), *Privatdozenten*, or assistants. And while "ordinary professors" (or holders of chairs) enjoyed an enviable social and economic position in imperial Germany, this was generally not true of other academics (Busch 1959, Burchardt 1988:163–88; Ringer 1988:96). As extraordinary professor at Freiburg, Eugen Fischer made less than the average German industrial worker (FP: *Antrag zum Budget* 1908–9). In this context, "anthropologists" without a personal fortune or other lucrative profession had to renounce academic careers for better-paying positions such as school teacher or librarian.

Nor did the field train new members in significant numbers. From 1870 to 1910, only three university "habilitations" (conferring the right to teach as private docent) in physical anthropology were granted in all of Germany: Schmidt in 1885, Luschan in 1888, and Birkner in 1904. Three others (among them Eugen Fischer) were habilitated in anatomy "including physical anthropology"; Rudolf Martin and Theodor Mollison acquired their habilitations in Zurich (Schwidetzky 1982:87–89). The academic calendar of 1902–3 indicates that physical anthropology proper was taught in only six of the twenty-one German universities: at Berlin, by Luschan and the anatomy professors Hans Virchow (Rudolf's son), Gustav Fritsch, and Wilhelm Krause; at Breslau, by Thilenius, as extraordinary professor of anthropology and ethnology; at Erlangen, by Arnold Spuler, docent in anatomy; at Freiburg, by Fischer, as docent for anatomy and anthropology; at Heidelberg, by Klaatsch, as extraordinary professor of anatomy; and at Munich, by Ranke (Ranke 1903).

The practical consequence of this low level of professionalization was that more than 90 percent of German "anthropologists" at the turn of the century, when not merely nominal members of the German anthropological society, were more or less amateurs, practicing physical anthropology as a secondary field or hobby. The socio-professional distribution of "anthropologists" can best be illustrated by the case of the Berlin society, which in 1899 counted 501 members, whose occupations were listed in the society's *Verhandlungen* (*VhB* 1899:3–15). Among the three hundred who resided in Berlin, fifteen (5 percent) held a position in the University or at the Berlin Museum as ethnologists or archeologists, but only one (Luschan) as physical anthropologist. A socio-professional analysis of this community shows how vague the boundary was between "professional" anthropologists and "amateurs" in this pre-professionalization period. Of those 501 ordinary members, 190 were private physicians, medical academics, or people with M.D.s working in non-medical fields; about 55 were non-medical academics, librarians or museum employees. The other 255 included tradespeople and accountants; painters and photographers; officials in government and colonial administration; school teachers and persons of private means; army or navy officers; scientists and professionals of various sorts; publishers or booksellers; priests or rabbis; travellers; and two ladies, one of them a novelist. In short, at least half the membership practiced anthropology as a "Sunday hobby" (Luschan 1916:18), and did not know much more about physical anthropology than Chamberlain or many of the race theoreticians.

To mobilize this relatively unprofessional and imperfectly institutionalized group against dilettantish and amateur racism was no small task. It was complicated by the fact that by 1900 physical anthropology itself had entered a period of internal scientific crisis. Prior to that time, however, Virchow and his colleagues were able for three decades to speak as the voice of a "scientific anthropology"—which, in late nineteenth-century contemporary terms, must be regarded as anti-racist.

The Racial Liberalism of German Anthropology under Virchow's Leadership

From the beginning of its institutionalization, German anthropology was staunchly monogenist, in contrast to France and the United States, where strong "polygenist" movements had developed in mid-century (Blanckaert 1981; Stanton 1960; Stepan 1982:44–46; Stocking 1968:42–68). The few German polygenist anthropologists, like the materialist Carl Vogt, had had to retire or emigrate because of their political radicalism and participation in the 1848 Revolution (Gregory 1977:51–73, 254). The two main organizers of the first meeting of German anthropologists in 1861, the Prussian aristocrat, anatomist, and embryologist Karl Ernst von Baer and the anatomist and physiologist Rudolf Wagner, were both deeply Christian defenders of the spiritual values of a universal humanity threatened by polygenism and the biological materialism of early Darwinians (Baer & Wagner 1861:24; Ottow 1966; Montgomery 1974:86). Almost all leading German anthropologists residing on the Reich's territory, from the founding of the German Anthropological Society in 1870 to World War I, professed a belief in the unity of the human species.

Although it was of course argued in scientific terms, monogenism was more than a purely scientific matter. Virchow confessed that behind his "penchant" for monogenism was a "traditional," even a "sentimental" idea: "I cannot restrain myself from thinking, when I look at the whole history of Mankind, that we are really brothers or sisters" (in Ranke 1887:233)—although as an empiricist he nevertheless noted the "apparent" unity of mankind had not yet been "exactly demonstrated," and that the problem of race formation was empirically "still unsolved" (Virchow 1896a:13, 43). Ranke took advantage of his position as permanent general secretary of the German anthropological society from 1878 to 1908 to drum into his colleagues, at the annual assemblies, the unity of mankind and the "equality of feelings and mental life of all humanity" (CoB 1893:82, 1896:91, 1906:106).

This tenet was so strong that reactions were instantaneous when some German anthropologists were tempted to expel some "savages" from humanity by "animalizing" them. When the Swiss-German explorers Paul and Fritz Sarasin, both members of the Berlin society, manifested a "certain tendency to rank the Veddas among the chimpanzees" in a volume they published in 1892, they were criticized by Ranke at the 1893 national meeting (CoB 1893:83–84). Occasionally, a nonconformist like the brilliant Americanist Paul Ehrenreich, a member of the progressive Jewish circles around Virchow in Berlin, might suggest that monogenism was simply a convenient scientific prejudice to prove "men were all brothers" (1897:18–21). But, for the most part, Germany remained the country of monogenism.

Within, or alongside this publicly proclaimed monogenism, however, there were occasional discreet manifestations of what might be called a "bigenist" hypothesis. Although Schaffhausen was a convinced ethical monogenist and liberal Catholic (Zängl-Kumpf 1990:24–25), from a scientific point of view he was inclined to think that mankind originated from two primitive stocks (Schaffhausen 1890:127–28). Ludwig Wilser, a non-academic Teutonist anthropologist, went a step further by relating two primitive human forms to the two main types of anthropoid apes in terms of both pigmentation and craniology (Wilser 1894:17–18); but because Wilser was notorious as a heated controversialist with marginal opinions, none of his colleagues at the 1894 meeting of German anthropologists reacted to his speech. However, this was not the case when Klaatsch, professor of anthropology in Breslau—previously an advocate of the unity of mankind (1902b)—made a dramatic about-face at the 1910 meeting. On the basis of comparative morphological study of prehistoric human races, Klaatsch argued that there were two main branches of human evolution: one Western stock from which emerged the gorilla and Neanderthal man, and one Eastern stock for the orang outang and the Aurignacian race (1910:91–99). The reaction, however, was immediate. Erwin von Bälz, for thirty years professor for internal medicine at Tokyo University, suggested that Klaatsch would meet "a heavy opposition"—citing the statement of Felix von Luschan that "we all agree that mankind has arisen only from one place" (CoB 1910:99).

While Klaatsch, seconded by Fritsch, persisted in his polygenism, the German anthropological community as a whole remained monogenist (Luschan 1909:202). This included even several younger men who were later to become Nazi anthropologists: Theodor Mollison, docent at Zurich, and Eugen Fischer, professor of anatomy and anthropology at Freiburg—who cited the high fertility of the hybrid population of Boer colonists and Hottentots he studied in German Southwest Africa as a definitive demonstration of the physiological unity of the human species (1913:227). At a time when the controversy between monogenists and polygenists seemed obsolete in many countries, German anthropologists still found it necessary to reaffirm the common origin of mankind.

The racial liberalism of German anthropology is also exemplified by its negative reaction to the emergence of modern anti-Semitism and Teutonic racism (Strauss & Kampe 1985). The rapid industrialization of Germany after its political unification and several economic crises during the "founding years" of the new Empire produced a host of critics of modernity, of individualistic liberalism, and of the people who were seen as their main agents: the Jews (Zmarlik 1982; Jochman 1976). More than traditional social and religious prejudice, the animosity against Jews became for many a general *Weltanschauung*, in which "the Jews" were seen as the key to an understanding and solution of all the problems, past and present, that affected European nations (Pulzer 1966; Rürup 1976). The fight against *Judentum* became a vital *Kampf*, a Manichean "struggle for life" of the German or Aryan *Volk* against its most dangerous "parasite." This dramatic turn in the late 1880s may be documented by the titles of such works as *Der Verzweiflungskampf der arischen Völker mit dem Judentum* (Ahlwardt 1890).

The change from what was first called the *Judenfrage* ("Jewish question") to a *Rassenfrage* ("racial question") occurred at about the same time. The most significant work symbolizing this transformation was *Die Judenfrage als Racen-Sitten- und Culturfrage*, published by the influential economist and philosopher Eugen Dühring in 1881—which by the third edition of 1892 had been retitled *Die Judenfrage als Frage der Racenschädlichkeit [racial toxicity] für die Existenz, Sitte und Cultur der Völker*. This intellectual assault was accompanied by a flood of popular papers and a campaign of political agitation, culminating in 1893 in the election of sixteen candidates of the anti-Semitic leagues and political parties (Rürup 1976). Although the tide of purely political anti-Semitism thenceforth slowly ebbed until the eve of the World War (Levy 1975), anti-Semitism as a social phenomenon did not vanish. Linked to the call for Germanic solidarity and purity, it spilled over as diffuse "cultural code" (Volkov 1978) or overt ideology into many different associations, political movements, and the popular press, spreading to large segments of German society, including most ominously the academic and medical community, and student organizations. In 1896, the German Students' Union decided to exclude not only Jews but baptized students of Jewish origin (Berding 1991:108). By 1910, one of these anti-Semitic academics could proclaim: "Today the idea of social anti-Semitism has become the common property of all academic circles" (in Jarausch 1982:356; see also Kampe 1988:54–107).

In various ways, however, leading German anthropologists did what they could to resist the anti-Semitic landslide. In 1880, when anti-Semitic leagues successfully collected several hundred thousand signatures on a petition to the Bismarck government, Virchow was one of the few officials to publicly protest against the collective Judeophobia. As deputy of the Progressive Party in the Reichstag, he challenged Chancellor Bismarck to explain his position on the issue. In Berlin, Virchow was the main political opponent of the notorious anti-Semite Stöcker, twice defeating him for office. Virchow was so opposed to the new political anti-Semitism that a legend spread in anti-Semite circles that he was himself a Jew; his Progressive Party's systematic opposition to anti-Semitism was such that adversaries spoke of it as the "Jews' Party" (Kümmel 1968). In the Berlin Anthropological Society, the substantial Jewish membership (12 percent in 1899) helped liberal anthropologists to form a block against anti-Semitic outsiders. At the peak of political anti-Semitism in 1893, Ranke, general secretary of the German Anthropological Society, declared at the society's annual meeting: "Before the tribunal of anthropological research, there is no justification for ethnic or racial hatred" (CoB 1894:179).

But if Virchow insisted in the Prussian Parliament on distinguishing between "race" and religious affiliation, his position on the matter of a "Jewish race" reflected an uncertainty characteristic of academic anthropology (cf. Kiefer 1991:7–31). On the basis of his pigmentation survey between 1871 and 1886 of almost seven million German pupils, which had shown that

11 percent of Jewish children had blond hair, blue eyes, and fair skin, Virchow had called into question their status as an anthropological "race," and later defined them instead as a "national race" (1886, 1896a:3). But in 1880 he spoke of a "Jewish race"; what he opposed was the idea that it was doomed, "by its nature, its dispositions, its instincts to be abominable"; on the contrary, it possessed "excellent aptitudes" and had accomplished the "highest achievements" (in Kümmel 1968:169). He did, however, still speak of a "striking difference between the Semites and the so-called Aryans," of "Semitic blood," "Semitic race," and of the "Jewish nose" as "so crooked, that it was enough for many of them to replace a birth certificate" (1885:225, 227–29; CoB 1900: 71, 113). Similarly, Johannes Ranke felt that the "slightly crooked nose, fleshy at the end," and the "pouting lips of the ancient Semites in Babylon" were "still characteristic of present Jews" (CoB 1907:99).

Most serious anthropological studies, however, from Kollmann in 1885 to Weissenberg in 1909, maintained that Jews were not a "race" but an aggregate of several types. Further, for these liberal anthropologists difference of race was not a hindrance to cultural assimilation. In Virchow's eyes, the numerous Jews driven by pogroms out of the Russian Empire to the more liberal environment of Germany could be as fully germanized as had been the French Huguenots forced out by the revocation of the edict of Nantes. Jews in Germany had become "for us, a powerful ferment of the progressive culture" (1872:317).

Luschan, who as holder of the Berlin chair of anthropology was the leader of the liberal tradition after Virchow's death in 1902, was equally opposed to anti-Semitism. In "The Anthropological Position of Jews" in 1892, he argued that Semites had built a civilization with epics, cuneiform script, and monumental palaces at a time when "we Germans were still living in caves and earth holes and had barely learned to transform silex [flint] into implements." No wonder then that the "educated European recognized in his Jewish fellow citizen not only the living witness and heir of an ancient and venerable culture, but also respects and esteems and loves him as his best and most faithful co-worker and fire-comrade in the fight for the highest goods of this earth, in the fight for Progress and intellectual freedom" (1892:99–100).

Luschan's article was, however, atypical insofar as "classical" German anthropology of the years 1890–1914 had in fact little interest in Jews, except insofar as they were on a few occasions used as an argument in the controversy on the permanence of types (Kollmann 1900b:3). Of the several thousand articles published in the four main anthropological reviews during this quarter century, there were only six dealing with Jews—the other five were by Samuel Weissenberg, a Ukrainian Jewish physician educated in Germany who with the financial backing of the Rudolf Virchow Foundation had studied Jews in Central Asia, the Caucasus, Crimea, and the Near East (Kiefer 1991:39–52; Weissenberg 1895, 1909).

A similar pattern of resistance by physical anthropologists was evident in the face of the efflorescence of Pan-Germanism and *völkisch* movements in the 1890s. Like anti-Semitism, Pan-Germanism and *völkisch* ideology were at first political and cultural (Stern 1961). The idea of the "German race" was not so much a biological concept as a synonym for ethnicity and political community, an ambiguous catchword mobilizing the public around the idea of a permanent specificity of the Germanic *Weltanschauung* and a correct way to behave in society. Until the beginning of the 1890s even Jews, if they converted to German nationalistic norms, could be assimilated. It was only then that the lineaments of a comprehensive philosophy of racism began to permeate Germanic and anti-Semitic movements, becoming well-defined "race theories" at the turn of the century (Chickering 1984:234).

When the first waves of Teutonic racism swept Germany in the 1890s, established anthropology reacted as critically as it had against anti-Semitism. At the 1894 national meeting of anthropologists, Virchow attacked the "Pan-Aryan dogma," speaking of the "blood superstition" of "nativist fanatics" as a "residue of prehistorical times," a "resurgence of the very old idea of the inferiority or even wickedness of barbarians or allophylen" ("foreign stocks") (*CoB* 1894:178–79, 1896a:16–17). On several occasions, he ridiculed "our enthusiasts, the Pan-Germanists," who tried to find Teutonic tribes in every important prehistorical site; for him, the "advantage of modern anthropology" was that it kept "as far as possible from pure hypothesis," striving instead "to help objective truth to gain recognition and to respect only such truth as science" (*CoB* 1897:70, 75).

Virchow's racial liberalism is well known. But far from being alone in the battle against Teutonic racism, he was supported by most of his leading colleagues. His second-in-command, Ranke, maintained his hostility to Teutonic or Nordic Race theories until his death. Writing for a Munich weekly in 1908, Ranke argued that headform was not a racial character (Geus 1987:13–14); his last book review, in praise of Friedrich Hertz's anti-racist *Rasse und Kultur* (1915), warned against the theories of racial antagonism that were "recently growing up in a alarming manner," and urged the need to instruct the public on how the works of Gobineau and Chamberlain "contradicted the real scientific facts" (*AA* 1917:73).

Julius Kollmann, the third most influential of the German physical anthropologists, was equally outspoken. At a general meeting of the German anthropological society in 1892, he insisted that all European races were "equally gifted for all cultural tasks." Playing off against each other the advocates of dolichocephalic and brachycephalic superiority, Kollmann suggested ironically that anyone "who wants to practice anthropology with a political flavor" was free to choose between the two (1892a). A decade later, when Chamberlain advertised his *Grundlagen des neunzehnten Jahrhunderts* in a popular Austrian cultural review, Kollmann immediately retaliated in the same journal with a denunciation of the "madness of racial purity." Attacking the notion of a "Germanic race," he insisted that race "no longer determined the life of nations." While it might be politically "convenient" for a nation to believe in the "unity of its race," it was in fact a "fairytale"—a "meaningless and "deadly word" which had caused a great deal of "disaster" (1900a).

Others besides these institutional leaders also tried to shield their anthropological society and to alert the German public against such tendencies. In 1903, when the amateur anthropologist and Teutonist Ludwig Wilser painted the tall, dolichocephalic, fair-haired, blue-eyed, white-skinned "master race"—the Homo Europaeus of the French anthroposociologist Vacher de Lapouge—as an "incomparable great influence" on "the civilization and evolution of our continent," Herman Klaatsch was "commissioned by many of his colleagues" to protest officially against "a speech which disparages the dignity of science" (CoB 1903:186–87). Similarly, Aurel von Török, who held the chair of anthropology at Budapest, denounced Lapouge's "fantastic speculations" and "fairytales" (1906b:115–16). Rudolf Martin, in taking up his post as director of the Zurich Institute, spoke for many of his colleagues by condemning as "unscientific and misguided" the attempt to "tug anthropology into politics" (1901:13, 17).

Following Virchow's death in 1902, the task of politically controlling the "scientific truth" was taken over by Felix von Luschan. Condemning those "completely fanatic men" who wanted to breed a pure race of dolichocephalic blonds, Luschan insisted that all the greatest European civilizations were the product of cross-breeding; only "incurable chauvinists still speak of an Aryan race" (1905:1, 1912:55). In his continuing correspondence with his "dear friend" Franz Boas—with whom he had worked at the Königliches Museum für Völkerkunde—he complained about race theorists such as the national-racist prehistorian Wolff, a disciple of the Pan-Germanist archeologist Kossina (and "notorious head of the criminal anti-Semites"), who in a prehistorical review had referred to the Jewish linguist Sigmund Feist as a "mongrel man of civilization" and a "world-citizen of the red and gold International" (Wolff 1914:309; LuP: FL/FB, 6/16/14).

The resistance of established anthropologists to Aryan, Teutonic, or anti-Semitic racism was facilitated by the fact that, until 1910, most "race theoreticians" were either outsiders or did not hold central positions in the German anthropological society. Until the founding of Buschan's and Schwalbe's new reviews in 1896 and 1899 (CeB & ZMA), the main anthropological journals were controlled, directly or indirectly, by the liberals Virchow, Ranke, and the ethnologist Adolf Bastian. Virchow was particularly concerned to control the scientificity and "political correctness" of all anthropology published in professional journals, and thanks to his huge personal influence, was able to bar access to those he considered politically or scientifically undesirable "amateurs" (cf. Andree 1976:I, 127). This situation was acknowledged even by racial theorists, one of whom commented that in the field of racial biology, "two groups are facing each other: the so-called race theorists and the scientific anthropologists." The former were usually described by the latter as "dilettantes who indulge in imaginative hypothesis and whose work consequently cannot claim a scientific value" (Driesmans 1904:241). And indeed, an analysis of the social status of the eight main German theoreticians of race during the 1890–1914 period indicates that only one of them (Otto Ammon) was an established figure in the institutionalized anthropological community.

The race theorists may be seen as three concentric groups. The largest embraced the countless "philosophers of race" and theoreticians of racial anti-Semitism who were completely outside of and rejected by the established anthropological community. Among them were Ludwig Schemann, Gobineau's apostle in Germany, who was a philologist and historian; Willibald Hentschel, advocate of the stud-breeding of the "Aryan race," who was a successful biochemist; and Houston Stewart Chamberlain, the most notorious of all, who remained an essayist, despite a doctorate in biology and brief study of anthropology under Carl Vogt at the University of Geneva (Nagel-Birlinger 1979: 25; Löwenberg 1978; Field 1981). None of these men published a single line in an anthropological review. While Schemann did attempt to establish contact with anthropologists, most racial theorists cared little for established science. Chamberlain in fact poked fun at craniologists and prided himself on his dilettantism (1913:lxviii–lxx et passim).

A second group included those at the margins of institutional anthropology, whose work was often published in sociological or medical reviews. In contrast to the first group, whose writings were not even reviewed in anthropological journals, these scholars were important enough to be taken into account scientifically, either positively or negatively. Among them were the anthroposociologist Ludwig Woltmann and the founder of German eugenics Wilhelm Schallmayer (Hammer 1979:8–30; Weiss 1986, 1987a), both of whom were physicians knowledgeable in anthropology. But although they had personal contacts among established anthropologists, and Schallmayer was a nominal member of the German anthropological society, neither man published in established anthropological reviews. Another who may be included in this group is Alfred Ploetz, organizer of the "Race hygiene" movement in Germany, who had studied medicine and psychiatry and did research on heredity; although he joined the Berlin anthropological society in 1903 (Weindling 1989:134), he did not in the pre–World War I period contribute to anthropological reviews or textbooks.

The third group of racial theorists—most notably, Otto Ammon and Ludwig Wilser—were active members of the German anthropological society and did work of the sort conventionally done by physical anthropologists (anthropometrical surveys, morphological studies, etc.). As the founder of anthroposociology in Germany, Ammon promulgated a Darwinian racial sociology that interpreted social class in terms of physical characteristics. Although he had no established university position, Ammon was quite influential by virtue of his classic anthropometric surveys of Baden and his position as general secretary of the anthropological commission of the Karlsruhe Anthropological and Archeological Society (Lichtsinn 1987:3–5). However, as the result of a financial dispute in 1889, Ammon effectively withdrew from the German anthropological society, refusing to attend meetings for the next twenty-one years. His coworker Ludwig Wilser, although serving for a time as president of the German Society of Natural Sciences, was a very difficult personality, constantly involved in disputes (even to the point of actual duels); although he made numerous contributions at the annual meetings, his bombastic style left him a marginal figure in the liberal and academically cautious environment of the German anthropological society.

Viewed as a single group, the racial theorists—each of them a *Privatgelehrter* without professorial status—were clearly marginal to the small community of established physical anthropologists and medical anatomists. Even those who were nominally members were without significant institutional positions within it. Throughout the period of Virchow's dominance, then, the anthropological establishment of Germany actively maintained what was in contemporary terms an "anti-racist position." From a present perspective, however, there were serious qualifications of this racial liberalism, especially when it came to those groups who did not share the "white" skins of European peoples; and with Virchow's passing, the nationalism of German anthropologists also began to take on a more imperialistic, pessimistic, and Darwinian character.

Colonialism, Nationalism, and the
Retreat from Racial Liberalism

In the period of belated imperialist expansion that began under Bismarck in the early 1880s, substantial numbers of "colored people" in Africa and Oceania came under German colonial rule. The attitudes of liberal anthropologists toward this historical process and the peoples it encompassed were complex and contradictory. Liberal anthropologists generally condemned the inhuman treatment of "inferior races." After a member of the Parliament in 1892 displayed in the Reichstag an instrument used on German ships for the corporal punishment of Negroes, Virchow presented it at a meeting of the Berlin anthropological society with the clear intention of horrifying his colleagues (VhB 1892:80). However, his early pacifist and anti-militarist opposition to Bismarck's colonial policy was sometimes cast in racial medical terms: he

thought that "our vulnerable race"—the "Teutonic race"—could not "racially" acclimatize in tropical countries (1885:237, 1887:297; Vasold 1988:
362–63). And as an anthropologist, Virchow quickly appreciated the opportunities that colonialism provided for the collection of anthropological data.
The ambiguity of his position is evident in remarks he made to the annual
meeting of the German anthropological society the year East Africa officially
became a German colony:

> Now that we have become a nation of navigators and our imperial colonies have
> very quickly increased, we are prompted to take care of our new fellow country-
> men, to establish spiritual relationship with them and to learn to value them, at
> least as far as their heads and brains are concerned. As we can obtain very few
> skulls, we cannot saw in pieces all those we receive. Thanks to the precious help
> of the government and of some travellers, I have been able to obtain until now
> some dozen skulls from our Eastern and Western African colonies. . . . Dr. Stuhl-
> mann investigated on a spot where a fight took place between two tribes. One
> of his assistants collected a certain number of heads on the scene, packed them
> in a bag and had them carried on the back of a boy to Zanzibar. As one could
> expect, they banged and bumped against each other during the trip, and their
> condition, when they arrived in Berlin, left a lot to be desired. Such are the
> conditions with which one has to reckon. (Virchow 1891:122)

This combination of generous humanitarian feeling and callous scientific utili-
tarianism was quite typical of the time. A similar tension is manifest in the
more strictly scientific writings of German physical anthropologists about non-
European peoples.

The harsh verdicts of slightly earlier times regarding Negroes, Asians, and
Australian Aborigines in fact tended to disappear in German anthropological
literature of the turn of the century. Assertions like the Austrian Friedrich
Müller's, in his *Allgemeine Ethnographie,* that "[T]he Negro can be trained [like
an animal], but it is exceptionally rare that he can be really educated" (1873:
155), are atypical of German anthropologists of the 1890–1914 period. When
such animalizing views were expressed in German anthropological publications, the authors, characteristically, were not Germans, and very often Anglo-
Saxon. German anthropologists of course shared the general European feeling
of cultural superiority, but, as humanitarian monogenists, they expressed it in
a softened manner: "these so-called 'savages'" were "perhaps, in many aspects,
children—but they are men like us, spirit of our spirit" (Ranke, in *CoB* 1906:
107). In general, German physical anthropologists sought to protect the
"lower races" from such "animalization," regarding it as the "speculation" of
"ape-fanatics." Savages—"our human fellows of faraway countries"—should
not be degraded to the status of "speculation objects" (Ranke, in *CoB* 1898:
8); the "missing link" of the "ape theory" was still missing, and the theory
itself remained a "pure speculation" (Virchow 1876:172).

As these references suggest, what was at issue scientifically, besides monogenism, was the status of Darwinian evolutionary theory. In the 1860s, Darwinians were eagerly looking for "traces of our ape ancestors" in present populations, for "links" between man and anthropoid apes, and very frequently Negroes, Veddas, and Australian Aborigines were depicted as such. For Carl Vogt, most of the characters of the Negro reminded us "irresistibly of the ape." For Ludwig Büchner, the "Ethiopian race" connected man "by a number of the most striking analogies with the animal world": his "long arms," "disgusting odor," and "shrieking voice" all linked him "to the ape" (in Hunt 1863: 46, 49). According to Ernst Haeckel, Negroes used their feet as hands just like the "four-handed" monkeys (1889:684), and the "lowest races," such as Veddas and Australians, were "psychologically nearer to the mammals (apes, dogs) than to the highly civilized Europeans" (1904:430; Gasman 1971:40). Even Schaffhausen, despite his "moral" monogenism, suggested that "savages" did not stand up like civilized people did, but were a little bent over like monkeys, using their feet for grasping in a manner similar to their ape-like ancestors (1890:123).

In general, however, the positivistic non-Darwinian monogenism which prevailed from 1870 to 1895 in institutional physical anthropology was sceptical of such views. Büchner, a physiologist turned philosopher, and Haeckel, a zoologist, were marginal to the German community of physical anthropologists; Vogt, exiled in Switzerland, could not hold a leading position in the German anthropological society, though he had helped to found it; Schaffhausen's Darwinism was quite atypical. For positivistic medical academics like Virchow, such animalizing statements were based methodologically on purely "philosophical speculations" about human origins (Virchow 1879:191). Their opponents' scientific vision was distorted by "ape-spectacles"—as in the case of pathological human microcephaly, which Vogt had wrongly interpreted as "ape atavism" (Vogt 1866; Virchow, in VhB 1895:349–50). In reaction, they insisted upon the human character of the "lower races." From a purely anatomical viewpoint, Virchow felt that the skulls of Negroes did not have a "low simian form"; and if Australians seemed to show a morphological relationship to apes, it was not so great that "the Australians are closer to the ape than to us. They will ever remain men in our sense" (1876:172). Similarly for the tribes of Tierra del Fuego: "that they are savages in other respects, or, if some prefer, barbarians, should not prevent us from admitting their purely human constitution" (Virchow 1887:291–92).

For much of the period, monogenist German physical anthropologists could also rely on ethnology in their resistance to the dehumanization of savages. Adolf Bastian, in particular—"the founder and main pillar of German scientific ethnology"—engaged in a "thirty years war" for "the equality and human dignity of all cultures, even for "the despised and neglected 'savages' one thought could be considered as half-animals" (CoB 1896:91). More detailed ethnographic studies, and the increasing use of ethnographic photography, also led some physical anthropologists to question "what was repeated again and again in the handbooks" (Kollman 1900a:76–77, 1900b). During this period one can in fact observe within anthropological literature a semantic evolution in the designation of "exotic" people. While the term "savage" continued to be used as an adjective—as in "savage tribes"—when used as a substantive it was placed in quotation marks or preceded by the qualifier "so-called" (Virchow, in VhB 1892:837; Ranke, in CoB 1891:33). And with the discovery of the Benin civilization and its beautiful bronzes in Black Africa in the late 1890s, Luschan suggested that African Negroes could no longer be thought of as "savages" or "half-apes." On the contrary, savages had very complex cultures, very different from each other (Luschan 1902:169, 1910:121; cf. Malgorzata 1990:15–16). Indeed, with growing ideological discontent about the effects of industrialization and urbanization, there was a tendency to return to romantic idealizations of the more "authentic," "natural," and "healthy" Naturmensch as opposed to a Kulturmensch threatened by "degeneration" with increasing civilization. Thus Ranke saw "sexual immorality" not as a "general infantile disease of humankind, but a product of increasing culture" (CoB 1893:83–84), and Rudolf Martin, after a journey to Malaysia, spoke of its "innocent" inhabitants as an "ideal for us" (1900:20).

But despite this softening of judgment, and despite the humanitarian liberalism, monogenism, and anti-Darwinism of the German anthropological community, most anthropologists continued, without any sense of contradiction, to hold a hierarchical evolutionary view of races and cultures. Accepting the generalized cultural progressivism of their day, they assumed that there was an evolution from savagery to full humanity—an evolution reflected in the traditional German dichotomy between Naturvölker and Kulturvölker ("nature peoples" and "culture peoples"). Naturvölker were people who were "poor in culture" or even entirely "without culture" (Luschan 1911b:66; Wohltmann 1891:30; Melk-Koch 1989:7). According to the liberal ethnologist Rudolf Steinmetz, who sharply criticized Teutonic race zealots at the turn of the century, ethnology as a discipline included "all phenomenon of the life of people without culture" (culturlos)—which was also Bastian's definition of the scope of ethnology (Steinmetz 1903:139).

Within this progressive linear framework—and despite the prevailing anti-Darwinist monogenism—cultural hierarchy was often assumed to have physiological and racial correlates. Thus Virchow, in a study of the skulls of "inferior human races," argued that brow ridges, though generally missing among races who were "the carriers of the highest cultures," were frequent among Australians, "who, objectively, have remained at the lowest level of culture," and who, even "after they came into contact with the Whites have not shown the slightest tendency for a higher form of civilization" (1880:16–26). Similarly, Virchow concluded (after having measured three skulls and comparing these to the results of other anthropologists) that the Veddas of Ceylon showed the "most striking contrast to the brain proportions of civilized races": "If we add to this the apparent very low ability of Veddas for mental development, the almost complete lack of any ideal orientation of thought, the incapacity to count and still less to make calculation, . . . then the question arises whether we are not dealing with microcephaly in the pathological sense of the word" (1881:131). So also, in the case of Ranke: despite his attempt to maintain the "lowest races" within the sphere of humanity, in this generalized evolutionary frame there was no absolute breach between anthropoid apes and man but rather a gradual progress: "the more the brain develops (in respect to the rest of the skull), the more the form becomes relatively human" (Ranke 1891:117–18). The generalized progressivist and evolutionary thinking shared by both Darwinians and "transformist" monogenists made it difficult, to deny some linkage between "low human evolutionary stage" and "apes." Somewhat reluctantly, Virchow admitted that the orbital arch of the Australians could be considered as a "pithecoid" or "simian" character, placing them (on a purely morphological level) "between orang-outang, and gibbon" (1880:25, 1896a: 9–11, 1896b:158). Ranke, who had long thought that Darwinian "ape-theories" had nothing to do with positive science, argued in the 1890s, on the basis of relative proportions of facial and cranial portions of the skull, that Australians and Papuans constituted the "most extreme form of the human skull" in the series from human to animal morphologies (1897:140–44).

What was problematic was the reasons for such differences, and whether the gap between lower and higher races was unbridgeable. An old but still current scientific question in the beginning of the 1890s was whether the "lowest savages" were a "primitive race in its original low level of evolution" or whether they represented the "degenerated remains of a more evolved population" (Virchow, in ZfE 1892:252; cf. Virchow 1881). In contrast to Darwinians, Virchow tended to attribute characteristics like microcephaly to pathological "degeneration," and optimistically to assume that it might be reversed (1892: 24, 32–33). Ever cautious, and inclined to express himself negatively rather than positively, he thought that no one had yet proven scientifically that blacks were "incapable of culture"—the more so since it had taken a very long time for Europeans to rise to civilization from a similarly low cultural state (1876:172–74, 1892:24–25).

For the most part, however, the implicit hierarchy was simply taken for granted by German anthropologists, whether or not they were Darwinian. And generally it was always the same peoples who occupied the bottom rungs of the ladder: the aborigines of Australia and Melanesia, and the Veddas of South India (Virchow 1892:23). African Negroes, in the German liberal view, were big children with all the innocent qualities and shortcomings of their age. They could understand practical things but could not grasp abstract ideas;

easily excitable, and liable to commit atrocities when "enraged," they required strong control (Luschan 1906:894).

German physical anthropologists were, however, generally too cautious to display their hierarchical assumptions in any fixed schemes or visual representations such as Haeckel's phylogenetic trees. And because these assumptions were rarely clearly defined, they remained open to reshaping. More important than hierarchy was the commitment to empirical method, and sometimes the purely craniometrical point of view could in fact contradict European ethnocentrism. Thus, after studying some skulls of Masai and other African tribes from a comparative anatomical viewpoint, Virchow remarked: "the concept of inferiority cannot be as easily applied to the factual circumstances as the theory suggests" (*VhB* 1893:495). Some German anthropologists were quite willing to have European races share first place in mankind's hierarchy, or even to give it to another race. Thus Ranke noted of Mongol skulls that they were "not only near the best European skulls but even often exceed them" (1897: 140). Similarly, in a speech on "culture and the brain" before the German anthropological society, Buschan argued that Chinese brain capacity exceeded that of Germans—explaining the difference in neo-Lamarckian terms as the result of a higher level of education (1904:130).

In the middle 1890s, after three decades of "eclipse" in German physical anthropology, the Darwinian perspective was strongly reasserted, and the fundamental question of the "hierarchy of races" and "existence of superior and inferior races" acquired again a central position in anthropology (Bartels 1904a:139; Stratz 1904b:193–94). Introducing the first number of his *Zeitschrift für Morphologie und Anthropologie,* Gustav Schwalbe, one of the main representatives of the second generation of this Haeckelo-Darwinian stream, insisted that the hierarchy of races was one of the crucial questions of evolutionist anthropology (1899:6).

For this new generation of Darwinists, the static and sterile "old craniometry" had to be replaced by a dynamic biological history of mankind, with human races organized in a genealogical tree, and traces of human ancestors sought among "living fossils" today (Alsberg 1906; Sarasin 1907:237–43; Luschan 1911:16)—a development signaled by the increasing use of the term "primitive." Such evolutionary thinking made it difficult even for those who fought against Aryan and Teutonic racism to escape a hierarchical point of view. Commenting on the First Universal Races Congress held in London in 1911, the same Kollmann who had defended the humanity of the Australian Aborigines now found the "equality" of colored races "incompatible" with the results of science. Reflecting the same widely prevalent view, even Franz Boas acknowledged, on the basis of the "correlation of anatomical structure and physiological function," that it would be "erroneous to assume that there are no differences in mental makeup of the Negro race and of other races" (1911: 272, 1909:328–29). And for those embracing the new Darwinian approach in German anthropology, the implications of racial evolutionary hierarchies were even more radical: the replacement of the previous humanitarian ethics by a biological and selectionist materialism more concerned with the inequalities of evolution than the universal brotherhood or spiritual unity of humankind.

Just as the progressive "anti-racism" of German physical anthropology was increasingly compromised by its attitude toward colonialism in the 1890s and its rapproachment with Darwinian evolutionism, so did the liberal nationalism of the German anthropological community change character toward the end of the century. Like Virchow, most of the leading anthropologists of the 1865–95 period were liberal, individualistic, confident of "Progress" and of the emancipatory value of "Science" (Smith 1991). They were also, however, strongly patriotic nationalists. The huge anthropometric survey Virchow undertook after 1871 was presented as a national task, an "anthropology of the Nation" (in Weindling 1989:54). Although he was critical of Pan-Germanist archeologists who tended to annex the unknown prehistorical past to the German nation and relate the greatness of all ancient and modern European nations to the achievements of Teutonic tribes, Virchow nevertheless admired his Gothic ancestors: a "powerful" and "iron" people that "we certainly may claim as German" (CoB 1891:67–68, 77–78). Similarly, Ranke proposed to erect, beside the new national parliament building which symbolized the political unity of Germany, a national museum which would illustrate the "development of the Teutonic tribes, from their very beginning to their merging in the new German Reich, in order to instruct the public, to promote science and to strengthen the love for motherland" (CoB 1892:78).

For the most part, however, Teutonic nationalism was manifest in German prehistorical archeology and folklore (Volkskunde) rather than in physical anthropology (Virchow, in CoB 1897:67; Henning, in CoB 1900:95). A major result of the first extensive anthropometric surveys was the conclusion that physical races were not something "national" (Kollman 1891:43–44). Quite the contrary, the various types established by physical anthropology in all European countries cut across the "existing political and linguistic units" (Virchow 1877:2). Moreover, leading German anthropologists generally did not assume that certain of these European "types" were superior to others. When Quatrefages, after France's defeat of 1870, wrote a tract against the "Prussian race," expelling it from the original Teutonic (and "Aryan") populations, and concluding that German national unity was founded on an "anthropological mistake," Virchow answered that national unity had nothing to do with the results of anthropology:

> Should we ask everyone, now that we build our State, to which ethnic group he belongs? To which race he is related? No, M. de Quatrefages, we do not carry on

such politics. Modern Germany is no longer the land of the old Teutonic tribes.
(1872:301–2, 317–18)

In his *Beiträge zur physischen Anthropologie der Deutschen*, Virchow saw the re-
current but fruitless attempts to find national "types" as the result of political
considerations "foreign to science." In a period when each European nation-
ality was striving to build its own state, politicians sought criteria of self-
identification, and because language could change several times in the history
of any one population, they were inclined to look for a "deeper, more natural,
physical background." But "happily," science had not made itself subservient
to these endeavours. On the contrary, the diversity of "types" in each country
shattered all the dreams of a biological foundation to nations (1877:2).

Rather than "scientizing" national unity, physical anthropology expressed
its national pride through the achievements of German science: the precise-
ness of German anthropometry, the discoveries made by German paleoanthro-
pologists and archeologists of human fossils and prehistoric sites, and the size
and richness of ethnological collections in German museums. In his presidential address to the German anthropological society in 1891, Virchow was
proud to announce the slight superiority that German archeology had gained
over other European nations in only a few decades (CoB 1891:67–68). After
a trip to France for the International Congress of Prehistorical Archeology and
Anthropology he admitted that Parisian museum collections of skeletons were
richer than those of Germany's decentralized university institutes, but insisted
that German anthropologists, "working harder, with more patience and more
method" on the material they possessed, had progressed a "little bit further"
than their French counterparts (CoB 1900:72). Nevertheless, Virchow had
close contact with liberal and radical French Republicans, and good relationships with French anthropologists like Léonce Manouvrier, one of the radical
leaders of the Paris anthropological society (Andree 1976:II, 122–23; Jenssen
& Ruprecht 1990.

In the 1880s, however, German nationalism took a new course, and there
was a turn in academic circles away from the liberal ideals of the *Vormärz*.
Students who were to provide the next generation of the German educated
elite were the first to convert to the more radical and anti-Semitic nationalism.
In 1880, a liberal professor prophesied: "If I am not mistaken, a national-
chauvinist generation . . . is about to emerge" (in Jarausch 1982:271). This
change of atmosphere among academics, combined with the spreading of anti-
Semitism, was reflected in 1888 in Virchow's defeat by a national conservative
in the election of rector of the University of Berlin. In 1893, Virchow's Liberal
Party, which had previously split into two wings, disappeared from the political
scene. Faced with a Marxist Social Democratic Party which had become the
country's largest political force in 1890, German academics championed the

conservative alternatives of "State Socialism" or "organic nationalism." In
the 1890s, German nationalism became increasingly imperialistic, militaristic,
pessimistic, and biologically oriented. Germany was perceived as losing ground
in the "struggle for life" of the world's imperialistic nations. With a declining
birth rate, the new industrial Germany felt threatened by its Slavic neighbors
and minorities in Eastern territories; now an importer rather than an exporter
of population, it accommodated about two million immigrant workers in 1906.
Eastern European Jews fleeing discrimination and pogroms poured into German towns and universities, heightening the fear of "national disintegration"
(Jarausch 1982:211; Kampe 1988:54–107).

   In this context, the nationalism of German anthropologists began to change
its character. By the 1890s, the founding liberal generation was already in its
seventies, and most of them were dead by the turn of the century (Andree
1969:79, 85, 97–98). While the survivors maintained their leadership and
political control over science until after 1900, they were soon to be replaced
by a new generation, less democratic and more Darwinian, which was to control German anthropological institutions and research for the next several decades. The contrast may be illustrated by comparing the two successive "ideological guarantors" of the discipline at the turn of the century: Rudolf Virchow
and Felix von Luschan, who as holder of the Berlin chair was to be the leader
of institutionalized physical anthropology after Virchow's death. Both men
were progressives, but their liberalism was of a different blend, in each case
symptomatic of its time. Virchow—a militant pacifist whom French newspapers called the "peace Apostle"—had opposed Bismarck's colonialism and
military budgets, viewing warfare as an evil that would return civilization to
barbarism, and condemning social Darwinian justifications of war as the
mouthings of "people poor in spirit" (Jenssen & Ruprecht 1990). By contrast,
Luschan was a "liberal imperialist" who took for granted the existence of the
German overseas empire, and the reality, necessity, and virtue of imperialist
competition.

   As far as dark-skinned races of the colonial world were concerned, Luschan's
position was in some respects similar to Virchow's. On the one hand, he cas-
tigated European colonists who treated them brutally, insisting on their common humanity: "[T]he more we now learn to know those 'savages' [*Naturvölker*], the more we realize there is never a border that sharply and surely
differentiates us from [them]" (LuP: lecture "Allg. Phys. Anthrop."; 1902:
169). On the other hand, like some other anthropologists of his generation,
Luschan had close connections to colonial institutions. In 1896 he contributed to the organization of the first German exhibition promoting German colonialism (Weindling 1989:54; Smith 1991:162–73; LuP: Deutsche
Kolonial-Austellung), and he saw anthropology as a potential contributor to
successful colonial policy (Luschan 1902:171, 1906:892–94).

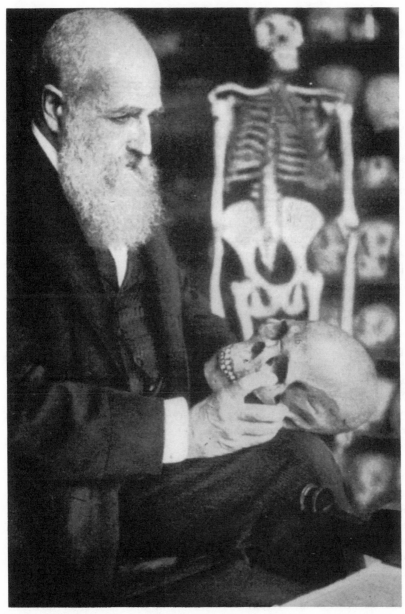

Felix von Luschan, Virchow's spiritual successor, and holder of the Berlin Chair after 1900, in the period of his turn toward eugenics, imperialism, and colonialism. (Courtesy of the Institut für Geschichte der Medizin der Frei Universität, Berlin.)

Luschan was particularly impressed by the colonial policy of Great Britain, which he held up as a model. Invited in 1905 to attend the British Association for the Advancement of Science meetings in South Africa, he commented on the recent transformation and modernization of the country: "before, bullock carriages, rebellious porters, insubordinate tribal chiefs; now, a dense railway network with luxurious express trains and perfect sleeping and restaurant wagons; then, shy and often hostile natives; today, obliging and communicative [ones]." The native African was "good and natural," but had an "essentially childish psyche"; brutal treatment was not only inhumane, but bad colonial policy: "[T]o one who has studied him the primitive man is easy to guide and 'to twist round one's little finger' like a little child." To postpone the inevitable extinction of the Bushmen, Luschan advised the British to gather them in reservations, where they could be given sheep to kill from time to time, in order to save cattle-raising white farmers from their depredations. Such preservationism was already undertaken for plants and animals, and it ought to be possible also "for the last remnants of the Bushmen." Luschan advocated a similar reservation policy for the German colonies in Oceania, to preserve "real Polynesians" for future ethnological study (1906:892–95).

If Luschan was paternalistic to natives who were quiet and docile, he was actively fearful of their rising political consciousness, and of the "color threat" posed by Asian and African demography. He condemned the immigration of "profligate and perverse" Chinese workers to European colonies, and worried that the Black and "colored" population was increasing more rapidly than White colonists, and might threaten European colonial interests and power. Worried by signs of incipient Pan-Africanism, which was financially supported by American Negroes, he felt it was necessary "either to nip it in the bud or at least to direct it into channels which are not so hostile against our own interests" (1906:892–95).

When the First Universal Races Congress brought together anti-racist white and "colored" intellectuals from all over the world in London in 1911, Luschan was one of a number of German anthropologists who were involved. As honorary vice president, he gave a talk on the "anthropological view of race," in which he argued that each human type was different by virtue of its adaptation to its surroundings, but was not "necessarily inferior." Criticizing the equation of "savage" and "colored people," he suggested that the only "savages" in Africa were "certain white men with 'Tropenkoller'" ("tropical madness") (1911:13–22).

On the other hand, Luschan—who was at this time president of the Berlin Gesellschaft für Rassenhygiene (Race Hygiene Society)—felt that the most serious problem was the "question of racial mixture." While a "certain admixture of blood" was "always a great advantage to a nation," he saw a great "danger to civilized nations" in the immigration of "coarser or less refined elements," including the "constant migration of Eastern Slavs" in Germany.

Quoting David Livingstone, Luschan felt that a mixture of Europeans with the "greater part of foreign races" was not desirable: "God created the white man and God created the black man, but the devil created the mulatto." Although neither eugenics nor "applied anthropology" yet offered reliable statistical information on "the moral and intellectual qualities of half-castes," it was nonetheless anthropologically better to have a "separate evolution" of both Whites and the "so-called colored races": "racial barriers will never cease to exist, and if ever they should show a tendency to disappear, it will certainly be better to preserve than to obliterate them" (1911:22–23). Although he fought against white American prejudices, and thought the cultural promotion of blacks was America's most important duty, he later advocated the construction of a "pure Negro Republic" in the South of the United States as the best way to avoid mixed marriages and "free the rest of the Union from undesirable elements" (in Rusch 1985:451).

After the Races Congress was over, Luschan (along with his "good friend" Boas) was one of three Western anthropologists who contributed to the published proceedings (Boas 1912). But in reporting to the German anthropological society, he dismissed the venture as bringing together a "large number of colored scholars from all over the world, theosophians, esperanto-people, idealists, peace-dreamers struggling to form an ill-assorted unified whole" (CoB 1911:179).[3]

Unlike Virchow, Luschan had no high opinion of "peace enthusiasts." Reacting to such endeavors as the International Peace Congress in the Hague in 1899, he spoke of "perpetual peace" as "an absurd utopia" and general disarmament as "the summit of mindlessness" (LuP:K15 "Heeres Ersatz," 23). A decade later, in a moment of naval competition between imperial Germany and imperial England, of international crisis between the Austrian and Russian Empires after the annexation of Bosnia, and between colonial France and colonial Germany over the control of Morocco, he suggested that "we will have always to be prepared for war and in the best case it will be only possible to postpone it. Perhaps the better armed we are, the longer we will be able to postpone it" (1909:205). In 1910, he warned of the danger of international disarmament and peace treaties for the "national existence" and security of Germany (1910:101). Granting that "the brotherhood of man" was a fine ideal, Luschan felt that "the struggle for life" was a "far better one"; national and racial antagonisms, in fact, kept mankind from becoming "like a herd of sheep" (1911:23).

Luschan's biologistic justification of war represented a "break with the

---

3. When German anthropologists received an invitation for a second World Race Congress in 1914, Fischer complained to Luschan that "the last time, by giving our signatures, we all fell into a trap": "now this swindle must stop," and "we should speak our opinion once and for all" (LuP: EF/FL 1/19/14).

humanitarian tradition" of German physical anthropology based on a secularization of Christianity (Sandmann 1990). Both Virchow and Luschan were
scientistic, believing that "Science" was both the crux of "Progress" and a solid
foundation for human politics (Mann 1969:5; Massin 1993b). But whereas
Virchow rejected Darwinism, Luschan converted to this modern "philosophy
of nature." Although he was not Pan-Germanist, he shared Pan-Germanists'
fears of Slavic immigration and their concern for a better-armed Germany and
a pro-birth eugenics policy in order to survive in the international "struggle
for life." On a visit to Australia on the eve of war in 1914, he suggested that
youth should be brought up imbued with the "ideal of a young and virile Nation, ready to conquer the Universe, fearing nothing and fearing inferior races
less than the rest" (LuP: "Culture and Degeneration," 12).

However, despite his move toward Darwinian nationalism and eugenics,
Luschan remained traditionally "liberal" in rejecting Nordicism, Aryanism,
and anti-Semitism. Others of his own generation and, more important, of the
generation born in the 1870s that was to come to the fore in the 1920s (including Eugen Fischer, Theodor Mollison, and Otto Reche) went a step beyond to embrace the Nordic doctrine of the anthroposociological school as a
means of strengthening Germany in the "competition for world supremacy"
(Buschan 1900:69–71).

The Crisis of Classical Physical Anthropology

If physical anthropology in Germany at the turn of the century became more
susceptible to racial theorizing emanating from without, it was, paradoxically,
because within the discipline itself, as elsewhere, the dominant mode of inquiry into racial differences seemed to many to have led into an epistemological, methodological, and conceptual blind alley (Mühlmann 1946:96–99;
Stocking 1968:163–69). The intense activity of the anthropological societies,
created for the most part in the midst of the positivistic period by anatomist
physicians and centered basically on physical anthropology and descriptive
anatomical techniques and measurement, had led to an inflation of the number and precision of anthropometric surveys. But the huge amount of work
accumulated during the three decades from 1860 to 1890 did not result in any
major scientific breakthrough. Anthropologists themselves, as well as scientists
from other disciplines, started questioning the value of physical anthropology—which a St. Petersburg anatomist saw as no more than a mass of incon-
gruous cranial measurements and the introduction of esoteric words of Greek
origin (Lesshaft 1896). At a joint meeting of the German and Vienna anthropological societies in 1889, Virchow ended his presidential speech by pointing
out that, two decades after its institutionalization, anthropology had in fact

retrogressed. Much of what was regarded as clear and definite when the Berlin society was founded in 1869 had been called into question (in Luschan 1912: 53). Addressing the Berlin society in 1896, Virchow noted that "for a long time, our field has not undergone so much inner controversy as in the past year. When we look to the coming period, it immediately appears we are in deeper confusion than we have been for a long time" (CoB 1896:76).

The discipline's claim to scientific status had been based largely on its veritable equation with anthropometry—the careful measurement of different human anatomical features, in substantial populations, for comparative study, in order more precisely to characterize human racial groups. Among these anatomical features, the most important was the human cranium, and from 1842, when the Swedish anatomist Anders Retzius used the ratio of width to length to distinguish dolichocephalic from brachycephalic heads and skulls, craniometry was the privileged mode of anthropometric inquiry. According to Virchow, the skull was critical because it enclosed "the most important organ of the body, the brain, and developed in a recognizable relationship to this organ (1892:3). Retzius's followers in France and Germany improved the metrical aspect and expanded the index categories, combining the cephalic index with the facial index and the facial angle to sort out different types of dolichocephals and brachycephals (Blanckaert 1989). Similarly, the number of facial index classes increased, from two with Virchow in the 1870s to nine with Kollmann in 1895 and twelve for Weissenberg in 1897 (Weissenberg 1897: 49–54).

The summit of craniometrical study was reached in 1890, when the German-speaking Hungarian anthropologist Aurel von Török, holder since 1881 of the first anthropological chair at the University of Budapest, made 5371 measurements on a single skull (Eickstedt 1940:178–79). But after having calculated 178 indices and more than 2500 angles, triangles, and polygons of determination, Török cast doubt on the whole venture: "to be honest and open," he could not say "how many of those measurements" might "prove useful" in determining "the general craniometric characters of the cranial form" (in AA 1891:284). Török was not alone in questioning his own craniometrical enterprise. By the end of the 1880s, craniometry was perceived by many physical anthropologists as in a state of "crisis," and they seriously wondered if they should "measure further or not" (Schmidt 1888; Hovorka 1898:289).

In this context, there were various attempts at reform. In 1892, the leading Italian anthropologist Giuseppi Sergi proposed the replacement of the cephalic index by a set of rather complicated categories based on morphological polygons, dividing long heads into "ellipsoid," "ovoid," or "pentagonal" and short heads into "sphenoid," "spheroid," or "platycephalic" (Sergi 1892). In 1909, Otto Reche, director of a section of the Hamburg Museum für

Völkerkunde (and later a zealous Nazi anthropologist), proposed to replace the
cephalic index by the index of the length of the occiput, which he felt was
what really distinguished the "dolichocephalic races." Adopting a new classification urged by Carl Toldt, the president of the Vienna anthropological society, he contrasted "plan-occipital" and "curvo-occipital" skulls (Reche 1911).

None of the reform attempts, however, were successful in reestablishing
paradigmatic consensus. Many of the fundamental problems confronting
physical anthropology were evident in the debate in the early 1890s between
Török and Kollmann. Török's herculean quantitative treatment of a single
skull, although initiated as an attempt to save the discipline, was contained in
a 1500-page critique of the current status of craniometry, in which he called
into question not only the value of the cephalic index, but also two of the
major postulates of the venture: the French paleontologist Cuvier's "law of
correlation," and the assumption that there was a homogeneous "pure type"
corresponding to every "original race" (Török 1890, 1891).

Kollmann replied to Török's critique in a long speech at the national meeting of the German anthropological society in 1891. Dismissing "the jumble of
Török's measurements" as "a dead end from which he himself could not find
the way out" (1891:37, 1892b:3), Kollman maintained that the European
population included two "completely different" and racially hereditary types
of face—one long and narrow (leptoprosop), the other short and broad (cha-
maeprosop)—and that by virtue of the law of correlation, each type showed a
harmony in every part, which was revealed by numerical ratios. To test the
validity of this law, Török had instructed a collaborator to examine 150 skulls
in his Budapest collection, only one of which showed the required correlations
(Kollmann 1891:42–43). Kollmann defended his position by arguing the
high degree of crossbreeding in Europe. The extensive pigmentation surveys
initiated by Virchow in Central Europe in the 1870s and 1880s had proved
that between a half and two-thirds of the people were "mixed-race." It was not
surprising that this general race-crossing would be evident in a series of facial
skulls. Even so, a correlation between facial index and cranial forms could still
be found, revealing the presence of underlying "pure types." To find these,
however, one should not work on random series as Török did; one must select
"typical skulls" of the different established "races." To make sure of finding the
correlated "type," one had to survey only "skulls of a unique type" (Kollmann
1892b:3–4).

In rejoinder, Török attacked the existence of Kollmann's five craniological
European "races," declaring the dominant craniology "a tedious pastime" that
achieved nothing but "self-deception" (1891:60–61). In response, Kollmann
justified his racial taxonomy by appeal to authority: they matched, with different names, the historical races established by the great names of German and
French anthropology. He then withdrew from the debate, and the Correspon-

denzblatt declared it closed, as far as its columns were concerned, on the grounds that it had taken a personal turn (*CoB* 1891:41, 61, 1892:2).

Kollmann left the debate without suffering too much damage, due both to his own authority and the fact that the Virchow-Ranke-Kollmann triumvirate which dominated the German anthropological society until 1900 was—as Luschan commented privately—a "Société d'admiration mutuelle" (LuP: K13). Török, however, kept up his attack on Kollmann and the dominant craniology in articles extending into the first decade of the twentieth century. According to Török, physical anthropology had reached a dead end because the whole craniometrical program was based on a wrong premise: the notion that the arithmetic mean would reveal the "type" of the "race." Within this paradigmatic frame, the more the measurements and indexes of a group of individuals neared the arithmetic mean value, the more those "racial types" were supposed to be "pure" and "free from crossbreeding"; the more individuals diverged from this ideal average, the more they were regarded as "crossbred." Török insisted that it was impossible for "a single mortal" to decide "merely by means of a series of craniological measurements, if he is dealing with 'racial purity' or 'blood crossing,'" and that "the use of the arithmetic mean does not make the thing the least bit more feasible." Craniometry was in fact "doomed to degenerate into the wizardry of a deceptive fortune-telling by skulls" because it rested on "a vicious circle." The whole approach, in fact, took for granted what it was designed to demonstrate: the existence of "pure races"—phenomena which "until now no one has succeeded in discovering . . . on the whole planet" (1901:402–3, 421).

> [O]ne briskly speaks of "pure" and "crossed" races as the most obvious things. . . .
> One chases headlong those "pure" races which, like will-o'-the-wisps, are the more elusive the more one tries to catch them. "Pure blood" races do not exist anywhere but in the fantasy of anthropologists—unfortunately too many of them. (422)

Török traced the flawed orientation of craniometry back to Retzius, who thought that each original race had a homogeneous headshape. In this typological perspective, the present huge variability of European populations was assumed to result from race crossings: "This idea was as such the fundamental hypothesis on which all the theory of dolichocephalic and brachycephalic races was based" (1906a:233–34). But logically, if the race-crossing hypothesis was correct, then the more one went back to remote times or the more one dealt with "primitive" isolated tribes protected from crossbreeding, the more one should find greater homogeneity of head shapes in comparison to present civilized nations in which a great deal of crossbreeding was historically documented. In fact, however, the prehistorical Swedish skulls studied by Gustav Retzius (son of Anders Retzius and founder of the Swedish anthropological society), which supposedly represented the "purest" Teutonic stocks, were very heterogeneous. Similarly, primitive tribes "still virgin from any contact with civilization" showed a variety of head shapes as great as the "most civilized Europeans"; conversely, it was quite possible for the most crossbred race to show an apparent "type." Thus the race-crossing hypothesis had no empirical foundation (Török 1906a:233–34).

In Török's view, Anders Retzius and his first followers could be optimistic about the future of his approach, since at that time there was still little evidence. But the more anthropologists learned about the different races of the earth, the less possible it was to "confirm the existence of 'pure' races." Unfortunately for science, however, rather than subject the theory to a proper criticism, craniologists preferred to save the whole scientific edifice by calling upon "blood-crossing" (or, in Kollmann's terms, "penetration") as "a *deus ex-machina* [to] help us out of trouble at any moment." But the impossibility of discovering even the smallest exclusively dolicho- or brachycephalic race was not primarily due to "blood-crossing." The real cause was "purely and simply that Retzius's hypothesis, according to which each stock should show one and only well-defined craniological form" was "fully inconsistent with the regularity of the law of variation of cranial shapes" (1906a:235, 1906b:116).

Taken seriously, the double conclusion of Török's critical analysis signaled the end of nineteenth-century racial craniometry. On one hand, the cephalic index—the most frequently used craniological implement for anthropological surveys—was irrelevant for racial differentiation (1906a:215–30). On the other hand, on the basis of the most detailed craniometrical study ever attempted in the history of anthropometry, Török could not find a more significant and valuable craniometrical parameter for race classification. It seemed that craniometry, taken by itself, did not provide an adequate basis for racial taxonomy. What was noteworthy about Török's critique was that it was purely internal. It came from a renowned craniologist who did not call on any external argument, such as the possible influence of environment or other factors; and although it became a personal conflict, it did not seem motivated by any specific ideological orientation. Nor was it the only expression of disillusion with traditional physical anthropology.

The discipline's difficulties were, in fact, exacerbated by various efforts of reform. None of the methodologies intended to save it were generally accepted, but simply intensified the methodological debate. At the 1891 meeting of the German society, Ranke suggested that in spite of the number of talents who had dedicated themselves to this discipline, craniology had not progressed much since Virchow's groundbreaking work in the 1850s (Ranke 1891: 115)—or, as he remarked later, even since the time of Blumenbach. Ranke suggested that there were two insoluble problems: on the one hand, the head shapes of the whole of mankind were distributed in a continuous series "in

which the most extreme members were connected by gradual and uninter-
rupted transitions"; on the other, the great individual variability within each
ethnic group surpassed the differences among the various "racial types" (1897:
139–46). And in the year before his death, Virchow himself doubted that any
of the present participants in the field could expect to see its final consolidation within their lifetimes, wondering even if by "mere measurements, it would
ever be possible to close the question" (1901b:137–39).

If members of the "old school" only gradually lost faith, many younger anthropologists were quickly convinced that craniology had reached a dead end.
Paul Ehrenreich, a disciple of Virchow who later became docent of ethnology
in Berlin, felt that craniology was "a complete fiasco"; despite the "endless
series of numbers published each year on cranial and corporal measurements,"
agreement could not be reached "on any single question" (1897:5–9). In
1898, a since forgotten doctoral student urged anthropologists to "come to
their senses" and recognize that "any attempt to classify mankind with the
help of craniology is doomed to fail" (Wohlbold 1898:148–51). In 1904, Paul
Bartels, an assistant at Berlin anatomical institute, remarked that craniometry
had fallen into "disrepute" with representatives of other scientific disciplines
(1904b:83). In 1911, the Polish anthropologist Stanislaw Poniatowski, working at the Zurich Institute of Rudolf Martin, suggested that given the number
of errors produced by arbitrary classification of the cephalic index, "its full
abolition would be a great step forward for anthropology" (1911:54).

It was not simply that the cephalic index seemed to many an arbitrary and
unreliable classification; there were those in this period who argued that the
phenomenon it alleged to index—headform— was itself unstable. The inter-
generational plasticity of headform discovered by Franz Boas in 1908 in his
study of immigrants to the United States was not an unprecedented result in
the German anthropological tradition. Virchow, with whom Boas had studied,
had previously insisted on "the possibility of change in cranial indices" (Ackerknecht 1953:236). And although, like Virchow, most turn-of-the-century
German anthropologists on the practical level worked implicitly within the
framework of static "types," many were, paradoxically, theoretically convinced
of the plastic character of headforms and races. Both monogenists and polygenists shared the Lamarckian assumption that the level of culture could influence the volume of the brain and thus the size and shape of the skull. Schaffhausen, a Lamarckian Darwinist, had argued that "the head shape of the same
ethnic group [Volk] does not remain unchanged, it is changeable"—if not with
climate, then with civilization, which made skulls broader (1890:127–28)—
and Klaatsch, Buschan, Ranke, and Alsberg all concurred (Buschan 1904:
127; Alsberg & Klaatsch, CoB 1911:101). Prior to 1900, there were not that
many German advocates of the complete fixity of races since prehistoric times.
Kollmann, the main proponent of the "persistency of races," noted that in

Germany his adversaries were much more numerous than his supporters (1898a:116–18). Responding to the charge that this belief contradicted his professed Darwinism, Kollmann adopted the mutation theory of De Vries, and spoke instead of the "temporary persistency of races" (1902). For the more consistent Darwinian Gustav Fritsch, constancy was the result of an interaction between the biological unit and its environment, and would continue only so long as the environment was stable (1898:161).

Virchow himself took an intermediate and sometimes contradictory position in this debate, depending on whether he opposed ultra-Lamarckian monogenists, Darwinists, Weismannists, or polygenists. In his 1887 speech on "Transformism" at the meeting of German naturalists and physicians, he declared that "ethnical dolichocephaly and brachycephaly are in a high degree hereditary": "[N]obody has ever proved that a dolichocephalic race could become brachycephalic" (1887:294–96). At the 1899 national meeting of anthropologists, he recognized that "his friend" Kollmann had partially proved the permanence of races since "diluvian times." But although he thought the advocates of permanence and of mutability both had good arguments, Virchow felt that both rested "on the ground of opinions" rather than "hard facts." Although his own research tended also to demonstrate their durability, he felt that an "absolute permanency of types" was "somewhat unlikely" (CoB 1899:81).

The failure of craniometry and the dispute over racial plasticity could not but have an inhibiting impact on what for decades had been the ultimate goal of physical anthropology: racial classification. Concluding as early as 1887 that "in the present state of our knowledge, all attempts to separate mankind in clear-cut groups (races or varieties) each having bodily properties not found in others, can have only a provisional value," Ranke himself refused to "increase the number of schematical classifications that cannot be precisely founded on a scientific level" (1887:II, 236). Otto Schoettensack, a prehistorian and paleoanthropologist who taught anthropology at the University of Heidelberg between 1904 and 1912, told students that "endeavours to classify mankind based on physical characteristics are countless," but could "not give very satisfying results" (SkP: "Volk II," 7). Paul Ehrenreich thought it was impossible to establish a purely somatic classification; although the three major "races" (white, black, yellow) were obvious, even these still lacked "scientific precision" (1897:5–39). The second generation of German Darwinian anthropologists at the turn of the century were particularly critical of all the previous attempts at racial classifications (Stratz 1904a:22). Gustav Fritsch, a comparative anatomist and physiologist at Berlin University, spoke in 1910 of the "total misery of our present racial classification." With the number of major races getting bigger and bigger and "our insight in the objective reality becoming smaller and smaller," Fritsch decided he would give up trying to establish a new "closed" and static system (1910:580–82). In a lively debate at the Berlin Anthropological Society in 1910 following Fritsch's attempt at an "open" evolutionary racial classification, Luschan suggested that "in the [current] state of our research," racial classifications belonged "rather to the realm of faith than that of knowledge" (ZfE 1910:927).

In 1912, Erwin von Bälz, back from Japan where he was the private physician of the Emperor Mitsu Hito, cast doubt on the possibility of any racial classification at the annual meeting of the German anthropological society. He began by rejecting any linguistic-based classifications such as those used by the zoologist Haeckel or the ethnologists Friedrich Müller and Paul Ehrenreich: "race" had nothing to do with linguistic systems. But the choice of physical taxonomic criteria seemed to rest on the arbitrary decision of the researcher. The founders of anthropology thought the color of skin was the clearest scale to divide mankind, but some people of India were as dark as African Negroes, despite the fact that they differed in other significant physical respects. After this had come headform, but craniometry, too, had failed to provide a reliable classificatory criterion. The craniological schemes of Sergi were "procrustean beds" in which real skulls could not be placed without violence. Similarly, the artificial geometrical combinations of cephalic and facial indices Kollman used to define his races often united ill-assorted individuals any layman would recognize as different. So also with hair form; during his thirty years in Japan, Bälz had noticed a non-negligible rate of curly hair in a "race" which was supposed to possess only sleek hair. Although the evolutionary classifications of the Darwinians Fritsch and Stratz and the "inferential-geographical" classification of Deniker seemed more fruitful, Bälz thought that this "highly disputed question" might never be solved in a satisfying manner (1912:110–13)—a position shared by Ranke's successor as professor of anthropology at Munich, Ferdinand Birkner (1912:532).

The skepticism of racial classification was paralleled by a growing suspicion of the central concept of physical anthropology: the very idea of "race" itself. Paradoxically, with the assimilation of statistical methodology by anthropological schools of the second half of the nineteenth century, the reality of races as physical entities was seriously compromised; constructed as statistical types, races lacked any precise biological definition (Virchow 1887:279; Stocking 1968:57). "Race" was now a pure construction of the mind and could never be fully achieved in an individual. In Virchow's terms, it was the ideal picture of a characteristic local population drawn from a multiplicity of individual variations around a mean; individual variations were in turn circularly defined as those variations which remained "within the typical norm" (1892:4, 22).

For supporters of the "inductive method," this transformation of the basic concept of physical anthropology under the influence of statistics led to a growing "nominalism" (Mühlmann 1986:99), which was reflected in the gradual substitution of the term "type" for that of "race." Virchow declared in 1896 that "the concept of race, which has always carried with it something undetermined, has recently become highly uncertain" (1896a:3). Luschan told students in his course on "general physical anthropology" at the University of Berlin that the word *race* was "just a word and a word behind which there is no clear concept" (LuP: K12, "Allg. Anthrop.," 1, 3). Török, concerned that people continued to speak lightheartedly of "races" despite the fact that the concept was scientifically dubious and the existence of human "so-called races" in a zoological sense had never been proved, urged that the word *race* be erased from the scientific vocabulary of physical anthropology (1890:14, 580, 1906b:117).

Even the concept "type" was called into question. After a few unfortunate experiences (e.g., "typical Teutonic skulls" which turned out to be "Slavic"), Virchow became very cautious (1900:110, 1901a:86). He thought it was impossible to fix the limits of variations within a definite stock and go back from those variations to the original specificity of the stock in a way that would enable anthropologists to define with certainty members of the different stocks: "the type was such a variable thing" (1901b:136; CoB 1896:80). The Russian anthropologist Koroptschewsky concluded that not only had "race" become "gradually a vague concept for a group without any scientific value," but that "type" was equally "very indefinite and nebulous" (CoB 1896:68).

With racial classification, "race," and "type" now seriously under question, physical anthropology was deprived of its central task, object, conceptual frame, and, consequently, the justification of its existence. The more purely positivistic anthropometry without "race" which was manifest at the end of the Wilhelmine period in Rudolf Martin's *Lehrbuch der Anthropologie* (1914) had lost much of its allure. Indeed, during the first decade of the twentieth century, physical anthropology seemed in danger of vanishing from the scientific field. If it did not do so, this was surely in large part because of its changing relation to Darwinism, to the new science of genetics, and to eugenics— as well as its eventual scientific adaptation to Germany's new political atmosphere.

The Eclipse and Revival
of Darwinism in Physical Anthropology

Despite the positive reception of Darwinism elsewhere in German intellectual and scientific life (Montgomery 1974:89; Kelly 1981), it was a very marginal stream in institutional physical anthropology prior to 1895 (Friedenthal 1900: 495). One of the few important Darwinian anthropologists in Germany was

Schaffhausen in Bonn—who in 1880 was described by a conservative journal as the only speaker at the general meeting of anthropologists who was "in cahoots with the theory of descent of Darwin and Haeckel," and who in 1857 was the first to interpret the skeletal remains of Neanderthal as ancestral to modern man. Until his death in 1893, Schaffhausen engaged in a lonely "35-year war" against Welcker, Mayer, and particularly Virchow, who had diagnosed the Neanderthal and a few other prehistorical skulls as pathological (Zängl-Kumpf 1990:24, 152–206, 277–85). At a time when "diluvial" skulls were quite scarce, it was very difficult to prove their non-pathological character against the opposition of Germany's leading pathologist.

For decades, Virchow did everything possible to save the "firm land" of physical anthropology from the "overflow" of the "tidal wave" of Darwinism agitating academic biology and the "half-educated" German public (CoB 1891:78), using his institutional power to bar Darwinians from positions of influence. In his 1894 presidential address to the German anthropological society, Virchow argued that the question of evolution in general did not concern anthropologists, and that the problem of human origins had been treated in an essentially speculative manner: "in this way, some people arrived at the Ape-theory; but it would have been just as possible to arrive at another theromorphic theory, for example, an Elephant-theory or a Sheep-theory." When no ape was discovered as human ancestor, the upholders of the "Ape-theory" had turned to "half-apes," anticipating that future geological discoveries would justify their speculation. Opposing "cool-headed anthropologists to Darwinists," Virchow insisted that anthropology could not allow such a methodology and remain scientific (CoB 1894:83–86). As Ranke suggested before the same audience, Darwinism was a "philosophy" rather than a science because it rested on the "deductive method," which did not want so much to "learn from nature as to teach nature." Thanks to "our master Virchow," that approach had for several decades had no footing in German physical anthropology (CoB 1894:177).

As Kollmann noted in 1905, the "eclipse of Darwinism" in German physical anthropology had been the result of two related factors: the critical reaction of Virchow, the most powerful figure in German anthropology, and the lack of sufficient evidence (1905:9). A third, more political background factor was the association of Darwinism, in the minds of both liberal and conservative anthropologists, with subversive ideas of radical materialist "philosophers" and socialist "terrorists" threatening the social order (Kelly 1981:55–74). However, when a series of new skulls were discovered in the last decade of the nineteenth and the first decade of the twentieth century, Virchow's position became difficult to maintain. In Europe, these included those of Spy in Belgium (1886), Krapina in Croatia (1899), Heidelberg in Germany (1907), and

Le Moustier (1908) and Combe Lachapelle (1909) in France. Even more important, however, was the discovery in Java in 1891 of *Pithecanthropus* by the Dutch anatomist Eugene Dubois (Theunissen 1989).

Initially, the reaction of German anthropologists to Dubois' discovery was quite cool. Many of them thought it was simply a reopening of the "Microcephal battle" they had won against Vogt and the first generation of Darwinists (*CoB* 1897:85). When Dubois' work was discussed at the Berlin anthropological society in 1895, Wilhelm Krause suggested that the tooth and the skull belonged to a big ape and the femur was that of a pathologically deformed man. (*VhB* 1895:78–80). Luschan, Waldeyer, and Virchow were also dubious, the latter speaking of Dubois' interpretation as "fantasy going far beyond all facts" (*VhB* 1895:81–87, 435–40). At the 1896 national assembly Virchow refused to recognize *Pithecanthropus* as a transition form, arguing that it was a now extinct giant gibbon (*CoB* 1896:81–83); and Ranke, who was frequently Virchow's parrot, saw the transformist interpretation of *Pithecanthropus* as evidence of the continuity of the romantic *Naturphilosophie* "under the leadership of Darwinism" (*CoB* 1896:25).

However, when leading anatomists, paleontologists, and zoologists in England, America, and France sided with Dubois, the positivistic anti-Darwinian fortress built by Virchow, Ranke, and Waldeyer began to crack after 1895. More and more voices started challenging the official rejection of Darwinism. At the 1899 national meeting, Hermann Klaatsch suggested that "in circles of specialists the conceptions of the theory of evolution, including man, have indisputably won the day." Unfortunately, "some leading anthropologists" had accepted the popular notion that this would be proven scientifically only when the "missing link" between ape and man was found. But the phylogenetic relationship of man to primates could also be demonstrated by embryology and comparative morphology. From this point of view, man in fact occupied an intermediary position between the anthropoids and the less specialized lower apes, which Klaatsch explained in terms of sexual and natural selection. In contrast to the anthropoid development of strong muscles and other bodily weapons for the struggle for life, man had instead developed intellectually, during a long period in which the pressure of natural selection diminished in favorable environments. This development could be reconstructed through comparative morphology, which Klaatsch felt would provide much more interesting results than the "much too one-sided anthropometry" which was now "fortunately overcome" (1899:154–57).

Responding to this pro-Darwinian attack on the "one-sided anthropometry" he had practiced for thirty years, Ranke noted the "deep contradiction" between Klaatsch's "painting rich in imagination" and "the conceptions and method of research generally defended in our society." In the absence of "hard facts," an appeal to zoology, paleontology, or anatomy was no more than mere

Rudolf Virchow (standing at the podium), at a gathering of German scientists on the occasion of his 80th birthday in October 1901. (Courtesy of the Bildarchiv preussischer Kulturbesitz, Berlin.)

"fantasy" (CoB 1899:157). Two years later, in 1901, Virchow offered the swansong of positivistic anti-Darwinism in his penultimate speech to the annual meetings of the German anthropological society. Responding to an essay by Gustav Schwalbe which disputed the pathological character of the Neanderthal skull and linked it to other recent discoveries (CeB 1901:339–41), Virchow insisted on what seemed to him pathological traits, including a chin that could still be found in patients of psychiatric hospitals. When Virchow (now over eighty) blundered by ascribing a fracture to the leg rather than to the arm, he overrode Klaatsch's immediate correction by insisting arrogantly on his authority as pathologist and denying the right of a mere anatomist to contest his judgment (1901a).

Defending the absent Schwalbe against "our honored old master" Virchow, Klaatsch argued that the similarities between the Neanderthal skull and the skulls of Spy greatly reduced the possibility that its unusual characteristics were pathological. The further argument that one or two specimens was not enough to reconstruct a race or a species ran counter to the ruling methodology in paleontology, where nobody would doubt the existence of Archeopteryx even though only two fossils had been found (CoB 1901:89–91).

Faced by a new generation of Darwinian anthropologists, Virchow was on
the verge of losing his long battle against Darwinism in anthropology. With
his death in 1902, the field was open for Klaatsch, Schwalbe, and their cohort,
the more so since Virchow's close supporters, most of them medical anatomists, lacked the new generation's knowledge of paleontology. A year later
Waldeyer evoked the "never too highly praised doctrine of Darwin" and his
"immortal work" in his presidential address (CoB 1903:68); in 1909, in a
speech for the fiftieth anniversary of the *Origin of Species,* he argued that the
animal origin of man had been definitively demonstrated by the paleoanthropological studies of Klaatsch, Hauser, and Schoettensack (Waldeyer
1909). During the intervening decade, books, articles, reviews, and lectures on
Darwinism sprang up like mushrooms after a sudden shower; in 1902, the
50,000 copies of Klaatsch's *Entstehung und Entwicklung des Menschengeschlechtes* were quickly sold out. Ranke, who had previously included such
works only under zoology in his annual summaries of literature, began to include them under anthropology. Reviewing all lectures on anthropology and
related disciplines in German universities in 1903, he found more devoted to
Darwinism and other evolutionary tendencies than to pure physical anthropology. Anthropological studies from an evolutionary perspective were becoming so sophisticated that it was difficult simply to reject them; in 1908, Ranke
even described the popular illustrated atlas *Vom Urtier zum Menschen* by the
Darwinian ecologist Konrad Guenther as a "splendid work" (CeB 1909:131–
32; CoB 1908:89). Schwalbe and Klaatsch, who had to keep a low profile
during Virchow's reign, became two of the most important men of the German
anthropological society, with Schwalbe responsible for directing planning for
a new anthropological survey of the German Reich (Schwalbe 1903). Although there were numerous reactions against the specific Darwinian mechanism of random variation and selection, by 1908 German anthropology was
celebrating the jubilee of Darwinism, and in 1910 Gustav Fritsch could claim
(although with some exaggeration) that most of the more famous scientists
had rallied to Darwin's evolutionary theory (CoB 1908:83; Fritsch 1910:581;
cf. Bowler 1983, 1986).

The surrender of a large segment of German physical anthropology to "Darwinism" entailed the methodological defeat of the inductive positivism that
had prevailed since the 1850s. Virchow's opposition to Darwinism did not
reflect a lack of respect for Darwin as scientist; it reflected more specific issues
of scientific methodology, and secondarily of politics. As a cellular pathologist,
Virchow felt that an understanding of the evolution of races and species had
to be based on serious research into our cellular mutability, rather than nebulous theories on "the ascent of Man." He was inclined to accept the transmission of secondary bodily modifications—the inheritance of acquired characters—and to explain change in terms of direct environmental influences

causing "pathological" (i.e., non-identical) cellular variation (Churchill 1976). He regarded the phylogenetic trees constructed by Darwinians like Haeckel as "deductive and speculative constructions" that went far beyond what was allowed by "positive facts" (*VhB* 1894:510). Honest anthropologists had to admit that on many points they "did not know" (*CoB* 1896:80–81).

It was commitment to this *docta ignorantis* that caused the anthropological establishment to resist Darwinian interpretations of paleoanthropological findings, as well as August Weismann's new theory of heredity of the germ plasm—though the latter was also resisted because most physical anthropologists before 1900 were neo-Lamarckians. In the face of the explosion of turn-of-the-century biological theories of evolution (De Vries, Semon, Eimer, etc.)—many of which were theoretically daring, given the scarcity of facts at their disposal (Bowler 1983, 1986)—German physical anthropology under Virchow's leadership was at once both empirically cautious and scientifically sterile. The same empiricism and methodological caution carried over also to issues of race. In a "positive" physical anthropology in which Neanderthal and Java Man were rejected as products of unproven theories, there was no place for an emotional metaphysics of race based primarily on theoretical constructions, to which the search for hard facts took second place.

However, the increasing accumulation of paleoanthropological evidence for the common origin of man and anthropoid apes, along with the indirect and progressive victory of Weismann's theory of heredity with the introduction of biometry, the emergence of Mendelian genetics in 1900, and Johannsen's concepts of "genotype" and "phenotype" in 1909, gave support to Haeckel's and Weismann's pleas for a hypothetical-deductive methodology (Kollmann 1886: 679; Haeckel, 1908; Churchill 1968:112, 1974:21, 27; Mayr 1985:323–24). The ultimate success of Darwinian paleoanthropology over Virchow's critical inductivism at the turn of the century opened the door to a more flexible attitude toward non-inductive approaches.

In the new epistemological context, any hypothesis was legitimate insofar as it could be fruitful and was not too conspicuously political. In anthropology, the shattering of the paradigm of the period 1860–95 brought to an end the consensual control of anthropology by a limited number of recognized authorities, and opened up a new phase of competing paradigms and heterogeneous approaches. In 1896, Virchow had warned his colleagues that he would not always be around to guard anthropology against "speculations" (*CoB* 1896: 84), and with his death no other anthropologist had the stature to fill the vacuum of authority he left. In such a dispersed environment of scientific crisis, any new theory had greater chances of gaining some acceptance from one or the other rival faction. There were too many doors, and too many of them were open, to keep the politically sensitive "science of race" under control.

The introduction of the Darwinian paradigm in physical anthropology itself led to a new set of political attitudes and values. Darwinism was not only a scientific guideline providing a methodology and orientation of research but also a "new *Weltanschauung*," a new philosophy of life with political implications (Schwalbe 1910:465). It proposed a model of biological evolution—humans included—based on inequality and the hard mechanisms of "struggle for life" and "natural selection." Insisting on biological evolutionary inequality, Darwinian anthropologists made much harder judgments of "backward races" than monogenist humanitarians: "modern science cannot confirm the exaggerated humanitarianism which sees brothers and sisters in all the lower races" (Klaatsch, in Bowler 1896:138). Darwinian scientists worried about the disastrous consequences of impeding "natural selection" in modern human societies, and praised the "cleansing power" of "selection." A coherent political ethics based on Darwinian biology implied a "healthy selfishness" for "superior" types, and the prevention of mixed marriages, if not the elimination of "inferiors" (Fischer 1910:28, 1913:302–4). If the Darwinism of the 1860s and 1870s could combine with optimistic social reformism or liberal *laisser-faire*, neo-Darwinism was politically pessimistic, and required therapeutic interventionist state politics, in tune with the growing illiberalism of the German elite. Followed to their logical conclusions, these biological theories of society demanded a rationalization of human sexual reproduction which was possible only in a technocracy directed by biologists and physicians, in which the state enforced a collective biological therapy (Weingart 1987; Weiss 1986, 1987a).

Society, Politics, and the Study of Human Heredity

These neo-Darwinian understandings of society made up only one form of the biologism which characterized European human and medical sciences from 1860 to World War I—a period in which biological concepts, methodologies metaphors, "laws," and hereditarian attitudes had a powerful influence in the "softer" scientific disciplines (Mann 1969:17). In the age of positivism, modernity was synonymous with science, and the science most pregnant with meaning was biology. "Organicism," "social Darwinism," "social Lamarckism," "hereditarianism," "criminal anthropology," "anthroposociology," and eugenics were in fact the various and sometimes competing facets of the same general phenomenon in the "age of the natural sciences" (Mann 1973; Weindling 1981).

In Germany, this "biologism" had first been advocated by materialist radicals and liberals who opposed the conservative Christian cosmogony (Gregory 1977). Science was used as a political weapon to refute the biblical conceptions of the traditional society—and as a result biology was banned from schools between 1882 and 1908 (Hanstein 1913:233–37). But it spread nevertheless through the university and through popularization, affecting various ideological camps from the most conservative imperialists to the most orthodox Marxists (Kelly 1981; Merten 1983:96–103). In the medical and human sciences, it influenced sociology, psychology, economics, historical sciences, criminology, pathology, and psychiatry (Mann 1969, 1973, 1983; Weindling 1989). The turn of the century was the high point of the imperium of biology, so much so that even those who had no reason to be delighted by this scientific imperialism acknowledged the fact. The theologian, church historian, and rector of Berlin University Adolf von Harnack deemed biology the central science, because it ranged from the "most elementary observations" of animal life right on through "the so-called human sciences" (in Hanstein 1913:233).

Within this pervasive biologism, quite divergent viewpoints could be accommodated. What might be called the "cerebralist" notion that there was a correlation between the size and shape of the brain on one hand and the level and form of mental activity on the other was shared by both neo-Lamarckian environmentalists and neo-Darwinian racists. In either case, large brains went with civilization and small brains with savagery (Nyström 1902:219; Woltmann 1903:295). The difference lay in the fact that neo-Lamarckians were optimistic about the beneficial influence of culture for the future development of small-brained peoples, while the neo-Darwinians thought they were barred from progress unless subjected to systematic selection. Even such critical observers as Virchow and Ranke could share some aspects of the cerebralist assumption; reminding his students to be wary of it in one chapter of his handbook, Ranke nevertheless remarked in the next on the influence of "culture and unculture" on the development of the skull (Ranke 1894:I, 557; II:224; Virchow 1892:23). Despite their encompassing biologism and their shared cerebralist assumptions, however, differences between neo-Lamarckians and neo-Darwinians were of considerable consequence, both scientifically and ideologically, when research and speculation about heredity became a central focus of biological thought in the last decade of the century. Prior to the 1890s, the inheritance of acquired characteristics was widely accepted in the scientific and medical communities, and anthropologists were no exception; it was a rare anthropologist who supported Weismann's new theory of the continuity of the germ plasm (CeB 1911:13). But when biometry and the rediscovery of Mendel's principles transformed the terms of the discussion of heredity after 1900, some anthropologists began to look to these new tendencies for a solution to the impasse in physical anthropology.

Among them was Franz Boas, who remained a member of the Berlin Anthropological Society, and who in 1899 hoped that Galtonian biometry would lead to a "definite solution of the problem of the effect of heredity and environment" (in Stocking 1968:173). In Germany, anthropological journals began publishing articles on biometry, which in 1909 Luschan believed might rescue anthropometry from its dead end (1909:201, 108). However, the first biometric studies on the inheritance of the cephalic index led to divergent results and interpretations, and a number of scientists, including Boas and the eugenicists Wilhelm Weinberg and Heinrich Poll, concluded that biometry alone did not easily distinguish between similarities induced by heredity and by environment. In a speech to the Berlin anthropological society in June, 1912, Boas concluded that statistics by themselves could only point to a bio-logical problem, which could only be solved by a biological methodology (1913a:4, 18, 22). In this context, a number of anthropologists turned to Mendelism and the genealogical study of alternating traits.

As early as 1905, Luschan had insisted on the necessity of establishing laws of heredity through race-crossing studies (Luschan 1905:4; Lehmann-Nitsche 1906:115). In 1911, Eugen Fischer, a disciple of Weismann at Freiburg, pre-sented to the German anthropological society the first results of a study he had undertaken in 1908 of the "Rehoboth Bastards" in German Southwest Africa, in which he defended the study of human heredity as a solution to the diffi-culties facing physical anthropology. Although anthropologists referred con-stantly to "race" and "crossbreeding" to explain phenomena, their knowledge of the biological processes involved was "close to zero." Fischer argued that "anthropobiology" would provide a solid scientific foundation by focussing on the mechanisms of racial inheritance and diversity (1911, 1912, 1913:1).

The integration of Mendelism and biometry and the shift from physical to biological anthropology were encouraged by three factors, each closely related to political issues. First, the dispute over the plasticity of headform (reopened in 1911 by the results of Boas' study—results which no one could adequately explain) threatened the whole edifice of anthropometry: what was the value of a statistical treatment of "type" if little was known about the racial or en-vironmental character of the features being measured? Although Fischer, like Luschan, accepted Boas' results, he believed that an answer to the relative influence of environment and heredity could only come from a comparative biometric analysis over several generations of families transferred into different environments, along with Mendelian studies of hybrids that would indicate which precise cranial features were hereditary (1914:26–29).

A second factor easing the conversion to a genetic paradigm was the na-tional or social eugenic concerns about the scope of heredity in the transmis-sion of pathological and racial "psychological characteristics." According to Luschan, there was "not a single social problem whose solution does not re-quire the knowledge of the laws of heredity." Whether it was feebleminded-ness, the "born criminal," the "Jewish question," or the consequences of alco-holism and venereal disease for "the future of the race," the key to the issue was heredity. While the state could enforce vaccination because of its obvious utility, it could do nothing about other biomedical problems threatening the nation's future, because medical scientists were only beginning to understand "the laws of heredity" (Luschan 1905:4, 1906, 1909:201–9).

A third burning political issue concerned the consequences of race mixture for fecundity, health, vitality, and the "mental and moral qualities" of a population (Luschan 1909, 1912:56; Fischer 1911, 1912; Retzenstein 1913). Fischer argued that the new "anthropo-biology" would include this "practical" aspect. Were racial hybrids as fecund as the pure types? What were the physical and psychological consequences of crossbreeding? Did one race dominate over the other? Were racial hybrids superior or inferior to the parents? Should Germany encourage or prohibit crossbreeding in the colonies, or at home between "Teutons and Semites?" Answers to these questions were of vital importance for the future of the nation, and would provide guide lines for the practical application of anthropology: race hygiene (1913:296–306).

It was to answer such questions that Fischer had studied the mixed Boer-Hottentot population of Rehoboth, examining a series of bodily characteristics (headform, stature, pigmentation, etc.) and physiological phenomena (tempo of growth, date of sexual maturity, fecundity). Although most characteristics were complexly determined, in general he felt that the results could be explained in Mendelian terms of dominant and recessive characters (1913:224, 306, 1914:13). Crossbreeding did not increase the number of "degenerate" individuals, nor did it lead to the establishment of a new "mixed" race intermediate between the parental groups. Although the occasional reappearance of apparently "pure" individuals was only the random recombination of separably heritable characteristics which gave the impression of a "pure type," the results seemed to demonstrate the hereditary persistence of various traits (223–27). Fischer's study was widely accepted in the German-speaking community as the first successful demonstration of Mendelian principles in human populations, and established his position as one of Germany's leading anthropologists—heir apparent to Felix von Luschan in the Berlin chair. To younger anthropologists, it provided a new basis for "the science of man"—which, according to the eugenicist Fritz Lenz, should henceforth be conceived as "the science of human genetic differences" (1913:363, 1914:523).

It was in this context, as well as that of the post-Virchowian loosening of inductive methodological vigilance, that there was a revival after 1900 of the "race" concept in German physical anthropology and human biology. In contrast to the fragile racial "types" obtained through extensive anthropometrical surveys and statistical reconstruction, the new "biological anthropology" sought to determine which bodily or physiological characteristics were inherited according to Mendelian laws and thereby offered support for "the racial nature of the morphologically distinguishable groups of the human kind" (Fischer 1913:2, 227). The first biometric and Mendelian studies on human heredity, carried on in Anglo-Saxon countries from 1901 to 1911 by Pearson's

school and by Davenport and Mendelians on the inheritance of single traits
such as eye, hair, and skin pigmentation, were taken to prove the genetic nature of most "racial" traits (Fischer 1914:6). Given the apparent strict inheritance of many "racial" traits, it was assumed that "races" were something real.
This conviction was reinforced by studies of tropical hygiene carried on since
the 1880s, which indicated that the various European races had differential
physiological resistances to tropical diseases (Retzenstein 1913:105–6). It
seemed possible that races which could not be firmly distinguished by craniometry might be differentiated by physiology (Révész 1907). The discovery of
the ABO blood system by Karl Landsteiner in 1900 also raised hopes for the
physiological distinction of "races." A serological study of several different racial groups undertaken in Java by the physician Carl Bruck was greeted in the
Zeitschrift für Ethnologie as providing, if confirmed, an "inestimable help for the
systematization of human races, for which anthropometric differences have
proved insufficient" (Bruck 1907; ZfE 1907:106–7).

The decline of positivistic empiricism following the surrender to Darwinism, along with the legitimacy given to the inheritance of racial traits by
bioanthropological studies, as well as the need for a simple typology in regional
and national surveys, led to a renewed interest in racial classifications, notably
those of Joseph Deniker, the librarian of the Museum d'Histoire Naturelle in
Paris, and of the American sociologist William Z. Ripley, both published in
1900. Drawing on the numerous existing surveys of millions of Europeans,
Deniker and Ripley made density maps of the geographical distribution of
physical traits in order to establish major "racial types"—six in the case of
Deniker, three in the case of Ripley. Although in principle subject to many
of the criticisms of previous typologies, these two classifications, combined and
modified in various ways, gained a widespread acceptance among German-
speaking anthropologists (e.g., AA 1902:170–88, 191–201, 1903:289, 1906:
42, 1909:255, 339, 1911:311–14)—even by those who were most critical of the legitimacy of racial classification (Luschan 1905:4; Martin 1914:
220–22).

There was, however, at the turn of the century, a new generation of "anti-
racist" scholars (including Hertz, Nyström, Weissenberg, and Zollschan) who
looked to neo-Lamarckism to support the plasticity of races. In their view, neo-
Darwinism supported the theory of "permanent racial characteristics," pre-
venting any racial progress through social change, and leading to "racial hatred" and "racial chauvinism" (Nyström 1902:642). Aside from its theoretical
and methodological implications for craniometry, the debate about plasticity
of headform took place in this broader political context. In the tradition of an
earlier monogenist environmentalism, the old Ranke, in discussing "the race
question," argued that the geographical distribution of head shapes in Bavaria
was a result of the transformative influence of mountains and plains (1908).

Such studies of the transformation of head shapes (including that of Boas) were used by opponents of race theories to prove the plasticity of human races in one generation in respect to what had been considered the "safest basis for racial differentiation": the cephalic index (Alsberg 1912:176).

The Lamarckian view was pushed even further in the work of popular anti-racist writers like Friedrich Hertz, to whom neo-Lamarckism meant social progress and hope, while neo-Darwinism implied pessimism, conservatism, or the inhuman use of biological "selection" to improve human races (1915:12). Neo-Lamarckism transformed the "racial problem" into an "illusion" that could be dissolved through appropriate cultural and social integration. Hierarchical cultural differences were not denied, and could even be linked to a biological hierarchy, but they were ascribed to the influence of environment (Zollschan 1911:254–97).

For anti-racists as well as for neo-Darwinian anthropobiologists, the "political issue of the racial question" depended on the outcome of scientific debates over "the question of heredity" (Zollschan 1911:223, 235). According to the biologist Paul Kammerer (later a suicide after the discovery of the "midwife toad forgery"), his own neo-Lamarckian experiments opened "an entirely new path for the improvement of our race"—"a more beautiful and worthy method than that advanced by fanatic race zealots" (in Bowler 1983:94–95). Anti-racist writers were confident that Weismann's theory had received its "finishing stroke" thanks to the "modern" experiments of neo-Lamarckian researchers like Kammerer and Semon (Finot 1906:48; Hertz 1915:15–18).

Over the longer run, however, the alliance of anti-racism and neo-Lamarckism proved counterproductive. Battling on the same scientistic and biologistic field with their adversaries, neo-Lamarckian anti-racists bound the fate of their political fight to what was to be the losing scientific camp. The rapid growth of experimental Mendelian genetics after the turn of the century paved the way for the eventual scientific defeat of neo-Lamarckism. Although more than two hundred supportive experiments were published between 1906 and 1909 in Europe and America, neo-Lamarckians had great difficulty developing an alternative "inductive" experimental framework for the laboratory study of heredity, and neo-Lamarckism fell more and more outside the main stream of genetics—"not because it lacked proof, but because Mendelian genetics proved so much easier to elaborate into a conceptual foundation for the study of heredity" (Bowler 1983:60, 76). Although there were still neo-Lamarckian anthropologists (such as Franz Weidenreich) around in the Weimar period, the scandal of Paul Kammerer's experimental forgery in the 1920s accelerated the disrepute of neo-Lamarckism among German geneticists and professional anthropologists (Hirschmüller 1991). By that time, the third generation of Darwinian (actually neo-Darwinian and Mendelian) anthropologists, men like Fischer, Reche, and Lenz—who were also ideological

Nordicists—could claim they had won the day. The scientific defeat of their anti-racist opponents left them with the monopoly of the "scientific truth" in human biology. Having secured a solid scientific position, they could propagate in German biomedical sciences the theory of permanent morphological and psychological features distinguishing the various "races," the necessity of a "selective" racial hygiene, and the implicit supremacy of the "Nordic race" (Proctor 1988b; Massin 1993a).

"Modern Race Theories" and the Redefinition of Physical Anthropology

In sharp contrast to the racial liberalism and skepticism of Virchowian physical anthropology, the turn-of-the-century period witnessed a major efflorescence of racial thinking elsewhere in German intellectual life. Leafing through newspapers and reviews from 1870 to 1895, looking for articles with the word "race" in their titles, one finds no more than two each year. Suddenly, in 1896, the number mounts to five and keeps growing geometrically to a peak of fifty-one in 1904. From then on "race" ceased to be a marginal theme, and became a public and political affair, with an average of thirty such self-defining articles per year (Massin 1990:128–34). In the first decade of the twentieth century, "race" and "race theories" became a major topic; the liberal sociologist Oppenheimer complained that "racial doctrine" was by this time one of "the most influential theor[ies] of the whole social sciences" (in Woltmann 1906:673). In fact, however, these "modern race theories" (Hertz 1904) had received at first a very mixed reception in the anthropological community.

In the form of the "Aryan Question," racial thinking had for some time been an important factor in disciplines very close to physical anthropology, including linguistics, prehistory, and archeology—many of whose practitioners were in fact members of the omnibus "anthropological" societies of the period, which in the case of the Berlin and national societies encompassed "Anthropologie, Ethnologie, und Urgeschichte." The "Aryans" (like the "Semites") had been initially the product of comparative philology, where they were hypothesized as the speakers and bodily transmitters of the earliest form of the Indo-European language and its attendant culture. Well before the end of the century, however, both linguists and physical anthropologists had called into question the tendency, characteristic of earlier nineteenth-century "ethnology," to equate linguistic and somatic categories. By 1880, positivistic physical anthropology had largely emancipated itself from the "tyranny of linguistics" (Poliakov 1987:289–295). On the linguistic side, even Max Müller, the philologist largely responsible for popularizing the Aryan concept, had acknowledged that "one can no more speak of an Aryan skull than of a dolichocephalic language"—though he continued to speak of an "Indo-European race" to which "all the greatest nations of the world belong" (in Römer 1989: 65, 125).

After 1880, the use of linguistic terms for racial classification by German physical anthropologists became less frequent. Anthropologists were mostly physicians or naturalists, and relied on craniology rather than linguistics; and every anthropometric survey showed that linguistic and national units did not coincide with any homogeneous physical types (Virchow 1886; Ammon 1890). However, the temptation to think in these terms was always present, and craniologists like the anatomist Kollmann had repeatedly to warn both the public and their colleagues: "Anthropology does not know any Germanic, Celtic, or Semitic race, it knows only nations bearing these names" (in Ehrenreich 1897:11). The emancipation from Aryan racial assumptions was imperfect even among the most cautious positivists. Although Virchow in the 1870s had rejected the possibility of identifying prehistorical Teutons, Celts, or Slavs from craniological material, he continued to refer to the "Semitic race," the "Teutonic race," the "Aryan race," and the "pure Aryan," including the Northern European populations under the stocks "which could be called Aryans in the purer sense" (1885:225–29, 1887:297). Even in 1891 he still thought it possible to determine from a skeleton whether an individual was related to the "Aryans or Indo-Europeans" (CoB 1891:79–80). And with the "complete fiasco" of craniology in the 1890s, some German scientists in fact sought to reintroduce linguistic classification in anthropology. The ethnologist Ehrenreich proposed replacing the taxonomy of the "white races" based on craniology and pigmentation by linguistic groups such as "Aryans" and "Semites" (1897:12, 29, 38); the Darwinian Gustav Fritsch, in his "open racial classification" of 1910, still used the linguistic concepts of "Indo-European" and "Aryan" (1910:583).

But even more than in physical anthropology, it was in prehistoric anthropology and archeology that specific linguistic groups and "races" were associated with prehistoric "cultural provinces," and in which attempts were made to establish the physical type and original home of the Aryans. Until 1880, most German philologists and archeologists (Virchow included) were convinced of the Asian origin of Indo-European cultures (Young 1968:26). But at the 1882 Frankfurt assembly of the German anthropological society, the controversial Pan-Germanist anthropologist Ludwig Wilser proposed that the original home of Germans and all their Indo-European "linguistic parents" was Scandinavia—unleashing thereby a "storm of protests" (Wilser 1900:146). Pursued by the Austrian prehistorian Karl Penka, the Scandinavian hypothesis reintroduced Gobineau's myth of the blond Aryan into serious academic German science (Penka 1883). Because of its political charge, the Scandinavian-Nordic race theory was a subject of continuing debates and intense research by both defenders and opponents. Indeed, in the last decades of the century, the question of the original home of the Aryans became such a subject of controversy that William Ripley, surveying European racial thought, concluded that "no other scientific question, with the exception perhaps of the doctrine of evolution, was ever so bitterly discussed or so infernally confounded at the hands of chauvinistic or otherwise biassed writers" (1900:454).

At this time, many of the greatest Indo-European linguists and archeologists were German or Austrian, and investigations and theoretical confrontations had a vibrant patriotic resonance—archeology and prehistoric anthropology more so, perhaps, than the statistical craniometry of contemporary populations. In addition to the original Aryan homeland, they defined the "national past" in relation to a specific territory, documenting, for example, the age of Teutonic (as opposed to Slavic) settlement in the eastern borderlands (Andree 1976:I, 89). Until his death in 1902, Virchow, who was greatly interested in the "patriotic" archeology of Prussia, was able to use his institutional power to channel patriotic enthusiasm into a rigorous methodological framework (Andree 1976:I, 168, II:116–17), and to keep politically "dilettantish" archeology out of the main anthropological and prehistorical journals. By the turn of the century, however, leading German academic archeologists and linguists, despite being critical of any direct identification of race and language, often tended implicitly to accept some sort of relationship, and were in most cases very eulogistic of the "Aryan" conquerors. Although the linguist and archeologist Otto Schrader insisted in 1901 that "we must keep away from the concept 'Indo-European original stock' everything that refers to the concept of 'race' established by anthropologists" (in Römer 1989:65), in a more popular book on *Die Indogermanen* he presented these warrior "conquerors" as the "strong master *Völker* of Asia and Europe" (*CeB* 1912:88).

The discussion of Indo-European origins was complicated by the fact that the several disciplines involved—including linguistics, artifact archeology, and prehistoric physical anthropology—each thought the others not in a position to solve the question, and controversy within each discipline did not allow the other two to draw safely on its results. With the growing specialization, no scientist mastered them all, and each field jealously monopolized its right to speak in its own name and to judge the scientific competency of its own members. Prehistoric anthropologists venturing into linguistics or linguists into prehistory risked their reputations as serious scholars. Communication between the disciplines and clarification of the dispute was made difficult by the fact that linguists generally did not take part in the meetings of the German anthropological society and after 1892 had their own review, *Indogermanische Forschungen*, which was certainly as abstruse to anatomist prehistorians as the anthropometric tables were to Sanskritists. Similarly, archeologists and prehistorians after 1909 tended to publish in Gustav Kossina's *Mannus* or Carl Schuchhardt's *Praehistorische Zeitschrift*.

Within archeology, the political and scientific line separating more "moderate" academic archeologists from amateur Pan-Germanists was not clear-cut. Amateurs were sometimes embarrassing but essential allies, inasmuch as the nationalist halo they created around these disciplines directly benefitted their professionalization and institutionalization. Penka, a retired high school teacher who started publishing in the proceedings (*Mitteilungen*) of the Vienna anthropological society in the early 1890s, was seen by academic archeologists as an erudite but armchair archeologist, and Wilser as a bombastic and biased "dilettante" mixing science with "patriotic rhetoric" (Hoernes, in *CeB* 1910: 358–59). But their Scandinavian theory nevertheless became quite influential, as more and more German scientists began turning to Europe for the original migration site (*CoB* 1908:89; Kraitschek 1910).

A potentially even more chauvinistic hypothesis would have located the original home of the "Aryans" in Germany itself. Proposed by the linguist-philosopher Lazarus Geiger in 1871 (Römer 1989:70), it was taken up by the Pan-Germanist archeologist Gustav Kossina, who, by providing the discipline with the "settlement-archeological method," was to be the most influential Germanic archeologist of the period 1900 to 1930. In 1903, Kossina argued that the Teutons were "synonymous with the ancestral nation of the Indo-Europeans, whose original site coincides with that of the Teutons" (*CeB* 1903: 118). In 1912, when he was professor of Germanic prehistory at Berlin University and director of the Gesellschaft für deutsche Vorgeschichte, Kossina published a book arguing that archeology proved Germany was the motherland of all the stocks that emigrated to produce the great Indo-European civilizations since antiquity, and that the fall of the southern and eastern Indo-European civilizations resulted from the contamination of the "Indo-European noble blood of the ruling classes" (1912:vi). Similarly, Kossina's main rival, the classical prehistorian Carl Schuchhardt, ascribed the Egyptian and Chinese civilizations to European prehistorical influences (Römer 1989:78).

That, of course, was the kind of Gobinesque thinking promulgated by the "modern race theorists" who stood just beyond the borders of German physical anthropology in this period. Almost unread in Germany in the 1860s and 1870s, Gobineau began to emerge from oblivion around 1880 thanks to his encounter with the composer Richard Wagner, who was so taken by the *Essai* that he read it several times. Quickly seizing their master's new fad, the Wagnerian circle of Bayreuth in 1881 devoted three articles to Gobineau in their review *Bayreuther Blätter*, which then became the main tribune of Gobinism and "Teutonic Christianity" in Germany. Among the younger Wagnerians who met Gobineau before he died in 1882 was the philologist and historian Ludwig Schemann, who had given up an academic career to become librarian at the University of Göttingen (Nagel-Birlinger 1979:25). Politically, Schemann combined ultra-conservatism, monarchism, anti-liberalism, nationalism, and Pan-Germanism, and under Wagner's and other influences developed his own Manichaean blend of anti-Semitism (1925:74). From 1889 on, he labored to spread the word of Gobineau in Germany. Having obtained the entirety of Gobineau's manuscripts, he published between 1898 and 1914 no less than twelve books by or about Gobineau, including the first German translation of the *Essai sur l'inégalité des races humaines* (1898–1901), a five-hundred-page analysis of Gobineau's reception in the world (1910), and a two-volume biography (1913–16).

When his first attempts to get a German translation of the *Essai* published were rejected on the ground that it was scientifically out-dated (Lémonon 1971:II, 245–47), Schemann in 1894 decided to found an organization to popularize Gobineau's work and secure funds for publication. The Gobineau Vereinigung reached its peak in 1914 with 360 members, including a high proportion of royal highnesses, aristocrats, influential political figures, and university professors (Lémonon 1971:II, 217–31). Through his connection with the president of the Pan-Germanist League, Schemann was able to get copies of the *Essai* distributed free to members, and from then on the League took the lead in the dissemination of Aryan racial theories.

Schemann, however, had only limited success in winning support from the organized anthropological community. Some archeological and philological societies joined (Lémonon 1971:II, 219), but no local anthropological society. The only leading member of the German anthropological society who enlisted in the Gobineau Vereinigung was the convinced Pan-Germanist archeologist Gustav Kossina, who in turn invited Schemann to join his prehistorical society, and organized a discussion of one of Schemann's publications at a meeting of the Berlin section in 1910 (SP: GK/LS 2/19/03, 3/9/03, 2/5/10). Although two Pan-Germanist anthropologists without professorial status, Otto Ammon and Ludwig Wilser, were also participants, the only established academic anthropologist who carried on a correspondence with Schemann was his Freiburg compatriot, Eugen Fischer, who in 1910 predicted that "racial thinking must and will win, even if not exactly in the Gobinian form." While caution "in front of the student youth" compelled Fischer to include "this great forerunner" among "race zealots," he nevertheless promulgated "the racial viewpoint" in his lecture courses (SP: EF/LS 1/16/10), and in a public lecture to an anthropological society spoke of Gobineau's having, "with premonition, sharply formulated and exposed this inequality of mental dispositions" (1910:18). Twenty-two years later, as director of Germany's most prestigious research institute for anthropology and human genetics, the Kaiser Wilhelm Institut für Anthropologie, Menschliche Erblehre und Eugenik, Fischer wrote Schemann that its foundation was "in part the accomplishment of the ideas you have supported for so many years" (SP: EF/LS 10/12/32). But if Fischer's role in the reorientation of German physical anthropology gave to his views, also, a premonitory significance, the fact remains that German physical anthropology did not immediately leap to embrace Gobinism as such.

The opposition between "modern race theory" and established physical anthropology was evident in the work of Houston Stewart Chamberlain, English-born son-in-law of Wagner, whose bestselling *Die Grundlagen des neunzehnten Jahrhunderts* (1899) transformed the "racial question" into a major subject of conversation and debates in German salons and academic circles. Although influenced by the Darwinism of his former professor Karl Vogt, Chamberlain had little use for official anthropology:

> The more you try to find out with specialists, the less you can see clearly. First linguists coined the collective concept of Aryan. Then came anatomist anthropologists. Once the dubiousness of linguistic deductions was proved, one moved on to cranial measurements. Craniometry became a profession and brought a huge mass of interesting material to light, but now "somatical anthropology" seems threatened by the same fate which linguistics underwent. . . . One of Virchow's best students [Ehrenreich] has concluded that it is a sterile pretension to want to solve ethnographical problems by measuring skulls. (1899:268–69, 1913:360–62)

For Chamberlain, race was not "a primitive phenomenon" but a constructed myth, not a hypothetical original purity to which one should strive to return, but an ideal to be achieved by selection (1899:289, 343). The best approach was not through an "objective" criterion such as measurement, but rather by the subjective impression given by the total appearance. If the learned anthropologist, with all his compasses and complicated measurements, could not distinguish between a Jew and a non-Jew, a child would immediately recognize a "pure blood" Jew by running away and crying (1913:679–80).

Given Chamberlain's attitude, it was not likely that "learned anthropologists" would flock to his standard. Although the liberal Kollmann complained in 1908 that the "conceptions of Gobineau and Chamberlain were prevailing almost exclusively" (*PAR* 1907/8:76), in fact, the influence of these two major representatives of the "philosophy of race" on German anthropology was rather less than that of other contemporary currents, including "anthroposociology."

"Anthroposociology" was developed in France by the social Darwinist Georges Vacher de Lapouge in the late 1880s, and in the next decade received a degree of intellectual and institutional recognition within French physical anthropology and the several currents of French sociology (Nagel 1975; Clark 1984; Massin 1992). But in France this period of scientific integration was rather brief; in 1898, Durkheim banned the topic from his review, and the next year Léonce Manouvrier, one of the new leaders of the Société d'Anthropologie de Paris, published a critique of "The cephalic index and the pseudo-sociology" which definitively ousted Lapouge from French institutional anthropology (Clark 1984:144–45; Mucchielli 1994). From that time on, in France Lapouge was able to publish only in local scientific reviews, and, in Germany, only in Buschan's *Centralblatt* and in the *Politisch-Anthropologische Revue* of the German racialist Ludwig Woltmann.

In contrast to the short-lived success of anthroposociology in France, this new discipline achieved a more lasting integration into organized anthropology in Germany, where it was independently developed by Otto Ammon, a former newspaper editor who turned to archeology and anthropology in the early 1880s. Ammon was general-secretary of the anthropological section of the Anthropological and Archeological Association of Karlsruhe, and when the German anthropological society held its sixteenth congress there in 1885, Ranke entrusted him with the task of investigating the physical characteristics of his fellow countrymen of Baden. Ranke, Virchow, and Kollmann all helped to supervise Ammon's lengthy survey of over 30,000 conscripts, as well as 2200 pupils and their families, and in 1890 his results were first published in a scientific collection directed by Virchow (Lichtsinn 1987:8–10, 21–42). They indicated that the urban populations were more dolichocephalic than the rural, which Ammon interpreted in social selectionist rather than environmental terms as a reflection of the greater aptitude of narrowheads for success in urban life—a result which he later formalized as "Ammon's Law" (1892, 1900).

Although his work won Ammon a certain international recognition, and was taken as a model by a number of regional surveys, Virchow was from an early point critical, complaining to Ranke in 1886 about the unreliability of Ammon's craniometric measurements and his "arbitrary" and "amateur" interpretations (Andree 1976:I, 86, II:410–11). After Ammon was denied an additional promised subsidy for his work at the 1889 national congress because of financial difficulties in the German society, he withdrew in anger from national meetings and did not return for the next twenty years (LuP: OA/FL 5/20/11). When he began publishing his more explicitly Nordic and social Darwinist anthroposociological essays in the early 1890s (1893, 1894, 1895), Virchow in fact denied him access to the forum of the Berlin society (Andree 1976:I, 86), and his work began to be excluded from anthropological journals controlled by Virchow, Ranke, and Bastian. And when Ammon finally published the full report of his thirteen-year project in 1899, Ranke for two successive years failed to mention it in his annual summaries of scientific work (LuP: OA/FL 5/20/11). Over a slightly longer run, however, Ammon and anthroposociology had a quite different destiny in Germany than in France.

The younger generation of Darwinian physical anthropologists, whose liberalism was compromised by aims of national expansion, and who were already committed to "selection" and "the struggle for life," responded much more favorably. For scientists seeking a new justification for a discipline in crisis, Darwinism provided a bridge toward what are retrospectively seen as "pseudo-scientific" social Darwinian doctrines, rehabilitating to some extent the previous theories of Haeckel, Woltmann, and Wilser, as well as those of Lapouge and Ammon. Felix von Luschan, in a journal Virchow did not control, praised Ammon's book on Baden as one of "the most significant enrichments of anthropological literature in the last ten years," and for showing the way in which "the anthropology of the future should progress" (1900). Georg Buschan published an equally eulogistic review in the *Centralblatt* he had founded in 1896, proclaiming it a "standard work" which presented substantial further evidence for Ammon's previous "theoretical opinions" (*CeB* 1900:18–23). Buschan in fact opened his review to Ammon, his "friend" Wilser, and even to Lapouge as authors and reviewers. Similarly, Schwalbe's *Zeitschrift für Morphologie und Anthropologie* invited Ammon to contribute (*ZMA* 1900:679–85, 1906:56–58) and published other articles on anthroposociology.

Schwalbe was the first important anthropologist to publically declare his sympathy to anthroposociology, at the thirty-fourth Congress of the German society in 1903—significantly, the year after Virchow's death. Adopting the three-race European typology of Lapouge, Sergi, and Ripley (Nordic, Alpine, Mediterranean), Schwalbe cited positively the surveys of Ammon, Lapouge, Collignon, and Livi, and accepted the basic postulates of anthroposociology:

> That a physical race is also equipped with specific psychological and behavioral characters appears more and more obvious to those who want to understand the historical process and not less to those who try to explain the causes of social stratification in one country. The various ways of thinking and behaving in politics and religion will be related to the various types of men, that is, to the various physical races. (1903:74)

Schwalbe was to pursue the issue in his presidential address on "the mission of anthroposociology" at the national congress in 1907 in Strasbourg. Indeed, this speech may be taken as the inflection point in the ideological reorientation of German anthropology from the liberalism of the second half of the nineteenth century to the strong racial biologism of the early 1930s (Massin 1993a). In it, Schwalbe characterized as "absolutely right" the "anthropological theory of history" of Gobineau, Chamberlain, Woltmann, Lapouge, and Ammon. Although he tried to reformulate their ideas in a more acceptable manner, he nevertheless conferred a scientific value on Aryanist, Teutonic, and Nordic race theories, some of which (like Chamberlain's) were notorious as well for their anti-Semitism. Schwalbe also accepted Lapouge's and Ammon's notions of European race psychology: "It is clear that the members of the Nordic race show another temperament, other moral conceptions, a wholly different type of thinking, another way of seeing the world, than those of the Mediterranean race" (1907:67–68). At the end of the decade, Ammon's scientific exile was ended when Luschan, the new leader of institutional anthropology, personally invited him to take part to the 1911 meetings of the German society.

Ludwig Woltmann, the young Marxist revisionist doctor who converted to Darwinism and racial determinism and founded the *Politisch-Anthropologische Revue* in 1902, did not live long enough to win this recognition. Save for a few Darwinian anthropologists such as Gustav Fritsch, most of its contributors were either non-academic German anthropologists or foreigners. But when Woltmann died in an accident in 1907, several dozen European scholars, ranging from the Marxist revisionist Eduard Bernstein to the Teutonic evangelist Houston Stewart Chamberlain and the Zionist race theorist Leo Sofer, as well as a few anthropologists, contributed obituary comments (*PAR* 1907–8:68). Even Luschan, who had previously refused to be involved (LP: LW/FL 11/20/02), spoke of the "heavy loss for anthropology" (72–73). Moritz Alsberg, a Jewish eugenist anthropologist, thought Woltmann's great merit was to have linked sociology to biology and racial anthropology—a connection of "great practical significance" for state policies (67–68). This broad political spectrum of support for Woltmann's enterprise was possible because in this period many medical social reformers were abandoning pure economic determinism for a new blend of materialism combining biological and sociological influences (Weindling 1989).

After 1900, Nordic anthroposociological ideas began to spread to official anthropological literature. In an article published in the *Archiv für Anthropologie* in 1902, an author adopted the racial psychology of Lapouge and Ammon, contrasting the dominating and "warlike" Nordic race with the "industrious and docile" Alpine (*AA* 1902:174). Between 1900 and 1904, Carl von Ujvalvy, a Hungarian aristocrat convert to anthropology, published no less than six "anthropo-historical" studies in the same review. Despite the fact that he extolled the "Gobineau school" and proclaimed the "inequality of human races," the editors of the *Archiv* valued him as "an excellent contributor" (*AA* 1904:ii). More generally, anthropological surveys began adding appendices relating physical type to intellectual or professional aptitudes (*AA* 1902:195, 208–9, 1903:337–38).

Even more than anthroposociology, it was eugenics which in the long run was to have the greatest impact on German anthropology. Prior to World War I, the study of human heredity was spread among several disciplines, including genealogy, psychiatry, hygiene, pathology, various other medical branches, and demographical or medical statistics; it was first united under the aegis and through the "scientific program" of eugenics at the turn of the century. From the late 1880s, anthropologists had shown great interest in medical pathology, including studies of the hereditary transmission of such anomalies as microcephaly, acromegaly, polydactyly, etc. (*CoB* 1890:101). At the Berlin society, Virchow and Ascher analyzed a family in which absence of teeth was linked to feeble-mindedness and this "sign of degeneration" was passed on through apparently healthy children (*VhB* 1898:114). In the late 1890s, genealogy, too, became a serious scientific study; in 1898, Ranke noted in his "scientific report of the year," that anthropology had been enriched by this new discipline tackling the most topical questions of the day (*CoB* 1898:83–84). In short, rather than being simply conquered by eugenics from the outside, physical anthropology was predisposed to eugenics by the growing internal interest in questions of heredity, and by the fact that most active physical anthropologists were trained in medicine, a field which early became impregnated by eugenics (Weindling 1989).

German eugenics emerged from the combination of two main factors: the (generally neo-Lamarckian) hereditarian conceptions of pathologies that prevailed in European medicine and psychiatry in the late nineteenth century, and the pessimistic view of the consequences of industrialization and urbanization, including the spreading of what were seen as hereditary diseases and the physiological "degeneration" of the whole population (Weiss 1987a:7–26; Weingart, Kroll, & Bayertz 1988:47–125; Weindling 1989:80–89). To these two elements, the two founders of German theoretical eugenics, the physicians Alfred Ploetz and Wilhelm Schallmayer, added an interpretation in terms of neo-Darwinian "selectionism." Because it was caused by the suppression of "natural selection" through medicine, social hygiene, and social welfare, which allowed "inferior elements" to survive and reproduce, "degeneration" could not be stopped merely by social politics, but required what Schallmayer called a "biological politics" (*CeB* 1907:71).

German eugenics became organized in 1905 with the founding by Ploetz of the Berlin Race Hygiene Society (Doeleke 1975). Ploetz had become a member of the Berlin anthropology society in 1903, and several of its leading members became members of Ploetz's new society, including Luschan, the ethnologist Richard Thurnwald, and Rudolf Virchow's son Hans (Weindling 1989:134; PP: *Mitgliederliste* 1913). Although Luschan retired as president of the Berlin society in 1912 after a lengthy feud with Thurnwald, who was then secretary, he remained sympathetic to eugenics, urging Australian and American students in 1914 to "make eugenic doctrines part of your religious creed" (LuP: *Sozialanthropologie* 14: "Hereditary" & "Culture and degeneration"; AP/FL 1/20, 1/22/12; Melk-Koch 1989:84, 132, 150).

In 1907 Ploetz moved to Munich, where he created the Munich Race Hygiene Society, in which he succeeded in involving Karl E. Ranke, a physician and anthropologist interested in biometry who was the son of Johannes Ranke. In 1909, Ploetz was able to announce to Luschan that "the old professor

Ranke," president of the German anthropological society, was also joining the
Munich society (LuP: AP/FL 5/30/09). A few months later, the elder Ranke
in fact proposed to Ploetz an amalgamation with the Munich anthropological
society, and they soon began to hold joint meetings (PP: JR/AP
11/29/09; Weindling 1989:142–43). A third local society was founded at Freiburg, where almost the whole medical faculty staff joined, along with the anti-
Lamarckian biologist August Weismann; when Eugen Fischer returned from
research in Southwest Africa in 1909, he became president. Among the anthropologists who joined the national society were Gustav Schwalbe, Theodor
Mollison, and Rudolf Pöch, holder of the chair of anthropology at Vienna
(*Mitgliederliste* 1909, 1913).

It is important to keep in mind that German eugenics was an extremely
broad stream uniting otherwise opposing political tendencies, with members
ranging from imperialists, race utopians, and anti-Semites on the extreme
right over to nationalistic state socialists, like Ploetz and Schallmayer, and
orthodox Marxist socialists like Karl Kautsky on the left (Graham 1977; Massin 1995). Although eugenics could be linked on the right wing with Nordicist
and anti-Semitic racism, this association was by no means systematic. And if
Ploetz sometimes expressed anti-Semitic views in his private correspondence,
and in 1910 established within the Munich group a "Secret Nordic Ring," he
kept a public distance from Aryan ideologues and did not integrate anti-
Semitism in his racial hygiene program (Weingart, Kroll, & Bayertz 1988:
92–93, 195; Weindling 1989:135–38). Like Luschan, he felt that the Jews
had played an "outstanding role" in the history of mankind, and placed them
on the same cultural level as the "Western Aryans." Far from supporting their
cultural or biological isolation, he favored a "full assimilation," as socially and
biologically advantageous for the Germans: crossbreeding was a good way to
enhance the "racial fitness" of both "races." Reacting in 1895 to the political
success of anti-Semitic candidates in 1893, he had suggested that anti-
Semitism would "slowly recede in the tide of natural science knowledge and
humane democracy" (1895:141–42; Weiss 1987b:202–3).

Wilhelm Schallmayer, the first theoretician of German eugenics, was not a
Nordicist. Opposing Ploetz's term "race hygiene" because he thought eugenics
had nothing to do with anthropological "races," he suggested replacing it by
the more neutral term "national eugenics" (1910:375, 384; Weiss 1987a:
103). In 1905 he reviewed favorably Friedrich Hertz's critique of *Moderne
Rassentheorien* in Ploetz's eugenical review, and although he criticized the neo-
Lamarckian Hertz for his lack of knowledge of genetics, and for tarring eugenics and racial theories with the same brush, Schallmayer "agreed with Hertz
on all essential points." He opposed the "politics of racial arrogance" of the
"Gobineau school," and prophesied that the "Aryan Gospel" would one day
achieve a "disastrous power for our nation and perhaps also for the destiny of

Europe" (*AfRGB* 1905:860–66). In the shorter run, Nordicism was likely to take the eugenic movement in "a direction that leads nowhere or nowhere good" (1910:374; Weiss 1987a:101).

It was possible, in short, for anthropologists and other scientists of rather diverse political views to feel a kinship with the eugenic movement.[4] When Ploetz founded the first German eugenical review, the *Archiv für Rassen- und Gesellschafts-Biologie* in 1904, he succeeded in attracting prestigious collaborators in a variety of fields, providing a forum for all debates on heredity, theories of evolution, racial biology and bio-sociology (*AfRGB* 1904:iii). Until World War I, Ploetz successfully maintained a political balance in his review between Nordicist anthropologists and race theorists like Ammon, Wilser, Kuhlenbeck, Fehlinger, and their opponents, between liberal Jews like Friedenthal and Zionist Jews like Auerbach, as well as between neo-Darwinian, neo-Lamarckian, Mendelian, and biometric biologists. Among the numerous anthropologists who participated in one way or another were (in addition to those already mentioned) Buschan, Fischer, Luschan, and Schwalbe, along with Birkner (University of Munich), Kohlbrugge, (Netherlands), Kollmann, Lundborg (Upsala, Sweden), Pöch (Vienna), Weinberg (Dorpat, Estonia), Weissenberg (Ukraine), and even Franz Boas (who published a rejoinder to criticisms of his headform study [1913b])—as well as leading ethnologists (including Achelis, Preuss, and Vierkandt), prehistorians (Kossina), and other scholars in disciplines at the margins of anthropology. During the first decade

4. The fact that many of the staunchest critics of Aryan, Teutonic, Nordic, and anti-Semitic race theories were Jews (including Hertz in Germany, Finot in France, and Boas in the United States), and that these critics were generally environmentalists, should not hide the existence of a strong current of "biologism" among the Central European Jewish intelligentsia—a phenomenon demonstrating the pervasive influence of "biologism" and "race theories" in the human and medical sciences in German-speaking countries at the turn of the century. Much of this biologistic literature by Jewish scientists and scholars appeared in three main journals: Woltmann's *Politisch-Anthropologische Revue*, Ploetz's *Archiv für Rassen- und Gesellschafts-Biologie*, and the Zionist Arthur Ruppin's *Zeitschrift für Demographie und Statistik der Juden*. Many Jewish anthropologists and biomedical scientists also supported eugenics, and even played a leading role in its propagation. These Jewish physicians were frequently radicals or liberals who supported a type of "reformed eugenics" coupled with social and sexual reforms (Weindling 1989:102–5). Among Zionist scholars, some also asserted the existence of a "Jewish race." Thus Elias Auerbach proclaimed, in Ploetz's eugenical review, that in the whole "Jewish racial history, the strongest resistance to racial mixture came not from the other nations but from the Jews themselves," because the Jews were "more keen on racial purity than any other civilized nation"; quoting Gobineau, Auerbach concluded: "I say that a nation will never die if it remains always composed of the same ethnical components" (1907:361). These Zionist authors sometimes used the same rhetoric against mixed marriages as did Nordicist anthropologists. Thus Ruppin was convinced that "crossing with very different races almost always has detrimental consequences," and hoped "to keep the race pure in the future" (1910:92). For more details on this issue, see Doron 1980, Kiefer 1991, Efron 1994, Massin 1995.

of the twentieth century there was, in short, an increasing degree of overlap between German anthropology and eugenics—which by 1914 was being taught, under one more traditional medical rubric or another, in one-fourth of German universities (Günther 1982:37–67). It was in this context that German physical anthropology took on a new life as a form of biological anthropology with a therapeutic agenda.

Toward a Biological Anthropology
Useful to the State

In contextualizing the turn-of-the-century transformation of liberal physical anthropology to Nordic racial biology, we have considered a number of disciplinary, intellectual, ideological, and social processes: the imperfect institutionalization of anthropology; ambiguities and contradictions in the racial liberalism of Virchow and his colleagues; the increasing influence of nationalism and imperialism; the growing disillusion with craniological anthropometry; the revival of Darwinism and the rejection of Virchow's inductive positivism; the emergence of new theories of human heredity and the turn to genetic approaches; the revival of the race concept and of European racial classifications; the Aryanism of surrounding disciplines and the vogue of "modern race theories," including especially anthroposociology and eugenics—with all of these linked to the emergence of a younger generation of physical anthropologists in the power vacuum left by the death of Virchow. Among the various further issues that might be addressed in a more systematic treatment of the transformation, there is one that may be briefly considered here: the claim by the younger, eugenically oriented physical anthropologists that their science might be of great practical utility to the state.

The low level of political and academic recognition of their discipline, which was reflected in the absence of chairs for anthropology in universities, was a matter of great concern to physical anthropologists at the turn of the century (Buschan 1900; Ranke, in CoB 1907:98). The usefulness of a science like chemistry was obvious for the industrial development and military power of Germany, but anthropology seemed to most officials a purely theoretical science with no application, a science where the only motivation was, as Bismarck put it in opening the annual meeting in Hanover, the gratuitous ideal of knowledge (CoB 1893:79). Physical anthropology had neither the obvious applicability of other "natural sciences" nor the prestige of traditional hu: manities. In contrast, ethnology could at least claim its utility in colonial policy (Buschan 1900:65; Martin 1901; Luschan 1906). Insisting on its importance in international colonial competition, Waldeyer, in an address at the joint meeting of the German and Austrian societies in Lindau in 1899, urged that no officials should be authorized to take up positions in colonies without training in ethnology (CoB 1899:74). Germanic archeology had for some time been thought of as a "national duty" (Virchow, in CoB 1897:67) and an "outstanding national science" (Kossina 1912). But what could physical anthropologists put forward in petitioning the government for more chairs? If anthropologists themselves were convinced of the interest and value of their discipline, they nevertheless realized that it would not be supported by those outside "as long as they do not see it could be profitable for practical life" (Mies 1891:125).

One area of possible social utility had been provided by the application of anthropometry for police identification of criminals, an approach developed in the late 1870s by Alphonse Bertillon (Mies 1891; Kollman 1891:28). But when Francis Galton created an easier and quicker method with fingerprints, the tedious anthropometrical measurement of criminals lost much of its interest after 1900 (Darmon 1987). A second opportunity in this field was afforded by "criminal anthropology," developed by the Italian forensic physician Cesare Lombroso. But although the Archiv für Criminalanthropologie was founded in 1897, German advocates of Lombroso were psychiatrists or jurists rather than anatomists or anthropologists—while the latter were often critical of his work (CeB 1899:20). Virchow thought it was simply another type of "speculation" lacking any serious scientific basis—a "pure caricature of science" (1896b: 157, 162).[5] Yet another administrative application was the use of anthropometrical surveys for the army and for school administration to determine the size of equipment. But to confine the "Science of Man" to the menial task of measuring criminals or the sleeping bags of conscripts was not very satisfying for scientists who thought that human biology could bring answers to pressing social problems.

It was in this context that scientists found anthroposociology and eugenics so attractive. Already in 1899, Waldeyer was commenting on the necessity of anthropology in the solution of the new demographical problem, which endangered German military strength (CoB 1899:74). But the first one really to apply anthroposociological ideas was Schwalbe, who, in the face of lack of enthusiasm in the various ministries, sought in 1903 to promote a new national bioanthropological survey of the Reich. Because of the historical and social significance of the various races, such a survey would be of great importance "not only for anthropologists, but also for . . . politicians and government people" (1903:74). In his presidential address to the 1907 national assembly in Strasbourg on the "Mission of Anthroposociology," Schwalbe

---

5. With the spread of eugenic thinking in anthropology, this attitude changed. In 1914, Luschan asserted that "as a rule, crime is hereditary disease, generally incurable and often enough also transmissible" (LuP: "Culture and Degeneration," p. 4).

argued that by facilitating the understanding of "the historical process," the new discipline might help prevent the threatening decline of Germany. Anthroposociology had transformed anthropology, until then purely theoretical, into a science "highly useful to the State and to the society." Consequently, the state had the "unimpeachable duty" to offer "its powerful support" to anthropology's efforts "to serve the State and the society" (1907:66–68).

Two years later, in a speech on the "present mission of anthropology" at the meeting of the prestigious Gesellschaft deutscher Naturforscher und Ärtze, Luschan also treated the problem of "applied anthropology." The most vital element for a state, when its "national existence" was under threat, was its "force of defense," which depended upon the quantity and quality of its population. In the struggle for life between nations, "in real war as well as in trade and commerce, the healthier ones, those who are physically and mentally healthy, win." Plato was quite aware of that when he recommended to statesmen the "elimination of inferiors." What, then, should happen to those "inferiors"? In nature, inferior animals were quickly wiped out according to the law of "survival of the fittest." In primitive human societies, individuals who were morally or bodily inferior were also quickly stamped out because they were useless and/or detrimental to the community. But in the case of civilized nations, things were more complicated. An incessant conflict opposed national interest and duty to "sentimental soft-heartedness, false humanity, crass selfishness, private prejudice, and social privileges, all of which protect precisely those who are inferior, and protect them even more, and even more vigorously, the more the culture is advanced, and they protect them always at the expense of the strong, healthy, and pure!" Inferiors of all sorts, the mentally ill, feebleminded, alcoholics, criminal recidivists, beggars, and so on, were increasing faster than the upper classes of the society. The clue to this problem was to be found in "applied anthropology" (Luschan 1909:201–8).

Repeating his warning at the 1910 and 1912 anthropological congresses, Luschan suggested that the "new science" of anthroposociology was "not only of the highest imaginable theoretical interest, but also possessed a direct practical significance, particularly in confronting the question of national suicide and the "degeneration of civilized nations" (1910, 1912:53–54). In his presidential address the following year, Luschan again spoke of "applied anthropology or anthroposociology" as having "vital importance for us as a nation and for the motherland" (CoB 1913:63).

If Luschan's "applied anthropology" was not Nordicist, the same was not true of his younger colleague Eugen Fischer. At the 1910 meeting of the Anthropological Society and the Society of Natural Sciences of his academic town, Freiburg, Fischer gave a talk on "Anthroposociology and its significance for the State," suggesting that it had been Gobineau's merit to have argued that European races were not only physically but also psychologically "extraordinarily different." While he considered "race theories" as often exaggerated, he believed that the "core" of the work of Chamberlain, Wilser, Woltmann, Lapouge, and Ammon "is right and will win general recognition." The brains of the various races were "differently organized," and their "whole psychology as well as their cultural achievement are extraordinarily different." The Nordics were the race responsible for "the highest and most intensive cultural achievement in Europe" from the beginning of history to now." Furthermore, the decadence of all European nations was due to the "elimination of the Nordic race." It was already eliminated in Italy, Spain, and Portugal, and France would be next; after that, Germany, "if it keeps on going like it has until now and like it does today!" (1910:18–23).

The only remedy was that offered by the new branch of anthropology called "race hygiene." During the last ten years, Fischer suggested, anthropology had begun to seize problems affecting "our daily life." Like medicine, anthropology had not only a theoretical dimension but also a "technical" and "therapeutical" one. Unfortunately, the warning calls of eugenicists and anthropologists were not heeded by official circles, even though the issues they broached involved the "most fundamental question for the existence of the State," as well as "the future of European nations." Governmental leaders should understand the importance of the teaching of anthropology in German universities, which was in fact the first step in the struggle against this peril. But "before the government takes a step, we have to take charge of this duty ourselves," by creating an International Race Hygiene Society to spread those ideas in the academic and cultivated public, governmental circles, and administration. To accomplish this ideological revolution, it was necessary especially to teach the youth that Germans must give up their "exaggerated humanity" and "pseudomorality," along with their "old and new ideas of expiation and individual hedonism," for a new ethic based on racial biology. Knowledge and will were the two most important things, because "if we have the will, we can do it." To control the future of Germany, it was necessary to control the biology of the nation, since in controlling reproduction "we" would be "masters of nature." "This doctrine will win; the study of race and thereafter the cultivation of certain racial components belongs to the future!" (1910:20–29). The first step to saving "our wonderful German Nation" was for scientists to influence public opinion through teaching and scientific propaganda; after that, laws and practical reform would come by themselves. Academics had only to "teach and prepare" (1910:25–30).

There was more to be done, however, than normal teaching. Fischer was an active evangelist to larger groups of the younger generation. In 1911, at the meeting of the Deutsch-Nationaler Jugenbund, he lectured his young audience on the importance of the "racial factor" in the life of nations, insisting that the race hygienist, like a surgeon for the whole nation, had to be ready to "cut

Eugen Fischer, in the period of his appointment as Rector of the University
of Berlin in 1933 and his subsequent rapprochement with the Nazi movement after their seizure of power. (From the *Festschrift* for Fischer in the
1934 volume of the *Zeitschrift für Morphologie und Anthropologie*, courtesy of
Robert Proctor.)

ruthlessly in where something was rotten" (1912). The program he proposed
was nothing less than an ideological revolution, through both teaching and
scientific propaganda, in which the next generation of the German elite was
the prime target. With that accomplished, the political revolution would follow by itself. And in 1933, it did.

In 1913, however, the triumph of National Socialism was still two decades
in the future. But even before the Great War it could no longer be argued that
German physical anthropology, even in contemporary terms, represented an
anti-racist tendency. Virchow, whose influence had largely sustained that position, was a decade gone from the scene. Franz Boas—whose physical anthro-

pology was very much in the Virchow tradition—had long since emigrated to the United States, where he had just published what was to be the most influential anti-racist work of the modern anthropological tradition. Felix von Luschan, Boas' friend and Virchow's successor at the University of Berlin, had embraced eugenics and race hygiene. The wave of the future was represented by Eugen Fischer, who was later to be Luschan's successor at Berlin, and who by 1914 had foreshadowed almost all of the ingredients (save Manichaean racial anti-Semitism) of what would later become Nazi "biological policy."

Acknowledgments

This paper is a greatly abbreviated version of a larger study, carried out at the Centre Koyré d'Histoire des Sciences of the École des Hautes Études en Sciences Sociales, Paris. Research for this study has been supported by a fellowship of the Mission Historique Française en Allemagne (Göttingen). I would like to thank Professor Dr. F. Kümmel and Professor Dr. R. Winau for two years of hospitality at the institutes for the history of medicine of the University of Mainz and the Free University of Berlin; also, Suzanne Gross-Solomon (Toronto), Paul Lerner (Columbia), and George Stocking for helping a non-native English-speaker to edit and reduce the text, as well as Paul Weindling (Oxford) for comments and Michael Hubenstorf (Free University, Berlin) for biographical assistance on German medicine.

References Cited

Abbreviations

AA	*Archiv für Anthropologie.*
AfRGB	*Archiv für Rassen- und Gesellschafts-Biologie.*
CeB	*Centralblatt für Anthropologie, Ethnologie und Urgeschichte.*
CIAPP	*Congrès International d'Archéologie et d'Anthropologie Préhistoriques, Compte rendu, 1866.*
CoB	*Correspondenz-Blatt der Deutschen Gesellschaft für Anthropologie, Ethnologie und Urgeschichte.*
MAGW	*Mitteilungen der Anthropologischen Gesellschaft in Wien, 1870.*
PAR	*Politisch-Anthropologische Revue.*
PZ	*Prähistorische Zeitschrift.*
VhB	*Verhandlungen der Berliner Gesellschaft für Anthropologie, Ethnologie und Urgeschichte.*
VhG	*Verhandlungen der Gesellschaft deutscher Naturforscher und Ärtze.*
ZfE	*Zeitschrift für Ethnologie.*
ZIAVL	*Zeitschrift für induktive Abstammungs- und Vererbungslehre.*

ZMA   *Zeitschrift für Morphologie und Anthropologie.*
ZSDJ   *Zeitschrift für Demographie und Statistik der Juden.*

Parenthetic references which do not refer to a specific entry in the list below (e.g., *VhB* 1897:2) refer to texts in journals (see abbreviations above) which are not articles, such as presidential addresses, interventions in debates, "scientific report of the year," book and article reviews, or articles which are otherwise incidental to the topics of this paper.

Ackerknecht, E. H. 1953. *Rudolf Virchow: Doctor, statesman, anthropologist.* Madison.
Ahlwardt, H. 1890. *Der Verzweiflungskampf der arischen Völker mit dem Judentum.* Berlin.
Alsberg, M. 1906. Neuere Probleme der menschlichen Stammesentwicklung. *AfRGB* 3:28–41.
———. 1912. Schädelform und Umwelt Einflüsse. *AfRGB* 9:175–84.
Ammon, O. 1890. *Anthropologische Untersuchungen der Wehrpflichtigen in Baden.* Virchow-Holtzendorff'sche Sammlung gemeinverständlicher wissenschaftlicher Vorträge, H. 101. Hamburg.
———. 1892. La sélection naturelle chez l'homme. *L'Anthropologie* 3:720–36.
———. 1893. *Die Natürliche Auslese beim Menschen.* Iena.
———. 1894. *Die Bedeutung des Bauernstandes für den Staat und die Gesellschaft: Sozialanthropologische Studie.* Berlin.
———. 1895. *Die Gesellschaftsordnung und ihre natürlichen Grundlagen: Entwurf eine Sozial-Anthropologie.* Iena.
———. 1899. *Zur Anthropologie der Badener.* Iena.
———. 1900. *L'Ordre social et ses bases naturelles: Esquisse d'une Anthroposociologie.* Paris (French trans. of 1895).
Andree, C. 1969. Geschichte der Berliner Gesellschaft für Anthropologie, Ethnologie und Urgeschichte, 1869–1969. In *Festschrift* 1969:I, 9–139.
———. 1976. *Rudolf Virchow als Prähistoriker.* 2 vols. Cologne & Vienna.
Auerbach, E. 1907. Die jüdische Rassenfrage. *AfRG* 4:322–61.
Baelz, E. von. 1912. Kritik der Einteilung der Menschenrassen. *CoB* 43:110–13.
Baer, K. E. von, & R. Wagner. 1861. *Bericht über die Zusammenkunft einiger Anthropologen.* Leipzig.
Bartels, P. 1904a. Über Rassenunterschiede am Schädel. *Internationalen Monatsschrift für Anatomie und Physiologie* 21:137–86.
———. 1904b, Untersuchungen und Experimente an 15 000 menschlichen Schädeln über die Grundlagen und den Wert der anthropologischen Statistik. *ZMA* 7:81–132.
Berding, H. 1991. *Histoire de l'antisémitisme en Allemagne.* Paris.
Bergner, G. 1965. Geschichte der menschliche Phylogenetik seit dem Jahre 1900: Ein Überblich. In Heberer, 1965a:20–55.
Birkner, F. 1912. *Die Rassen und Völker der Menschheit.* Berlin.
Blanckaert, C. 1981. Monogénisme et polygénisme en France de Buffon à P. Broca (1749–1880). Doct. diss., University of Paris I.
———. 1989. L'indice céphalique et l'ethnogénie Européenne: A. Retzius, P. Broca, F. Pruner-Bey (1840–1870). *Bull. & Mém. de la Soc. d'Anthrop. de Paris* NS 1:165–202.

Boas, F. 1902. Rudolf Virchow's anthropological work. In Stocking 1974:36–41.

———. 1909. Race problems in America. In Stocking 1974:318–30.

———. 1910. *Changes in bodily form of descendants of immigrants.* Washington, D.C.

———. 1911. *The mind of primitive man.* New York.

———. 1912. The instability of human types. In Stocking 1974:214–18.

———. 1913a. Veränderungen der Körperform der Nachkommen von Einwanderern in Amerika. *ZfE* 45:1–22.

———. 1913b. Die Analyse anthropometrischer Serien, nebst Bemerkungen über die Deutung der Instabilität menschlicher Typen. *AfRGB* 10:290–302.

Bowler, P. J. 1983. *The eclipse of Darwinism: Anti-Darwinian evolution theories in the decades around 1900.* Baltimore.

———. 1986. *Theories of human evolution: A century of debate, 1844–1944.* Baltimore.

Bruck, C. 1907. Die biologische Differenzierung von Affenarten und Menschlichen Rassen durch spezifische Blutreaktion. *Berliner Klinische Wochenschrift* 26:793–97.

Burchardt, L. 1988. Naturwissenschaftliche Universitätslehrer im Kaiserreich. In Schwabe 1988:151–214.

Busch, A. 1959. *Die Geschichte des Privatdozenten: Eine soziologische Studie.* Stuttgart.

Buschan, G. 1900. Die Notwendigkeit von Lehrstühlen für eine 'Lehre vom Menschen' auf deutschen Hochschulen. *CeB* 5:65–72.

———. 1904. Cultur und Gehirn. *CoB* 35:127–33.

Chamberlain, H. S. 1899. *Die Grundlagen des neunzehnten Jahrhunderts.* 2 vols. Munich (3d. ed., 1901).

———. 1900. Die Racenfrage. *Die Wage* (Vienna) 3:31–32, 138–41.

———. 1913. *La genèse du XIXe siècle.* 2 vols. Paris (French trans. of 1899).

Chickering, R. 1984. *We men who feel most German: A cultural study of the Pan-German League 1886–1914.* London.

Churchill, F. B. 1968. August Weismann and a break from tradition. *J. Hist. Biol.* 1: 91–112.

———. 1974. William Johannsen and the genotype concept. *J. Hist. Biol.* 7:5–30.

———. 1976. Rudolf Virchow and the pathologist's criteria for the inheritance of acquired characteristics. *J. Hist. Med.* 31:117–48.

Clark, L. L. 1984. *Social Darwinism in France.* Birmingham, Ala.

Darmon, P. 1987. Bertillon, le fondateur de la police scientifique. *L'Histoire* 105:42–48.

Deniker, J. 1900. *Les races et les peuples de la terre: Eléments d'anthropologie et d'ethnographie.* Paris.

Doeleke, W. 1975. Alfred Ploetz (1860–1940) Sozialdarwinist und Gesellschaftsbiologe. Doct. diss., University of Frankfurt.

Doron, J. 1980. Rassenbewusstsein und Naturwissenschaftliches Denken im deutschen Zionismus während der Wilhelminischen Ära. *Jahrbuch des Instituts für deutsche Geschichte* (Tel Aviv) 9:389–427.

Driesmans, H. 1904. Rassentheoretiker und Anthropologen. *Baltische Monatschrift* 57: 241–45.

Dühring, E. 1881. *Die Judenfrage als Racen-, Sitten- und Culturfrage.* Karlsruhe.

———. 1892. *Die Judenfrage als Frage der Racenschädlichkeit für die Existenz, Sitte und Cultur der Völker.* Berlin.

Efron, J. M. 1994. *Defenders of the race: Jewish doctors and race science in fin-de-siècle Europe*. New Haven.

Ehrenreich, P. 1897. *Anthropologische Studien über die Urbewohner Brasiliens.* Braunschweig.

Eickstedt, E. von. 1937. Geschichte der anthropologischen Namengebung und Klassifikation. *Zeitschrift für Rassenkunde* 5:208–63; 6:36–96, 201–10.

———. 1940. *Die Forschung am Menschen*. Vol. 1: *Geschichte und Methoden der Anthropologie*. Stuttgart.

Festschrift zum Hundertjährigen Bestehen der Berliner Gesellschaft für Anthropologie, Ethnologie und Urgeschichte 1869–1969. 1969. Berlin.

Field, G. G. 1981. *Evangelist of race: The Germanic vision of H. S. Chamberlain*. New York.

Finot, J. 1906. *Das Rassenvorurteil*. Berlin.

Fischer, E. 1910. *Sozialanthropologie und ihre Bedeutung für den Staat*. Freiburg.

———. 1911. Zum Inzuchts- und Bastardierungsproblem beim Menschen. *CoB* 42:105–9.

———. 1912. Zur Frage der Kreuzungen beim Menschen. *AfRGB* 9:8–10.

———. 1913. *Die Rehobother Bastards und das Bastardierungsproblem beim Menschen*. Iena.

———. 1914. Das Problem der Rassenkreuzung beim Menschen. Freiburg (reprint from *Verhandlungen der Gesellschaft deutscher Naturforscher und Ärzte*, 85th meeting in Vienna).

F P. See Manuscript Sources.

Friedenthal, H. 1900. Über einen experimentaldess Nachweis von Blutverwandtschaft. *Archiv für Anatomie und Physiologie*, 494–508.

Fritsch, G. 1898. Ueber die Entstehung der Rassenmerkmale des menschlichen Kopfhaares. *CoB* 29:161–64.

———. 1910. Die Entwicklung und Verbreitung der Menschenrassen. *ZfE* 42:580–86.

Gasman, D. 1971. *The scientific origins of national socialism: Social Darwinism in Ernst Haeckel and the German Monist League*. New York.

Geus, A. 1987. *Johannes Ranke (1836–1916): Physiologe, Anthropologe und Prähistoriker*. Marburg.

Gobineau, A. de. 1853–55. *Essai sur l'inégalité des races humaines*. 4 vols. Paris.

Graham, L. R. 1977. Science and values: The eugenics movement in Germany and Russia in the 1920s. *Am. Hist. Rev.* 82:1133–64.

Gregory, F. 1977. *Scientific materialism in nineteenth century Germany*. Dordrecht.

Grimm, H. 1986. Felix von Luschan als Anthropologe: Von der Kraniologie zur Humanbiologie. *Ethnogr.-Archäol. Zeitschrift* 27:415–25.

Günther, M. 1982. Die Institutionalisierung der Rassenhygiene an den deutschen Hochschulen vor 1933. Doct. diss., University of Mainz.

Haeckel, E. 1868. *Natürliche Schöpfungs-Geschichte*. Berlin (8th ed., 1889).

———. 1904. *Die Lebenswunder*. In *Ernst Haeckel Gemeinverstandliche Werke*, ed. H. Schmidt. Vol. 4. Leipzig (1924).

———. 1908. *Unsere Ahnenreihe: Kritische Studien über phyletische Anthropologie*. Iena.

Hammer, W. 1979. Leben und Werk des Arztes und Sozialanthropologen Ludwig Woltmann. Doct. diss., University of Mainz.

Hammond, M. 1980. Anthropology as a weapon of social combat in late-nineteenth-century France. *J. Hist. Beh. Scis.* 16:118–32.

Harwood, J. 1984. National styles in science: Genetics in Germany and the United States between the World Wars. *Isis* 78:390–414.

Heberer, G., ed. 1965a. *Menschliche Abstammungslehre: Fortschritte der "Anthropogenie" 1863–1964.* Stuttgart.

———. 1965b. Zur Geschichte der Evolutionstheorie, besonders in ihrer Anwendung auf den Menschen: Von Darwin bis zum Ende des 19. Jahrhunderts. In Heberer, 1965a:1–19.

Hertz, F. 1904. *Moderne Rassentheorien.* Vienna.

———. 1915. *Rasse und Kultur: Eine kritische Untersuchung der Rassentheorien.* Leipzig.

Hiltner, G. 1970. *Rudolf Virchow.* Stuttgart.

Honigmann, P. 1990. An der Grenze zwischen anthropologischem Interesse und Rassismus: A. von Humboldts Auseinandersetzung mit J. A. Comte de Gobineau. In G. Mann & F. Dumont 1990:427–36.

Hovorka, O. 1898. Sollen wir weiter messen oder nicht? *CeB* 3:289–94.

Hunt, J. 1863. *On the Negro's place in nature.* London.

Jarausch, K. H. 1982. *Student, society, and politics in imperial Germany: The rise of academic illiberalism.* Princeton.

Jenssen, C., & T. M. Ruprecht. 1990. "Abrüsten oder Untergehen." Ein Interview mit Rudolf Virchow aus dem Jahre 1895. *Medizinhistorisches Journal* 25:252–68.

Jochman, W. 1976. Struktur und Function des deutschen Antisemitismus 1878–1914. In Mosse & Paucker 1976:389–477.

Kampe, N. 1988. *Studenten und 'Judenfrage' im deutschen Kaiserreich.* Göttingen.

Kelly, A. 1981. *The descent of Darwin: The popularization of Darwinism in Germany, 1860–1914.* Chapel Hill.

Kiefer, A. 1991. *Das Problem einer "Jüdischen Rasse."* Frankfurt am Main.

Kiffner, F. 1961. Felix von Luschan: Eine biographische Skizze aus persönlichen Erinnerungen und Äusserungen seiner Zeit. *Wissenschaftliche Zeitschrift der Humboldt-Universität zu Berlin, Math.-Naturwiss.* 10:231–39.

Klaatsch, H. 1899. Die Stellung des Menschen in der Primatenreihe und der Modus seiner Hervorbildung aus einer niederen Form. *CoB* 30:154–57.

———. 1902. *Entstehung und Entwicklung des Menschengeschlechtes, Weltall und Menschheit.* Vol. 2:1–338. Berlin.

———. 1910. Menschenrassen und Menschenaffen. *CoB* 41:91–100.

Kollmann, J. 1886. Review of A. Weismann, "Ueber die Bedeutung der geschlechtichen Fortpflanzung für die Selektionstheorie" and of R. Virchow "Ueber Akklimatation." *Biologisches Centralblatt* 5:673–79, 705–10.

———. 1891. Die Kraniometrie und ihre jüngsten Reformatoren. *CoB* 22:25–29, 34–39, 41–46.

———. 1892a. Die Menschenrassen Europas und die Frage nach der Herkunft der Arier. *CoB* 23:102–6.

———. 1892b. Noch einmal Herr von Török. *CoB* 23:2–5.

―――. 1898. Ueber die Beziehung der Vererbung zur Bildung der Menschenrassen. *CoB* 29:115–21.

―――. 1900a. Die Rassenfrage. *Die Wage.* 3:76–78.

―――. 1900b. Die angebliche Entstehung neuer Rassentypen. *CoB* 31:1–5.

―――. 1902. Die temporäre Persistenz der Menschenrassen. *Globus* 82:383–87.

―――. 1905. Neue Gedanken über das alte Problem von der Abstammung des Menschen. *CoB* 36:9–20.

Kossina, G. 1902. Die indogermanische Frage archäologisch beantwortet. *ZfE* 34:161–222.

―――. 1912. *Die deutsche Vorgeschichte: Eine hervorragend nationale Wissenschaft.* Mannus-Bibliothek 9. Würzburg.

Kraitschek, G. 1910. Das Indogermanenproblem. *MAGW* 40:30–31.

Kümmel, W. 1968. Rudolf Virchow und der Antisemitismus. *Medizinhistorisches Journal* 3:165–79.

Lehmann-Nitsche, R. 1906. Schädeltypen und Rassenschädel. *AA* 5:110–15.

Lémonon, M. 1971. Le Rayonnement du Gobinisme en Allemagne. 2 vols. Doct. diss., University of Strasbourg II.

Lenz, F. 1913. Review of Eugen Fischer, "Handwörterbuch der Naturwissenschaften." *AfRGB* 10:362–70.

―――. 1914. Review of Martin 1914. *AfRGB* 11:522–24.

Lesshaft, P. 1896. Der anatomische Unterricht der Gegenwart. *Anatomischer Anzeiger* 12:H. 17.

Levy, R. S. 1975. *The downfall of the anti-Semitic parties in imperial Germany.* New Haven.

Lichtsinn, H. 1987. *Otto Ammon und die Sozialanthropologie.* Frankfurt am Main.

Lilienthal, G. 1994. Die jüdischen "Rassenmerkmale." Zur Geschichte der Anthropologie der Juden. *Medizinhistorisches Journal* 8:173–98.

Löwenberg, D. 1978. Willibald Hentschel (1858–1947): Seine Pläne zur Menschenzüchtung, sein Biologismus und Antisemitismus. Doct. diss., University of Mainz.

LuP. See Manuscript Sources.

Luschan, F., von. 1892. Die anthropologische Stellung der Juden. *CoB* 23:94–100.

―――. 1900. Review of Ammon 1899. *Naturwissenschaftliche Wochenschrift* 18:213–15.

―――. 1902. Ziele und Wege der Völkerkunde in den deutschen Schutzgebieten. *Verhandlungen des Deutschen Kolonial Kongresses,* 163–74.

―――. 1905. Zur physischen Anthropologie der Juden. *ZSDJ,* 1/H.1:1–4.

―――. 1906. Bericht über eine Reise in Südafrika. *ZfE* 38:873–95.

―――. 1909. Die gegenwärtigen Aufgaben der Anthropologie. *VhG* 1910, 2:201–8.

―――. 1910. Angewandte Anthropologie im akademischen Unterricht. *CoB* 41:100–101.

―――. 1911. Anthropological view of race. In *Papers on inter-racial problems, communicated to the First Universal Races Congress held at the University of London,* ed. G. Spiller, 13–24. London.

―――. 1912. Die Wichtigkeit des Zusammenarbeiten der Ethnographie und der somatischen Anthropologie mit der Prähistorie. *CoB* 43:52–56.

―――. 1916. Gustav Schwalbe (1844–1916). *CoB* 47:15–18.

Malgorzata, I. 1990. *From Spree to Harlem: German 19th century anti-racist ethnology and the cultural revival of American blacks*. Sozialanthropologische Arbeitspapiere 27, Free University. Berlin.

Mann, G. 1969. Medizinische-biologische Ideen und Modelle in der Gesellschaftslehre des 19. Jahrhunderts. *Medizinhistorische Journal* 4 : 1 – 23.

———, ed. 1973. *Biologismus im 19. Jahrhunderts*. Stuttgart.

———. 1983. Sozialbiologie auf dem Wege zur unmenschlichen Medizin des Dritten Reiches. In *Unmenschliche Medizin*, ed. Förderkreis Bad Nauheimer Gespräche, 22 – 43. Mainz.

Martin, R. 1900. Über eine Reise durch die maylayische Halbinsel. *Mittelungen der Natur wissenschaftlichen Gesellschaft in Winterthur* 2 : 1 – 21.

———. 1901. *Anthropologie als Wissenschaft und Lehrfach: Eine akademische Antrittsrede*. Iena.

———. 1914. *Lehrbuch der Anthropologie in systematischer Darstellung: Mit besonderer Berücksichtigung der anthropologischen Methoden*. Iena.

Massin, B. 1990. *Fragments et éléments bibliographiques pour une histoire des théories raciales et de leurs principales critiques de Gobineau à Günther (1855 – 1945): Science et idéologie*. Paris.

———. 1992. Ammon, Otto (2206); Chamberlain, Houston Stewart (2323 – 25); Gobineau, Arthur (1796 – 97); Vacher de Lapouge, George (2898 – 900); Woltmann, Ludwig (2943 – 44). In *Les oeuvres philosophiques: Dictionnaire*, ed. J. F. Mattei. 2 vols. Paris.

———. 1993a. Anthropologie raciale et national-socialisme: Heurs et malheurs du paradigme de la 'race.' In *La science sous le Troisième Reich*, ed. J. Olff-Nathan, 197 – 262. Paris.

———. 1993b. De l'anthropologie physique libérale à la biologie raciale eugénico-nordiciste en Allemagne (1870 – 1914): Virchow-Luschan-Fischer. *Revue d'Allemagne et des Pays de Langue Allemande* 25(3): 387 – 404.

———. 1995. Intellectuels et scientifiques Juifs, eugénisme et théoriciens sionistes de la "race juive" dans la fin de l'Allemagne wilhelmienne (1900 – 1914). In *La race: Idées et pratiques dans les sciences et dans l'histoire*, ed. A. Ducros & M. Panoff, ms. Paris.

Mayr, E. 1985. Weismann and evolution. *J. Hist. Biol.* 18 : 295 – 329.

Melk-Koch, M. 1989. *Auf der Suche nach der menschlichen Gesellschaft: Richard Thurnwald*. Berlin.

Merten, H.-G. 1983. *Sozialbiologismus: Biologische Grundpositionen der politischen Ideengeschichte*. Frankfurt.

Mies, J. 1891. Ueber Körpermessungen zur genauen Bestimmung und sicheren Wiedererkennung von Personen. *CoB* 22 : 124 – 28.

Montgomery, W. M. 1974. Germany. In *The comparative reception of Darwinism*, ed. T. F. Glick, 81 – 116. Austin.

Mosse, W. E. & A. Paucker, eds. 1976. *Juden in Wilhelminischen Deutschland 1890 – 1914*. Schrift. wiss. Abh. Leo-Baeck Inst. 33. Tübingen.

Mucchielli, L. 1994. L'abandon de la notion de race chez les sociologues durkheimiens dans le contexte "Fin de siècle" (1885 – 1914). In *La race: Idées et pratiques dans les sciences et dans l'histoire*, ed. A. Ducros & M. Panoff, ms. Paris.

Mühlmann, W. E. 1946. *Geschichte der Anthropologie*. Wiesbaden (1986).

Müller, F. 1873. *Allgemeine ethnographie*. Vienna (1879).

Müller-Hill, B. 1989. *Science Nazie, science de mort: L'Extermination des Juifs, des Tziganes et des malades mentaux de 1933 à 1945*. Paris.

Nagel, G. 1975. *Sozialdarwinismus in Frankreich: G. Vacher de Lapouge, 1854–1936*. Freiburg.

Nagel-Brilinger, M. D. 1979. Schemann und Gobineau: Ein Beitrag zur Geschichte von Rassismus und Sozialdarwinismus. Doct. diss., University of Freiburg.

Nyström, A. 1902. Ueber die Formenveränderungen des menschlichen Schädels und deren Ursachen: Ein Beitrag zur Rassenlehre. *AA* 27:211–31, 317–36.

Ottow, B. 1966. K. E. von Baer als Kraniologe und die Anthropologen-Versammlung 1861 in Göttingen. *Sudhoffs Archiv* 50:43–68.

Penka, K. 1883. *Origines Ariacae: Linguistische-ethnologische Untersuchungen zur ältesten Geschichte der arischen Völker und Sprachen*. Vienna & Teschen.

Pestre, D. 1995. Pour une histoire sociale et culturelle des sciences. *Annales ESC*, ms.

Ploetz, A. 1895. *Die Tüchtigkeit unserer Rasse und der Schutz der Schwachen*. Berlin.

Poliakov, L. 1987. *Le Mythe Aryen: Essai sur les sources du racisme et des nationalismes*. Brussels.

Poniatowski, S. 1911. Über den Wert der Indexklassifikationen. *AA* 10:50–54.

PP. See Manuscript Sources.

Proctor, R. 1988a. From *Anthropologie* to *Rassenkunde* in the German anthropological tradition. *HOA* 5:1988:138–79.

———. 1988b. *Racial hygiene: Medicine under the Nazis*. Cambridge, Mass.

Pulzer, P. G. 1966. *Die Entstehung des politischen Antisemitismus in Deutschland und Österreich 1867–1914*. Gütersloh.

Querner, H. 1969. Die Anthropologie auf den Versammlungen der Deutschen Naturforscher und Ärzte bis zur Gründung der Gesellschaft für Anthropologie 1869. In *Festschrift* 1969:1:143–56.

Ranke, J. 1887. *Der Mensch*. 2 vols. Leipzig.

———. 1891 Zur Frankfurter Verständigung und über Beziehungen des Gehirns zum Schädelbau (and debate with Lissauer & Szombathy). *CoB* 22:115–23.

———. 1894. *Der Mensch*. 2 vols. Leipzig (2d ed.).

———. 1897. Über die individuellen Variationen im Schädelbau des Menschen. *CoB* 28:139–46.

———. 1903. Die im Studienjahr 1902/3 an der Universitäten Deutschlands, Österreichs und der Schweiz abgehaltenen Vorlesungen und Curse aus dem Gesammtgebiete der Anthropologie. *CoB* 34:53–58.

Reche, O. 1911. Längen-Breitenindex und Schädellänge. *AA* 10:74–90.

Reimer, J. L. 1905. *Ein pangermanisches Deutschland: Versuch über die Konsequenzen der gegenwärtigen wissenschaftlichen Rassenbetrachtung für unsere politischen und religiösen Probleme*. Berlin & Leipzig.

Retzenstein, F. von. 1913. Zur Mischehenfrage. *CoB* 44:103–10.

Révész, B. 1907. Rassen und Geisteskrankheiten: Ein Beitrag zur Rassenpathologie. *AA* NF6:180–87.

Ringer, F. K. 1988. Das gesselschaftliche Profil der deutschen Hochschullehrerschaft 1871–1933. In Schwabe 1988:93–104.

Ripley, W. Z. 1900. *The races of Europe: A sociological study*. London.

Römer, R. 1989. *Sprachwissenschaft und Rassenideologie in Deutschland*. Munich.

Ruppin, A. 1910. Der Rassenstolz der Juden. *ZDSJ* 6:88–92.

Rürup, R. 1976. Emanzipation und Krise: Zur Geschichte der Judenfrage in Deutschland. In Mosse & Paucker: 1–56. Tübingen.

Rusch, W. 1985. Der Beitrag Felix von Luschans für die Ethnographie. *Ethnogr.-Archäol. Zeitschrift* 27:439–53.

Sandmann, J. 1990. *Der Bruch mit der humanitären Tradition: Die Biologisierung der Ethik bei E. Haeckel und anderen Darwinisten seiner Zeit*. Stuttgart.

Sarasin, F. 1907. Über die niedersten Menschenformen der südostlichen Asiens. *Verhandlungen der schweizerischen naturforschenden Gesellschaft* 1:237–44.

Schaffhausen, H. 1890. Das Alter der Menschenrassen. *CoB* 21:122–28.

Schallmayer, W. 1891. *Über die drohende körperliche Entartung der Culturmenschheit und die Verstaatlichung des ärztlichen Standes*. Neuwied.

———. 1910. *Vererbung und Auslese in ihrer soziologischen und politischen Bedeutung*. Iena.

Schemann, L. 1910. *Gobineaus Rassenwerk: Aktenstücke und Betrachtungen zur Geschichte und Kritik des 'Essai sur l'inégalité des races humaines.'* Stuttgart.

———. 1913–16. *Gobineau: Eine Biographie*. 2 vols. Strasbourg.

———. 1925. *Lebensfahrten eines Deutschen*. Leipzig.

Schmidt, E. 1888. *Anthropologische Methoden: Anleitung zum Beobachten und Sammeln für Laboratorium und Reise*. Leipzig.

Schott, L. 1961. Zur Geschichte der Anthropologie an der Berliner Universität. *Wissenschaftliche Zeitschrift der Humboldt-Universität zu Berlin, Math.-Naturwiss.* 10:57–65.

Schwabe, K., ed. 1988. *Deutsche Hochschullehrer als Elite 1815–1945*. Boppard.

Schwalbe, G. 1899. Ziele und Wege einer vergleichenden physischen Anthropologie. *ZMA* 1:1–15.

———. 1903. Ueber eine umfassende Untersuchung der physisch-anthropologischen Beschaffenheit der jetzigen Bevölkerung des Deutschen Reiches. *CoB* 34:73–83.

———. 1907. Eröffnungsrede: Aufgaben der Sozialanthropologie. *CoB* 38:65–68.

———. 1910. Über Darwins Werk: "Die Abstammung des Menschen." *ZMA* 12:441–72.

Schwidetzky, I. 1982. Die institutionelle Entwicklung der Anthropologie; Die inhaltliche Entwicklung der Anthropologie; Die Anthropologie und ihre Nachbarwissenschaften. In *Maus und Schlange: Untersuchung zur Lage der deutschen Anthropologie*, ed. I. Spiegel-Rösing & I. Schwidetzky, 75–200. Munich.

Sergi, G. 1892. Sur une nouvelle méthode de classification des crânes humains. *CIAAP. Compte Rendu lle session* T. 2:297–304. Moscow.

SkP. See Manuscript Sources.

Smith, W. D. 1991. *Politics and the science of culture in Germany 1840–1920*. New York.

SP. See Manuscript Sources.

Stanton, W. 1960. *The leopard's spots: Scientific attitudes toward race in America, 1815–1859*. Chicago.

Steinmetz, S. R. 1903. Die Aufgaben der Social-Ethnologie. *CoB* 32:139–43.

Stepan, N. 1982. *The idea of race in science: Great Britain 1860–1960*. London.

Stern, F. 1961. *The politics of cultural despair: A study in the rise of the Germanic ideology*. Berkeley.

Stocking, G. W., Jr. 1968. *Race, culture and evolution: Essays in the history of anthropology*. New York.

————, ed. 1974. *The shaping of American anthropology, 1883–1911: A Franz Boas reader*. New York.

————, ed. 1988. *Bones, bodies, behavior: Essays on biological anthropology*. HOA 5. Madison.

Stölting, E. 1987. Die anthroposoziologische Schule: Gestalt und Zusammenhänge eines wissenschaftlichen Institutionalisierungsversuch. In *Rassenmythos und Sozialwissenschaften in Deutschland: Ein verdrängtes Kapitel sozialwissenschaftlicher Wirkungsgeschichte*, ed. C. Klingemann, 130–71. Opladen.

Stratz, C. H. 1904a. *Naturgeschichte des Menschen: Grundriss der somatischen Anthropologie*. Stuttgart.

————. 1904b. Das Problem der Rasseneinteilung der Menschheit. *AA* 1:189–200.

Strauss, H. A., & N. Kampe, eds. 1985. *Antisemitismus: Von der Judenfeindschaft zum Holocaust*. Bonn.

Sudhoff, K., ed. 1922. *Rudolf Virchow und die deutschen Naturforscherversammlungen*. Leipzig.

Theunissen, B. 1989. *Eugen Dubois and the ape-man from Java: The history of the first "missing-link" and its discoverer*. Dordrecht.

Török, A. von. 1890. *Grundzüge einer vergleichenden Kraniometrie: Methodische Anleitung zur kraniometrischen Analyse der Schädelform für die Zwecke der physischen Anthropologie, der vergleichenden Anatomie sowie für die Zwecke der medizinischen Disziplinen und der bildenden Künste*. Stuttgart.

————. 1891. Entgegnung auf Herrn Kollmann's Angriffe. *CoB* 22:60–61.

————. 1901. Inwiefern kann das Gesichtsprofil als Ausdruck der Intelligenz gelten? Ein Beitrag zur Kritik der heutigen physischen Anthropologie. *ZMA* 3:351–484.

————. 1906a. Neue Untersuchungen über die Dolichocephalie: Ein Beitrag zur nächsten Aufgabe der Rassenforschung. *ZMA* 9:215–38.

————. 1906b. Versuch einer systematischen Charakteristik des Kephalindex. *AA* 4:110–20.

Tschepourkovsky, E. 1903. Ueber die Vererbung des Kopfindex von Seiten der Mutter. *CoB* 34:172–75.

Vasold, M. 1988. *Rudolf Virchow: Der grosse Artz und Politiker*. Stuttgart.

Virchow, R. 1872. Über die Methode der wissenschaftlichen Anthropologie: Eine Antwort an Herrn de Quatrefages. *ZfE* 4:300–319.

————. 1876. Die Ziele und Mittel der modernen Anthropologie. In Sudhoff 1922: 170–82.

————. 1877. *Beiträge zur physischen Anthropologie der Deutschen*. Berlin.

————. 1880. Über einige Merkmale niederer Menschenrassen am Schädel und über die Anwendung der statistischen Methode in der ethnischen Craniologie. *ZfE* 12:1–26.

————. 1881. *Über die Weddas von Ceylon*. Verhandlungen der Königliche Akademie der Wissenschaften. Berlin.

———. 1885. Über Akklimatation. In Sudhoff 1922:214–39.

———. 1886. Gesammtberichte über die von der deutschen anthropologischen Gesellschaft veranlassten Erhebungen über die Farbe der Haut, der Haare und der Augen der Schulkinder in Deutschland. AA 16:275–446.

———. 1887. Über Transformismus. In Sudhoff 1922:277–98.

———. 1891. Zur Frankfurter Verständigung. CoB 22:121–24.

———. 1892. Crania Ethnica Americana: Sammlung Auserlesener Amerikanischer Schädeltypen. Berlin.

———. 1894. Aino-Schädel. VhB, 175–78.

———. 1896a. Rassenbildung und Erblichkeit. In Festschrift für Adolf Bastian, 3–43. Berlin.

———. 1896b. Ueber Criminalanthropologie. CoB 27:157–62.

———. 1900. Ueber das Auftreten der Slaven in Deutschland. CoB 31:109–13.

———. 1901a. Über den prähistorischen Menschen und über die Grenzen zwischen Species und Varietät. CoB 22:83–89.

———. 1901b. Über Schädelformen und Schädeldeformation. CoB 22:135–39.

Vogt, C. 1866. Mémoire sur les microcéphales ou hommes-singes. Geneva. German version in AA (1867) 2:129–279.

Volkov, S. 1978. Antisemitismus as a cultural code. Leo-Baeck Institute Yearbook 23:25–46.

Waldeyer, W. 1909. Darwins Lehre, ihr heutiger Stand und ihre wissenschaftliche und kulturelle Bedeutung. Deutscher medizinischer Wochenschrift 8:345–49.

Weinberg, R. 1904. Rassen und Herkunft des russischen Volkes. PAR 3:484–508.

Weinberg, W. 1908. Über Vererbungsgesetze beim Menschen. ZIAVL 1:377–92, 440–60; 2:276–330.

Weindling, P. 1981. Theories of the cell state in imperial Germany. In Biology, Medicine and Society 1840–1940, ed. C. Webster, 99–155. Cambridge.

———. 1989. Health, race and German politics between national unification and Nazism 1870–1945. Cambridge.

———. 1993. The survival of eugenics in 20th-century Germany. Am. J. Hum. Genetics 52:643–49.

Weingart, P. 1987. The rationalization of sexual behavior: The institutionalization of eugenic thought in Germany. J. Hist. Biol. 20:159–93.

Weingart, P., J. Kroll, & K. Bayertz. 1988. Rasse, Blut und Gene: Geschichte der Eugenik und Rassenhygiene in Deutschland. Frankfurt am Main.

Weiss, S. 1986. Wilhelm Schallmayer and the logic of German eugenics. Isis 77:33–46.

———. 1987a. Race hygiene and national efficiency: The eugenics of Wilhelm Schallmayer. Berkeley.

———. 1987b. The race hygiene movement in Germany. Osiris 3:193–236.

Weissenberg, S. 1895. Die südrussischen Juden. AA 23:347–423, 531–79.

———. 1897. Ueber die verschiedenen Gesichtsmasse und Gesichtsindices, ihre Eintheilung und Brauchbarkeit. ZfE 29:41–58.

———. 1909. Die kaukasischen Juden in anthropologischer Beziehung. AA 8:237–45.

Wilser, L. 1894. Klima und Hautfarbe. CoB 25:17–19.

————. 1900. Die 'Kruger-Penkasche Hypothese': Ein Beitrag zur Geschichte der arischen Frage. *Globus* 78:144–47.

Wohlbold, H. 1898. Die Kraniologie, ihre Geschichte und ihre Bedeutung für die Classification der Menschheit. Doct. diss., University of Erlangen.

Wohltmann, F. 1891. Die Sambaquis in Brasiliens (Anthr.-Naturwiss. Verein Göttingen). *CoB* 22:14–15, 30.

Wolff, Karl. 1914. Die Urheimat der Indogermanen. *Mannus* 6:309–20.

Woltmann, L. 1903. Politische Anthropologie. In *Woltmanns Werk*, ed. O. Reche. Vol. 1. Leipzig (1936).

————. 1906. Bemerkungen zur Rassentheorie. *PAR* 5:673–682.

Young, E. J. 1968. *Gobineau und der Rassismus: Eine Kritik der anthropologischen Geschichtstheorie.* Meisenheim.

Zängl-Kumpf, U. 1990. *Hermann Schaffhausen (1816–1893): Die Entwicklung einer neuen physischen Anthropologie im 19. Jahrhundert.* Frankfurt am Main.

Zmarlik, H.-G. 1982. Antisemitismus im Deutschen Kaiserreich 1871–1918. In *Die Juden als Minderheit in der Geschichte*, ed. B. Martin & E. Schulin, 249–70. Munich.

Zollschan, I. 1911. *Das Rassenproblem unter besonderer Berücksichtigung der Theoretischen Grundlagen der Jüdischen Rassenfrage.* 2d. ed. Vienna.

Manuscript Sources

The research for this paper involved the consultation of a number of different manuscript archives, including the following, which are cited by acronyms in the text:

FP   Fischer File of Freiburg (1900–14, academic letters), Universitätsarchiv Freiburg (Breisgau), Germany.

LuP   Luschan Papers, Staatsbibliothek, Berlin.

PP   Ploetz Papers, through Paul Weindling, Wellcome Unit in the History of Medicine, University of Oxford.

SkP   Schoettensack Papers, Universitätsarchiv, Heidelberg.

SP   Schemann Papers, Universitätsbibliothek, Freiburg (Breisgau), Germany.

GERMAN CULTURE AND GERMAN SCIENCE IN THE *BILDUNG* OF FRANZ BOAS

JULIA E. LISS

The last entry in Franz Boas' compendium of his life's work, *Race, Language and Culture* (1940) is "The Study of Geography" (1887)—a peculiar but nonetheless well-marked place for an essay seminal to Boas' anthropological and scientific point of view. This is not, however, a seminal work in the sense of laying out a research strategy for future development. Couched as a defense of geography, it in fact explores more elusive questions about the temperament of scientists and styles of scientific inquiry. Considered in conjunction with his early life and career, it enables us to see the scientific and the personal as mutually reinforcing and illuminating, and to appreciate the basis of certain enduring and unresolved tensions in Boas' life and work.

In the most immediate sense, "The Study of Geography" addressed these tensions through a comparison between the historical and physical sciences. Both, Boas suggested, started from the "foundation" of "the establishment of facts" and aspired "to the same end—to find the eternal truth." But in method, assumptions, and temperament the two moved along different trajectories. Whereas the first stressed "the investigation of phenomena themselves," for "their own sake," the latter sought the discovery of laws in which the phenomena were only a means to that end. Like cosmography and the historical sciences with which it was allied, geography allowed for the "subjective connection" arising in "the mind of the observer." In contrast, the physical sciences focussed on phenomena that were presumed to have an "objective unity." Although Boas sought to justify geography and cosmography as worthy

Julia E. Liss is a member of the History Department of Scripps College in Claremont, California. She is presently working on a study of Franz Boas, cosmopolitanism, and the development of American anthropology (University of Chicago Press, forthcoming).

155

scientific enterprises, he granted the legitimacy of both approaches. Because each of them originated "in a different desire of the human mind," a choice between them could only be subjective, "being a confession of the answerer as to which is dearer to him—his personal feeling towards the phenomena surrounding him, or his inclination for abstractions; whether he prefers to recognize the individuality in the totality, or the totality in the individuality." The temperament of the scientist decided that choice: on the one hand, the "logical and aesthetic demands" of the physicist; on the other the "'affective' impulse" of the cosmographer (1887:641–43, 645).

Ultimately, Boas provided few answers in this essay. If anything, he heightened tensions which endured in his own future work, between wholes and parts, universals and particulars, objective and subjective interpretations, and emotional (affective) and rational (aesthetic) approaches. At the end of the essay, Boas spoke of "the impulse which induces us to devote our time and work to this study" as a matter of "gratifying the love for the country we inhabit, and the nature that surrounds us" (1887:647). At the time the essay was first published, in English, that country was the United States, to which he had just immigrated at the age of twenty-nine. But the country in which he had grown up, and the nature that he had enjoyed from childhood, was that of his native Germany. It was there that he had struggled with these emotional, intellectual, and epistemological tensions as he encountered them in his formal education, in the dynamics of family relations, and in his psychological development. That Boas wrote in these same terms about these very problems in his correspondence with family and friends provides not only evidence about his state of mind as a young man, but, more significantly, casts light on the confluence of person, culture, and profession which, Boas himself suggested, helped to define the scientific enterprise.

Observing Nature, Understanding Culture: Religion, Science, and Humanism in the Minden *Gymnasium* Years

Born in Minden, Westphalia, a province of Prussia, on July 8, 1858, Boas was raised in a solidly middle-class, Jewish family. His relationship to his religious heritage was ambiguous. Much later, he felt that his limited religious education made it difficult to understand the power of religious belief for others, and blamed his upbringing for the shock of finding that a friend adhered to the "authority of tradition" (Boas 1938:201). But according to his daughter, Franziska, Boas "originally was brought up as an orthodox Jew," and his sister, Hedwig Lehmann, recalled that all the children received religious instruction, even though their parents were free-thinkers. The family's Jewish identity seems to have been more a matter of tradition and family loyalty than of faith. Although Meier Boas kept the Jewish holidays out of respect for his religious mother, the family celebrated Christmas as a German holiday (Franziska Boas 1972:10–11; Yampolsky n.d.). Later Boas viewed the matter in terms of a balance between emotional attachment and intellect: although his parents "had broken through the shackles of dogma," his father "had retained an emotional affection for the ceremonial of his parental home without allowing it to influence his intellectual freedom" (Boas 1938:201; cf. Glick 1982:545–65; Messer 1986:127–40). At the time, however, he seems to have found the tensions between family ideals and spiritual experience somewhat troublesome, and turned to private religious experimentation. He and his sister Toni, to whom he was extremely close, discussed mysticism, prayed together, and punished themselves when they thought they had sinned (Lehmann n.d.), and he criticized his free-thinking mother for being ignorant of his own spiritual questioning (BPP: FB/TB 10/5/76, 9/27/73). Despite his later claims to have surmounted religious dogma, at the time religious experience was an attractive if not fully realized alternative.

That Boas appreciated its attractions is evident in his later response to the religious questioning of his own children. Writing to his wife Marie in 1894 regarding their young daughter's queries about God, he suggested that

> one could maybe say, See the world around you! How is it made, who told the leaves to grow and drop in the fall? We don't know. We only know that spring is beautiful and so is winter when it snows. We are just happy about it . . . and we want to thank somebody for the beautiful world because we enjoy it as we enjoy the presents our parents give us. We all feel like this. For some people this means to thank God, others call it to enjoy the world. That is the same thing. (BPP: FB/MB 11/27/94)

Boas himself had felt the emotional need to explain the phenomena of the natural world, and if he did so by embracing science as an alternative, it provided a comparable sense of wonder and joy to that of religious faith.

From his early childhood, it was nature that provoked his own greatest fascination. In the *Curriculum Vitae* he wrote upon graduation from *Gymnasium* at the age of eighteen, he tried to put the history of his preoccupation in the context of his own upbringing and developmental influences. Early on, his mother had encouraged him to "observe nature," and in kindergarten he had participated in play activities and tasks "which at the same time were directed toward awakening our minds, especially our interest in nature by games which imitated animal life, and by keeping our own flower beds which we had to sow, water and care for" (Boas 1876–77:2). These early interests honed his powers of observation and his sense of the importance of critical detail, helping him

Franz Boas in 1868, at age ten, at the time of his entrance into the Minden *Gymnasium*. (Courtesy of the American Philosophical Society.)

develop a heightened awareness of his environment and an inquisitiveness about its diversity. Family vacations and trips to the seashore during periodic childhood illnesses allowed the young Boas to collect algae and sea anemones. By the age of ten or eleven, he began to take himself seriously as a scientist, reporting to his uncle Abraham Jacobi that he had written a piece on natural history treating the origin of tides, life in the sea, the origin of the earth, fossils, and the difference between land and water animals (BPP: FB/AJ 1/3/[68?]; BPM: FB/AJ 9/22/69). In the *Gymnasium*, Boas' education followed similar paths. In particular, he enjoyed physical geography, mineralogy, astronomy, geology, and the study of plant and animal life in their "transient geographical distribution"—at one point making maps of the geographical distribution of lichen and mosses near Minden. Later, his interests moved from botany to zoology, where "the external description of animals interested me less than their inner form"—which he studied by comparing whole bones of animals (especially geese, ducks, and hares), or their heads (Boas 1876–77:3–5, 13).

This shift from descriptive to comparative science was quite self-conscious. In an unusual piece of youthful self-criticism, Boas recalled the shortcomings of his early perspective in a manner foreshadowing his later concern with a multifaceted, integrative approach to natural and human phenomena. He felt that his early readings about nature "had the disadvantage of teaching me to pay attention to details only, while they awoke no understanding at all for nature in general"—although he allowed that "this may also have been due to the fact that I was too young then to be able to have an eye for more than details." Eventually, however, he decided that "merely collecting and recognizing plants did not please me anymore," and he turned his attention to natural history, and the interrelation of things and their structures. "True science," he now thought, "does not consist in describing single plants but in the knowledge of their structure and life and in the comparison of all classes of plants with one another " (Boas 1876–77:2, 3, 6).

From the time he was a child, Boas had linked this fascination with the natural world to visions of escape. Here his affinities with Humboldtian cosmography were explicit. He was particularly interested in exploration, especially the voyages of Alexander von Humboldt, and he dreamed of travelling to Asia and Africa. While at the *Burgerschule* he developed a yearning

> to see and get acquainted with foreign countries, a longing which has not yet left me. At that time my desire was always directed toward Africa, chiefly to the tropics, and I still remember very well that I ate as much as possible of certain foods which I did not like in order to accustom myself to deprivations in Africa. (Boas 1876–77:3)

Writing at the age of twelve to his sister Toni—to whom he frequently confided his innermost thoughts—he said that after graduation from the *Gymna-*

sium he would like to go to the university and study medicine, and then, if he passed his doctoral exam, make a north- or south-polar expedition and travel through Australia or Africa. "But—But—But," he continued, he had to finish his studies, "because without being thoroughly equipped, what fruit would be borne from such a trip?" (BPP: FB/TB 12/3/70). This was more than a passing fancy. In June of 1871, he told Toni that he wanted to be an African traveller and explore both the unknown lands and "those already known—the "Galla-, Banda, Kaffern, Hottentotten Volker"—to learn about the habits and customs of peoples, about the plant and animal life, and even about their geological relations (BPP: FB/TB 6/20/71).

Boas' fascination with the study and exploration of the natural world did not, however, preclude an interest in more traditional humanistic topics. Letters on his scientific activities often included sections in Latin, as well as carefully written bars of Mendelssohn (BPP: FB/TB [1871], 5/3/74). His interests were in fact markedly eclectic and wide-ranging, including history and literature, music and art, as well as natural science. This breadth of cultivation was consistent with the educational ideal of the German *Gymnasium*, which was epitomized in the word *Bildung*, meaning "cultivation," "formation," or "education" in a spiritual sense. Reflecting an idealist conception of human development, *Bildung* referred to a process by which the individual was formed organically through an affective immersion in the material of learning. In these terms, education was an integral experience distinct from mere memorization or analytical skills (Ringer 1969:86–87). Assuming a "theoretical unity of knowledge," *Bildung* encompassed both a dedication to "pure scholarship" and a general education "defined as the full development of the student's mind, spirit, and character" (Ringer 1979:35).

In the process of molding students as individuals, the *Gymnasium* curriculum placed great emphasis on the tradition of classical humanism. The young Boas studied the Greek myths, Xenophon and Ovid, and the classics of German literature, especially Schiller and Goethe, including lyric poetry such as Schiller's *Wilhelm Tell* and *Die Jungfrau von Orleans* (1876–77:8–10, 16, 17). He read Cicero and translated Homer and Horace, at one point trying to be faithful to the original choice of words and their arrangement (BPP: FB/TB 10/2/76, 10/5/76). He enjoyed music, especially the "old classical masters," not the modern composers (1876–77:15).

When he recounted his studies in more detail, however, what Boas emphasized was not the values embodied in great works and great men, but rather the history of culture, which he complained was neglected in the school curriculum. Focussing on the "history of peoples not of single men," he was concerned with the Celts and their religious and "cultural position" rather than their wars with Caesar. His interest in Homer included history as well, especially that of ancient Egypt, Assyria, and Babylon, and their culture and art. In this respect, his humanistic studies resembled closely his orientation toward natural history exploration, signaling a move from details to the larger picture of their inter-relatedness (1876–77:8, 11–12).

But if he was primarily interested in the ways of peoples rather than leaders, in literary and artistic studies Boas tried nevertheless to master the great works in the humanist canon, worrying about developing correct taste and discriminating judgment. Although these approaches point to a differentiation between what became an anthropological "concept of culture" and a genteel definition of "high" or elite culture as the fruits of civilization, what is impressive in these early years is that the two approaches coexisted. Moreover, they reveal an ambivalence toward received tradition that was rooted in Boas' aspirations to be an insider while feeling essentially an outsider to the culture, an ambivalence which was mediated through adopting a position of detachment.

Along with his penchant for detailed observation, Boas brought to his study of art, literature, and music a concern for the process of learning and understanding. He was preoccupied with methodological questions rather than the objects of study themselves. In a letter to his sister, Toni, for instance, he asked what her impressions of Paris were: "I believe, if one wants to profit from such a trip, one must remain a longer time than you stayed, and study all the galleries and museums in detail before you go, so that you know the particular things you want to see, because it is impossible to see everything" (BPP: FB/TB 9/29/76). Treating her trip just as he would have a journey of exploration, Boas focussed on proper preparation and attention to detail, from the position of a distanced observer.

Boas' interest in the problem of art and taste developed from his reading of Lessing's *Laocoön*, a landmark in the literature of the German Enlightenment and the study of aesthetics. In his autobiography, Goethe had written that "one must be a young man" in order "to recognize what effect Lessing's *Laocoon* had upon us. It carried us from the region of poverty-stricken notions to the open country of thought" (in Gay 1973:454; see also Gay 1966:265–73). Boas was the same age as Goethe had been when he reported to Toni that "in school we have just begun to read Laokoon (naturally by Lessing)," adding that "these periods are the most interesting of all that we have" (BPP: FB/TB 9/29/76). Reading Lessing was important to Boas not just because he thereby partook of the legacy of the German Enlightenment, but also because it helped him compensate for what he perceived to be childhood deficiencies. As he wrote Toni, he was trying to develop the ability "to judge good works with taste," a skill which, in his view, he should have acquired with frequent exposure during his childhood, when "the particular qualities of good works would

have been so deeply stamped into our flesh and blood that we, even if unconsciously, would certainly have noted their absence in every inferior work"
(BPP: FB/TB 9/29/76).

Even in music, where the Boas children had better preparation, Franz
stressed the importance of prior experience and methodological preparation
over creative or affective engagement. He played Haydn, Mozart, and Beetho-
ven in four-handed arrangements to gain knowledge of their orchestral pieces:
"The greatest advantage which I have in learning to play the piano lies less in
the fact that I myself can play the things than in the fact that I can understand
them to a certain extent when I hear them played by artists, because I was
previously able to become acquainted with them. For that reason my aim is
not to play everything really beautifully . . . but to be able to understand the
others" (1876–77:15).

Boas' worries about the development of taste and his interest in method and
in rational understanding reflect his problematic relationship to German culture and the ideal of *Bildung*. On the one hand, like many members of the
middle class for whom the classical education of the *Gymnasium* provided entry into an elite, Boas shared the desire to develop correct taste and make
appropriate distinctions in aesthetic matters. But being also "of Hebrew origin," as he identified himself on the first page of his *Curriculum Vitae*, he was
an outsider to the dominant culture. While the inculcation of *Bildung* facilitated the assimilation of Jews in the post-Enlightenment period of Jewish
emancipation, Boas' concern with acquiring aesthetic judgment suggested that
these distinctions did not come naturally to him and were, he thought, absent
from his immediate (familial) environment. He felt himself on the margins of
the world which by virtue of his education he was supposed to enter. The
posture of careful observer he characteristically adopted both manifested and
was the means by which he attempted to resolve this predicament. In this Boas
was much like his contemporaries Erwin Panofsky and Ernst Cassirer, who
emphasized a belief in reason in the development of aesthetic judgment. For
Panofsky this meant understanding a work of art through classical language,
history, and rigorous study; for Cassirer it meant a "rational critique of culture"
in order to control irrationality, not unlike Boas' aims for anthropology as a
science of culture. Boas' dilemmas, therefore, were not idiosyncratically personal, but an expression of cultural conflict translated through individual experience (Mosse 1985:42–53; see also Meyer 1988; Liptzin 1944).

Boas' early intellectual and social development was thus defined by his
struggle for a sense of self as mediated by his family milieu, the enculturation
of the German education system, and by his search for meaning beyond the
boundaries of his immediate surroundings. As an outsider to the dominant
culture, he was ambivalent about his experience as an insider educated at the
elite *Gymnasium*. At the same time, however, he interpreted his development

largely in terms of the priorities of German culture, especially the ideals of science and *Bildung*. The conflicts between these two cultural experiences were the defining moments of Boas' development. But as he came to maturity, the universalism represented by science played an increasingly important role in his life, as a source of personal commitment and as a way to transcend the limits of his immediate social and intellectual world.

Responsible Manhood
and Personal Fulfillment:
The Crisis of Career Choice

Throughout his teens, Boas was plagued by illness, which caused him to miss almost two years of school. According to his sister, Hedwig Lehmann, the illness consisted of severe headaches and nervousness, and no organic cause was ever found (Boas 1876–77: 15, & added note). It does not seem unlikely, however, that his difficulties reflected the conflicts he experienced in thinking about his own future, which played themselves out in the dynamics of his family relationships. On the one hand, there was his businessman father, who thought in terms of the practical considerations of assured income; on the other hand was his idealistic mother, who was more inclined to encourage his drive for personal fulfillment. It was only after an extended period of internal and familial discussion, in the context of Boas' own developing sense of independence, that the issue came to crisis, and was resolved in the decision that his university studies should be devoted to science.

Initially, Boas shared family expectations that he would study medicine, although even early on he hoped to pursue his own interests as well. In the years before he was to graduate from the *Gymnasium*, he thought frequently about his future. Writing to Toni in the summer of 1873, when he was fifteen, he wondered what he would become. "If there is more time, then I can surely think about it. . . . Now, it seems to hover before my eyes that I will then study medicine, and then natural sciences in addition, so that in case of emergency I can turn to medicine. But these are all now castles in the air . . ." (BPP: FB/ TB 8/22/73). As the "awkward" question in life, "What do you want to be?" persisted, Boas was unsure of his own inclinations. Writing to Toni in May 1874, he felt that he wanted to study botany, but feared that if he did so, he would be "forced to become a teacher, which will not be much of a pleasure for me," because he would "have to waste my precious time with dumb school boys and would not distinguish myself above the others." Medicine did not "entice" him "in the least"; of other possibilities—zoology, mineralogy, physics, chemistry—"if anything, the last. If only I could choose, but then no time would remain for botany" (BPP: FB/TB 5/4/74).

The problem was complicated by the pressure of practicality, and his own desire to reach responsible manhood. Along with his parents, Boas worried about how he could earn a living. "If it weren't for the matter of money," as he put it to Toni in the same letter, "everything would already be good, but . . . one must take it into consideration." Anticipating the all-too-quick passage of his youth, he worried that after completing *Gymnasium* at eighteen, with "one year to serve in the military" and four further years to study, he would arrive at the ripe age of twenty-three with no clear, established, and profitable profession, and would "have to get on however others do"— although, he noted, he might "relish teaching once [he] has tried it" (BPP: FB/TB 5/4/74).

His worrying about pragmatic considerations, however, was largely a defensive response to his parents' expectations; what concerned Boas primarily were his efforts to fulfill himself as an individual. Boas had a strong drive for personal independence, which he spoke of in 1876 as a mixture of commitment to his particular interests and faith in his own initiative. Unlike his sister, who was "always equally despondent and [had] no confidence in [her]self," Boas suggested to Toni that "I always (at least mostly, not to exaggerate) remain in good spirits and hopeful for the future, where my strength brings me further, where my wishes shall be met." Even so, he felt he was worse off than she was, because he had "no strength left for things which could make me a well-rounded man," and "on top of that, I have no better prospects for the future, i.e. none, as far as versatility is concerned." Whereas she could "calmly follow the ideal life-calling which [she had] chosen," he had "the secure inner conviction that medicine is absolutely not the right field for me, and that I never can become distinguished in it":

> My main interests find no true nourishment [in medicine], and I will therefore always remain hungry as a doctor, hungry for knowledge, hungry for understanding. And I am sure if I were to complete *my* studies, then I would keep enough time for all sorts of different things, and could still achieve something thoroughly in my subject. You see, if I now nevertheless become a doctor, then what else is left to me? So I trust in my strength which will bring me to my true calling [*Beruf*]. (BPP: FB/TB 10/5/76)

Like his contemporary Max Weber, Boas measured his self-fulfillment in terms of a calling or vocation rather than a mere occupation, especially one for which he felt ill-suited and which stood only for financial security (Weber 1922:129–56; Jameson 1988:33–34). In this context, science took on the sacred and unequivocal responsibility usually attributed to religious faith, an equation which Boas himself had drawn in his own reflections on the relationship between religious and scientific understanding.

What was at stake was nothing less than Boas' sense of himself. He framed the issue to Toni as a quest to prove his freedom of will, recalling the motto of the early sixteenth-century German humanist and crowned poet Ulrich Hutten: "Ich habs gewagt" ("I have dared"). Though small and physically weak, Hutten had run away from home at the age of seventeen to avoid a monastic life and to dedicate himself to fighting tyrannical authority. His ardent nationalism and opposition to papal rule made him a rallying point during Bismarck's *Kulturkampf* of the 1870s (Mosse 1964:163; Craig 1978:78; Garland 1986: 931–32), and his powerful drive to fight injustice made him a perfect hero for young Franz:

> Now I can shout with Ulrich Hutten: "I have dared!" And I have ventured on a daring game because the price would be a missed life or —— You see, I am therefore the architect of my own fortune and so are you and so is everyone else. One must strike while the iron is hot. (BPP: FB/TB 10/5/76)

In the same passage, Boas went on to contrast his own Huttenesque identity with that of a more ambiguous role model, "the Idealist," to whom he compared Toni:

> You suffer from the same malady from which the Idealist, whose memoirs I am reading, suffers. She wants to be a free person and yet still believes that fate is to blame for everything. Mostly, she didn't strike while the iron was hot. (BPP: FB/ TB 10/5/76)

It seems possible that "the Idealist" was Mathilde Franziska Giesler Anneke, a suffragist and educator who, like Boas, was born in Westphalia. Raised a Catholic, married young and soon divorced, Anneke fought for the custody of her child, became a woman's rights activist, and after the Revolution of 1848 emigrated with her second husband to America, where she continued her educational and humanitarian endeavors (Zucker 1950:272–73). Despite her failures of decision, the "Idealist" had thus demonstrated a persistence of values which Boas found powerfully attractive. Several days later, he wrote to Toni that "a quality of the Idealist has struck me":

> her full devotion to the idea and the object to which she directly dedicates her life. She lives and acts for the idea, or rather the ideal (wherefore she is called the idealist!), so that everything that she does she does with respect to the ideal. About what her ideal is she never really speaks directly; she says, at most, [that it is] the unification of the nation into one people which will not be separated into high and low [or rich and poor]. (BPP: FB/TB 10/8/76)

What shone through to Boas was not any particular program or agenda, but the importance of idealism, pure and simple, and the sense that one could frame one's life around a coherent set of goals and principles.

Boas read these memoirs at an opportune time. They seemed to reveal the pattern of his experience and to provide an inspiration for his future as well. Although he did not make the connections explicit, the Idealist's dreams existed side by side with his own; he reviewed her life and commitments as he struggled to define his own future. A few days later, when he explained once again why he had such faith in himself, his words echoed his description of the Idealist's idealism.

> Because for me self-confidence and hope are the same, and you know indeed how willingly one hopes. Because if my strength does not convey to me another calling, then I must go through my life as a doctor, and I am not made for that, even though you don't want to believe it. And therefore I trust my strength, and I will work until I have achieved this goal. You must not believe that I imagine I can attain something without work, I want only to work until I have achieved something. (BPP: FB/TB 10/12/76)

Despite such emotional tribute to his dreams, Boas settled for less than he hoped. Having at this point only eclectic scientific interests, more idealistic than practical, Boas ended his *Curriculum Vitae* with a statement of his desires poignantly measured by familial loyalties. Striking an unenthusiastic compromise, he agreed to study medicine with the possibility of switching later. "So I hope with my whole heart that this desire which determines my whole life will still be fulfilled for me" (1876–77:20).

In the continuing struggle to follow his heart into science, the advice of his uncle, Abraham Jacobi, helped Boas to determine and achieve his goals. Jacobi, an accomplished doctor of pediatric medicine, active in social and political causes, had been married to Franz's mother's sister and emigrated to New York after a period of imprisonment after the Revolution of 1848. As a child, Franz had shared his budding scientific interests with Jacobi, and now he wrote of his joy at passing his exams and his difficulty deciding what to do. Saying he would choose his profession as his uncle advised, Franz added that his promise to study medicine in his *Vita*, despite the fact that his teachers and school director told his father he should study mathematics, was a practical solution only; he planned to switch later (BPP: FB/AJ 2/14/77).

It was Boas' mother, however, who most explicitly enlisted Jacobi's support to enable Franz to pursue a scientific career in the face of his father's opposition. In her own letter to her brother-in-law, she reported that Franz had passed his exam with excellent grades in mathematics, so high, she boasted, that his teacher said he had a "genius for mathematics" and should be a docent and follow a scientific career. She asked for advice about selecting a university and urged encouragement and praise so that Franz's father would not object if he did not want to study medicine. In support of her campaign, she sent a copy of his *Vita*, written in her own hand. "You are the only one who can give us sensible advice," she said later (BFP: SB/AJ 2/15/77, 3/2/77; BPP: FB/TB 2/25/77).

By the beginning of March, 1877, Boas had a sense that he would have his way (BPP: FB/TB 3/4/77). Waiting for his father's return from a business trip in Saxony and Berlin, Boas expected to "besiege Papa once more": "He appears to me much more flexible than previously. I have only one fear, that he

will say, do what you want, but I do not want to assume any responsibility."
The fear that he might be free from his father's imposing will and yet be dependent on him for financial support, gave Franz a helpless, paralytic feeling.
He passed the time reading texts by two authors whose works had done so
much to shape his ambitions: Humboldt's *Cosmos,* which had inspired his
dreams of natural history and exploration; and Goethe's *Faust,* the quintessential work about the pursuit of truth and knowledge (BPP: FB/TB 3/12/77 and
[3/15/77]). He was at once feeding his hunger for scientific knowledge and
laying the groundwork for battle.

Finally, in March of 1877, came the confrontation with his father. In relating the news to Toni, "a brother who floats in seventh heaven" described the
events as a triumph, once again on the model of Ulrich von Hutten:

> I have dared! I may now also carry out my life like Ulrich von Hutten, because I
> have dared to tell Papa that I want to study mathematics and natural sciences. I
> already spoke with Papa several days ago upon his return, but then he told me,
> we have to wait for the news from Uncle Jacobi, and today it came. He writes
> the decision should be left to me, and since Papa said I should decide and doesn't
> want to stand in my way, . . . now the whole responsibility rests on my shoulders,
> and I said I want to study mathematics and natural science. Now the entire
> future lies in my hands and let's hope that I succeed. I have dared! (BPP: FB/TB
> 3/18/77)

If all moved according to schedule, he imagined, he would receive his doctorate in three years, take the state examination, and qualify as a lecturer and
private docent. "Will it be as I think? What secures the future for me only time
will tell. . . . I have no wishes because all my wishes are fulfilled. . . . I can
become what I want . . ." (BPP: FB/TB 3/18/77). By the end of March he had
decided to go to Heidelberg to study mathematics and chemistry and then
elsewhere in the fall for physics (BPP: FB/TB 3/27/77).

The Ambivalence of Belonging and Exclusion in the Life of the *Burschenschaft*

Like many young men of his generation, Boas began his university career by
immersing himself in a communal world of student fellowship and excess. He
did so, however, in a manner which marked the problematic character of his
own identity, poised, in a period of rampant anti-Semitism, between the labels
of Jew and non-Jew. Writing to his parents, he expressed an alienation from
the society of Jewish students (BPM: FB/Family 4/21/77, FB/Mother 4/30/77;
BPP: FB/Parents 5/3/77). But as he wrote a childhood friend, he also scorned
the mainstream culture of "our much praised, glorious German youth, steeped

A studio portrait of Boas' *Burschenschaft* in Bonn, 1878. Boas is standing, beer stein in hand, second from left in the lower left-hand corner. (Courtesy of the American Philosophical Society.)

in vulgarity"; moving "powerfully to the left," he felt that a revolution would be required to change everything. Even so, he wanted to join a *Burschenschaft*, or students' association, because the people in it were the "best," and without joining one would have few friends (BPM: FB/R. Krüer 5/18/77).

After migrating from Heidelberg to Bonn, Boas, over his parents' objections, joined the Allemannen. Because Jews were not yet excluded from the student associations, his new fraternity helped him differentiate himself from the "Jewish society," filled the gap in his social life, provided him with a distinct social standing, and nevertheless allowed him to protest the mainstream "vulgar" student life of nationalism and anti-Semitism which abounded around him (cf. Jarausch 1982). Boas threw himself enthusiastically into the corporate subculture of his association, at one point occupying himself with administrative and official responsibilities (BPP: FB/Parents 2/10/79; Liss 1995). Like others in his group, he also engaged in drinking and duelling, which early on brought a series of *Schmisse*, or scars (cf. Gay 1992). However, the occasions which provoked his defense of honor were not all typical of others in the Allemannen. Familiar with anti-Semitic challenges since his childhood (BPP: FB/TB 10/6/70), Boas engaged in public confrontations on university campuses (BPP: FB/Parents 1/18/81), and later in his student career warned his mother that he was bringing home "this time for the last time again a few cuts, one even on the nose! I hope you will not say too much about it, because with the damned Jew baiters this winter one could not survive without quarrel and fighting" (BPP: FB/Mother 4/6/81). What had begun as an attempt to join the mainstream of student life ended up as a means of self-defense against the exclusive anti-Semitism of that world.

Boas' anger and resistance did not lead, however, to a heightened attachment to his own Jewishness. Instead, he seems to have been aware of his ethnicity only as a result of external designation rather than through any subjective identity. For this reason, his experience contributed to what might seem otherwise a paradoxical orientation: he grew increasingly impatient with prejudice, especially that deriving from generalizations about racial or physical characteristics, while at the same time trying to prove himself as part of the mainstream culture.

Like other students, however, he relished those moments when conventional distinctions were abandoned and he could immerse himself in a larger, undifferentiated fellowship. Writing to his mother from Bonn, he described the Shrove Tuesday festivities: "The uniformed students' association was suspended . . . because we consider ourselves no more as students belonging to the uniformed association, but rather as students and fools, and on Sunday afternoon the festival was opened in which we put on peasants' smocks and peaked caps." Marching to the market, "where all Bonn had assembled," they later gathered in a tavern and "talked and sang until late at night":

> There we sat together among students entirely unknown to us—naturally all in smocks and peaked caps—and drank to brotherhood [*Brüderschaft*], or called each other *Du* [the familiar form of address] anyway. In general, everyone there, every girl, every gentleman [*Herr*], was addressed with *Du*. You have no idea of such a tavern, since it was too wild. (BPP: FB/Mother 3/7/78)

No matter how much the community of the *Burschenschaft* fulfilled a need for closer personal relationships and the suspension of differences, Boas still saw a conflict between his emotionalism and his need for control, on the one hand, and the social realities of Bismarck's Germany that would place him forever on the margins, on the other. His admiration of communal fellowship was always expressed in the voice of an outside observer, and even in his enthusiasm Boas continued to hold up a model of more controlled behavior. He contrasted his Shrove Tuesday excesses, for instance, with a more acceptable rationality. After staying up all night drinking, Franz marched through the streets, was pelted with plaster pellets by the Bonn women's dance club, and drank beer in the morning for so long that he forgot lunch and again stayed up late drinking and dancing. It was a "wanton night," he wrote his mother, "and about it I have a terrible moral hangover." Although he had been "in these days clearly mad," and had "celebrated Shrove Tuesday really more wildly than any one of us," he had now "thank God, again become rational"

(BPP: FB/Mother 3/7/78). These half-hearted expressions of guilt notwith-standing, they demonstrated a more persistent pattern: the opposition of emo-tion to intellect and the need to place unreason under rational control. Al-though a convention of Kantian dualism, these were no mere abstractions for Boas; they were deeply embedded in his increasingly conflicted sense of himself.

Boas' moments of irrational emotionalism were linked to his unfulfilled ro-mantic yearnings, which signified for him both the frustration of his emotional needs and his inability to control himself. At one point he told a friend that he made "sacrifices to Bacchus" because Venus had rejected him (BPM: FB/RK 6/27/77). More generally, he contrasted his intellectual drives with his out-of-control passions, and explained his raucous sociability as a release from in-ner torment. In one letter to his parents, he explained why he did not write more often:

> Sometimes I work intensely and a lot, sometimes a little. In any case, I can reassure you about my state of mind: that I never lose sight of the goal that hovered before me; it hovers before me just as clear and pure as the aim of truth and I want to pursue it just as much as ever. No, dear parents, trust me, such a passion does not pull me into the dirt, but you can not imagine how it robs me of the calm of work. . . . Dear parents, I want to make an effort to control myself as much as possible and to be as reasonable as possible, but it doesn't work, how-ever. Of course I have days when I am half crazy and I can't endure being at home, and I seek the loudest society possible, while on other days, I prefer quietly to retreat into myself. (BPP: FB/Parents 7/10/79; cf. 2/10/79)

But if personal turmoil led him to seek release for irrational impulses, and if the rites of student life offered camaraderie and standing in a close knit social world, his position as a Jew made his honor and status precarious. By the time he finished his degree in 1881, Boas increasingly turned to science as a way to reconcile the unfulfilled promises of his social existence and escape the limi-tations of this social world. Science allowed him to transcend the boundaries which he could not surmount from within the exclusive community of the German university or through the ritualistic acts it encouraged. It was more than a coincidence of the academic calendar that, upon his graduation, he promised his mother he would no longer fight duels: "I am no longer a student and have had, as a matter of fact, enough of it!" (BPP: FB/Parents 7/8/81). The need for community and the desire for authority, status, and honor persisted, but they would have to be achieved instead through science. Through the pursuit of truth and free interchange of ideas, Boas would seek simultaneously to escape the limitations of his world and fulfill the needs that it had created. Science became a channel for his passions, a way to control them and assert his strength in a disciplined way. Increasingly, his energies turned in this direc-tion, and in his studies he worked through the same problems of belonging and exclusion, and expressiveness and control which had always preoccupied him.

From Physics to Geography:
The Interaction of the Organic
and the Inorganic

When Boas first arrived at Heidelberg, his interests were still very broad: "My science has indeed an awfully wide field, and I don't know at all how I shall manage the whole thing in the short college days." Writing to his parents, he listed mathematics, chemistry, and physics—in which he thought he might specialize—among those subjects he was studying. By November, when he was at Bonn, he was taking courses in elasticity theory, geography, integral calculus, heat theory, experimental physics, crystallography, and seminars in mathematics and physics (BPP: FB/Parents 7/4/77, 11/9/77). Eventually, however, this breadth became the source of frustration. As he later wrote his uncle Jacobi,

> I have now, unfortunately, studied 6 semesters, in which I have basically learned only what and how endlessly much there is to learn, and that at first one must be very modest with one's plans, particularly one's working plans. When I went to the university I imagined that I would study in sequence mathematics, physics, chemistry, physiology etc., but when I reached the second semester I saw that I would have enough to do with mathematics and physics. (BPP: FB/[AJ] 3/31/80)

Given the high demands Boas placed upon himself, even this narrower range often wore him out and made him distraught, and, as he had in childhood, he often looked to nature for relief (BPP: FB/Mother 1/21/78, FB/TB 6/2/78, 6/23/78). But while putting aside his books to walk in the countryside might refresh him, it did not help him bring his education under control. That involved what he later called "a compromise" in his university studies: "On account of my intense emotional interest in the phenomena of the world, I studied geography; on account of my intellectual interest, I studied mathematics and physics" (Boas 1938:201). By his fourth semester, Boas had begun to study geography with Theobald Fischer, who soon became a role model for him, even though his main interests were still mathematics and physics. In the spring of 1879, he wrote to his parents telling them that Fischer, who had "only been a private docent for five semesters!" had been appointed as a university professor at Kiel: "I would like it if later I had such success" (BPP: FB/Parents 5/26/79). That fall, he left Bonn to join Fischer at Kiel, planning to take his degree in both geography and physics.

The shift toward geography enabled Boas to pursue his childhood dreams of exploration. Looking ahead, he proclaimed to his Uncle Jacobi that he wanted to "get out into the world" for a few years, in order to "supplement my theoretical knowledge with personal experience. . . ." He had heard that "you North Americans" send out expeditions, especially to the Rockies, and asked if Jacobi could find out about them (BPP: FB/AJ 3/31/80).

Boas' interest in geography was part of a change in outlook which occurred during his university years. Critical to this shift was the Kantian revival of this period, which was compatible with his rigid empiricism and his desire for complete knowledge through an interdisciplinary command of phenomena, but which drew him away from the materialism of his youth. In one of his first letters from Heidelberg, Boas commented on Kuno Fischer, one of the foremost neo-Kantians of the time, whose lectures on aesthetics helped him to articulate "all that I have felt unconsciously but about whose causes I have never reflected . . ." (BPP: FB/Parents 7/4/77). By the time he had received his degree, he spoke not only of a shift in scientific interests, but also in his epistemological standpoint. "The objectives for which I studied changed quite a bit during my university years," he wrote his uncle in 1882.

> At first they were mathematics and physics, but by studying the natural sciences I became aware of other questions which prompted me to take up geography. This subject fascinated me to such an extent that I finally chose it as my major study. The direction of my work and study was, however, strongly influenced by my training in natural sciences, especially physics. I was led to the conviction that the materialistic worldview—for a physicist a very real one—was untenable. This gave me a new point of view and I recognized the importance of studying the interaction between the organic and inorganic, above all the relation between the life of a people and their physical environment. Thus arose my plan to make as my life's work the following investigation: In how far may we consider the phenomena of organic life, especially those of the psychic life, from a mechanistic point of view? And furthermore what conclusions may be drawn from such a consideration? In order to solve such a question I must at least have a general knowledge of physiology, psychology, and sociology, which up to now I do not possess and must acquire. (BPP: FB/[AJ] [4/10/82]; cf. Stocking 1968:138)

The research for Boas' doctoral dissertation marked an important moment in this shift. His thesis, a study of the penetration of light in water, raised unexpected questions about perception and variable cognition. In January, 1881, he wrote home that he was regrouping, after trouble with his equipment and methodology. Consoling himself that "Helmholtz and other people have made similar mistakes," he narrowed his dissertation to "a modest opus" which would examine single photometers in addition "to the investigation on the color of water" and avoid other issues which "would lead me into territory that would take me too far afield." Nonetheless, his difficulties delayed his degree until July and caused repeated frustration and self-doubt. More than purely mechanical or technical problems, the "disagreeable dissertation nuisance" revealed to Boas the limitations of his assumptions and delivered the final blow to his youthful materialism (BPP: FB/Parents 1/8/81, 1/18/81). A half century later, in his "Anthropologist's Credo," Boas revealed just how significant and discomforting this adjustment was. "In preparing my doctor's thesis," he wrote,

I had to use photometric methods to compare intensities of light. This led me to consider the quantitative values of sensations. In the course of my investigation I learned to recognize that there are domains of our experience in which the concepts of quantity, of measures that can be added or subtracted like those with which I was accustomed to operate, are not applicable. (Boas 1938:201)

In marked contrast to the difficulties he encountered in his physical research were the ease and enthusiasm with which he pursued geography. By September 1880 he had arranged to take his exams in January, and in keeping with the current emphasis on natural over man-made divisions, had already prepared "Africa except for political geography, which is insignificant . . ." (BPP: FB/Parents 9/26/80) Postponing his exams on Fischer's advice, he began to plan for further training in cartography at Gotha, the principle center for map-making, and where a position opened up starting in August. "There is now on earth no better geographic institute and no better opportunity to learn than this," he wrote his parents. It would not only provide an "opportunity . . . to learn something properly" and meet people who "could be very useful to me later," but it also permitted him to carry out his military term of service simul-taneously (BPP: FB/Parents 3/27/81, 7/8/81; see also Freeman 1961:44). Al-though in the event Boas apparently did not go to Gotha, his career objectives had clearly shifted, and his desire "to learn something properly" centered no longer on physics but on geography.

Boas' changing priorities were borne out in his exams. Approaching the university with "trembling and horror," suffering "anguish" before the exam and battling amnesia during it, Boas managed to gain enough "equilibrium of temperament" to do quite well. Not, however, before having some difficulty with the physics: "Karsten questioned me first and most unpleasantly and about very particular things. . . . First I was very anxious and could hardly bring a word out of my throat, but afterwards it went very well" (BPP: FB/Father 7/24/81; Kluckhohn & Prufer 1959:8). Fischer's questions gave him less trouble, perhaps because the two had developed a close working relationship. He had previously discussed his work on the "history and criticism of the theory of isotherms" with Fischer, who at his request agreed to give him this topic on the exam (BPP: FB/Parents 7/8/81). During the exam, Fischer also asked him about "depictions of terrain," ocean currents, the geography of is-lands and of New Zealand. He was examined also on "the most important agricultural states of North America and China," including "the conditions of their development, above all geological and climatic conditions, . . . the con-ditions for Siberian cultural development," and "the ethnography of North Asia" (BPP: FB/Father 7/24/81). In the final part of his exams, Benno Erd-mann, a leading neo-Kantian, questioned him on philosophy, including psy-chophysics, logic, and the "development of materialism" (BPP: FB/Father 7/24/81; cf. Stocking 1968:143).

Initially, Boas felt that his epistemological concerns might be explored by

The Boas family, sometime after 1882 (as indicated by the volume of the *American Art Review* prominently displayed upon the living-room table). From left to right: Franz, his mother Sophie, his father Meier, his older sister and confidante Antoinette (Toni), and his younger sister Hedwig (Heti). (Courtesy of the American Philosophical Society.)

the quantitative experimental methods of psychophysics, and in the interim between his graduation and the beginning of his required military service in the fall of 1881, he undertook a series of psychophysical studies, the published results of which he sent to Erdmann (Stocking 1968:137, 143). But although he later reported to his Uncle Jacobi that he had in mind "the exact outline of a book on the subject," for "various practical reasons" he committed himself instead to geography. It was "the science that I have thoroughly learned," and "to obtain a position I must work in my field"—and it also had the further attraction of enabling, indeed requiring, him to fulfill his childhood dreams of travel and exploration. Resisting his parents' encouragement to take the state examination that would qualify him as teacher in a *Gymnasium*, Boas discussed his plans for further research in a series of letters to Jacobi. In addition to a study of isotherms, he had in mind "a larger plan" to "investigate the influence of the configuration of the land on the acquaintance of peoples with their near and far neighborhoods," and to pursue it, he hoped that Jacobi might help him to get a fellowship at the Johns Hopkins University in Baltimore. Although initially he felt that he "did not yet feel competent to undertake trips with valuable scientific results," by April, 1882, he was "studying the dependence of the migration of the present-day Eskimo on the configuration and physical conditions of the land," and by the end of November he was making plans for an expedition to Baffinland. Fortunately, his father had consented to support his studies for one more year, and upon the completion of his military service in October, 1883, Boas left for Berlin to carry on further preparatory studies and to garner support for his expedition plans (BPP: FB/AJ 1/2/82, 4/10/82, 11/26/82, 5/2/83).

Entering the Metropolitan World of German Science: From Berlin to Baffinland

Because Boas conceived his researches as geographical, and exploited contemporary interest in the field to garner support, it is important to keep in mind the current tendencies in geographical studies. The year in which he conceived his Arctic expedition was also the year in which Friedrich Ratzel published his *Anthropogeographie*, which Boas later recalled had given "systematic representation of the ideas which I had then in mind, and which I desired to study in one particular field" (Boas n.d.). The specific "geographical problem" he had selected—"the dependence on the knowledge of the land and the range of wandering of peoples on the configuration of the land," which would lead in turn to a "psychological study about the causes for the limitation of the spreading of peoples"—could easily be glossed as an attempt to solve problems suggested by Ratzel's *Anthropogeographie* (BPP: FB/AJ 5/2/83). It suggests as well the close relationship of geography to the studies he was to make his life's work: ethnology and anthropology.

Soon after Boas arrived in Berlin, he was introduced to a vibrant circle of geographers and anthropologists through whom he received training and sought support for his planned expedition. A week or so after he arrived, Boas met the "noted geographer" Reiss, vice president of the anthropological and geographical societies, who recommended a cartographer from the geographical society to give Boas lessons and invited him to the anthropological society, where he promised to introduce him to Adolf Bastian and Rudolf Virchow, with whom he had already discussed Boas' plans (BPP: FB/Parents 10/20/82).

Although the prospect of these meetings offered the most promising opportunities yet, Boas suffered acutely from the anxiety of youth, inexperience, and social marginality. Terrified at first to call on Reiss, his "heart pounding," Boas had arrived with a "well-prepared speech." But he "hardly had sent in my visiting card, [when] Dr. Reiss appeared in the door and welcomed me as if I were a good old acquaintance." Putting aside his "big speech," Boas was able to "explain to him pleasantly who I was and what I wanted" (BPP: FB/Parents 10/20/82). Prior to the anthropological society meeting, Boas asked his parents to "keep your fingers crossed" as he tried "to inspire Bastian with interest for me" (BPP: FB/Parents 10/20/82). Arriving there, he knew no one, and "felt rather unhappy until, after some time Dr. Reiss appeared, in order to introduce me to the gentlemen" (BPP: FB/Parents 10/24/82). Even with such entree, it was not easy:

> I try very hard in society to be courteous, but you know that it is very hard for me. I hope I shall learn some of this here in Berlin. Even though it is not necessary to control a society, it is, however, most uncomfortable if one is an obviously passive member. (BPM: FB/Parents 11/17/82)

Despite his fears, Boas was able to take advantage of his introduction into a network of scientific men whose interests overlapped his own. His efforts to further his expedition centered on impressing Bastian and Virchow, the leading figures in organized German ethnology and anthropology (Ackerknecht 1953; Koepping 1983). Although Boas was taken aback when Reiss, anticipating his future rather than his immediate interests, introduced him to Bastian "as the Dr. Boas of whom he had already spoken to him, and who is preparing himself for a journey to Northwest America," he did his best to take advantage of the situation. When Bastian "rushed up" with the question, "When do you want to leave?" Boas was "entirely dumbfounded, but considered the question and answered immediately, when I have learned enough!" Boas went on to explain his research plans, and thought Bastian appeared interested, although he "didn't understand the entire relationship of ideas." Reiss continued to introduce Boas around "as a future northwest American" and, when they retired to a tavern after the meeting, introduced him to Virchow, to whom he explained his "plan" as well. Bastian joined them, and after listening again to what Boas had to say, offered his assistance, inviting him to visit him soon at the Berlin Ethnographic Museum. He then authorized Boas to work with "the Eskimo things on hand" and also referred him to the director of the local observatory to learn position-finding, and meteorological and magnetic observations (BPP: FB/Parents 10/24/82). Also with Bastian's encouragement, Boas began measuring skulls with Virchow—who years before had been an associate of his Uncle Jacobi, and who, as cautious empiricist and institutional entrepreneur, became for Boas a scientific role model (BPP: FB/Parents 1/13/83; cf. BPP: FB/Parents 1/21/83; Boas 1902; Ackerknecht 1953:30).

Taking advantage of his newly established connections, Boas was at "great pains to interest the appropriate circles here in the matter," including not only Virchow and Bastian, but also scholars in Bremen and Copenhagen, Scottish whalers, and some New Yorkers who might be interested (BP: FB/AJ 11/26/ 82). He asked his Uncle Jacobi about possible contacts with the American Geographic Society because "its sponsorship is a guarantee of success," and considered applying for a Humboldt and Ritter grant, although it did not materialize (BP: FB/AJ 11/26/82; BPP: FB/Parents 1/13/83; cf. BPP: FB/Parents

1/7/83). In the end, he relied on his own ability to bluff his way, convincing the editor of the *Berliner Tageblatt* to give him 2500 marks in exchange for a series of articles on the expedition. Acknowledging to his parents the bravado of his statements, he declared that the trip would interest many because it would trace the last of the unexplored coastal regions of arctic America and because of the unusual means of the travel. When he "bragged" about his connections, the editors were impressed by the "Wissenschaftlichen Protectoren" he named, and he promised to write a sample piece "as elegant and popular as possible": "I shall begin the essay this afternoon, the Arrival of a Ship at an Eskimo Village—a highly colored account" (BPP: FB/Parents 1/23/83). The additional support of the German Polar Commission made his funds generous enough to pay for a servant to accompany him (BP: FB/AJ 2/8/83).

In the year and a half between his graduation and his departure for Baffinland, Boas had moved beyond the momentary and marginal community of student life to gain a foothold in a metropolitan scientific community of worldwide influence—influence which he was able to mobilize to realize his own scientific ends (not to mention his childhood dreams of exploration and travel). A foothold, however, did not assure a future. Boas might aspire to follow in Fischer's footsteps to the quick achievement of a professorial chair, but that was not an easy goal, especially for a Jew. In 1882, it was by no means certain that he could or would become a permanent member of the German academic scientific community. Late that year, he had reassured his Uncle Jacobi that he had not sought the fellowship at Johns Hopkins "because I thought I would get ahead better there than here." Rather, he wanted "to have the opportunity to continue my studies without being a burden to Papa, and to learn things that I must know as a geographer"—things that were absolutely necessary for the achievement of his scientific goals. His "dearest aim" had always been, "and still is, the achievement of a German professorship." And then, with no more break than a semicolon, he added, "of course I concede that if I had a better chance to achieve an assured existence over there, I would go without hesitation" (BP: FB/AJ 11/26/82).

Science and Cultural Identity in the German Emigré Community of New York City

By the time Boas left for Baffinland, the pull of America had grown much stronger. On a vacation in the Harz Mountains in 1881, he had met and fallen in love with Marie Krackowizer, the American-born daughter of Austrian Forty-Eighters who were part of his Uncle Jacobi's New York circle. Boas' newfound but still secret love for Marie helped give him the inner strength necessary for his daring venture in the Arctic; its success would make it possible to declare his feelings to her (BPP: FB/AJ 5/4/83). Scientific enterprise promised to bring together his professional and his personal life—but in yet another location.

Boas' voyage to Baffinland, and his protracted return to Germany by way of New York, only served to exacerbate the sense of displacement Boas already felt (Liss 1995). His stay among the Eskimo—recounted in letter diaries to Marie—heightened his sense of alienation from the "good society" of contemporary Germany, strengthening his belief in the "relativity of all *cultivation* [*Bildung*] and that the evil as well as a value of a person lies in the cultivation of the heart" (in Cole 1983:33) Distressed by the rising nationalism of Bismarck's Germany, frustrated by the limited opportunities of German academic life (BPP: FB/MK 7/21/85, 7/24/85, 12/12/85, 1/14/86), and anxious to enter married life with Marie Krackowizer—who had been born and brought up, and still lived, in New York City—Boas had major personal and professional choices to make upon his return from Baffinland.

Initially, Boas yielded to the pressure of his parents and his mentor, Theobald Fischer to continue pursuing a scientific career in his homeland. After some months in the United States, he returned to Germany in the spring of 1885, where at Fischer's urging he tried to qualify himself as *Privatdozent* in geography at the University of Berlin, offering as his habilitation thesis the first formulation of his Baffinland researches (a Ratzelian anthropogeographical work which he later described as a "thorough disappointment"). But his appointment was not realized for more than a year, during which he worked again under Bastian at the Berlin Museum, laying plans for the Northwest Coast expedition that would take him back to America in the fall of 1886 (Stocking 1968:151–52).

Torn by conflicting loyalties and goals, Boas weighed the relative advantages of staying in Germany and moving to America. Despite his alienation from German social and academic life, he still identified himself with the strongly institutionalized intellectual power of German science, which on several occasions he contrasted with the unformed and amateurish state of science in America. Writing to Marie from Hamburg soon after his return in 1885, he noted the contrast: "[H]ere there is unified striving and living," but "that is not so in America." He immediately went on, however, to see America as a field of personal scientific opportunity: "[I]f only I could create that [unified striving] there for geography" (BPP: FB/MK 4/10/85). Ironically, what attracted him to America was the chance to realize German scientific goals and the idealistic values he had proclaimed in the crisis of his late adolescence. Writing to his sister Toni after he had travelled to the Northwest Coast in the fall of 1886, Boas hoped that she would

> understand why I would prefer to be in America than in Germany. You say that
> [Felix] Adler's work fascinates you greatly. I am also convinced that one feels

best, when one works for others and that I wish very much to do so in my way. . . . Here I see a broad field open for my activities and I hope I shall have the privilege to work in it. In this respect I am and will remain an incurable idealist—and you and I have our mother to thank for this. (BPM: FB/TB 12/10/86)

Writing to Marie only five days later, Boas said that he wanted to stay in America "to bring scattered efforts into focus scientifically and above all, in my small way, thus to work for the German idealism, which I possess and which is my driving force" (BPM: FB/MK 12/17/86). Although he felt marginal to both worlds, Boas felt he could best pursue his German aims by coming to America. Affirming his commitment to scientific work as self-fulfillment and social duty, he looked to new sources of allegiance and identity, and he found these in New York City among a circle of German emigré reformers, relatives and family friends.

The local community of German immigrants into which Boas integrated himself epitomized the combination of German heritage and universalistic values. At the center of this circle was Marie's father, Ernst Krackowizer, a scientist, physician, and reformer, who even after his death in 1875 served as a model of the cosmopolitan spirit within the community of expatriates. In a memorial address delivered before the New York Academy of Medicine, Abraham Jacobi spoke of his friend and associate from revolutionary Vienna as having been committed to medicine both as "an exact science and a social and humane institution." "Eminently a German," in education and "memories" Krackowizer was at once "universal in his knowledge, cosmopolitan in principle, and national in politics" (Jacobi 1875:46–47; 51–52). More than an abstract set of ideals, Krackowizer's universalism was rooted in the value system of this particular immigrant community of German-Americans, expatriate scientists, social and political activists. When he was still in Baffinland Boas had looked to Krackowizer's humanitarian commitment to justify his own emigration to America (Boas 1883–84: 1/22/84). Visiting Krackowizer's grave at Sing Sing shortly after his arrival in New York, he wrote to Toni wishing that he might have known "that man whom all people preserve in memory," hoping that he might "sometime be worthy of him. How small all selfish efforts seem in comparison to [his] work of sacrifice in the service of mankind" (BPM: FB/TB 10/29/84).

Although he did not settle permanently in New York until 1896, Boas was able from the beginning to make use of his pre-established ties to this circle, which included not only his Uncle Abraham Jacobi, but other well-known and influential figures such as Felix Adler, the leader of the Ethical Culture movement, and Carl Schurz, who had served as Secretary of Interior before playing a leading role in the unsuccessful Liberal Republican movement of 1872. Drawing on the connection between Jacobi and Schurz, Boas met Felix Adler and others who were interested in his work (BPM: FB/MK 5/9/86; cf.

Franz Boas and Marie Krackowizer, at the time of their marriage in New York City in 1887. (Courtesy of the American Philosophical Society.)

FB/TB 12/10/86). Shortly before he left for British Columbia in the fall of 1886, Schurz introduced him to directors of museums, and, on the recommendation of Jacobi, he attended the American Association of the Advancement of Science meetings in Buffalo (BPM: FB/Parents 8/28/86, FB/MK 8/24/86). At a party in his honor after his return from the Northwest Coast, Boas showed off his collection from his recent trip to assembled guests, including Albert Bickmore of the American Museum, the Schurzes, and the Putnams, to whom Jacobi was connected through his wife, the feminist physician Mary Putnam Jacobi (BPM: FB/MK 1/8/87; BPP: FB/Parents 1/28/87; Link 1949).

Through these connections, Boas also met Columbia University psychologist James McKeen Cattell, the editor *Science,* which was the journal of the American Association for the Advancement of Science. Like other academic scientists who had studied in Germany, Cattell recognized the scientific values symbolized by a German doctorate, and he invited Boas to take charge of the magazine's geographical section. Feeling that American science, and New York's in particular, was underdeveloped, Boas seized what seemed an opportunity to establish himself there, and in the spring of 1887, he and Marie were married. Justifying his decision to his parents some months later, he hoped that they would "realize that I have greater opportunity here to accomplish something than in Europe." The very backwardness and unformed character of American science would make it possible for him quickly to establish himself:

> It is possible to be more active [because] in science everything is so far behind in comparison to Europe that a young man, as I am, is able to accomplish much more. And this kind of activity makes me happy. I am beginning to be known as well here as I am on the other side, of course only in my small scientific circle. (BPP: FB/Parents 12/20/87; cf. 12/2/87)

Despite his optimism, Boas' early attempts to establish a secure scientific position for himself were frustrated, at least in part because his vision of an unformed scientific field awaiting the fructifying genius of Germanic science was not appropriate to the realities of the American scientific scene. Writing to his parents after an early attempt to reorganize the long dormant New York–based American Ethnological Society did not bear fruit, he complained that while "there is no lack of Ethnologists here," it seemed "that the 'push' Americans are supposed to have in business is lacking in any other undertaking" (BPP: FB/Parents 12/20/87; cf. 12/2/87). By February of 1888, Boas had resigned from *Science* because he felt it was too much of a "trade journal" (BPP: FB/Parents 12/7/88), and was trying to stimulate interest in a travel journal on the model of successful European enterprises such as the French publication, *La Tour de Monde,* or the German one, *Globus* (BP: FB/Charles Scribner's Sons [2/88], 2/6/88). Unexpectedly, Boas' European standards for scientific endeavor, which he had thought would give him a career advantage, became a source of discontent. For the better part of a decade, until his New York connections facilitated his appointment at Columbia University and the American Museum, he had to accommodate himself to the demands of a series of employers whose scientific goals were frequently at odds with his own scientific vision.

Paradoxically, Boas' early efforts to establish himself in America had the effect of affirming a German identity which, as a Jew in Germany, had been very problematic for him. Frustrated by the resistance he met in American science, he wrote to his parents that "it is strange but the American scholars are of quite a [different] type than ours." Noting that they were "much greater dilettantes" frequently lacking "the fundamentals," he said that "scientifically," he felt "like a German" (BPM: FB/Parents 6/10/88). Politically as well, he felt "very little Americanized," and even turned his anthropological eye homeward with new understanding. Commenting on Toni's harsh judgment of Germans, he wrote that while he too hated nationalism and Bismarck worship, he understood why they existed: "It shows how difficult it is to remain uninfluenced by one's environment" (BPM: FB/TB 11/30/88). When his parents back in Germany worried about his income, he chided them ironically as "the bad Americans who wish only to make money" while he, in America, was still "the idealistic German" (BPM: FB/Parents 2/14/88).

"The Study of Geography," published in *Science* soon after Boas assumed his editorial duties, when he was still optimistic about his entry into American science, was the quintessential statement of the scientific vision he had brought with him from Germany to the United States. As much an expression of his personal enculturative experience as of his prior scientific work and epistemological reflection, it was a juxtaposition rather than a synthesis, simultaneously legitimizing two distinct approaches to "eternal truth": on the one hand, the search for universal, objective scientific laws, valid for all times and all places; on the other hand, a more subjective mode of understanding, closer to art than to physical science, which was expressed in the appreciation of the particularities of historical moment and geographic place. The former would produce "the history of the whole earth," the latter, "that of a single country" (Boas 1887:647) Although both approaches were to inform Boasian cultural anthropology, it was the latter which distinguished it from the evolutionary tendencies Boas encountered during his early anthropological career in the United States (cf. Stocking 1974, 1979).

References Cited

Ackerknecht, E. W. 1953. *Rudolf Virchow: Doctor, Statesman, Anthropologist*. Madison.
BFP. See Manuscript Sources.
Boas, Franz. 1876–77. Curriculum vitae, written as a requirement on completing the Gymnasium. Trans. Helene Boas Yampolsky(?). BPP.
———. 1883–84. Diary of Arctic expedition, 1883–84. BPP.
———. 1887. The study of geography. In Boas 1940:639–47.
———. 1902. Rudolf Virchow's anthropological work. *Science* 16:441–45.
———. 1938. An anthropologist's credo. *The Nation* 147:201–4.
———. 1940. *Race, language and culture*. New York (1982).

————. n.d. Baffinland and the Eskimo. BPP.

Boas, Franziska. 1972. Reminiscences of Franziska Boas. Interview by John Cole (August and September 1972). Trans. Oral History Research Office, Columbia University.

BP. See Manuscript Sources.

BPM. See Manuscript Sources.

BPP. See Manuscript Sources.

Cole, D. 1983. "The value of a person lies in his *Herzensbildung*": Franz Boas' Baffin Island letter-diary, 1883–1884. *HOA* 1:13–52.

Craig, G. A. 1978. *Germany, 1866–1945*. New York.

Freeman, T. W. 1961. *A hundred years of geography*. London.

Garland, H., & M. Garland. 1986. *The Oxford companion to German literature*. 2d ed. Oxford.

Gay, P. 1966. *The Enlightenment: An interpretation*. Vol. 2: *The science of freedom*. New York.

————, ed. 1973. *The Enlightenment: A comprehensive anthology*. New York.

————. 1992. Mensur: Cherished scar. *Yale Review* 80:94–121.

Glick, L. 1982. Types distinct from our own: Franz Boas on Jewish identity and assimilation. *Am. Anth.* 84:545–65.

Jacobi, A. 1875. Biographical sketch of Ernst Krackowizer, M.D. In *In memory of Ernst Krackowizer*, 33–65. New York.

Jameson, F. 1988. The vanishing mediator: or, Max Weber as storyteller. In *The ideologies of theory: Essays 1971–1986*. Vol. 2: *The syntax of history*, 3–34. Minneapolis.

Jarausch, K. 1982. *Students, society, and politics in imperial Germany: The rise of academic illiberalism*. Princeton.

Kluckhohn, C., & O. Prufer. 1959. Influences during the formative years. In *The anthropology of Franz Boas: Essays on the centennial of his birth*, ed. W. Goldschmidt, 4–28. San Francisco.

Koepping, K.-P. 1983. *Adolf Bastian and the psychic unity of mankind: The foundations of anthropology in nineteenth century Germany*. St. Lucia, Queensland.

Lehmann, H. n.d. Reminiscences of Franz Boas. BPP.

Link, E. 1949. Abraham Jacobi and Mary P. Jacobi: Humanitarian physicians. *J. Hist. Med.* 4:382–92.

Liptzin, S. 1944. *Germany's stepchildren*. Philadelphia.

Liss, J. 1995. Patterns of strangeness: Franz Boas, modernism, and the origins of anthropology. In *Prehistories of the future: The primitivist project and the culture of modernism*, ed. E. Barkan and R. Bush. Stanford.

Messer, E. 1986. Franz Boas and Kaufmann Kohler: Anthropology and Reform Judaism. *Jewish Social Studies* 48:127–40.

Meyer, M. A. 1988. *Response to modernity: A history of the reform movement in Judaism*. New York.

Mosse, G. L. 1964. *The crisis of German ideology: Intellectual origins of the Third Reich*. New York.

————. 1985. *German Jews beyond Judaism*. Cincinnati.

Ringer, F. 1969. *The decline of the German mandarins: The German academic community, 1890–1933*. Cambridge.

————. 1979. *Education and society in modern Europe*. Bloomington.
Stocking, G. W., Jr. 1968. From physics to ethnology. In *Race, culture and evolution: Essays in the history of anthropology*, 133–60. New York (1982).
————. 1974. The basic assumptions of Boasian anthropology. In *A Franz Boas reader: The shaping of American anthropology, 1883–1911*, ed. Stocking, 1–19. New York.
————. 1979. Anthropology as *Kulturkampf*: Science and politics in the career of Franz Boas. In *The uses of anthropology*, ed. W. Goldschmidt, 33–50. Washington, D.C.
Weber, M. 1922. Science as a vocation. In *From Max Weber*, ed. H. Gerth & C. Mills, 129–56. New York (1946).
Yampolsky, H. n.d. Reminiscences of Helene Boas Yampolsky. Taken down by Robert Yampolsky. BPP.
Zucker, A. E., ed. 1950. *The forty-eighters: Political refugees of the German revolution of 1848*. New York.

Manuscript Sources

I have drawn on four major collections of Franz Boas' papers which are held by the American Philosophical Society, Philadelphia, Pa., and indicated here by the following abbreviations:

BFP   Boas Family Papers
BP   Boas Papers (available also on microfilm)
BPM   Boas Papers Miscellany: miscellaneous materials and translations
BPP   Boas Personal Papers

THE ETHNOGRAPHIC OBJECT AND THE OBJECT OF ETHNOLOGY IN THE EARLY CAREER OF FRANZ BOAS

IRA JACKNIS

In early 1887, a twenty-nine-year-old, relatively inexperienced anthropologist chose the pages of *Science* to launch an attack on the establishment of American anthropology. Returning from his first field trip to the Northwest Coast, Franz Boas had stopped in at the United States National Museum to study the Eskimo and Northwest Coast exhibits, which had been arranged by curator Otis T. Mason. Criticizing the classification and arrangement of specimens, Boas observed that Mason had juxtaposed objects from diverse cultures on the basis on physical resemblances, arranging them in a putative evolutionary order. Boas argued instead that these appearances were often misleading, insisting that one must first place the artifact in the setting of its generating culture, and, by extension, those of its neighbors, before its true "meaning" could be understood. With this, he shifted the goal of ethnography from the study of discrete objects, in a universal perspective, to a focus on their cultural context, in a local setting (1887c & d).[1]

Over the long run, Boas' critique of Mason established the epistemological grounding for a radically different approach to the study of culture. Ironically, however, Boas' ethnographic work over the next decade and a half did not fulfill the implications of his critique. For the most part, his research resulted

---

Ira Jacknis is Associate Research Anthropologist, Phoebe Hearst Museum of Anthropology, University of California at Berkeley. His professional interests include the art and culture of the Indians of Western North America. He is currently researching the career of Alfred Kroeber and anthropology at the University of California.

1. Studies of this episode include Buettner-Janusch 1957; Stocking 1965:155–57, 1974c; Mark 1980:32–36; Hinsley 1981:98–100; Jacknis 1985:77–83; Gruber 1986:178–79.

in the collection or creation of discrete objects, many of them not very different from those created by the fieldwork of the evolutionary scholars of the
Smithsonian Institution. It was only gradually, and occasionally, that the basis
for a fundamentally different ethnography was, imperfectly, realized. The reasons for this are complex. They reflect Boas' own conceptual and methodological predilections, as well as those of the discipline, and of the institutions that
funded his work. They reflect the limitations of the various techniques in his
ethnographic "tool box"—some of them quite traditional, some more uncon-
ventional, some even experimental (cf. Tomas 1991:76; Jacknis 1984:2–4).
They reflect also the cultural situation and acculturation of the peoples he
studied—in a style that was for the most part quite different than that we have
come to associate with "participant observation." These and other factors affected the various kinds of ethnographic "objects" that he collected and the
way he conceived and manipulated them.

Boas used the tools of Western ethnographic technology to collect or produce an extraordinary array of ethnographic objects. For, in addition to what
might be called first-order tangible objects such as native-made artifacts,
which might be directly collected, there were also second-order ethnographic
objects constituted by the ethnographer as part of the process of ethnographic
interpretation and representation. Thus, in physical anthropology, in addition
to skeletal material, there were plaster casts, measurements, and photographs.
For other ethnographic purposes there were, in a visual mode, maps, drawings,
photographs, and films. In the aural sphere, there were sound recordings and
musical transcriptions; in a verbal medium, there were various kinds of native
texts, informal prose, and ethnographic notes, as well as vocabularies and
grammars for linguistics.

Although Boas, by the standards of the day, was quite reflective about the
nature of such objects and the purposes and methods of their collection and
constitution, he did not reflect systematically upon the various senses in which
he used the term "object" and its cognates. In his debate with Mason, he complained that "in the collections of the national museum, the marked character
of the North-west American tribes is almost lost, because the objects are
scattered . . ." (1887c:62). That same year, in "The Study of Geography," he
insisted that "the whole phenomenon, and not its elements, [was] the object
of the cosmographer's study" (1887a:140). Again, in the Mason debate, he
spoke of "the main object of ethnographical collections" as "the dissemination
of the fact that civilization is not something absolute, but that it is relative . . ."
(1887d:66). To these must be added his usages of the cognate form "objective"—as in "objective unity" (contrasted with "subjective unity") or "objective criticism."

But if his usage reflects at various points an awareness—increasing over
time—of the differing semantic significance of these varying inflections and

phrasings, he did not speculate about the matter systematically, or in the same terms that we might today. Thus there is little evidence of a generalized concept of "objectification," of the process by which disciplines construct their objects and "in the process make themselves" (Kirshenblatt-Gimblett 1991: 387).[2] Nor shall systematic speculation on such matters be undertaken here. But such nuances of signification, in different contexts and points of time, will be implicitly at issue in much of what follows, as we examine the various kinds of ethnographic objects that Boas collected and produced in the field, or caused to be collected or produced by others, over the first two decades of his career. By considering how and why they were created, and the shift in Boas' ethnographic goals in relation to his changing theoretical orientation and the evolving goals of his anthropology, we may cast additional light not only upon Boas' place in the history of ethnography, but offer a more general case study of how ethnographic knowledge is generated, how theory and practice confront each other in the field.

Ethnographic Objects and the Objects of Ethnology in Boas' Major Fieldwork Phase: 1886–1900[3]

Boas' critique of Mason's museum methods came at a critical transitional juncture in his career. Just returned from his first trip to the Northwest Coast, newly married to the daughter of an emigré Austrian, he had decided to settle permanently in the United States, and had taken a job as the geography editor of *Science*. In contrast, Mason, as curator at the United States National Museum, was an important member of the Washington anthropological establishment led by John Wesley Powell, the most powerful figure in American anthropology, who had at his disposal what were then substantial funds for anthropological research; for Boas to confront Mason was a way to define a position for himself and to announce his availability (Hinsley 1981). Confident of the authority of his German scientific training, Boas had a slightly disdainful attitude toward American science, and for a brief time apparently felt that he could quickly establish his own position in American anthropology by volunteering a dose of German methodological and epistemological

2. For recent treatments of the role of objects in culture, see Appadurai 1986; Dominguez 1986; Miller, 1987; Reynolds & Stott 1987; Handler 1988; Bronner 1989; Hedlund 1989; Cruikshank 1992.
3. The extensive literature on Boas' fieldwork and ethnography includes Smith 1959; Codere 1959, 1966; White 1963; Rohner 1966; Harris 1968:250–318; Stocking 1974a:83–127, 1974b, 1974c, 1977, 1986; Cole 1983, 1985; Cole & Muller-Wille 1984; Maud 1982:47–99, 1986, 1989; Krupat 1990; Sanjek 1990:193–203; Murray 1991:100–109.

sophistication. What he had to offer was the distillation—applied to the specific problem of museum arrangement—of the dualistic scientific orientation which underlay all of his later work, and which he had recently articulated in *Science* in the essay on "The Study of Geography." An amalgam of his own early enculturation in the classical German intellectual tradition; his university studies in Helmholtzian physics, post-Humboldtian human geography, and neo-Kantian German philosophy; and his post-graduate attempt through psychophysics and ethnogeography to study the conditions of human knowledge of the external world, this essay postulated an opposition between two methods of knowing the world—methods which in the German tradition were distinguished as those of the *Natur-* and the *Geisteswissenschaften*. On the one hand was the method of the physicist, who was motivated by an "aesthetic" impulse and studied phenomena that had an "objective unity," resolving these into their elements and investigating each separately and comparatively in the hope of establishing or verifying general laws. On the other hand was the method of the cosmographer/historian, motivated by an "affective" impulse, who insisted on the validity of a holistic study of complex phenomena that had a "merely subjective" unity, and whose elements "seem to be connected only in the mind of the observer (1887a:140–41). Although in this essay Boas had insisted on the legitimacy of both approaches, his position in the debate with Mason was clearly an attempt to justify, in the anthropological realm, the priority of the cosmographer against the physicist (Stocking 1968; see also Bunzl, Liss, in this volume).

Over the longer span of Boas' career, there is an evident movement away from physics toward cosmography. But the tension between the aesthetic and the affective modes was never resolved in his own work, and in the immediate aftermath of the debate there was a clear shift back toward the elemental analytic and comparative approach characteristic of evolutionary anthropology (see Bunzl, in this volume). This seems in part to have been a reflection of the sponsorship and the circumstances of his own early fieldwork, which was supported both by Powell's Bureau of American Ethnology and by the Northwest Coast Committee of the British Association for the Advancement of Science, chaired by the British evolutionary anthropologist E. B. Tylor. But aside from any accommodation he may have made to the physicalist theoretical preferences of his evolutionist sponsors, Boas' object-oriented ethnographic method was quite consistent with prevailing research modes, both in anthropological and other forms of inquiry, as well as with certain technical innovations of the period.

By the time of the 1887 debate, Boas had already completed two field expeditions. In carrying out his geographic and ethnographic research in Baffinland from August 1883 to August 1884, he produced an impressive array of methodological objects, including maps (his own and those created by the

Inuit at his request), meteorological observations, tidal measurements, and a collection of natural history and geological specimens. He made drawings and photographs, compiled a census of all the settlements in Cumberland Sound, made physical measurements and musical transcriptions, and took texts in the native language, as well as collecting over one hundred artifacts—ethnographic objects in the more usual material sense (Cole & Muller-Wille 1984; Cole 1983; Liss 1990:125–79; Stocking 1965). Although he would never again use quite so many instruments to create such a broad array of data, a similar multi-media approach would characterize the rest of his fieldwork methodology.

In the fall of 1886, Boas began his Northwest Coast research. Like his Baffinland journey, this trip was self-funded. It was an amazingly productive and comprehensive expedition; he collected primarily linguistic material and folktales, but also gathered artifacts and skeletons. During his first two weeks, he obtained tales and linguistic data—essentially out-of-context—from Tsimshian, Bella Coola, Bella Bella, and Tlingit informants on the coastal steamers or visiting Victoria. His practice was to jot down brief notes which he would laboriously copy out in augmented form in the evenings, forming a cumulative manuscript. Of necessity, he worked with interpreters or with the Chinook Jargon trade language. Much of his work was still dedicated to geographical questions, which were to be partially embodied in an ethnogeographic map of Vancouver Island. For his ethnological survey, an essential problem was to determine the relationship and distribution of ethnic and language groups. On this trip he first encountered the Kwakiutl, who would become the principal subject of his ethnography. In the Kwakiutl village of Nuwitti, Boas carried out a kind of participant observation fieldwork—giving a feast, witnessing dances, sketching their material culture, collecting artifacts, and recording tales (Boas 1969; Codere 1959:63–64).

Between 1888 and 1894, Boas made five trips to British Columbia sponsored by the British Association for the Advancement of Science. Working under the supervision of Canadian philologist Horatio Hale, he was principally preoccupied with survey research (Gruber 1967:18–34). In a series of detailed letters, Hale requested "not so much a minute and special study of any one or two stocks or tribes . . . as a general outline or 'synopsis' of the ethnology of the whole province, which may hereafter be completed by such special studies, in the way of monographs, by yourself or others" (BP: HH/FB 4/30/88). In addition to maps and several small artifact collections, Boas was instructed to get limited vocabularies and brief grammatical sketches. His documentation on these trips consisted primarily of notebooks of verbal material—both native as well as his own—which he incorporated into a series of reports to the British Association Committee (Stocking 1974a:88–106). In 1890 and 1891, his trips received funding from the Bureau of American Ethnology; accordingly, he spent most of his field time not in British Columbia, but with the Salish and Chinook of Oregon and Washington. Along with anatomical measurements, he focused on recording vocabularies and tales (Hymes 1985).

The first four of Boas' British Association fieldtrips were during the summer months, when he was free from academic duties at Clark University. After resigning his position in the faculty revolt of 1892, he worked for two years as chief assistant to Frederic Ward Putnam, the director of Harvard's Peabody Museum, who was in charge of the anthropological exhibits for the World's Columbian Exposition in Chicago. Although Boas did not conduct fieldwork during this period, he collected, directly or through intermediaries, a large body of physical anthropological data. He also worked closely with George Hunt, the son of an English Hudson's Bay Company trader and a high-ranking Tlingit woman, who had grown up among the Kwakiutl, and whom Boas had met in 1886. Boas had commissioned Hunt to bring an artifact collection to the fair, along with a group of Kwakiutl who, as living exhibits, were to perform ceremonials and demonstrate techniques. While Hunt was in Chicago, Boas taught him an orthography that would allow him to transcribe Kwakwala, and in the ensuing years Hunt played a major role in collecting his ethnographic data (Jacknis 1991a).

Although Boas worked briefly for the Field Columbian Museum when the Chicago fair closed, he did not get the permanent position he had hoped for, and for more than a year was without regular employment. In the fall of 1894, he traveled again to British Columbia. The three weeks that he spent during this period observing the winter ceremonials among the Kwakiutl at Fort Rupert marked an important moment in his ethnography, his most sustained period of fieldwork in something approximating the participant observation mode (Boas 1969:176–90).

With his appointment as curator of anthropology at the American Museum of Natural History late in 1895, followed shortly thereafter by a permanent appointment at Columbia University, Boas' institutional position was secured, and he was freer to direct his ethnographic research along his own methodological and theoretical lines. But although he was chief organizer of the Museum's Jesup North Pacific Expedition, it was essentially a continuation, on a much grander scale, of the survey work he had been carrying on under British Association auspices (Jonaitis 1988:154–312; Freed, Freed, & Williamson 1988). This time, however, Boas did not have to do it all himself; the effort involved a multi-person team, spread out over two continents and five years. This scale allowed Boas to combine the more intensive investigation of single cultures with a comparative perspective. Boas himself took to the field during only two seasons—1897 and 1900. In 1897, he visited the Coast Salish, Bella Coola, Haida, and Tsimshian (allowing Hunt to work with the Kwakiutl). In

A Kwakiutl hamatsa dancer, crouching, with other Kwakiutl at the Chicago World's Fair, in the summer of 1893. The standing figure on the left is George Hunt's son, David. (Courtesy of the Peabody Museum, Harvard University; photograph by John H. Grabill, neg. no. N29640.)

1900, however, he worked only with the Kwakiutl, did his last artifact collecting, and began to rely even more heavily on Hunt.

The major phase of Boas' fieldwork came to an end with this last Jesup trip of 1900 (cf. White 1963:9–10). In 1905 he resigned from the American Museum of Natural History, devoting himself to a full-time teaching career at Columbia University (Jacknis 1985). He would not return to the field until 1911, when he carried out some archeological research in Mexico. After that, he did several short periods of fieldwork in the American Southwest between 1919 and 1923, and returned to the Northwest Coast briefly in 1914 and 1923, and for three months in 1930. But with these exceptions, his influence as ethnographer after 1900 was dependent on the work of his students, and the several native ethnographers whom he recruited—most notably, George Hunt (cf. Berman, in this volume).

The Northwest Coast fieldwork of Boas' *fin-de-siècle* major phase was formed by several personal, institutional, and ethnographic influences. Most of his fieldwork came during a personally precarious period when, still a recent immigrant establishing a family, he had yet to achieve permanent employment in a profession which itself was not yet firmly established. On these early trips, Boas was trying to prove himself—to come away with results that would get him a job and professional respect in American anthropology. This compelled him to work with great intensity. Especially on the 1894 trip, when he was unsure if he would be able to return again to the region, he felt under great pressure to produce ethnographic objects which he could later analyze and publish (Cole ms.).

In this context, it is not surprising that Boas should have drawn back from his confrontation with Mason, once Powell had entered the debate with a strong defense of Mason's position, or that for the next few years his ethnographic work should have been largely along lines consistent with the orientations of the institutions funding his research, whether directly or by purchase of the ethnographic objects that it produced. To cover his research expenses, he sold his 1886 artifact collection to the Berlin Ethnographic Museum and to the United States National Museum (Cole 1985:108–9); in subsequent years he sold linguistic manuscripts to the Bureau of Ethnology. In the late nineteenth century, bones, artifacts, and texts were part of the political economy of anthropological research, and, like that of other ethnographers, Boas' ethnography had a petty entrepreneurial aspect (cf. Stocking 1985: 112–14).

The specific needs of the sponsoring institutions varied, of course. Although they had also a significant research function, museums were institutions devoted to the public exhibition of physical objects. During this early work for fairs and museums, Boas was genuinely interested in scientific popularization, devoting serious thought to how ethnographic objects might be presented in a way that would call into question the viewer's taken-for-granted assumptions of the superiority of European culture (Jacknis 1984:32–33, 1985:86–88). Institutions with no exhibitional function, like the British Association Committee or the Bureau of Ethnology, were driven more by research goals, and were more likely to be interested in second order ethnographic objects of the sort here called "methodological"—vocabularies, texts, measurements. In any particular case, the objects of Boas' ethnography (the kinds of objects to which it was directed) were largely a matter of instruction by or negotiation with particular institutional sponsors.

During these early years, Boas was often forced to combine disparate sources of funding in a series of overlapping contracts: in 1890 and 1891 he was supported both by the British Association and the Bureau of Ethnology; his trip in 1894 had triple support from the Association, the United States National Museum, and the American Museum. Joint support by institutions with different collecting agendas naturally demanded a multi-purpose field activity and produced a varied array of ethnographic objects. It was only on his two Jesup trips, after he had secured his own institutional base at the American Museum and Columbia University, that Boas was more or less free to follow his own agenda, and, even then, much of the activity he organized followed along already established lines.

That this was the case reflects the agendas and assumptions of late nineteenth-century anthropology, as they were affected by the ethnographic situation on the Northwest Coast. Among the more relevant elements of this local cultural setting were: an ethnic situation in which racial, linguistic, and cultural groupings did not neatly correlate, and in which cultural relationships reflected complex patterns of cultural diffusion; elaborate family privileges and iconography, which associated extended verbal accounts with artifacts; rank and private ownership, which restricted access to these stories; and severe depopulation and acculturative pressures (such as the Canadian anti-potlatch law), which pressured Boas to create documents of native cultures before they were irrevocably transformed (Codere 1990; Harris 1968:301; Stocking 1974a:84).

In this context (and indeed, generally, in this period), the need for initial survey and mapping was felt with an urgency that is hard to appreciate today. When Boas began his work very little was known about Northwest Coast cultures (Suttles & Jonaitis 1990), and it was he who first described much of what we now take for granted. Boas' goals on the Jesup Expedition, for example, reflected traditional disciplinary concerns with the movement and development of peoples over large spans of space and time (in the broadest sense, the peopling of America), as well as his own interests in tracing local geographic and historical cultural relationships. For despite his criticism of the evolutionary assumption, his own anthropology, too, was diachronically oriented. The past that he sought to reconstruct was a more recent and shorter run past than that of evolutionism, but it was a past that lay behind the experience of European contact, a past whose evidences were widely felt to be rapidly disappearing, a past which for the most part had to be reconstructed rather than directly observed (Burton 1988; Gruber 1970). The challenge for Boas and his collaborators was how to leave a permanent record of a culture that was simultaneously unwritten, changing, and disappearing. The solution was either to collect their tangible artifacts or to create objects out of ephemeral sights, sounds, and words. The objects were conceived of as records for posterity, for science and all mankind, not the native peoples themselves, whom, Boas assumed, would be radically changed if they did not become extinct.

Given these various pressures, it is not surprising that Boas' early fieldwork had a mixed quality. Most of it was survey; little of it could be called "intensive." On these early trips, he moved around constantly, visiting diverse groups—interior and coastal—and investigating disparate research questions regarding physical form, material culture, social custom, language, folklore.

Although his three weeks in Fort Rupert in 1894 were distinctive, it was only in 1900 that he went to one place (the Kwakiutl village in Alert Bay) and stayed for an entire field season (Boas 1969:245–66).

Over the period of its major phase, however, there was an evident shift in the style of Boas' fieldwork, and in the sorts of objects that he collected or created—a shift corresponding to shifts in the objects (as aims) of his ethnological research. As articulated in the Mason debate, the latter had both a historical and a psychological aspect; in fact, these were intimately related, since it was the historical experiences of a people which formed their habits or thought and worldview (1887c:64). If, earlier on, it was historical problems that predominated in Boas' work, his interest over time shifted from the study of historical relationships to the study of their psychological implications, which were more clearly manifest in textual material than in material objects (Jacknis 1985; Stocking 1974c). With this in mind, we will look more closely at two distinctive tendencies in Boas' ethnographic practice, which may be called the "objective" and the "contextual."

"To Collect Certain Things": The Objective Orientation

In an era obsessed with objects—objects as goals of social aspiration, objects as embodiments of achievement, objects as measures of status, objects as products and as the means of knowledge—museums played a central role in the constitution of anthropological knowledge (cf. Bronner 1987, 1989; Orvell 1989:40–72). As Otis T. Mason declared, "[T]he true history of our race is written in things, . . . the material expressions of the human mind" (in Hinsley 1981:89). In similar tones, E. B. Tylor claimed that "to trace the development of civilization and the laws by which it is governed, nothing is so valuable as the possession of material objects" (in Van Keuren 1989:26). Entering anthropology in the midmorning of its "museum age," Boas spent a good bit of his early career in museum settings (Jacknis 1985), and much of his ethnographic work was devoted to collecting objects of various sorts, ranging from the physical remains of human beings to the products of their art and industry to the traces of their thought—from the tangible to the textual. Although the human subjects of the objectifying process were, characteristically, dark-skinned non-European "others," ethnology covered the full array of human variabilities, and Boas did not neglect any of its forms.

At one end of the scale were the bones of native peoples. In October of 1894, Boas sold to the Field Museum for $2,800 a personal collection of 238 items of skeletal material that he had accumulated since 1886, primarily from the Salish and the Kwakiutl (Cole 1985:168–69, 119–121; cf. Jantz et al. 1992). Although Boas had acquired a portion of the bones himself—including some stolen from graves (1969:88), most were gathered for him, largely by James and William Sutton (brothers from the Vancouver Island town of Cowichan). Aside from collecting actual physical remains, Boas created a number of second-order objects to document the physical appearance of the region's natives. Such multiple encoding was a frequent aspect of Boas' methodologically self-conscious anthropological style; all were different ways of creating permanent records of transient bodies, records which could complement or be compared with one another. For instance, in 1897 he systematically attempted to compare the plaster casting and photographic documentation of a set of individuals (Jacknis 1984:20).

Whether collected or created by the researcher, the objects of physical anthropology offered limited insight into the historical or psychological problems central to Boas' ethnological project. In contrast, native artifacts were essential tools. In his debate with Mason, Boas insisted that ethnological collections "were indispensable" for "a study of native art and its development" (1887c: 63); outlining his further collecting plans to E. B. Tylor in 1888, Boas hypothesized that "the arts and industries of the various races [of the Northwest Coast] were originally distinct, . . . but a decisive answer can only be given by collecting systematically. . . . A collection of this character showing the arts and industries of the various tribes and the style peculiar to each would be of great value to the student" (BP: FB/EBT 8/17/88).

It had been artifacts brought back to Berlin by J. A. Jacobsen during the year Boas served under Bastian at the Berlin Ethnographic Museum which had attracted Boas to the Northwest Coast in the first place (1909:307). His sense of the deficiencies of the Jacobsen collection, as well as his need to finance his own research, helped motivate his own most important collecting effort in 1886, when he acquired seventy well-documented Kwakiutl pieces, including "all the ornaments that belong to one dance" (1969:40). In addition to collections Boas made for the Berlin Museum, he also collected artifacts for the United States National Museum, and especially for the American Museum of Natural History, as well as minor collections for other institutions (Jacknis 1989:49–52; Cole 1985:141–64; Jonaitis 1988:122–217, 1991).

His most important early analysis of this material was his classic study of Northwest Coast decorative art (1897a), the first scholarly exposition of the basic principles of Northwest Coast design. Artifacts were also deeply embedded in Boas' other monograph of 1897—a contextual study of Kwakiutl ceremonialism and social organization (1897b). With these and other publications, Franz Boas effectively founded the study of Northwest Coast art and artifact. Among the topics he considered in his writings were materials and techniques, formal analysis, social and ritual context, iconography, and historical development. Apart from his own research in the field, Boas encouraged many students and colleagues, whose work he reviewed in his summary study of *Primitive Art* in 1927.

In addition to the study of native-made objects, Boas was an innovator in several modes of second-order objectification. Although his ultimate questions were historical and psychological, his fundamental empiricism demanded that one start with careful contemporary observations. To this end, he employed both visual and audial recording devices. He used his own camera on his first field trip to the Baffinland Eskimo in 1883–84, and again in 1886. In 1888, 1893, and 1894 he worked with professional photographers; during his last fieldwork in 1930–31, he experimented with a 16-millimeter movie camera (Morris 1994:55–66). His most extensive use of photography came in the fall of 1894, when he was assisted by Oregon C. Hastings, a professional photographer from Victoria, B.C., and by George Hunt. The team took 189 photographs, ranging from architecture and material culture, to portraits (mostly "physical types" for purposes of physical anthropology), to a ceremonial series (including the first images of a Kwakiutl potlatch). As a result, his 1897 monograph was one of the earliest ethnographies to be illustrated by original field photographs (Jacknis 1984:36, 51).

Given his own musical interests, it is not surprising that native music was also a continual focus of Boas' research (Boas 1887b, 1888, 1896b, 1944, cf. also 1897b). In addition to twenty-three songs he transcribed in Baffinland, and another four when Jacobsen's Bella Coola troop visited Berlin in 1886 (Cole 1982:118), his most extensive music research was among the Kwakiutl. He was especially interested in questions of song text, rhythm, and stylistic repertory, and collaborated throughout his career with a number of leading ethnomusicologists (Christensen 1991). He was one of the first ethnologists to make mechanical sound recordings, working with John C. Fillmore at the Chicago fair to record 116 cylinders of Kwakiutl songs. Together with James Teit, Boas himself used the phonograph in 1897 to record Thompson Salish songs, and he continued to use the phonograph on later field trips.

Boas also exploited sound recording for the study of linguistics. In 1902 he instructed his student H. H. St. Clair to use the phonograph to record Comanche speech (Stocking 1974b:460). Summarizing the experiment to the Bureau of Ethnology's W. H. Holmes, he suggested that "the phonograph makes it easy to collect good texts by having old men dictate into the phonograph, and by having younger people repeat the dictation from the phonograph" (BP: FB/ WHH 6/2/03). Again in 1914 he discussed the use of the phonograph for linguistics, with the texts "written out from re-dictation." While he noted that "so far, no extended series has been collected in this manner" (1914:452), his correspondence with Edward Sapir (also a musician-linguist) suggests that he was still interested in the 1920s in the possibilities of improved technology for recording language (BP: FB/ES 10/17/23).

As these passages suggest, over time the privileged place in Boas' ethnographic tool box was given to the collection of texts in the native language. Boas was not the first to collect texts. Among precedents he himself cited were the 1864 Eskimo texts of H. Rink, the Danish explorer (BAE: FB/WHH 9/23/03), and those of several Bureau of Ethnology researchers, including Albert Gatschet, James Mooney, and James Owen Dorsey, whose collaboration with George Bushotter, a Teton Dakota, was a clear precursor for Boas' work with George Hunt (Boas 1914:451–52, 1917:199–200). It was Boas, however, who made the text the methodological center of his ethnography, and "the foundation of all future researches" (in Stocking 1974a:123).

In the beginning, Boas seems to have been attracted by the object-like character of texts as "natural objects"—bounded and enduring entities, and regarded as such by indigenous peoples themselves, of myths, tales, and songs. Such materials had practical ethnographic advantages, insofar as they could often be transcribed out of context on brief survey trips, supplying the necessary material for later analysis. On his first Northwest trip and during the British Association survey, the texts he collected were mostly materials of this sort. They provided the basis of an analysis, culminating in the *Indianische Sagen* of 1895, which was carried on in the "aesthetic" physicalist mode of his postmuseum debate period. Because mythic types and particular motifs were readily transmitted across cultural and even linguistic borders, Boas felt he could employ a quantitative elementaristic approach to trace the geographical relationships of neighboring tribes, and thereby reconstruct the prior history of non-literate peoples (Jacknis 1984:48–49; Stocking 1974a:85–86). During the period of his active fieldwork, however, Boas made a slow, but critical, shift in the kind of verbal objects he produced.

While later texts sent in by Hunt also include some indigenous genres (such as the mourning cry, a kind of family history), they were usually much more discursive and open-ended. To this extent, they were less object-like. From Boas' point of view, however, they were nonetheless object-ive, insofar as they were presumed to exclude the point of view of the European observer and to be "a presentation of the culture as it appears to the Indian himself." If he had "spared no trouble to collect descriptions of customs and beliefs in the language of the Indian," it was "because in these the points that seem important to him are emphasized, and the almost unavoidable distortion contained in the descriptions given by the casual visitor and student is eliminated" (1909:309).

From another point of view, however, such texts retained in an important way an object-like character, insofar as they constituted a body of material that would endure through time and provide the basis for future analysis and interpretation. Without such texts in the native language, Boas maintained, "a control of our results and deeper studies based on material collected by us will be all but impossible":

> Besides this we must furnish in this way the indispensable material for future linguistic studies. What would Indo-European philology be, if we had only grammars made by one or two students and not the live material from which these grammars have been built up, which is, at the same time, the material on which philosophic study of language must be based. . . . As we require a new point of view now, so future times will require new points of view and for these the texts, and ample texts, must be made available. (BP: FB/WHH 7/24/05, in Stocking 1974a:123)

Although texts only achieved a tangibly permanent character as the result of the ethnographer's intervening augmentation of an otherwise unwritten language, Boas regarded them as enduring expressions of the native mind, objects analogous to those preserved in the libraries and other institutional loci of the European humanist tradition. Like the records of early European civilizations, ethnographic texts might survive the passing of the peoples who produced them, constituting, for the vanishing primitive, a permanent archive which could serve as "the foundation of all future researches" (in Stocking 1974a:123, cf. 1977).

Insofar as exigencies of fieldwork and the goal of comprehensiveness allowed, the archives and collections thus created would be full of multiples. Boas felt that the collection of so-called "duplicates" in ethnological museums was "absolutely necessary," because "they are the only means of determining what is characteristic of a tribe, and what is merely incidental" (1887c:63). Textual variants played a similar empirical role: "[W]e now desire that each tale be obtained from several informants and from several places, in order to enable us to gain an impression of its importance in the tribal lore, and to insure the full record of its contents and of its relations to other tales" (1914: 452). Beyond their value as documentation of native cultural diversity, variants would also tend to guard against the inevitably distorting frame of the observer, and against the dangers of "arbitrary" or "premature" classification (Stocking 1974c:2–3).

Although the focus of Boas' ethnography shifted over time from the tangible to the textual, his fieldwork practice in the 1890s remained firmly object-centered. This fact accounts in part for what seem from present perspectives to constitute serious limitations in his ethnography, including the production, study, and representation of objects apart from their "natural" cultural, behavioral, and performative contexts. For instance, much of Boas' analysis of Kwakiutl song was based on the sound recordings he and Fillmore made at the Chicago fair. These were paralleled in the visual mode by the photographs that John Grabill made of Kwakiutl singing and dancing, and which Boas used in his 1897 monograph with the backgrounds retouched away (Jacknis 1984:38–42). And in his 1930 film of the Kwakiutl, Boas was seemingly content to photograph chiefs simulating potlatch oratory during daylight in a front yard (Ruby 1980:8). Although such practices no doubt reflected technological constraints, Boas apparently felt that the cultural rules informing such expressions (which were largely unconscious) would still be expressed in an altered context.

Even so, one cannot help but be struck by the passages in his letters in which the behavioral enactment of those cultural codes was seen as an interruption to their study: "There is a small or large potlatch almost every day which of course interrupts my work. But since I know what to expect, I make use of the time for drawing." A few days later he again complained: "I had a miserable day today. The natives held a big potlatch again. I was unable to get hold of anyone and had to snatch at whatever I could get" (1969:38). Even on his last field trip in 1930, he noted: "My work here is going along so-so. There are many interruptions—dances, dinners, speeches, etc." (1969:296). Boas, however, defined his work not as the observation of potlatches but as the collection of texts. Even his most carefully observed cultural performance, the 1894 Fort Rupert potlatch, seems much less colorful in published versions than in the accounts preserved in his family letters (Maud 1982:60–61; Sanjek 1990:201–2). In general, his letters from the field to his parents and wife contain vivid descriptions of acculturative features like urban Indians and salmon canneries (1969:28, 251–53), topics conspicuously absent from his formal ethnography. Boas carefully observed such aspects of native life, but they did not answer his theoretical questions—the reconstruction of precontact aboriginal history and traditional worldviews.

Although Boas' own ethnography never systematically focussed on cultural behavior in the present, in time the more holistic and contextual ethnographic tendency so strongly manifest in the 1887 debate with Mason came more to the fore in his work, and after World War I it was to become even more prominent in the work of his students (Stocking 1976). But in the most succinct statement of his ethnographic goals he offered in the early period, the object-centered approach was still strongly manifest. In 1903, Boas was called upon to testify before a committee investigating the administration of the Bureau of American Ethnology. Worried that monies allocated for ethnographic research might have gone astray, the committee wanted to know what had happened to the ethnographic objects the funds were intended to purchase. In explaining the disposition of objects produced on jointly funded expeditions, Boas reported that he instructed his students

to collect certain things and to collect with everything they get information in the native language and to obtain grammatical information that is necessary to explain their texts. Consequently the results of their journeys are the following:

they get specimens; they get explanations of the specimens; they get connected
texts that partly refer to the specimens and partly simply to abstract things concerning the people; and they get grammatical information.

In this context, Boas assured the committee that the division of ethnographic spoils between the two funding institutions was quite straightforward:
"[T]he grammatical information material and the texts go to the Bureau, and
the specimens go to the New York Museum" (in Stocking 1977). For present
purposes, however, the point is rather that every*thing* the students brought
back was precisely that: either a tangible object or ethnographic information
embodied as such, a "thing" which could be collected, preserved, and studied.

"The Whole Culture of a Tribe": The Contextual Orientation

During three weeks in the fall of 1894, Boas finally got his chance to do the
kind of intensive fieldwork from which Horatio Hale had dissuaded him.
While much of his field season was a continuation of the survey work funded
by the Bureau and the British Association, his time in the Kwakiutl village at
Fort Rupert was quite different. Here, Boas lived among the Indians, observing
their potlatches and winter ceremonials. Sitting among the guests during the
long evenings, he took shorthand notes which he revised and expanded the
following mornings with George Hunt's assistance (Boas 1969:176–90; see
also Sanjek 1990:201–2; Suttles 1991:117–33). In contrast to his earlier survey work, and most of his later ethography, he focussed here on sequences of
behavior, played out in a limited space and time, and his resulting account was
structured around these observations of cultural practices in process and in
context.

What were the reasons for the special observational quality of the 1894
episode? Undoubtedly, Boas was motivated by two museum commissions to
produce life-group dioramas, one for the American Museum on Kwakiutl domestic crafts (the uses of cedar), and another for the National Museum depict-
ing the dramatic return of the *hamatsa* (or cannibal dancer) initiate (Jacknis
1985:81–82). It seems likely also that the special focus of this visit can be
viewed as an ethnographic response to his exposure to Kwakiutl ceremonialism at the Chicago fair (Jacknis 1991a:101–6). While Boas had seen Kwakiutl ceremonial dancing in October, 1886, he had not previously seen the
hamatsa, which were the most important dances (Maud 1986:47). While
no doubt radically modified in their hot summer performance in a Euro-
American-exhibition context, these vivid and spectacular ceremonial dances
must have made Boas eager to see them on their home ground.

Kwakiutl fool dancers (left to right, Charlie Wilson, Mungo Martin, Peter Pascaro, Spruce Martin, and unidentified man) during the hamatsa ceremony at Fort Rupert, British Columbia, November 30–December 3, 1894. (Courtesy of the American Museum of Natural History; photograph by Oregon C. Hastings, neg. no. 106706.)

This episode brought to the fore the contextualist aspects of Boas' thought which had been so strongly expressed in the museum debate of 1887, but which had been muted in his early fieldwork. Against Mason's decontextualized comparison of elements, Boas had argued that classification based on external appearances was deceiving: because the "character" of an ethnological phenomenon "is not expressed by its appearance, by the state in which it *is*, but by its whole history," the "outward appearance of two phenomena may be identical, yet their immanent qualities may be altogether different" (1887c: 66). And just as these immanent qualities could only be understood in historical context, so also did they require an understanding of the larger contemporary cultural context:

> From a collection of string instruments, flutes, or drums of "savage" tribes and the modern orchestra, we cannot derive any conclusion but that similar means have been applied by all peoples to make music. The character of their music,

which is the only object worth studying, [and] which determines the form of
their instruments, cannot be understood from the single instruments, but requires a complete collection of the single tribe. (1887b:62)

The obverse of the affective holistic approach Boas had inherited from the
romantic tradition was of course a systematically critical attitude toward aesthetic physicalist methodologies based on the comparison of analytically derived elements. To avoid "premature classification" on the basis of "outward
appearances" it was necessary to study the processes that produced apparently
similar phenomena. From the beginning, and increasingly over time—and in
all areas of his anthropology—Boas emphasized the importance of studying
process. In his 1896 essay on "The Limitations of the Comparative Method,"
he insisted that "customs and beliefs themselves" were not "the ultimate objects of research," but that "the object of our investigation is to find the processes by which certain stages of culture have developed" (1896a:276).

Given this context of underlying assumption, it is understandable that Boas'
commitment to the "objective" ethnographic orientation was from the beginning qualified, and critical, and over time became more so. In contrast to the
collections brought back by Smithsonian scientists, which often numbered in
the hundreds and thousands of pieces (Parezo 1987), Boas rarely brought back
as many as one hundred. From his first Northwest Coast fieldwork, he was
sensitive to the limitations of museum specimens and the importance of verbal
and social contexts. One of his major concerns on the 1886 trip was to document Johann Jacobsen's collection in Berlin (Jacknis 1984:5). Despite his use
of visual aids—paintings and photos of museum artifacts—to help elicit information on use and iconography, he found that the Kwakiutl could not tell him
these cultural meanings if they had not owned the pieces in question, if they
did not have the relevant ancestral privileges (1890). In making his own artifact collection among the Kwakiutl, Boas therefore attempted to record the
tale for each mask: "It is the only collection from this place that is reasonably
well labeled" (1969:40). In his letters of instruction to George Hunt, Boas
always impressed upon him the need to obtain the accompanying traditions
("It is better for us to get a few pieces less and the story belonging to each. We
do not want to grab everything, and then not know what the things mean"
(AMNH: FB/GH, 4/14/97; cf. Jacknis 1991b:190). When the United States
National Museum commissioned Boas to prepare an annotated catalogue of its
Northwest Coast collection, he insisted instead on publishing his research
on the ceremonial context of Kwakiutl ritual objects (1897b; Jacknis 1985:
104–5).

Although Boas published an excellent formal analysis of Northwest Coast
art based on museum specimens (1897a), questions of iconography and meaning often remained unclear. Even after he interviewed Charles Edenshaw, "one

of the best artists among the Haida" in 1897 (Boas 1926:275; cf. 1969:223, 225, 229; Jonaitis 1992), he expressed doubt on several points of Edenshaw's interpretation, feeling that he needed "more than this one man, to feel safe" about the identification of objects (1969:228). After further research, he concluded that some ambiguity seemed to be inherent in Northwest Coast art (1927:212).

Boas extended and generalized these insights in his writings on primitive art. In several essays published during his tenure at the American Museum, he demonstrated the disjunction between form and meaning (1903:562). From a consideration of given forms (the triangle, for example) associated with different meanings by different tribes, Boas concluded that forms were generated by technical processes, with meaning later "read into" them:

> [T]he explanation of designs is secondary almost throughout and [is] due to a late association of ideas and forms. . . . The two groups of phenomena—interpretation and style—appear to be independent. . . . Different tribes may interpret the same style by distinct groups of ideas. On the other hand, certain groups of ideas may be spread over tribes whose decorative art follows different styles, so that the same ideas are expressed by different styles of art. (1903:562)

The argument was in fact quite consistent with his general cultural theory of the role of "secondary explanation," and no doubt was a factor in its development (Stocking 1968:221–25).

It was not only artifacts that were problematic ethnographic objects for Boas. He was equally if not more dubious of the utility of archeological and osteological materials. Although during the Jesup Expedition he encouraged Harlan Smith to investigate what there was, local conditions of terrain and climate on the Northwest Coast produced a relative paucity of prehistoric sites, and in general Boas felt that "the natural destruction of material makes it quite impossible to make archaeological collections systematic" (1907:928). In a posthumous evaluation of his archeological work, J. Alden Mason recalled a remark attributed to Boas: "If a man finds a pot, he is an archaeologist; if two, a great archaeologist; three, a renowned archaeologist!" Mason felt that "Boas had little interest in objects per se," but was interested in them only "as they presented, or helped to answer, a problem . . ." (Mason 1943:58).

Boas was equally critical of the utility of bone collecting. After reviewing the major American osteological collections he noted that "investigations of osteological material, particularly on material collected among modern tribes, are always unsatisfactory, in that the identification of the skull, regarding its tribe and sex, often remains doubtful" (1894, in Stocking 1974a:192). And it was often difficult to determine whether the individual was a full- or mixed-blood. Boas concluded that the study of Native American physical anthropology had to rest on measurements from living individuals.

Boas was similarly concerned with complicating factors in the use of the new photographic and phonographic recording devices. Although he never explicitly commented on photography as an ethnographic medium, one can find in his writing evidence that he was uncomfortable with its privileging of a particular moment of inscription (Boas 1927:71–72; cf. Jacknis 1984:44–45). Boas believed that the only reliable ethnographic objects were those which had been repeatedly elicited from as many informants as possible. Many texts and songs could be checked in this way; photographs could not. The photograph was also suspect as an object produced by the observer rather than a native. While photographing in Fort Rupert in 1894, Boas witnessed the dramatic sight of "cannibal" dancers covered with blood, carrying skulls that they licked clean. Yet he was forced to admit, "George [Hunt] was not here, and so I did not know what was going on" (1969:188). And although Boas did instruct George Hunt to take pictures, he did not seem to have realized the possibilities of native photography in conveying a native world of thought and meaning (Jacknis 1992a).

Boas was always concerned about the technical problems of these new recording devices, such as the inability of cameras of his time to take pictures of potlatches in a darkened house. Similarly, early phonographs could not accurately record rhythm, faint notes, or the sounds of the choral singing common on the Northwest Coast, and the wax cylinders could only record for short periods. During his 1893 World's Fair session, Boas overcame this limitation by recording a single song across two cylinders (cf. Shelemay 1991:280). But since Kwakiutl musical performances lasted hours, the effect of technological limits was to create the song as a bounded musical object and unit of ethnomusicological study. Boas clearly realized that there was more to a song performance than the physical sound. Recording Thompson Indians in 1897, he noted the vivid acting and gestures that accompanied the singing he was recording (1969:202–4). While Boas did not comment on the machine's failure to record such gestures, he did contrast mechanical sound recording with musical notation as a method of preservation. Comparing the Kwakiutl songs he had "written down from the singing of the Indians themselves" with those of John C. Fillmore "obtained from phonographic cylinders," which he then corrected by re-eliciting the songs, he concluded that most of the differences were minor (1896b:1). Boas was similarly cautious about the utility of phonograph recording for linguistics. Although he acknowledged its value in recording cadences and its speed in capturing text recitation, he doubted its importance for phonetics. It rendered "only the physical characteristics of the spoken sound, while the primary object we have to investigate is the physiological method of producing the sound," which could only be obtained "by closest observation of the speaker" (FB: FB/WHH 11/3/06).

Even native texts had their limitations for Boas as an ethnographic medium. Compared to artifacts, "texts" in a non-literate culture had a more intangible or conceptual existence. They were manifest only in performance, either for a native audience or as constituted in dialogue by the informant and anthropologist. Boas was aware that the manner of transcription greatly affected the status of the final product. Recording texts verbatim was a slow procedure, making it "difficult for the narrator to employ that freedom of dictation that belongs to the well-told tale, and consequently an unnatural simplicity of syntax prevails in most of the dictated texts." Those created by literate natives were much better: When "a native has once acquired ease in the use of the written language, the stylistic form becomes more natural, and refinements of expression are found that are often lost in slow dictation." But texts produced by natives who had been educated in white schools were also problematic, insofar as their vocabulary, grammar, and phonetics may have been modified. Even if this were not the case, the work of "single individuals [could] not replace the dictated record, because the individual characteristics of the writer become too prominent, and may give a false impression in regard to syntactic and stylistic traits" (1917:200).

However problematic the construction of texts may have seemed to Boas— or may seem today (cf. Berman, below)—it is clear that he came to regard them as the best ethnographic entrée into the thought-world of native peoples. Of the various types of objects he collected, they were the least subject to the distorting processes of objectification, the most likely to carry relevant and accessible aspects of context. This shift was marked in 1905 by Boas' resignation from the American Museum in a dispute over the purposes of museum exhibition. Two decades after entering the artifactual world of American museum anthropology, he left it; two years later, he made it evident why he had done so, in an essay on "Some Principles of Museum Administration." Also published in *Science*, it echoed at many points the argument and the language of his 1887 debate with Mason. Although the essay ranged widely, at its core was Boas' belief in the inadequacy of artifacts as ethnographic sources. Because museum specimens were "primarily incidental expressions of complex mental processes that are themselves the subject of anthropological inquiry," there was an inevitable imbalance between a culture's objects and its concepts. In a passage closely paralleling one he had used in 1887 with reference to a different artifact (a rattle), he argued that objects "used in the daily life of the people" received "their significance only through the thoughts that cluster around them": "a pipe of the North American Indians is not only a curious implement out of which the Indian smokes, but it has a great number of uses and meanings, which can be understood only when viewed from the standpoint of the social and religious life of the people" (1907:928). And if one object could have many meanings, it was also frequently the case "in anthropological collections that a vast field of thought may be expressed by a single object or by no object whatever, because that particular aspect of life may consist of ideas only; for instance, if one tribe uses a great many objects in its religious worship, while among another practically no material objects are used, the religious life of these tribes, which may be equally vigorous, appears quite out of its true proportions in the museum collections" (1907:928). Because any array of objects was necessarily "only an exceedingly fragmentary presentation of the true life of a people," the "psychological as well as the historical relations of cultures, which are the only objects of anthropological inquiry, cannot be expressed by any arrangement based on so small a portion of the manifestations of ethnic life as is presented by specimens" (1907:928).

Two years previously, in a lecture on "Some Philological Aspects of Anthropological Research," Boas made the case for a more systematically holistic ethnography. Implicitly referring to his own early experience, Boas acknowledged that the "general breakdown of native culture, the fewness of numbers of certain tribes, [and] the necessity of rapidly accumulating vanishing material" might "compel the student, much against his will, to adopt methods which he recognizes as inadequate." But the time must come when "collections of traditions obtained by means of the garbled English of interpreters, descriptions of customs not supported by native evidence, [and] records of industries based only on objective [sic] observation of the student, must be considered inadequate." Against this, he posed the "ideal" of an ethnography conducted by students who had taken time "to familiarize themselves sufficiently with native languages to understand directly what the people whom they study speak about, what they think, and what they do," and who would "record the customs and beliefs and traditions of the people in their own words, thus giving us the objective [sic] material which will stand the scrutiny of painstaking investigation" (Boas 1906:183–88). In that shift from "objective" as externally observed to "objective" as culturally constituted was implicit a major reconception of the ethnographic object and the object of ethnology.

The Heritage of Boas' Objectivism:
Delayed Closure, Secondary Reinterpretation,
and Cultural Self-Constitution

In 1900, Franz Boas wrote to fellow collector Charles Newcombe, reporting the completion of his Kwakiutl research in anticipation of a concluding monograph (1909): "I have finished this summer my rather protracted studies on the Kwakiutl" (BCARS: FB/CFN 9/9/00). In fact, however, Boas continued his Kwakiutl researches until his death, carrying on ethnography at a distance with the assistance of George Hunt, along lines established in the 1890s. But although their joint ethnographic venture produced volume after volume of new textual materials, it is the principal irony of Boas' career as ethnographer

Franz Boas demonstrating the pose of the Kwakiutl hamatsa dancer for model makers at the United States National Museum in February, 1895; the life group exhibit of the hamatsa dance subsequently installed in the National Museum. (Courtesy of the National Anthropological Archives, Smithsonian Institution, neg. nos. 8304 and 9539.)

207

that, despite preaching cultural holism to Mason, he never embodied the whole of Kwakiutl culture in a single monograph (cf. White 1963).

The closest approximation to such an ethnography was his report on the 1894 trip during which he had observed the winter ceremonial. Instead of the museum "catalogue" that he was commissioned to produce, Boas wrote the most sustained contextual account of his career. It was divided into two basic parts: a general review of an ideal winter ceremonial, with the cast of dancers and mythological characters, followed by a description of the actual events that he had witnessed, in a narrative organized by date. Each cultural element—mask, song, dance, oration—was first placed in a kind of metaphoric system of equivalences and meanings. Next, Boas rendered aspects of Kwakiutl culture in their metonymic contiguity as he had experienced them, including such circumstantial factors as a confusion in the ceremonial order caused by the three participating subtribes. The observational quality of the field work is underscored by his "action" photographs; the resulting account was his only work to be illustrated with field photographs taken at the same time as the research. By these devices Boas created a kind of "ethnographic present" found nowhere else in his ethnography (1897b:passim).

Despite this striking observational quality, the ethnography was not the recording of an actual speech performance that it purported to be, but a verbal reconstruction (Sanjek 1990:200). Although Boas was a witness and at times a participant, each morning he worked with George Hunt translating and fleshing out his brief notes. After Boas returned to New York, Hunt sent him further Kwakwala texts from the event, which Boas incorporated into his 1897 monograph. These bits of indigenous verbal data—myth, song, or speech—were then integrated into the ethnographer's explanatory prose, producing Boas' most complex, variegated piece of ethnographic writing. It stood alone, however, in the "five foot shelf" of Boas' ethnography, which included over ten thousand pages of texts—at least a third of them collected by George Hunt under Boas' direction (White 1963:21–34; cf. Berman, below).

It has recently been suggested that both in its "urge to include and collect" and in "its deferral" of closure, Boas' work was "characteristic of a certain set of anthropological assumptions"—here, the romantic holism of the Mason debate and the idea of salvage ethnography—"in which the fragmentary and provisional nature of the actual materials, and of the relation to a changing culture is played down, is seen as a temporary transition between the cultural whole which preceded the work (the actual Kwakiutl lifestyle which was disappearing), and the scientific whole which will be reformed at some point in the future (knowledge)" (Murray 1991:109). From this perspective, "the collecting of texts acted as a way of not coming to conclusions, an endless deferral of the generalising or synthesising which would constitute an ethnography" (Murray 1991:101). This delaying of closure was a general characteristic of Boas' work: just as he retreated from formulating general laws, so did he retreat from writing general ethnographic summaries (cf. Stocking 1974c). One might also suggest, however, that cultural wholes, whether represented in the forms of artifact collections or monographs, are not the "natural" phenomena Boas apparently thought they were: "Just as the ethnographic object is the creation of the ethnographer, so, too, are the putative cultural wholes of which they are a part. . . . 'Wholes' are not given but constituted, and often they are hotly contested" (Kirshenblatt-Gimblett 1991:389).

How Boas might have responded to such a postmodern critique one can only speculate. A century ago, however, he persisted in the collection of texts, encouraging his students to follow suit. While they did so, the first generation—still oriented toward a past "ethnographic present"—also devoted much of their effort to "memory ethnography," working with surviving elders. Over the next several decades, however, ethnographic method evolved— along lines consistent with shifts in Boas' interests—toward a more presentoriented, participant observation mode, in which the assumption of cultural holism became even stronger than it had been for Boas (Stocking 1976). And over time, as Boas had hoped, those interlineal Kwakwala texts he produced with George Hunt became a major resource for cultural reanalysis—the very unboundedness of their documentary richness a stimulus to holistic interpretation (Goldman 1975, 1980; Walens 1981; Berman 1991, 1992). More recently, they have been seen, paradoxically, as a precursory manifestation of the boundary-resistances of postmodernism (cf. Krupat 1990). There has even been a new appreciation of the long-neglected artifact collections (Fitzhugh & Crowell 1988; Jonaitis 1991).

Ironically, these objects and texts are also of vital concern to the Kwakiutl themselves. For while Boas hoped that his ethnography would be used by future students, he did not anticipate—though he surely would have welcomed—that they would include members of the very group which he, along with others of his generation, assumed was disappearing. In their U'mista Cultural Centre in Alert Bay, B.C., the Kwakiutl today consult the Kwakwala texts for language instruction, and many Kwakiutl artists study Boas' collections and publications for inspiration (Jacknis 1989; Ames 1992:62). In a manner somewhat different than Boas intended, these ethnographic inscriptions have continued to live in our world—not simply as objects salvaged for the scholarly reconstruction of a cultural past, but as objects serving as resources for a continuing cultural self-constitution.

Acknowledgments

Versions of this paper were presented in 1988 at the annual meeting of the American Anthropological Association in Phoenix, and in 1992 at a symposium on Boas at Barnard College, New York. I am indebted to George Stocking for his insightful comments in the formulation of this essay; in many ways, it is an elaboration on his brief note on "The Aims of Boasian Ethnography" (1977). For assistance in research and writing, I also wish to thank Marlene Dullabaun Block, Thomas Buckley, Douglas Cole, Richard Handler, Curtis Hinsley, Belinda Kaye, Nancy Parezo, Sheila O'Neill, and Peter Welsh.

References Cited

Ames, M. 1992. *Cannibal tours and glass boxes: The anthropology of museums.* Vancouver.
AMNH. See Manuscript Sources.
Appadurai, A., ed. 1986. *The social life of things: Commodities in cultural perspective.* Cambridge.
BAE. See Manuscript Sources.
BCARS. See Manuscript Sources.
Berman, J. 1991. The seals' sleeping cave: The interpretation of Boas' Kwakw'ala texts. Doct. diss., University of Pennsylvania.
———. 1992. Oolachan-woman's robe: Fish, blankets, masks, and meaning in Boas' Kwakw'ala texts. In *On the translation of Native American literature,* ed. B. Swann, 125–62. Smithsonian Essays on Native American Literature. Washington, D.C.
Boas, F. 1887a. The study of geography. *Science* 9:137–41. In Boas 1940: 639–47.
———. 1887b. Poetry and music of some North American tribes. *Science* 9:383–85.
———. 1887c. The occurrence of similar inventions in areas widely apart. In Stocking 1974a:61–63.
———. 1887d. Museums of ethnology and their classification. In Stocking 1974a: 63–67.
———. 1888. On certain songs and dances of the Kwakiutl of British Columbia. *J. Am. Folklore* 1:49–64.
———. 1890. The use of masks and head-ornaments on the Northwest Coast of America. *Internationales Archiv für Ethnographie* 3:7–15.
———. 1895. *Indianische Sagen von der Nord-Pacifischen Kuste Amerikas.* Berlin.
———. 1896a. The limitations of the comparative method of anthropology. In Boas 1940:270–80.
———. 1896b. Songs of the Kwakiutl Indians. *Internationales Archiv für Ethnographie* 9:1–9.
———. 1897a. The decorative art of the Indians of the North Pacific Coast. *Bulletin of the American Museum of Natural History* 9:123–76.
———. 1897b. *The social organization and the secret societies of the Kwakiutl Indians.* Report of the U.S. National Museum 1895:311–738. Washington, D.C.
———. 1903. The decorative art of the North American Indians. *Popular Science Monthly* 63:481–98. In Boas 1940:546–63.
———. 1906. Some philological aspects of anthropological research. In Stocking 1974a:183–88.
———. 1907. Some principles of museum administration. *Science* 25:921–33.
———. 1909. *The Kwakiutl of Vancouver Island.* The Jesup North Pacific Expedition, Memoir of the American Museum of Natural History V. New York.

———. 1914. Mythology and folk-tales of the North American Indians. In Boas 1940: 451–90.

———. 1917. Introduction to the *International Journal of American Linguistics*. In Boas 1940:199–225.

———. 1927. *Primitive art*. Cambridge.

———. 1940. *Race, language, and culture*. New York.

———. 1944. Dance and music in the life of the Northwest Coast Indians of North America. In *The function of dance in human society*, ed. Franziska Boas, 7–18. New York.

———. 1966. *Kwakiutl ethnography*, ed. H. Codere. Chicago.

———. 1969. *The ethnography of Franz Boas: Letters and diaries of Franz Boas written on the Northwest Coast from 1886 to 1931*, ed. R. P. Rohner. Chicago.

BP. See Manuscript Sources.

Bronner, S. J., ed. 1987. *Folklife studies from the gilded age: Object, rite, and custom in Victorian America*. Ann Arbor.

———. 1989. Object lessons: The work of ethnological museums and collections. In *Consuming visions: Accumulation and display of goods in America, 1880–1920*, ed. S. J. Bronner, 217–54. New York.

Buettner-Janusch, J. 1957. Boas and Mason: Particularism versus generalization. *American Anthropologist* 59:318–24.

Burton, J. W. 1988. Shadows at twilight: A note on history and the ethnographic present. *Proceedings of the American Philosophical Society* 132:420–32.

Christensen, D. 1991. Erich M. von Hornbostel, Carl Stumpf, and the institutionalization of comparative musicology. In *Comparative musicology and anthropology of music: Essays on the history of ethnomusicology*, ed. B. Nettl & P. V. Bohlman, 201–9. Chicago.

Codere, H. 1959. The understanding of the Kwakiutl. In *The anthropology of Franz Boas: Essays on the centennial of his birth*, ed. W. Goldschmidt. San Francisco.

———. 1966. Introduction. In *Kwakiutl Ethnography*, ed. H. Codere, xi–xxxii. Chicago.

———. 1990. Kwakiutl: Traditional culture. In *Northwest Coast*, ed. W. Suttles. Vol. 7 of *Handbook of North American Indians*, ed. W. C. Sturtevant, 359–77. Washington, D.C.

Cole, D. 1982. Franz Boas and the Bella Coola in Berlin. *Northwest Anthropological Research Notes* 16(2): 115–24.

———. 1983. "The value of a person lies in his *Herzensbildung*": Franz Boas' Baffin Island letter-diary, 1883–1884. *HOA* 1:13–52.

———. 1985. *Captured heritage: The scramble for Northwest Coast artifacts*. Seattle.

———. Ms. "Ambition, personality, and circumstance: The fin-de-siècle apogee of Franz Boas."

Cole, D., & L. Muller-Wille. 1984. Franz Boas' expedition to Baffin Island, 1883–1884. In "Boas' footsteps: 100 years of Inuit anthropology." *Etudes Inuit Studies* 8(1): 37–63.

Cruikshank, J. 1992. Oral tradition and material culture: Multiplying meanings of 'words' and 'things.' *Anthropology Today* 8(3): 5–9.

Dominguez, V. 1986. The marketing of heritage. *Am. Ethnol.* 13(3): 546–55.

Fitzhugh, W. W., & A. Crowell. 1988. *Crossroads of continents: Cultures of Siberia and Alaska.* Washington, D.C.

Freed, S. A., R. S. Freed, & L. Williamson. 1988. Capitalist philanthropy and Russian revolutionaries: The Jesup North Pacific Expedition (1897–1902). *Am. Anth.* 90(1): 7–24.

Goldman, I. 1975. *The mouth of heaven: An introduction to Kwakiutl religious thought.* New York.

———. 1980. Boas on the Kwakiutl: The ethnographic tradition. In *Theory and practice: Essays presented to Gene Weltfish*, ed. S. Diamond, 331–45. The Hague.

Gruber, J. W. 1967. Horatio Hale and the development of American anthropology. *Proceedings of the American Philosophical Society* 111:1–37.

———. 1970. Ethnographic salvage and the shaping of anthropology. *Am. Anth.* 72: 1289–99.

———. 1986. Archaeology, history, and culture. In *American archaeology, past and future*, ed. D. J. Meltzer, D. D. Fowler, & J. A. Sabloff, 163–86. Washington, D.C.

Handler, R. 1988. *Nationalism and the politics of culture in Quebec.* Madison.

Harris, M. 1968. *The rise of anthropological theory: A history of theories of culture.* New York.

Hedlund, A., ed. 1989. *Perspectives on anthropological collections from the American Southwest: Proceedings of a symposium.* Arizona State University, Anthropological Research Papers 50.

Hinsley, C. M., Jr. 1981. *Savages and scientists: The Smithsonian Institution and the development of American Anthropology, 1846–1910.* Washington, D.C.

Hymes, D. 1985. Language, memory, and selective performance: Cultee's Kathlamet sun's myth as twice-told to Boas. *J. Am. Folklore* 98:391–434.

Jacknis, I. 1984. Franz Boas and photography. *Studies in Visual Communication* 10: 2–60.

———. 1985. Franz Boas and exhibits: On the limitations of the museum method of anthropology. *HOA* 3:75–111.

———. 1989. The storage box of tradition: Museums, anthropologists, and Kwakiutl art, 1881–1981. Doct. diss., University of Chicago (forthcoming, 1997).

———. 1991a. Northwest Coast Indian culture and the World's Columbian Exposition. In *The Spanish borderlands in pan-American perspective*, ed. D. H. Thomas, 91–118. Washington, D.C.

———. 1991b. George Hunt, collector of Indian specimens. In Jonaitis 1991: 177–225.

———. 1992a. George Hunt, Kwakiutl photographer. In *Anthropology and photography, 1860–1920*, ed. E. Edwards, 143–51. New Haven.

———. 1992b. The artist himself: The Salish basketry monograph and the beginnings of a Boasian paradigm. In *The early years of Native American art history: The politics of scholarship and collecting*, ed. J. C. Berlo, 134–61. Seattle.

Jantz, R. L., D. R. Hunt, A. B. Falsetti, & P. J. Key. 1992. Variation among North Amerindians: Analysis of Boas's anthropometric data. *Human Biology* 64(3): 435–61.

Jonaitis, A. 1988. *From the land of the totem poles: The Northwest Coast Indian art collection at the American Museum of Natural History.* New York.

————, ed. 1991. *Chiefly feasts: The enduring Kwakiutl potlatch*. New York.

————. 1992. Franz Boas, John Swanton, and the new Haida sculpture at the American Museum of Natural History. In *The early years of Native American art history: The politics of scholarship and collecting*, ed. J. C. Berlo, 22–61. Seattle.

Kirshenblatt-Gimblett, B. 1991. Objects of ethnography. In *Exhibiting cultures: The poetics and politics of museum display*, ed. I. Karp & S. Lavine, 386–443. Washington, D.C.

Krupat, A. 1990. Irony in anthropology: The work of Franz Boas. In *Modernist anthropology: From fieldwork to text*, ed. M. Manganaro, 133–45. Princeton.

Liss, J. 1990. The cosmopolitan imagination: Franz Boas and the development of American anthropology. Doct. diss., University of California, Berkeley.

Mark, J. 1980. *Four anthropologists: An American science in its early years*. New York.

Mason, J. A. 1943. Franz Boas as an archaeologist. *Mem. Am. Anth. Assn.* 61:58–66.

Maud, R. 1982. A guide to B.C. Indian myth and legend: A short history of myth-collecting and a survey of published texts. Vancouver.

————. 1986. Did Franz Boas witness an act of cannibalism? *J. Hist. Beh. Scis.* 22(1): 45–48.

————. 1989. The Henry Tate-Franz Boas collaboration on Tsimshian mythology. *Am. Ethnol.* 16:158–62.

Miller, D. 1987. *Material culture and mass consumption*. Oxford.

Morris, R. C. 1994. *New worlds from fragments: Film, ethnography, and the representation of Northwest Coast cultures*. Boulder.

Murray, D. 1991. *Forked tongues: Speech, writing, and representation in North American Indian texts*. Bloomington.

Orvell, M. 1989. *The real thing: Imitation and authenticity in American culture, 1880–1940*. Chapel Hill.

Parezo, N. 1987. The formation of ethnographic collections: The Smithsonian Institution in the American Southwest. In *Advances in archaeological theory and method*, 10:1–47.

Reynolds, B., & M. A. Stott, eds. 1987. *Material anthropology: Contemporary approaches to material culture*. Lanham, Md.

Rohner, R. P. 1966. Franz Boas: Ethnographer on the Northwest Coast. In *Pioneers of American anthropology*, ed. J. Helm, 149–222. Seattle.

Ruby, J. 1980. Franz Boas and early camera study of behavior. *The Kinesis Report* 3:6–11, 16.

Sanjek, R. 1990. The secret life of fieldnotes. In *Fieldnotes: The makings of anthropology*, ed. R. Sanjek, 187–270. Ithaca.

Shelemay, K. 1991. Recording technology, the record industry, and ethnomusicological scholarship. In *Comparative musicology and anthropology of music: Essays on the history of ethnomusicology*, ed. B. Nettl & P. V. Bohlman, 277–92. Chicago.

Smith, M. 1959. Boas' 'natural history' approach to field method. In *The anthropology of Franz Boas: Essays on the centennial of his birth*, ed. W. Goldschmidt, 46–60. San Francisco.

Stocking, G. W., Jr. 1965. From physics to ethnology: Franz Boas' Arctic expedition as a problem in the historiography of the behavioral sciences. *J. Hist. Beh. Scis.* 1: 53–66.

————. 1968. *Race, culture, and evolution: Essays in the history of anthropology.* New York.

————, ed. 1974a. *The shaping of American anthropology, 1883–1911: A Franz Boas reader.* New York.

————. 1974b. The Boas plan for the study of American Indian languages. In Stocking 1992: 60–91.

————. 1974c. The basic assumptions of Boasian anthropology. In 1974a: 1–19.

————. 1976. Ideas and institutions in American anthropology: Toward a history of the interwar period. In Stocking 1992: 114–77.

————. 1977. The aims of Boasian ethnography: Creating the materials for traditional humanistic scholarship. *Hist. Anth. Newsl.* 4(2): 4–5.

————. 1985. Philanthropoids and vanishing cultures: Rockefeller funding and the end of the museum era in Anglo-American anthropology. *HOA* 3: 112–45.

————. 1986. Franz Boas and the history of humanistic anthropology. Paper presented at the annual meeting of the American Anthropological Association, Philadelphia.

————. 1992. *The ethnographer's magic and other essays in the history of anthropology.* Madison.

Suttles, W. 1991. Streams of property, armor of wealth: The traditional Kwakiutl potlatch. In Jonaitis 1991: 71–133.

Suttles, W., & A. Jonaitis. 1990. History of research in ethnology. In *Northwest Coast,* ed. W. Suttles. Vol. 7 of *Handbook of North American Indians,* ed. W. C. Sturtevant, 73–87. Washington, D.C.

Tomas, D. 1991. Tools of the trade: The production of ethnographic observations on the Andaman Islands, 1858–1922. *HOA* 7: 75–108.

Van Keuren, D. 1989. Cabinets and culture: Victorian anthropology and the museum context. *J. Hist. Beh. Scis.* 25: 26–39.

Walens, S. 1981. *Feasting with cannibals: An essay on Kwakiutl cosmology.* Princeton.

White, L. 1963. *The ethnography and ethnology of Franz Boas.* Texas Memorial Museum Bulletin 6. Austin.

Manuscript Sources

AMNH   American Museum of Natural History, Department of Anthropology Archives, New York.

BAE   Bureau of American Ethnology Archives, National Anthropological Archives, Smithsonian Institution, Washington, D.C.

BCARS   British Columbia Archives and Record Service, Victoria, Charles F. Newcombe Papers, Add. ms. no. 1077, box 1.

BP   Franz Boas Papers, Professional Correspondence, American Philosophical Society Library, Philadelphia.

"THE CULTURE AS IT APPEARS TO THE INDIAN HIMSELF"

Boas, George Hunt,
and the Methods of Ethnography

JUDITH BERMAN

I had a miserable day today. The natives held a big potlatch again. I was unable to get hold of anyone. . . . It is unfortunate that the work here has to stop for a while.

(Franz Boas 10/12/86, in Rohner 1969:38)

the Head chief nɛgadẕe told this story on the 25 of Dec. last in a feast he gaved to the Kwagoł tribes. nɛgadẕe is the Head chief of the gegɛlgɛm nɛmemot. and in this feast he told this story ontill Every Body nearly went off[f] to sleep. as for me as soon as I see that he was going to neᵉweła or tell his History in a feast. for his son. I took my Book out of my Pocket and I took notes of what he was saying.

(BPC: George Hunt to Boas 1/15/24)

Franz Boas published voluminously on the subject of his primary ethnographic interest, the people he called the "Kwakiutl." [1] Most of his publications, however, are not what is now thought of as traditional ethnography. Nearly four

---

Judith Berman is a Research Associate at the University of Pennsylvania Museum. Her writings on the Boas-Hunt texts include a dissertation, "The Seals' Sleeping Place: The Interpretation of Boas' Kwak'wala Texts," and several articles. Her current research is on the history of the Taant'akwáan (Tongass) division of the Tlingit during the eighteenth and nineteenth centuries.

1. Three terms will be used in this paper in place of Boas' "Kwakiutl": Kwagulh, Kwak'wala, and Kwakwaka'wakw. Strictly speaking, "Kwakiutl," properly Kwagulh or k̓agul, applies only to

thousand pages, about four-fifths of the total, consist of translated but unan-
notated Kwak'wala-language text. Boas filled five volumes exclusively with
myth and other narrative materials (1910, 1935–43; Boas & Hunt 1905,
1906) and another six with ethnographic data on subjects ranging from cooking and hunting methods, to chiefly inheritance and succession, and to prayers, dreams, and the bird-souls of human beings (Boas 1909a, 1921, 1925a,
1930). Still another massive volume of mostly non-narrative texts was in
preparation at the time of Boas' death (HCU XIV). These texts dwarf his
more analytic work in sheer size; they are also the major source of data for his
analysis.

For many anthropologists, the salient characteristic of Boas' texts is how raw
and undigested they appear. Printed in a now-archaic orthography, they are
arranged on the page in a single block that is frequently unbroken even by
paragraphing. Other than the translations, and the occasional introductory
note on provenience, they are almost completely bare of annotation or commentary. All this combines to lend Boas' texts on air of naked, unbiased ethnographic authenticity:

> In a [Boas] text, the ethnographer has acquired data in which he is out of the
> picture. . . . [It has] a high degree of objectivity as ethnographic data [and] . . .
> considerable self-dependence. . . . It is free of hearsay and is of the sort no witness
> is led into giving. (Codere 1966:xiii–xvi)

The very nakedness of the texts—the degree to which the reader feels deprived of the ethnographer's mediating and interpreting presence—as well as
their detail and sheer quantity, has overwhelmed succeeding generations of
North American anthropologists, who have hardly known what to make of
them (cf. Codere 1966:xxx–xxvi). At the worst, the texts have been held up

---

four out of the more than twenty political divisions, or "tribes," as both Boas and Hunt called
them, of a native people of coastal British Columbia, Canada. The four Kwagulh "tribes" once
lived in separate villages, but relocated to the Hudson's Bay Company post of Fort Rupert, near
the northern end of Vancouver Island, shortly after its establishment in 1849. The Kwagulh shared
a language, now called Kwak'wala, and many but not all cultural practices with the other sixteen-
odd tribes. These tribes as a group have been known to anthropology as the "Kwakiutl" or
"Southern Kwakiutl." The native term Kwakw̲a̲ka'wakw, which means "speakers of Kwak'wala,"
will be used here instead. While the tribes counted as belonging the Kwakw̲a̲ka'wakw have
changed over the last century, the term is equivalent to the anthropological taxon "Southern
Kwakiutl" according to usage common today. "Kwakw̲a̲ka'wakw" also has the important virtue of
reducing ambiguity of reference.

Three orthographies are used in this paper for writing Kwak'wala words. Names such as "Kwak-
w̲a̲ka'wakw" are spelled in the orthography of the U'mista Cultural Centre, Alert Bay, B.C. In
quotations taken from Boas or Hunt the words are spelled as they wrote them. Except for the
somewhat Anglicized spelling of "Kwagulh," all other Kwak'wala words are given in an orthography that closely follows that used in Lincoln and Rath (1980), with, however, the addition of
non-phonemic schwa (ə) for ease of reading.

as objects of ridicule, emblematic of everything wrong with Boas' anthropology—a collection of endless ethnographic trivia by someone with no higher vision for anthropology (e.g., Murdock 1960:xiv; Harris 1968:261).

This is a distortion. In collecting and compiling these texts, Boas was motivated by an important theoretical principle. Furthermore, the collection process itself was structured and purposeful—though the structure and purpose are obscured by the texts' published form.

The extent to which Boas' texts have been misunderstood is symbolized by the frontispiece of Boas' posthumously published *Kwakiutl Ethnography* (1966: vi). The photograph shows a text in manuscript and is labelled "Kwakiutl field notes by Franz Boas." The manuscript shows not field notes, but rather a page from a finished composition. The handwriting reproduced there is not Boas', either, but that of a man named George Hunt.

Until recently, most anthropologists knew little of Hunt's central role in Boas' ethnographic research (see, however, White 1963:31–34; Codere 1966: xxviii–xxx; Canizzo 1983; Jacknis 1991; Berman 1991b, 1994). George Hunt was not simply an "informant," not simply Boas' native guide and interpreter in the field. Guided by Boas' mailed instructions, Hunt authored most of the Kwak'wala texts. He was, in a real sense, a partner in an ethnographic collaboration. The collaboration was complex and synergistic, and the respective roles of Boas and Hunt are not obvious from the final published product.

Boas' collaboration with Hunt was important to him not just for the ethnographic data it produced. The crucial point was the *means* by which the data were gathered—i.e., through Hunt. For Boas, his work with Hunt solved a methodological problem that arose directly from his notion of culture: the problem posed by what we now call relativity.

"The Culture as It Appears to the Indian Himself"

Boas' role as a gatherer of ethnographic data has not received the attention that other facets of his intellectual life have done. Existing studies have focussed largely on his field trips, especially those to the North Pacific Coast (White 1963; Codere 1966; Rohner 1969). Commentary on the subject offers widely varying interpretations. Boas was "first of all . . . a fieldworker" (Lowie 1937:131), "engaged in participant observation of Kwakiutl life long before that dubious phrase had been invented" (Codere 1966:xxiv). Alternatively, Boas was an "austere visitor" whose participation in native life was confined to "mingling politely with the natives, . . . always with some discomfort" (Jacobs 1959:127). His goal was "to sit down with a good informant and fill his notebooks—and then go home." Far from acting as a participant observer, "there is no indication whatever . . . that he ever tried to take part in their daily life and become personally acquainted with the people" (White 1963: 49; Rohner & Rohner 1969:xxviii–xxix). A reading of Boas' early letters from the field (Rohner 1969) suggests that the truth lies somewhere between these opposing viewpoints. In what may seem paradoxical to today's anthropologists, however, Boas cannot be assessed as an ethnographer solely on the basis of what he did or did not do "in the field" as a "participant observer." His notion of ethnographic endeavor is very different from the picture of classical anthropological fieldwork. To criticize him, as some have done, for his failure to spend a prolonged period of his life in a native village, or produce a "complete, integrated ethnography" (Rohner & Rohner 1969:xxiii), is to miss altogether what Boas was attempting to accomplish.

Boas did not often use the word "ethnography," relying instead upon such phrases as "descriptions of customs and beliefs" of a people, or the "presentation of the culture" (1909a:309). His views on the methods and goals of ethnographic description, while developing somewhat over time, are nevertheless remarkably consistent in many ways from his first field trips in the 1880s to his mature writings in the teens and twenties. The following analysis presents Boas' thoughts on the practice of ethnography, according to distinctions both implicit and explicit in his writings.

Boas distinguished between two kinds of "descriptions of customs and beliefs." On the one hand, there were raw, unprocessed ethnographic materials direct from the natives of a culture, including native-language texts as well as music and objects of material culture. On the other hand, there were more summarizing, analytic or interpretive "second-hand accounts" (1911a:56) of a culture closer to what we think of as ethnography today. Although both primary and secondary materials contributed to the science of ethnology, Boas felt that the collection and publication of primary materials was absolutely vital, partly because of the accelerating disappearance of many Native American peoples in his time. As Boas wrote William Holmes, "My own published work shows that I let this kind of work take precedence over practically everything else, since it is the foundation of all future researches" (7/24/05, in Stocking 1974:90–91).

Boas envisioned bodies of primary materials as scholarly resources comparable to the historical records and remains of civilizations of the Old World. The fact that many in his own day did not understand the need for primary materials on Native American cultures was evidence of the lack of scholarly rigor in current ethnological practice. "Nobody would expect authoritative accounts of the civilization of China or of Japan," he complained, "from a man who does not speak the languages readily, and who has not mastered their literatures" (1911a:56).

Primary ethnographic materials provided raw linguistic, folkloric, ethnographic, and historical data (Jacobs 1959). The fundamental importance of primary materials, however, lay in *how* this data was present in them. Primary materials embodied what we would now call "the native point of view" (cf. Codere 1966:xiv–xvi). As Boas explained his research among the Kwakwa̲ka'wakw:

> It seemed to me well to make the leading point of view of my discussion, on the one hand an investigation of the historical relations of the tribes to their neighbors, on the other hand a presentation of the culture as it appears to the Indian himself. For this reason I have spared no trouble to collect descriptions of customs and beliefs in the language of the Indian, because in these the points that seem important to him are emphasized, and the almost unavoidable distortion contained in the descriptions given by the casual visitor and student is eliminated. (1909a:309)

The reason that so much of this material consisted of texts of traditional oral literature was that

> the [myths and] tales probably contain all that is interesting to the narrators and . . . in this way a picture of their way of thinking and feeling will appear that renders their ideas as free from the bias of a European observer as is possible. Matters that are self-evident to the Indian and that strike the foreign observer disappear while points of view will be expressed that may be entirely overlooked by the student. (1935:v, cf. 1936:306)

In these passages, Boas juxtaposes the "almost unavoidable distortion" and the "bias" of the outside observer against "all that is interesting" to the natives of a culture, the "points that seem important" to them, the natives' "ideas," their "way of thinking and feeling." These two sets of phrases hold the key to Boas' thinking on texts and the native point of view.

For Boas, ethnology was "the science dealing with the mental phenomena of the life of the peoples of the world." "Manifestations of mental life" included such domains as visual art, narrative, law, social customs, etc. (1911a:59). All such mental phenomena—all of what we would now call cultural phenomena—were shaped by an unconscious classification system that was specific to each culture (1911a:63–66). While Boas' notions of "distortion" and "bias" have received considerable attention in the literature, the theory of classification that underlies them has not—partly, perhaps, because he did not fully develop it himself (cf. Hymes 1970). It was based not on cognitive categorization solely, but on the pairing of what we would now call cognition and affect (1911a:22–23, 65–66).

Boas used the term "ideas" and "interests" to refer to connected but distinct aspects of cultural classification. He did not ever explain precisely how he conceived of these notions, or how they were connected, but he did sketch the general outlines of his thought on the subject. "Ideas" were the cognitive aspect of classification, the cognitive or semantic categories themselves. "Ideas" could include larger-scale cultural categories such as "modest behavior," but also fine-grained categories such as those for different ages and genders of, say, a seal. Boas did not refer to the ethnographer's need to discover how such basic categories of culture are constituted, except in his brief discussion of the semantic structure of lexicon (1911a:21–23). It is clear from his correspondence with George Hunt, however, that this was a matter of at least occasional concern to him, especially in the last decades of his life. For example, he queried Hunt in detail about the Kwakwaka'wakw notion of spiritual "excitement" (Kw. x̌as-):

> When a man goes out and meets a being that makes him a shaman, or when a
> young man is initiated in the winter ceremonial and comes back excited and has
> to be quieted down; how is the idea underlying this? Is his excitement due to the
> fact that he has been with a spirit, and that his mind in this way becomes ex-
> cited; or is there an idea that the spirit is near him and has to be driven away; or
> is the spirit in him and has to be driven out? . . . I should like to know exactly
> how the Indians think of this. (BPC: FB/GH 5/18/27)

"Interests," on the other hand, were, or were closely linked to, the cultural foci of emotion, the "points that seem important" to the native (1909a:309), "the passions of the people" (BPC: FB/GH 12/6/26). An "interest" would appear to be, in part, simply the affectual component of a certain "idea," as for example the feelings of shame or censure connected to the "idea" of immodest behavior (cf. 1911a:66). The term also seems to refer, however, to the amount and quality of cultural attention given a certain category, as for example the strong "interest in rank and privileges" exhibited by Kwakwaka'wakw myths (1966:315). For Boas, "interests" were more fundamental than "ideas"; the semantic structure of the lexicon depended upon, arose from, "the chief interests of a people." That is why the Eskimo, hunters of seals, have many different words for the different ages, genders, and circumstances of seals (1911a:22).

For Boas, cultural classification posed *the* major methodological problem facing ethnographers. The universality of classification, the variation from culture to culture in *how* "interests" and "ideas" were constituted, and especially the largely unconscious nature of classification, made defects in ethnographic recording by outsiders inevitable. Observers experiencing the "manifestations" of another culture inevitably filtered what they saw through their own cultural categories (cf. 1889). For Boas, as a consequence, minimizing what he called "distortion" or "bias" was the key to accurate and authentic ethnographic data.

Primary materials, especially native-language texts, were his means to accomplish this. Only the expressions of the native's own mind—whether myths or masks, dreams or dinner menus—could convey the nature of the native's world without distortion. Primary materials were cultural "manifestations" complete in and of themselves, in which the native's mentality was transparently crystallized, and readily accessible.

In Boas' theory, the visual arts, music, law, and other domains of culture were as much expressions of the mental life of a people as their language and literature. He made important collections of material culture, and he transcribed and made phonograph recordings of native music. Both he and his students, however, exhibited a certain prejudice in favor of texts, of *verbal* expressions of native mentality. In part this was a practical response to the vast ethnographic task Boas saw confronting anthropologists. For cultures on the verge of extinction, often with only one or two elderly members surviving, verbal accounts were all that could be obtained. And since he was interested in the supposedly pure and uncontaminated state of Native American cultures before European influence, it was necessary "to rely upon accounts of customs from former times recorded from the mouths of the older generation" (1911a: 56). Texts also functioned as records explaining other kinds of cultural objects, especially specimens of material culture (in Stocking 1977:4). Finally, only verbal accounts in the native language could properly "convey information relating to the religious and philosophic ideas or to the higher aspects of native art, all of which play so important a part in Indian life" (1911a:55).

Boas mentioned three potential sources of good ethnographic data, of both the primary and secondary kind. These are what we may label the "resident outsider," the "professional anthropologist," and the "native fieldworker." While the discussion that follows isolates them as distinct types, Boas clearly did not see them as mutually exclusive categories, and the men and women who were his students, protégés, and correspondents combined the types in various ways.

The first source of good data was the observer who had lived for a long time in close proximity with the natives of a culture, "who [had] command of the language, and who [was] on terms of intimate friendship with the natives." Such an observer did not have to have professional training. Boas suggested that, in fact, a "general review of our ethnographic literature shows clearly how much better is the information obtained by [such] observers" than that obtained by more scholarly types who had to work "through the medium of interpreters" (1911a:57). Whenever Boas encountered such knowledgeable laypersons, he encouraged them to write down their observations, as extracts from his letters from the field demonstrate:[2]

There was also a Mr. Clayton, a nice man whom I had met up there. He has many interests and understands Bella Coola well, having lived among them for a long time. I talked to him so much that he promised to write down stories during his free time in the winter and send me copies. (10/26/86, in Rohner 1969:48)

2. His early field trips on the North Pacific Coast, however, seem to have given him a prejudice against missionaries and he subsequently disregarded their ethnographic endeavors (Stocking 1974:68–69).

> I have obtained the address of a missionary in the interior from Good and have
> asked him for notes on the grammar of the language. . . . I have asked Bishop
> Ridley for a sketch of the Tsimshian, a certain Collins for one of the Haida, a
> Mr. Small for [illegible], and Hall for translations from the Kwakiutl. I hope very
> much that they will honor my requests. . . . (12/4/86, in Rohner 1969:70–71)

Not all such attempts bore fruit. Of those people mentioned above, only
Hall responded to his urgings, publishing a Kwak'wala grammar that failed to
impress Boas (Hall 1889; Boas 1911b:428). Boas' greatest success in this line
was with James Teit of Spences Bridge, B.C., who ended up publishing extensively on various Salishan groups, most notably the Thompson (Teit 1898,
1900, 1906, 1909, 1912; in Boas 1917a). Teit was the ideal resident outsider,
who had married an Indian woman and settled among her people, and who
was "fully conversant in the language of the Thompson Indians" (Boas 1900;
9/21/94, in Rohner 1969:139).

A second, and not necessarily superior, means of acquiring ethnographic
data was the labor of the professionally trained anthropologist. In most cases,
professional anthropologists could be only "casual visitors" (1909a:309) to a
community, and their data ran the risk of containing more distortion than that
of lay ethnographers who had lived for many years in friendship among natives. In Boas' time, too, when many native North Americans spoke no English, professional anthropologists faced a serious language barrier.

> [T]he number of trained investigators is very small, and the number of American
> languages that are mutually unintelligible exceedingly large. . . . Our investigat-
> ing ethnologists are also denied opportunity to spend long continuous periods
> with any particular tribe, so that the practical difficulties in the way of acquiring
> languages are almost insuperable. . . . [W]e must insist that a command of the
> language is an indispensable means of obtaining accurate and thorough knowl-
> edge, because much information can be gained by listening to conversations of
> the natives and by taking part in their daily life, which, to the observer who has
> no command of the language, will remain entirely inaccessible. [Yet] it must be
> admitted that this ideal aim is, under present conditions, entirely beyond our
> reach. (Boas 1911a:56)

Boas therefore recommended "a theoretical knowledge of native languages"
that would enable ethnographers "to collect at least a part of the information
that could be best obtained by a practical knowledge of the language" (1911a:
56). An anthropologist capable of at least writing down and reading back
utterances in the native language, and of quickly grasping the general significance of the utterances, was in a position to obtain much information otherwise inaccessible. Although this method was entirely "a makeshift," it was still
better than working without any knowledge of the language at all. By this
means the anthropologist could get information firsthand, without having to
employ an interpreter, "who may mislead him." The range of subjects that
could be covered was far greater, because this method avoided the linguistic

limitations of the interpreter, or of the trade language. "[U]nder present conditions," Boas concluded, professional anthropologists were "more or less compelled to rely upon an extended series of texts as the safest means of obtaining information from the Indians" (1911a:57).

This prescription for ethnographic fieldwork describes Boas' own field methods. Gifted with a fine ear and an almost astonishing ease of acquiring the grammatical and phonological rudiments of American languages, so very different from Indo-European languages, he often passed from complete ignorance of a language to collecting texts in it in the space of a day or two. For example, on his 1886 field trip to the North Pacific, he spent two weeks at the Kwakwaka'wakw village of Newiti (i.e., X̱wamdasbi') off northern Vancouver Island. Using Chinook Jargon as a contact language (which he apparently had begun learning only two weeks before), he obtained a small body of Kwak'wala texts. He had no translations for these texts, and had only a general idea of their content, but already his transcriptions were sufficiently competent that when he pulled them out in another village, he was able to report that "the Indians always understand when I read to them" (10/23/86, in Rohner 1969: 45–46). He apparently found this method so useful that for the rest of his life he was ready to recommend it to every fieldworker, whether or not that person shared his linguistic abilities.

Boas was not, however, without reservation about texts taken down in this manner. Anticipating a later criticism of his method, he pointed out that the slowness of dictation often brought forth unnatural diction and syntax (1917a: 200). Further, text collectors, including himself, were guilty of bias toward traditional narratives. While these narratives had considerable value from an ethnographic point of view (1935:v), they often differed substantially from other kinds of speech in both style and vocabulary. "[W]e have hardly any records of daily occurrences, everyday conversation, descriptions of industries, customs, and the like" (1917a:200–201).

The work of resident outsiders and professional anthropologists, while important, nevertheless did not produce the most authentic ethnographic data. The third, and most valuable, source of ethnographic information was the native speaking for himself.

> The best material we possess is perhaps contained in the naïve outpourings of the Eskimo, which they write and print themselves, and distribute as a newspaper, intended to inform the people of all the events that are of interest. These used to contain much mythological matter and much that related to the mode of life of the people. . . . Some older records on the Iroquois, written by prominent members of the tribe, also deserve attention; and among the most recent literature the descriptions of the Sauk and Fox by Dr. William Jones [who was part Fox] are remarkable. . . . (1911a:57–58; cf. 1917a:200)

As the above quotation suggests, ethnographic information authored by natives of a culture could range from "naïve outpourings" of the untutored, intended only for consumption by other members of the culture, to the work of professionally trained Ph.D.'s. Mastery of the native language was crucial, although the data did not have to take the form of text. Although Boas did not address the issue, in this third category of fieldworker, the distinction between what we have been calling primary and secondary materials could well become blurred. Depending upon the form it took, a description of the culture written by a native might be a pure "manifestation" of native "mental life," or it might be some kind of very superior "second-hand account" that expressed in part the native point of view, and in part, because written for members of another culture, the interests and ideas of that culture.

Boas was not content to rely upon writings that natives generated for their own consumption, or the occasional work written by natives in English for a larger public. As in the case of resident outsiders, he deliberately sought out Indians who were willing to produce, or collect, ethnographic data. George Hunt is only the best-known and most productive of the native North Americans with whom Boas worked in this fashion. Boas seems to have enlisted any Indian with the requisite native-language ability and literacy skills whom he could interest in the task. He had already begun scouting for such persons on his first trips to the North Pacific: in 1886, for example, he met a young girl from Bella Bella, whom he taught to take down folktales in Heiltsuk (10/26/86, in Rohner 1969:48; BPC: FB/GH 3/13/17).

As with Boas' recruitment of resident outsiders, only some of these contacts resulted in substantial ethnographic endeavor. Boas employed the Tsimshian Henry Tate much as he did Hunt, mailing questions and paying by the page for his Tsimshian-language replies. For twelve years until his death in 1914, Tate transmitted oral-literary and ethnographic texts, which Boas published as *Tsimshian Texts, New Series* (1912; BPC: FB/HT 3/7/06, W. Tate/FB 5/6/14; Maud 1982:96–99, 1989, 1993). Boas' collaboration with William Beynon, also of Tsimshian heritage, produced an even larger corpus of texts, but few of these have been published (BPC: WB/FB 10/7/35 ff., FB/WB 4/14/41; Tsimshian Chiefs 1992; see Halpin 1978). Boas also worked briefly with Louis Shotridge, a Tlingit from Klukwan, who had been hired by G. B. Gordon to collect and curate Tlingit materials for the University of Pennsylvania Museum. Gordon arranged for Shotridge to study with Boas so that Shotridge could learn to write Tlingit (UPM: GG/FB 10/17/14, GG/LS 11/19/14, FB/GG 10/20/14, 11/23/14; Milburn 1986). The result was Boas' *Grammatical Notes on the Language of the Tlingit Indians* (1917b), which also contains a text composed by Shotridge.[3]

3. Shotridge himself published a number of articles based on his knowledge of Tlingit culture and history and on field research (1917, 1919a, b, & c, 1921, 1928, 1929; Shotridge & Shotridge 1913).

Franz Boas with George Hunt and his family at Fort Rupert, British Columbia, in 1894. (Courtesy of the American Philosophical Society; photograph by Oregon C. Hastings.)

Other native fieldworkers received more substantial professional training from Boas. One of Boas' first Ph.D.'s, William Jones, part Fox Indian, authored several major works, including *Fox Texts* (1907), *Kickapoo Tales* (1915), *Ojibwa Texts* (1917), and *Ethnography of the Fox Indians* (1939). All but the first were published posthumously; in 1909 Jones was killed by hostile Ilongots in the Philippines, where lack of funding had forced him to accept an appointment (Fisher 1939; Boas 1909b). Another of Boas' Indian students was Archie Phinney, a full-blooded Nez Perce who also died young, a little more than a year after publishing a text volume (1934). Mention must also be made of Ella Deloria, an Oglala Lakota, who worked at Columbia University and in the field with Boas and Ruth Benedict for fourteen years. Among her other publications, Deloria produced a text volume (1932), and, with Boas, a grammar (1939).

The relationships of these fieldworkers to the communities they studied, and the degree to which Boas supervised or collaborated in their work, varied considerably. What they shared was their common labor in the service of Boas' quest for the most authentic ethnographic materials. This quest was not, however, without its ambiguities. Although Boas called bodies of texts presentations of "the culture as it appears to the Indian himself" (1909a:309), his collaboration with George Hunt shows that, there, at least, the reality was rather more complicated. A closer look at how the Boas-Hunt texts were produced reveals that Boas was rarely "out of the picture," as Codere asserted, and that the "objectivity" and "self-dependence" she found in the texts are less than might at first appear (1966:xiii). Boas' relativism, as practiced, was fraught with tensions and paradoxes that arose partly from his specific methodology, but also, more fundamentally, from his underlying goals.

"It Is Well if I Live like One of You"

Boas held up the mentality manifested in Hunt's texts as representative in some way of the Kwakwaka'wakw, calling the text volumes *Kwakiutl* texts, *Kwakiutl* tales, *Kwakiutl* ethnology. George Hunt was not Kwakwaka'wakw, however. His father was a Hudson's Bay Company employee from Dorsetshire, England (Healey n.d.:19). His mother was a high-ranking Gaanax.ádi clanswoman from the Taant'akwáan (Tongass) division of the Tlingit (Barbeau 1950:651–54). By the reckoning of the matrilineal Tlingit, Hunt was a full member of the Raven House of the Taant'akwáan Gaanax.ádi (Olson 1967: 46, 87; ROP:VII). Hunt was indeed born at the Hudson's Bay post of Fort Rupert, British Columbia, in 1854, three years after the four Kwagulh divisions of the Kwakwaka'wakw had established a new village there (BPC: GH/FB 4/7/16, 1/16/19; Boas 1921:973–77). But he grew up at the Fort, and not, strictly speaking, among the Kwagulh. Furthermore, Hunt had plenty of contact with other Tlingit in his childhood and youth, in Fort Rupert and especially in Fort Simpson in the north, where his father was stationed from 1868 to 1871 (BPC: GH/FB 8/2/20; Barbeau 1950:654–55; Judd, Simonsen, & Scopick 1989:50). Hunt's first language was evidently Tlingit, rather than English or Kwak'wala; his Kwak'wala transcriptions have a noticeable Tlingit accent, and are not without the occasional grammatical error (see Berman 1994).

Hunt was an outsider in the Kwagulh community at Fort Rupert. He nevertheless had unique opportunities to observe the inner workings of Kwakwaka'wakw society from childhood. Because his birth was said to have brought peace between the Kwagulh and the Taant'aḵwáan, the elderly chiefs began inviting him to their exclusive gatherings once he reached nine years of age, and he was apparently a guest at many other, lesser gatherings as well (BPC: GH/FB 1/6/19; cf. HCU XIV:2816; Boas 1921:1115, 1363–88). As he said to Boas, his prolonged exposure to the activities at these chiefs' feasts taught him all about the social organization and

> all the famely History [ninəwiləm] of the Defferent Brother tribes [descent
> groups] of the four Defferent tribes [divisions] of Forts Ruperts [Kwagulh]. (HCU
> XIV:2193–95; cf. BPC: GH/FB 1/6/19)

Because Hunt had participated in the winter ceremonial as a young man, and as an adult had to sponsor the ceremonial himself, he knew about the great ritual complex of the Kwakwaḵa'wakw (Boas 1966:179–91 ff.; BPC: GH/FB 6/27/27). He was well-versed in Kwakwaḵa'wakw shamanism because he had gone "all through the Rules of the shamans" (4/27/22). He learned the true "old Fashion" Kwak'wala in all its richness and complexity (6/9/30, 3/15/30, 2/17/31)—and he spoke it fluently and by and large correctly, despite the occasional grammatical lapses (Berman 1994). Hunt married a Kwagulh chief's daughter in 1872, the year after his family's return from Fort Simpson (Boas 1966:56–57; HCU XIV:2193–2238). Through his marriage, and in the course of raising sons who had inherited chiefs' positions among the Kwagulh, Hunt learned about the intricate and culturally central Kwakwaḵa'wakw potlatch (cf. HCU XIV:2196; BPC: GH/FB 5/31/23). Transformed by his marriage from an interested outsider to an in-law with a stake in the proceedings, Hunt thereafter became ever more deeply involved in Kwakwaḵa'wakw culture and society (see Berman 1991b:21–23).

One point that would seem to affect significantly the viewpoint of Hunt's texts is the degree to which Hunt was raised as a Tlingit as opposed to a white, since the cultural distance between the Tlingit and the Kwakwaḵa'wakw was much less than that between the latter and the colonial whites. On this point we have little information, except to note that Hunt knew his Tlingit family crests and traditions, that he chose to spend his life among Indians, and the quality of his observations in his letters, though sometimes skeptical or distancing with regard to Kwakwaḵa'wakw practices, seems more Indian than white.

Hunt apparently had no single ethnic affiliation. In one of his rare comments on the subject to Boas, he stated, "I am not . . . asham that I am Half Blood that come from my mother from the north . . . and a white man my Father R. Hunt" (HCU XIV:2193). It seems significant that Hunt worked as

an interpreter and middleman his whole life—for the Hudson's Bay Company,
the Royal Navy, the Canadian Indian Reserve Commission, for a missionary,
for the colonial court system, and ultimately for collectors and ethnologists
(Jacknis 1991:181). The one thing that seems clear is that he never saw himself as Kwakwaka'wakw—characteristically, he calls his wife's relatives "these
Kwagoɬ," "these Indians."

The Kwakwaka'wakw, for their part, perceived Hunt to be a "real man"
(bak̯'əm), that is, an Indian (Codere 1966:xxix); but they considered him to
be a foreign Indian, a Tlingit (Boas 1966:190–91, 1930:II, 258, cf. HCU
XIV:2193). To this day, Hunt's descendants among the Kwakwaka'wakw are
sometimes jokingly referred to as Tlingit and foreign. On the other hand,
Hunt acted towards his children as a Kwakwaka'wakw father, not as a Tlingit
or white one, giving potlatches and feasts for them according to Kwakwaka-
'wakw custom. And in Kwakwaka'wakw fashion, he passed on his mother's
Tlingit crests and privileges, which by Tlingit reckoning were his only by virtue of matrilineal descent, to his sons and his daughters' husbands (Boas 1966:
188–89, 1921:1354; Barbeau 1950:654–60). Perhaps Hunt's most definite
statement on this subject is that given in a speech to the Kwagulh in 1894,
recorded by Boas: "It is well if I live like one of you, and it is well if I act like
one of the northern tribe, because my mother was of high blood among her
tribe" (1966:191).

Boas learned about Hunt's non-Kwakwaka'wakw origins at an early date in
their relationship,[4] but he did not always make them perfectly clear to his
readers. He did acknowledge Hunt's background briefly in the prefaces to
some, but not all, of the text volumes (1930 I:ix; Boas & Hunt 1905:3), and
he occasionally made somewhat cryptic references to it elsewhere (e.g., 1921:
1001, 1966:191). In general, however, Boas was silent about the fact that the
author of the texts was a foreigner among the Kwakwaka'wakw.

Boas also failed to identify Hunt in most accounts in which Hunt was not
just a recorder but also an actor. Boas included one account, a first-person
description of Hunt's shamanic initiation and training (Boas 1930:I, 1–40),
in a publication in which the Kwak'wala texts were placed in one volume and
the English translations in another. A preface mentioning Hunt's origins appears in the Kwak'wala volume, but the content of the preface to the volume
of translations is completely different. Lévi-Strauss, for one, missed Boas' explanation, basing his discussion of the psychological realities of shamans and

4. It is unclear when Boas learned that Hunt was not Kwakwaka'wakw. In Boas' first encounters
with Hunt's family, in 1886, and with George Hunt himself in 1888, he had no inkling that Hunt
was Tlingit on his Indian side (Boas 10/19/86, 6/12/88, 6/13/88, 6/17/88, in Rohner 1969:43–
47, 90–91). But by 1894, if not before, the facts of Hunt's origins had become clear to him, for in
that year he witnessed Hunt defending himself against prejudice towards the "northern tribe"
(1966:190–91).

their patients in "The Sorceror and his Magic" (1963a) upon an account by a "Kwakiutl Indian."

Another account well known in the anthropological literature is Boas' description of the 1894 winter dances at Fort Rupert (1897; see also 1966:179–241). Though disguised for most readers behind their Indian names, George Hunt and his family were featured rather prominently. Hunt was called both Nułqułəla (his winter name) and the "father of Yag̲is." His eldest son David was referred to as N̓əmug̲is (his secular name), as Yag̲is (his winter name) and as the "principal Cannibal dancer of the *Kwaguł*"; Hunt's mother, the Tlingit noblewoman Mary Ebbetts Hunt, was called by the Kwak'wala name Musg̲əmxx̱ala. Boas presented the Hunts' activities during the events as typically Kwakwaka'wakw, despite the fact that Mary and George Hunt and many of the prerogatives they displayed were Tlingit, and were considered to be Tlingit by the Kwakwaka'wakw (Boas 1966:183–91 ff.).

Elsewhere, Boas presented the story of Hunt's marriage to his first wife Lucy without ever mentioning Hunt's name or origins. It begins as follows:

> As an example of the elaborate procedure, I will describe a marriage which occurred in 1872, about which the husband told me in great detail. The wife of the chief, Ten-Fathom-Face, proposed to the young man to marry the granddaughter of Property-Coming-Up, "a sensible girl." Since the young man had no relatives but was highly respected, Ten-Fathom-Face took charge of his marriage. (1966:56–57)

As Boas knew, Hunt had plenty of relatives in Fort Rupert. He merely had no Kwagulh relatives. While it seems likely that large portions of his marriage took place according to the usual Kwagulh practice of the time, other portions of it were distinctly unusual, if not unique. Given that nineteenth-century Kwakwaka'wakw lived in corporate descent groups, and were capable of reckoning genealogies of twenty generations or more in depth, it would have been unlikely to find a young man with *no* relatives. Any young person of noble birth who had lost parents or even grandparents by misfortune would still have had a number of more distant relatives willing to act on his or her behalf. One interesting question raised by the account of Hunt's marriage is why Chief Ten-Fathom-Face (Nəqaƀənkəm, a well-known warleader of the mid-nineteenth century) and his wife agreed to sponsor the entry into Kwagulh society of the son of a Tlingit mother and a white trader. Boas does not mention that Hunt's proposed bride was Ten-Fathom-Face's ƛuʔligas, his "sister's or brother's daughter," certainly an important factor in the equation (the original first-person account by Hunt is to be found in HCU XIV:2193–2283).

Other published accounts that feature George Hunt include one that ends with the succession of his sons to chief's seats among the Kwagulh (Boas 1921:952–1002), one that ends with Hunt's second marriage (1921:1003–74), and an account that is of one of his younger sons' marriages (1925a). In these third-person accounts Hunt's identity is mentioned only once, in a footnote, as "the narrator, who by descent is not a member of the tribe" (1921:1001).

Boas' usual precision with ethnic and social divisions where provenience was concerned makes his apparently deliberate concealment of Hunt's identity in these accounts difficult to understand. Boas may have been attempting to protect Hunt from the unwelcome attention of the law (Wayne Suttles, personal communication). In Hunt's time, participation in Indian dances or potlatches was a criminal offense, and Hunt's involvement in the ceremonial and political life of the Kwakwaka'wakw, as well as the investigations he undertook for Boas, made him no favorite with the missionaries or the Indian Agent. They frequently harassed and threatened him (BPC: GH/FB 1/15/94, 8/12/01, 12/20/04). In 1900 he was arrested and tried (but acquitted) "for going to see Lawits'is tribe winter Dance, a Hamats'a Eating Daid corps[e]" (3/15/00).

This does not explain, however, why Boas failed to disclose Hunt's origins in other places where he made Hunt's involvement, in a general sense, perfectly clear (e.g., 1921). Boas evidently believed that Hunt was so close to being fully Kwakwaka'wakw as to make no difference. He told his family that Hunt *was* Kwakiutl (FB/M. K. Boas 9/13/1897, FB/A. Wohlauer 12/8/23, in Rohner 1969:243, 287). In obscuring Hunt's antecedents, Boas may have been trying to deflect scholarly quibbling over the authenticity of his texts, or confusion over how to interpret the events described therein. The ceremonies at Hunt's marriage, after all, were not Tlingit but were arranged and undertaken by Kwakwaka'wakw. The winter ceremonial Hunt sponsored for his son and daughter was, despite the presence of Tlingit elements, scripted and carried through as a Kwakwaka'wakw event. Boas was surely correct that Hunt's Tlingit-ness, or his white-ness, for that matter, did not rob these accounts of ethnographic value.

Hunt's origins, however, do call into question whether his texts are pure "manifestations" of the "mental life" of the Kwakwaka'wakw. While Boas apparently thought it a negligible problem, no matter how completely Hunt might have adopted Kwakwaka'wakw customs and beliefs, his "interests" and "ideas" could not be exactly those of a native of that culture, if only because he was considered to be, and considered himself to be, an outsider. One wonders what, or if, Boas thought about this question, but he never addressed it in writing.

It may be that some of the difficulties encountered by a modern anthropologist, searching for intellectual and imaginative access to the texts, arise from the fact that Hunt came close to the Kwakwaka'wakw viewpoint without ever reaching it. Despite Boas' interest in "mental life," the texts focus on procedures, incidents, cultural facts, rather than ideas and meanings (BPC: FB/E. Sapir 5/28/24). It is as though Hunt himself were still focused on the rules that would allow him to play the game, and lacked the idiomatic familiarity that would have allowed him to consider the whys and wherefores of it.

There is another aspect of Hunt's near-assimilation that may affect what is expressed in the texts. Boas and Hunt had very different attitudes toward the object of study. Boas' interest in Kwakwaka'wakw culture was largely intellectual, and he approached a good portion of the research out of a sense of scientific duty. He gathered so many Kwakwaka'wakw myths, for example, not because he enjoyed them, but because they documented the material culture collections he was making and shed light on questions of diffusion, and because he assumed, a priori, that they expressed the "interests" of the tellers. He considered the myths themselves "lacking in variety of subject matter and skill in composition," and showing little "general human interest" or "imaginative power" (1935:190; Codere 1966:xvi). Hunt, on the other hand, collected the stories because they appealed to him, perhaps at many levels. He enjoyed going to potlatches, too. He enjoyed the food, the singing, the storytelling, and the chiefs' political posturing. "I feel glad to Hear them try to Beat Each other with there storys," he told Boas (HCU XIV:2195–96).

It is possible to make too much of Boas' complaints that he could not get any fieldwork done while the Indians were potlatching (Rohner 1969:38 ff.; cf. White 1963:49), and it is possible to contrast those complaints too sharply with Hunt's ethnographic eagerness. Boas' earliest trips to the field, where these complaints surface the most frequently, were conducted with fairly specific research goals in mind, and with very limited time and money. Hunt's permanent residence at Fort Rupert, his ready comprehension of Kwak'wala, and his unique position in Kwagulh society, also gave him opportunities unavailable to Boas. It would not be unfair, though, to say that Boas, while respecting Kwakwaka'wakw individuals and Kwakwaka'wakw culture, did not identify with them or have any wish, romantic or otherwise, to be accepted into their society. Hunt, in contrast, chose to live among them. In a sense, Hunt's whole life was participant observation. His enthusiasm for the culture may have been that of the newly converted; that may be why, even when all the other guests grew sleepy from long speeches, Hunt was still eager to observe something he had not heard or seen before (BPC: GH/FB 1/15/24).

"I Took Notes of What He Was Saying"

Boas' consideration of how "interests" and "ideas" were expressed in texts was confined almost exclusively to the *content* of speech (e.g., Boas 1935). He did not examine the ways in which mental life was manifest in *forms* of speech, in what we would now label pattern, genre, style, and so on. This is not to say that he gave no thought to the existence of such things (see, for example, 1914:454–55, 1917a:208–9, 1925b:491–502), only that he did not explore their presence in his ethnographic materials.

Thus, we do not know if Boas ever questioned whether the means by which the texts were produced had any consequences for their authenticity as primary materials. In retrospect, we can see that they clearly must have had. We now understand that internal form, genre, style, context, and the content of speech are interconnected. The means of production, what we could call George Hunt's ethnographic practice, is thus an important issue in examining their collaboration.

Hunt's Kwak'wala texts were written largely but not exclusively in response to specific questions posed by Boas, who usually transmitted them through the mail one or two at a time. During the few periods when the two worked face to face, Boas also drew up lists of questions that he left with Hunt. In answering Boas' questions, Hunt often used himself as a source of information. Hunt believed that through his experiences he had become an expert in the authentic, pre-European life of the Kwakwaka'wakw (BPC: GH/FB 1/6/19). According to Hunt, the Kwagulh at Fort Rupert shared his opinion of his expertise, especially regarding social ranks and prerogatives, and the proprietary myths (9/28/18). Hunt also consulted other Kwakwaka'wakw extensively, usually having to pay for the information they gave him (e.g., 7/23/99, 10/27/08, 10/14/20). He travelled long distances in pursuit of stories, information, and objects, once planning to spend an entire winter in Kingcome Inlet gathering stories at the Dzawada'enuxw village there (e.g., 9/16/98, 1/23/06, 10/7/16, 11/12/21; Rohner 1966:214; Codere 1966:xxix).

A third source of the information in Hunt's texts was his direct observation of the life unfolding around him. In aid of this, Hunt kept a series of "memorandum books," beginning, perhaps, in his adolescence in the first years of his employment by the Hudson's Bay Company (HCU XIV:2238), and continuing until the last years of his life. In these notebooks he kept his accounts, and he also jotted observations on various events and practices as they occurred (and he took notes in them during, or after, consulting sessions). Although Hunt sometimes took notes on a practice about which Boas had specifically inquired (HAR: GH/FB 1/15/95), they were often a spontaneous response to something of interest to him.

> the head chief nEgadze told this story on the 25 of Dec. last in a feast he gaved to the Kwagoł tribes. . . . as soon as I see that he was going to . . . tell his History [myth] in a feast. for his son. I took my Book out of my Pocket and I took notes of what he was saying. (BPC 1/15/24; see also GH/FB 7/21/16, 5/31/23, 5/9/25; GH/FB 4/21/25)

In these practices, Hunt acted much like a classic "participant observer," except that he was required by Boas to write up his observations in Kwak'wala.

Overall, Hunt seems to have been a reliable and conscientious fieldworker (Boas 1921:45, 1467, 1930 I:ix–x). Although Boas did occasionally wonder about the source of Hunt's information (e.g., BPC: GH/FB 9/17/18), he did not require Hunt to specify whether the information had been obtained through introspection, consultation, or direct observation, or some combination of the three. Boas' lack of interest in such distinctions extended to how the texts were presented in published form. In consequence, only in the rare first-person narratives is it clear where the information comes from. These accounts include both descriptions of events experienced or witnessed by Hunt, as well as discussions or narrations in which he is interlocutor or audience of another speaker (e.g., Boas 1930:II, 1–41, 101–12, 177–81, 257–60, 278–83, 1921:713–28, 1317–18; HCU XIV:2193–283).[5] For many of the other texts, the only clue to the source of information is the name of the Kwakwa̱ka'wakw man or woman from whom Hunt first heard the story or other data, which Boas placed at the head of the text. Many texts do not even have this much.

In his letters to Boas, Hunt did often explain the provenience of a text, sometimes in vivid detail. For instance, there is his report on how he came by a rare example of a woman's storytelling genre, the text of which Boas, in the published version, merely identifies as the "Wail of ʟ!aʟ!ɛqwasila, a Gwaᵉsɛla woman" (1921:836–85):

> I hear a woman crying for the Death of her Brother. and in her crying she start to tell the whole History of her family. she Began from the Whale before it turn into a man. and this man came to marrie to the Kwaguł tribe. She kept on crying or singing from 7 o clock untill nearly 3 o clock. and after she finished. I went to her and asked her if I could write the story of her cry song. she said that she would be proud of it. . . . no Body is allowed to sing it But the oldest Daughter of the family she Belongst to. (BPC: GH/FB 7/4/16)

Hunt evidently took notes on her "cry song" (Kw. lag̱aləm), a kind of recitative, while it was in progress, or at any rate consulted the woman after it was over. He reported that he obtained seventeen generations of the genealogy in the song while the woman was in Fort Rupert, and then undertook a journey to Smith Inlet to obtain the remaining five generations from her after she had returned home (BPC: GH/FB 7/4/16, 10/14/16).

It is important to note that when sitting as an audience for Kwakwa̱ka'wakw storytellers, Hunt did not take down texts into his notebooks from dictation, as Boas did in the field. The texts did not originate as transcriptions of spontaneous or even elicited performances of a native oral-literary genre. Rather, Hunt made notes on a custom practiced, a point explained, a story told, then wrote it up fully *in his own words* (BPC: E. Sapir/FB 3/19/24, FB/ES 5/28/24).

5. Hunt sent much other information, not in text form, to Boas that was based directly on his own experience. Some of this was published and some of it is still unpublished. Hunt's detailed house-by-house censuses of Fort Rupert (BPC: GH/FB 8/20/19, 10/4/19), the linguistic information, and the translations of geographical and personal names with which he supplied Boas, are among these materials (HCF: FB/GH 6/20/02, 12/5/04; HAR: GH/FB 7/15/02).

Hunt took notes in a mix of English and Kwak'wala, and wrote the full story
first in Kwak'wala, later adding English interlineations (HMB; BPC: GH/FB
12/16/25). In the published versions of Hunt's narrative texts, the storyteller
named at the head of the story is the person from whom Hunt originally obtained his information, not the immediate narrator. The only texts taken directly from dictation were collected by Boas himself, and they appear in just
two of the text publications (1910, 1935–43).

The bulk of the texts in Boas' collections were composed by Hunt with the
goal of creating written Kwak'wala texts for Boas. Significantly, Boas did not
publish Hunt's *English* responses to questions. The written ethnographic text,
of course, was not a form native to Kwakwaka'wakw culture. Hunt, who spent
long hours even as a child listening to the narratives and oratory of the oldest
Kwagulh chiefs (BPC: GH/FB 1/6/19; HCU XIV:2193–95), must have
drawn in whole or part upon the rules and properties of existing Kwakwaka-
'wakw oral genres of explanation, description, and narration. In the end, however, he must be understood as the immediate author of his texts, and as an
author writing in a novel and artificial form. Nothing like these texts would
ever have been made if Boas had not trained and paid Hunt to do it, and
guided him with questions as he did do it.

To understand the relationship between Hunt's texts and native Kwakwaka'wakw discourse forms, it is necessary to distinguish the several aspects of
discourse form mentioned above: internal patterning, style, genre, and performance context. Hunt's narrative style, for example, is formal and wordy in
comparison to texts collected by others from dictation, or by tape recorder
(Boas 1910:1–243, 1935–43 passim; Levine 1977; KWFN; see, however,
BPC: FB/E. Sapir 5/28/24). It appears, however, to be an authentic Kwakwaka'wakw speech style formerly used in the myth recitations that were common
in nineteenth-century potlatches (BPC: GH/FB 2/28/17, 5/12/18; Berman
1994). The story referred to above, told by "the head chief nɛgadze . . . in a
feast," may well have been narrated in this style originally. The informal style
of domestic storytelling, as represented in texts collected at various times from
other speakers, was rather different. The stories Hunt heard in consulting sessions may well have been narrated in the informal style, and may have undergone a significant stylistic shift when Hunt wrote them down.

During a public recitation, the content and internal patterning of that particular oral performance of the myth would have depended on the occasion,
the audience, and the personal or political agenda of the chief doing the nar-
rating (BPC: GH/FB 5/12/18; also Berman 1991b:117–33). In the head
chief's story, something is known of the original performance context through
one of Hunt's letters. Any direct link between this performance context and
Hunt's version is lost, though, because we do not know enough about how he
took notes or how he then reworked the notes into a narrative text.

In this particular case, the story Hunt wrote down is his retelling of a single oral narrative performance. In other cases, in the pursuit of greater accuracy, Hunt had the storyteller give him the story more than once before committing his version to paper (BPC: GH/FB 12/16/25). When from a single storyteller, elements of the original narrator's voice do sometimes persist in a text (Berman 1991b:248–50; Wilson 1993:357–58). Nevertheless, when Hunt combined several versions of the story he obscured the shape of each single performance. While repeated narration was a traditional method of transmitting stories from one adult to another (Ford 1941:248), one cannot take the internal form of written texts that resulted from this process as necessarily reproducing the original narrator's literary art.

Sometimes Hunt's text is an amalgamation of versions from several different people from different social groups:

> I Dont go to and take these stories from one man the owner of the story[.] after this man who Belong to the nɛmemot [corporate descent group] the story Belong to tells his story then I go to the Rival nɛmemot and ask him to tell the same story. . . . then I go to the third man and ask him to tell me the same story. then I get the Whole story By Doing this. (BPC: GH/FB 11/21/26; cf. 1/15/25)

Where Hunt combines his own observations and recollections with stories or information from several others (e.g., 1921:1363–80), the situation is even more confused. Overall, Hunt's texts can only embody native discourse forms to the extent that Hunt himself had internalized Kwakwaka'wakw ethnopoetics (see Berman 1991b). It would seem that to a large degree he had done this, but further study is needed on this point.

"You Cannot Be Too Detailed in Getting Information"

One of the most important issues bearing on the texts is, of course, the relationship between Boas and Hunt. Even supposing George Hunt were pure Kwakwaka'wakw, and created texts that were authentic transcriptions of Kwakwaka'wakw oral discourse, the texts still would not be perfect embodiments of Kwakwaka'wakw culture springing from his mind parthenogenetically and full-grown. The texts emerged out of the intersection and interaction of two different personal and cultural frames of reference.

Boas and Hunt had a personal relationship that lasted forty-five years. Boas' written questions and Hunt's texts answering them were each guided and shaped by their own needs as well as by assumptions about the emotions, desires, knowledge, and ignorance of the other person. Their Kwakwaka'wakw ethnography was an epistolary ethnography. One reminder in the texts of this interactional context, lost in English translation, are Hunt's metanarrative comments that use such Kwak'wala third-person-near-second-person demonstrative forms as yu, yəxux̱, and laxux̱, meaning "this thing [i.e., the text] that is near you." In his Kwak'wala, Hunt explicitly marked the fact that the texts were communications addressed *to* someone. Another reminder of the inter-actional context is the formal public style Hunt used, which seems to tell us something about how Hunt conceived of his task and of his relationship to Boas.

The complex personal context of their collaboration lies beyond the bounds of this paper. Other aspects of the collaboration are, on the other hand, of immediate concern. These include the anthropological, scholarly frame of ref-erence that guided the research from Boas' end, and the local cultural frame(s) of reference, Tlingit, colonial white, or Kwakwaka'wakw, that shaped Hunt's response to Boas' requests, and informed and gave significance to the collected data. These both are crucial to understanding the texts, and both are missing from the published accounts.

Boas paid Hunt to write texts as a way of collecting Kwakwaka'wakw eth-nographic material that would be free of his own perceptual and interpretive bias. Yet the scope and focus of the textual material arise largely from the non-Kwakwaka'wakw framework within which Boas was working. The published form of the epistolary ethnography leaves out Boas' side of the correspondence, which reveals that his directions to Hunt were far more highly structured than one would ever gather from the way in which he presented Hunt's material. Boas' investigations proceeded in a logical order that is not obscured by nu-merous digressions, overlaps, and minor changes of course. In the 1890s, Boas was most concerned with collecting material culture for museums; in the first decade of the twentieth century he moved from this to an exami-nation of technology, foodways, ethnozoology, and ethnobotany. By the latter part of the decade he had started on social organization, a subject he actively pursued until the 1920s, when he began questioning Hunt about "the way the Indians think and feel" (BPC: GH/FB 9/29/20). By the end of this decade he had become interested in the socialization and training of children (5/22/28).

The correspondence shows that Boas planned his route years in advance. The outline for the fifteen-plus years of research that culminated in his massive 1921 publication, *Ethnology of the Kwakiutl*, was first laid out for Hunt in Janu-ary of 1899:

> When you continue writing for me, I would ask you to write first of all what I suggested to you last summer, namely, the cooking-book of the Kwakiutl, and then you might also ~~study~~ [sic] write down all the curious ideas they have about cooking, all the superstitions they have referring to it, and when you are through with that, you might ask some of the highest chiefs about their great great grand-fathers, or however far they can remember, and let them tell you the whole history of their family. (HAR: GH/FB 1/13/99)

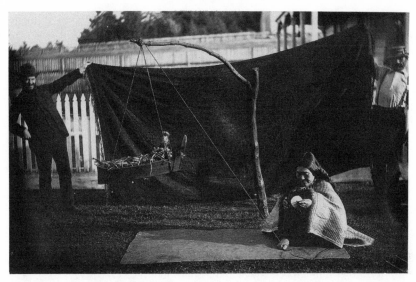

Boas and Hunt hold a backdrop behind a woman posed in precolonial clothing for a photograph session in 1894. Pickets and buildings of the former Hudson's Bay Company post at Fort Rupert can be seen in the background. (Courtesy of the American Museum of Natural History; photograph by Oregon C. Hastings, neg. no. 11604.)

Boas and Hunt did not start collecting the "recipes for cooking and preparing food," which fill most of the first volume of the 1921 publication, until nearly five years later (HCF: FB/GH 11/3/04, 10/31/05; HAR: GH/FB 12/6/04). In 1906, Boas and Hunt began the family histories and studies of social organization that take up a good part of the second volume, but did not really get them underway until 1911 (BPC: FB/GH 3/6/1906, 11/5/1906, 4/3/1911, 5/20/1911). In the meantime, Boas had expanded his plan to include "the carpentry work, the fishing, sealing and . . . a good many important tales we have not got yet" (HCF: FB/GH 10/31/05). Texts on carpentry and related topics, nearly all obtained before 1910, were published partly in a separate 1909 volume (1909a), partly in the section called "industries" in volume 1 of the 1921 publication. Oral literature texts collected throughout the fifteen-year period were added to volume 2.

The frequent pauses and digressions in Boas' broad progression were brought about by several factors. External circumstances, such as the need to ready previously written Hunt manuscripts for publication, the requirements of Boas' funding sources, or questions referred to him by other ethnologists, caused a number of delays. Boas' and Hunt's various labors for the Jesup North Pacific Expedition put off commencement on the cookbook for five years. One digression was set in motion when a museum in Cambridge, evidently the Peabody, requested information on some coppers available for purchase in Fort Rupert (BPC: FB/GH 10/27/21, C. Willoughby/FB 12/29/21). Boas started another digression, about special treatment of bears, trying to obtain information for Irving Hallowell's dissertation on bear ceremonialism (Hallowell 1926: 76–77; BPC: FB/GH 11/10/24). Interruptions also occurred when Hunt decided to pursue matters on his own initiative, or simply as a result of the circumstances of his life. Hunt's investigations were often held up by other work, by illness, by (especially in winter) the demands of traditional social life, and, at certain points, perhaps, by lack of enthusiasm. The deaths of Hunt's first wife and eldest son, the first in 1908 and the second in 1925, also caused significant hiatuses.

On any given topic, Boas pursued information in an orderly and systematic fashion. For example, he began his in-depth investigation of traditional social organization by asking Hunt for a description of the residents of a single big-house (guk̆), and how they were related. When Hunt sent back a diagram and description with much genealogical information (BPC: GH/FB 2/9/06), Boas responded,

> Day before yesterday your description of the people of YaxLEns house came into my hands. While I am very much pleased with what you have given me, I think that your statement might be even a little fuller. Thus I should like to know to what brother tribe [Kw. ṅəṁimut "descent group"] YaxLEn and omx[ᵉ]it belong by birth, whether it was their father's or their mother's brother tribes, what names they have had since they were children, and to what brother tribes these names belonged, also whether with these names they took their seats in the different brother tribes, then what their winter names were, and where they got them. You have given some of this in regard to YaxLEn['s] children, but I should like to have the whole thing just as full as possible. (BPC: 3/6/06)

Later that year, Boas moved from residence and descent to the topic of marriage proscriptions.

> One of the things in which I am very much interested is to know what marriages are forbidden by the Kwakiutl. For instance, would a man marry his cousin on his father's side? Can a man marry his cousin on his mother's side? Must a man, after his brother's death, marry his brother's widow? May two brothers marry two sisters? (BPC: 11/5/06)

By 1911, he had begun his study of social organization in earnest.

> There are still a number of points that I do not understand very clearly in the laws of the Kwakiutl; and I believe that the best way to make it clear to me is if you will take the trouble to take any one of the families of Fort Rupert, which

you know so well, and begin the life of a few particular men and women from the time of their birth. . . . You will see what I should like to have is the real family history of a number of people. We have a good many of their laws, but I shall understand them very much better if I can see how they really work out in the case of a number of particular men and women. . . . I hope you will take all pains to . . . write it out with all possible detail. (BPC: 5/20/11)

Boas has been criticized for the endlessness, obscurity, and triviality of his texts; yet those "obscure" texts are Hunt's responses to perfectly standard anthropological queries on such topics as the use of a particular plant species or the possibility of parallel-cousin marriage. The family histories, to take just one example, were intended by Boas to be case studies to help him sort out the still controversial areas of Kwakwaka'wakw descent, inheritance and marriage. They are full of particularist detail because, as he told Hunt with regard to inheritance and succession,

You know that the question of position in inheritance among the Kwakiutl is so difficult that you cannot be too detailed in getting information, and I think the best way of straightening the matter out is to get the actual position and the actual changes in position in the case of some people and their families. (BPC: 3/6/06)

Another aspect of the missing anthropological frame of reference that strongly shaped the texts is Boas' attitude toward internal cultural diversity. His notion of systematic inquiry also included inquiry that sought "all the differences of opinion on a subject" (BPC: FB/GH 3/30/21). This point came up periodically in his work with Hunt. "You know as well as I do that you or me cant find two Indians tell a storie alike," Hunt complained to Boas in the early years of their association (HAR: 10/21/95; BPC: 11/5/95). Over twenty-five years later he was still warning Boas that they would never find perfect agreement among the Kwakwaka'wakw (BPC: 3/22/21). Boas reassured him that he expected "a good many conflicts of opinion and [that] some may say one thing and others another and if that is the case, we ought not to try to make it uniform, but simply say what everyone tells" (BPC: 3/7/21, 4/21/25). Boas' attitude, combined with the lack of cultural consensus on many issues, explains, for example, why the myth volumes contain multiple versions of a number of stories, and why some texts on cosmology are records of arguments rather than explications of a single view of the universe (Boas 1930:II, 177–78, 180–81, 257–60).

The epistolary background of the texts explains not only what is present in them, but also what is absent. For example, Boas has been criticized for his "neglect of commoners": "A major deficiency in Boas' work with the Kwakiutl was his neglect of the patterns and behavior of the lower classes: his nearly exclusive concern with the nobility and his presentation of this picture as representative of Kwakiutl life . . ." (Ray 1955:159; cf. Codere 1966:xvi). This neglect, found in Boas' analytic writings as well as in the texts, has a significance that has been completely misunderstood. Boas made a concerted effort to extract such information from Hunt:

> If I am to understand the whole matter thoroughly, I ought to know also about the names of some of the chiefs of lower rank . . . ; and also the same for some of the common people. For me the names and the rights of the common people are just as important as those of the people of high blood. (BPC: 10/13/17)

And, months later, when this appeal drew no response:

> There is one thing that I have very much at heart. You always tell me about the chiefs and the highest men in the tribe. If I am to understand the matter clearly, I ought to know also the names of some of the people of low rank—how they get them, whether they come from father to son, and how they are obtained in marriage. If I am to understand really [sic] the Kwakiutl, the rights of the common people are just as important as those of the people of high blood. (BPC: 1/16/18)

When Hunt finally replied, it was with the terse statement, "[about] the Poor men . . . this is hard to get for they shame to talk about themselves" (BPC: 2/4/18). The "neglect of commoners" did not arise from *Boas'* frame of reference, but, apparently, from that of the Kwakwaka'wakw (cf. BPC: FB/GH 3/20/29; HCU XIV:4604–23, 4559–63; also Boas 1902:314).

"This Way . . . Shows You More to Learne"

Knowing the questions that generated the texts sheds considerable light on the nature of Boas' scholarship. As the preceding example shows, it also allows us to look at the way in which Hunt answered Boas' questions (or failed to do so), which in turn reveals much about the frames of reference within which Hunt was operating. If we assume that Hunt frequently used the Kwakwaka-'wakw frame of reference, this is then an important source of information about Kwakwaka'wakw "interests" and "ideas."

For example, when Boas began to investigate "how the Indians think and feel," he repeatedly asked Hunt for "as clear and systematic a description as possible" of Kwakwaka'wakw cosmography (BPC: 3/7/21, 2/1/21, 9/8/21). Hunt never supplied this systematic description. His response, instead, was to seek out and record myths that contained cosmographic information (found in Boas 1935–43:II, 189–209). For Hunt, Kwakwaka'wakw myths were not simply stories about a long-ago Kwakwaka'wakw past; they were one of the most important sources of information about the nature of the traditional, pre-European Kwakwaka'wakw present, a kind of straightforward ethnographic description. There were certainly aspects of traditional culture and practice for which Hunt could not discover a mythic explanation, but he always assumed that the myth existed. Thus, when Boas asked him about the Kwakwaka'wakw view of eclipses, he replied,

> Now about the Eclipse of the moon and sun. I am trying to find out about the story of the great mouth in the Heavens that swallow the moon or sun. But so far I could not get any one to tell me. . . . in the old time when there is Eclipse of the moon or sun I heard the Indians all cry out Hogwä, Hogwä or Vomet, vomet the Indians calls Eclipes nɛgɛkw. or swallowed. so . . . there must Be a story about it. or Else the old People would not know about the great mouth of the Heaven that is Right on the Road of the sun and moon. (BPC: 10/20/21)

Similarly, when Boas asked Hunt "whether there is any particular reverence paid to the bear" (BPC: 11/10/24), Hunt replied not just with texts of prayers addressed to the bear, but also with at least two myths about bears (BPC: GH/FB 12/16/25, 1/9/26, FB/GH 1/4/26, in Boas 1935–43:I, 17–23, 219–27).

To take another example, when they began working on the "cooking-book," Boas evidently expected that Hunt would present him with a more or less orderly series of recipes for different dishes somewhat like the series Boas ultimately published (in 1921:305–602). Hunt began in this way, writing on preparation and cooking of salmon (HAR: GH/FB 12/6/04, 1/20/05, 2/20/05). When he moved on to halibut, however, Hunt decided that the whole matter would be better explained if he began at the beginning—and the beginning of halibut cooking was with the making of halibut hooks and the methods of halibut fishing (HCF: GH/FB 12/9/05). "[A]ll the . . . things Belong to the works," he told Boas, "should Be put in all the way from the Beginning to the Last" (BPC: 12/23/05). "I think . . . this way writing it, shows you more to Learne than any we have Been Doing Before" (BPC: 3/10/08).

Hunt did worry that this approach might not be the one that Boas wanted (BPC: GH/FB 12/23/05, 3/10/08). As far as is known, however, Boas never tried to shepherd him back to the original plan, and at any rate Hunt continued in this style. Boas was evidently much interested in hook-making and fishing methods. His response to Hunt's departure from the plan, however, was simply to break Hunt's texts apart for editorial purposes.

Boas separated the text on halibut, for instance, into several pieces. He placed the first section, on making the hooks and fishing, in the 1909 volume (1909a:472–80); a second, on cleaning and drying halibut after they have been caught, in a long section labelled "preservation of food" in the 1921 volumes (pp. 241–49); a third, on cooking and eating fresh halibut heads, in the section labelled "recipes" (357–59); a fourth, on drying again, under "preservation of food" (249–52), and one last one, a long one, on eating dried halibut, under "recipes" again (360–79). The text can be reconstructed without too much difficulty because Boas left footnotes explaining where the text had broken off and where it was continued.

Boas does not point out, and indeed he may have assumed that it was obvious to readers, that the sections of this series of texts that went in the 1909 volume dealt with what was mostly men's work (carpentry, fishing, etc.), while the sections that went into the 1921 volume, under "recipes" and "preservation of food," described what was largely a woman's domain. What is interesting is that Hunt felt the two, the fishing and the cooking, belonged together as one connected set of activities. For Hunt, the important conceptual boundary was not that dividing men's from women's work but that encompassing husband and wife together as an economic unit. Cleaning, preserving, and cooking fish is not what a *woman* has to know, but "what a man['s] wife has to know." Hunt was fascinated by his researches for the cookbook, because despite over thirty years of marriage, he never had any idea "that a . . . man who goes out to catch salmon in these Rivers has to have a wife who got to know so much" (HAR: GH/FB 12/6/04).

It needs to be repeated that not all of Hunt's material was written in response to questions from Boas. Hunt not infrequently initiated investigation of topics entirely on his own. For example, he seemed always on the lookout for myths they had not yet recorded, even when Boas was firmly focussed on other topics, and even when the myth did not illustrate some other point about which Boas was asking. Hunt apparently felt a strong affinity for the myths that seems to have been partly a matter of personal taste (cf. HCU XIV: 2194–95), partly a reflection of the traditional importance of myth among the Kwakwaka'wakw (myth was also important to the Tlingit), and partly, perhaps, a response to Boas' own abiding interest in them. Hunt was thus personally responsible for collecting most of the myth material recorded after 1905. For instance, after his remarriage he learned and wrote down the long, secret version of a proprietary myth from his wife's family that he and Boas had acquired in its short, public form before (BPC: GH/FB 2/28/17). Another myth he happened to hear in a potlatch and wrote down (BPC: GH/FB 1/15/24). In December of 1925, he discovered that an old woman living in Fort Rupert had "lots of fine old stories that I never Heard of Befor" and he began collecting myths from her (BPC: 12/16/25, 1/9/26). Once, when going through an old "memorandum book," he discovered a story he had been told by a Gusgimaxw chief in 1899 but had never sent. "You Dont know How glad I was when I found it" (BPC: 10/11/27). Another myth a man had promised to tell him only after his mother died; as soon as she passed away Hunt went and obtained the story (BPC: 12/17/27, 3/28/28).

Boas generally made no comment, encouraging or discouraging, when Hunt took the initiative. Sometimes, however, he responded enthusiastically. For instance, after Hunt's first wife had been ill for many months, Hunt wrote:

> Now here after I will try to get all the Deffrent kind of Indian mediciens such as wind caller and to stop the South East [wind] and medicens to kill or to take life Back, and all the old fations mediciens for there sick people what was used in the old times. one of this Indian medicien I am using on my wife this last 5 Weeks and it is the only thing that is Doing lot of good. So I think it is good to have all this in you Museum. (BPC: 12/6/99)

Boas replied:

> I am very glad to think that . . . you are trying to get all the different kinds of Indian medicines. . . . You know that we have nothing of that kind in our collections so far, and it is a very good thing that you are beginning to get them. I wish . . . after you are through with the [story] you are sending me now, that you would write down whatever you can learn about these medicines. (BPC: 12/22/99)

At another time, the incumbent of a winter-ceremonial ritual office died, and the new office-holder was willing to talk to Hunt about things that before had always been "strickly secret" (BPC: 6/15/26). Hunt immediately began to send texts to Boas on the full, secret myth of the ceremonial's origin and on the secret procedures of the initiates. Boas was "very much interested" and soon began transmitting questions for Hunt (BPC: 8/26/26). This began several years of investigation into various aspects of the winter ceremonial.

"People Do Not Want to Be Bothered with Reading Indian Names"

While these instances illustrate Hunt's role in shaping the scope and focus of the texts, they also show how Boas organized and edited Hunt's texts after they were written. Hunt wrote about halibut cooking from the beginning to the end; Boas broke that text apart into examples of "industries," "recipes," "preservation of food." Hunt wrote about the cosmos as revealed through Kwakwaka'wakw myth; Boas placed those myths together with others that meant something different to Hunt.

Their winter ceremonial investigations supply another example. Hunt actually wrote down two versions of the myth of the ceremonial's origin, a short one, and the more detailed, secret one, referred to above, that he learned much later. The added details refer to the actions of the winter ceremonial initiates, and do not affect the overall shape or style of the myth, which differs little in those respects from the short version. Boas, however, presented the two versions in quite different ways. The short version he published in a volume of myth texts without any mention of its special function in the ceremonial (Boas & Hunt 1906:103–13); the more detailed one he placed in a topical volume, *Religion of the Kwakiutl* (1930:57–86), where it is included among largely non-literary texts under the heading "The Winter Ceremonial" as a description and explanation of the actions of real-life initiates in Hunt's day.

Boas' editing altered primary materials and disguised many indications of his native fieldworker's "interests" and "ideas." To take myth once more as an example, there does appear to have been a basic intersection between Boas' interest in myth and that of the nineteenth-century Kwakwaka'wakw: both thought that myths were important. Beyond this, however, their interests and ideas diverged. Boas was interested in myths as a source of scientific data. The Kwakwaka'wakw, and presumably also Hunt, were interested in myths because of the functionality of myth within their own lives. Boas never discussed the significance of myth in Kwakwaka'wakw life as a whole, whether as an overall cultural category (Kw. nuyəm), or in its various subdivisions. In fact, however, myth was a pervasive force in many separate domains of nineteenth-century Kwakwaka'wakw culture. There were at least two broad categories of myth: "house-stories" (nuyəmił), owned by noble descent lines, and another type that lay in the public domain. Apparently, for Boas both categories of myth were equally expressions of the Kwakwaka'wakw experience and so had equivalent significance within his research scheme. He did not indicate in the published versions of texts which narratives belonged to which category. These two categories of narrative, however, were emphatically not equivalent. As Boas well knew, they had different social functions, different performance contexts, different and even opposing thematic concerns. For the high-ranking, narration of one's house-story was practically obligatory in every large feast (e.g., BPC: GH/FB 2/28/17, 5/12/18). The house-story was so important to notions of personal and social identity that on the basis of her fieldwork, conducted over twenty years after Boas' final visit to the field, Helene Codere speculated that

> it was the Kwakiutl themselves who insisted [to Boas] on the knowledge and recording of their myths. Even in 1954, elderly Kwakiutl tended to begin any association with an anthropologist with "Do you know my story?"—that is, lineage myth [i.e., house-story]. (1966:xvi)

The category of "house-stories" was further divided between the public versions heard by Codere, which also make up many of the myth texts recorded by Hunt and Boas, and the special longer, secret versions known only to family members (BPC: GH/FB 2/28/17, 3/10/17; see also Boas 1921:1222–248). Boas did not label the few texts that were the secret versions, nor even note the existence of that sub-category.

Boas grouped texts together according to his own preferences. His editorial categories sometimes have a connection to Kwakwaka'wakw cultural categories, sometimes not. He left no explanation of his editorial decisions in this regard, and almost no annotation or commentary on the subject of cultural categories and meanings, even things he knew from Hunt's correspondence if not his own fieldwork. A look at Boas' English translations to the texts shows that this manner of treating Kwakwaka'wakw concepts and categories was not confined to the arrangement of texts for publication. It is also found at the level of English word choice and phrasing. Because of this, the translations cannot be relied upon for more than the general sense (cf. Berman 1991b:49–56, 1992, where these issues are examined in greater detail).

Boas' understanding of Kwak'wala was not a superficial one. His posthumous grammar (1947) and unpublished dictionary (BLC) are among the most significant accomplishments of his career. He also had Hunt's English interlineations on which to base his translations. His translations contain few errors with Kwak'wala in a narrow sense. Nevertheless, he introduced many "distortions" into the text.

For example, Boas often translated terms for Kwakwaka'wakw cultural categories inconsistently. Thus the Kwak'wala word nuyəm was rendered variously as "myth," "tale," "story," "legend," and "tradition." From the translation alone it cannot be learned that all of these refer to a single ethnoliterary genre. There is a further point, one of considerable methodological significance. Boas' emphasis on the need to record the native's thinking in his own words did not apply to the native's *English* words. All of Boas' glosses from nuyəm differ from George Hunt's gloss, which was, simply, "History." Again, for the term kisʔu, which refers to the inherited, myth-derived prerogatives of the Kwakwaka'wakw nobility, Boas gives "crest," "privilege," "dance," "mask," and even "name." Hunt, in his interlineations, also gives more than one gloss for this term, but he prefers the word "title," apparently in the legal sense, and he calls the one in possession of the title, kisʔunuk, the "title owner" or the "Hereditry [*sic*] owner" (e.g., HCU XIV:3919).

Similarly, Boas often did not preserve important semantic distinctions embedded in grammar and lexicon, particularly the topological precision that was so much a part of nineteenth-century Kwak'wala. For instance, Kwak'wala then distinguished between vertical and horizontal orientation of many objects. In one of Hunt's texts, the hero reaches what Boas calls the "edge of the world" (Boas & Hunt 1905:72). This "edge of the world" is not, as Western readers might expect, the edge of a horizontal plane that overhangs nothingness. The Kwak'wala word is derived from kuk-, which Hunt translated as "Reast on by the edge" (HCU XIII:2180), and means, literally, something like "[large] plane stands vertically on edge." The Kwakwaka'wakw "edge of the world" was a wall that *enclosed* the world.

Conversely, Boas' translations contain terms that *appear* to correspond to Kwakwaka'wakw cultural categories but do not. One example is "Kwakiutl" itself, or, as Boas sometimes wrote it, with seemingly greater authenticity, Kwaguł. Boas used this term to refer to various ethnological and linguistic categories, few of which correspond to the native cultural categories with which the term is associated (Berman 1991b:50–51, 111–14). Another example is Boas' use of the word "potlatch" as an analytical term for the activity of, as he defined it, "distribution of property" (1966:77, 1897:341). As others have pointed out, the word "potlatch" derives from Chinook Jargon, and it did not originally correspond to any single named taxonomic category in Kwakwaka'wakw culture (Curtis 1915:142; Goldman 1975:131–33)— though it may well do so today. In the Kwak'wala of Hunt's era, the variety of types of social events that Boas called "potlatches" were referred to by a corresponding variety of terms, the use of which depended upon the status and role of the recipient, on the kind of property being distributed, and on the immediate function of the event (see Berman 1991b:51–53).

Boas' translations erase native metaphors and literary imagery at least as often as they distort native cultural and semantic categories. He frequently replaced a term whose meaning is part of a rich Kwak'wala metaphor with a non-metaphorical term. For instance, one myth text describes a conflict over control of the weather, fought between the thunderbirds of the upper world and the ordinary birds of earth. The chief of the latter is named Ğəldəm (Boas & Hunt 1905:295–317). On the face of it, ğəldəm refers to the bird we call the "flicker," a member of the woodpecker family. The word derives from the Kwak'wala stem ğəlt- ("fire, to be on fire"), and Hunt's gloss for the whole word was "fire [on his] side" (BPC: GH/FB 12/12/04).[6] More recently, a Kwakwaka'wakw elder has given "makes fire" as a gloss for the name (Wilson 1993: 355). The name probably refers to the flame-colored wing- and tail-linings visible as the flicker flies overhead (Peterson 1961:138–39). That the chief fighting for summer and sunny weather is named "Fiery," or "Fire-maker," is an important part of the story imagery, but this point is completely lost in Boas' translation, which was, simply, "Woodpecker."

Another aspect of Boas' treatment of cultural categories and metaphor is his tendency to focus on detail rather than on pattern. For example, the names of Kwakwaka'wakw spirit beings are often descriptive of their attributes, i.e., Hayelbalisəla ("Crossing the world in a single day") for a loon who can do precisely that; Ķənķənx̌əliga ("Thunder following behind") for the thunder-

---

6. The nominalizing suffix following the stem in this name is presumably the formative suffix =əm, which has no somatic connotations. If this is the case, a more literal gloss would be, perhaps, "fiery one." The suffix could be the "instrumental" =əm, in which case the gloss might be the "means of causing fire" (Boas 1947:301).

bird; and Aʔuxⱡəʔa ("Trying to carry away in a pack-basket") for a kind of ogre who searches for children to carry off. Had Boas recognized the pattern in this practice, he might have realized that the flicker-chief's name was probably intended as description of an actual attribute of the character, and have been more likely to give a literal gloss for the name.

Interestingly, translation of names was a subject that generated a certain amount of correspondence between Boas and Hunt. This was because Hunt did not give a gloss in his English interlineations for many of the Kwak'wala names. Sometimes he did so because the names appearing in texts derived from neighboring languages such as Comox or Heiltsuk, and did not have a translation from the Kwak'wala. Often it was because the names were not simple to translate despite containing recognizeable Kwak'wala elements. Boas, however, would send back lists of the untranslated names and ask Hunt to try again. And try again Hunt did.

Boas often did not use the translations supplied by Hunt (Berman 1991b: 246–47), and he seemed puzzled by contradictions between different translations Hunt had given at various times for the same name. Boas and Hunt evidently had two rather different understandings of what translating the names meant. Hunt, it seems, was often trying to impart the sense of the name, even if that sense could not be understood from the name itself but only by knowing the metaphor or metaphors that lay behind the name. This was the case, for example, with his explanation of the personal name Q̓'əmxəlagəlis, for which Boas gave the translation "rockslide everywhere" (BLC:364):

> if I come to three old men. ask them the meaning of the name q!om|x·āᵉ|lā| gᴇᵉ|les . . . well one of the old men say. the meaning of this name is Propert Rolling Down Mountian. and the other say People Rolling Down from his Highness. and the third one say. all time Property Rolling Down from him. now you will see in this name is told in three Defferent ways By three men. now here when a mountian the stone and trees keeps on comeing Down a land slide. the Indeans calls it q!om|x·āᵉ|lā| gᴇᵉ|les all times Rocks Rolling Down mountian. this means that the cheef is a mountian. and Property that he gives away to the Defferent tribe is the Rock Rolling Down from his Body or Highness. So the Right meaning is all times Property Rolling Down from his Body (the mountian). (BPC: GH/FB 9/28/18)

At another time, Hunt said, "now to tell you the truth I dont [know] that there is any one who can translate these names Rightly for there are mare [more] like a Parables" (GH/FB 12/7/28 in HCU XI:2362a; also HAR: GH/FB 7/15/02). Boas, on the other hand, was not interested in these "parables," which would have made a fascinating subject of ethnographic study in and of themselves. His concern instead seems to have been primarily editorial: "The English translation reads ever so much easier," he told Hunt, "if we can give a translation of these names, because most people do not want to be bothered with reading Indian names" (HCF: 7/3/02).

Boas' indifference to this rich vein of native thought may have more than one source. It may be that Boas felt that no English translation could be perfect, because all translation involves the cognitive and semantic categories of another language and culture and thus inevitably introduces distortion. Serious scholars of the texts would learn Kwak'wala to study the texts.[7] Translations only had to be good enough for the casual reader, and for the casual reader Boas just wanted to tell the story in a simple and straightforward way. Or it may be that, just as some people are tone-deaf or color-blind, Boas had a kind of literary handicap with regard to word choice, image, and metaphor— so that he never really knew when he had stepped on something in his translating and crushed it out of recognition. That he was somehow unaware of the profusion of imagery in Kwakwaka'wakw myth is suggested by his statement that the mythology was lacking in "imaginative power" (1935:190).

There is probably some truth in both of these suppositions, however much they seem to contradict other aspects of Boas' work. Boas was the first to draw attention to the issue of cultural classification, and his interest in Kwakwaka-'wakw metaphor is evidenced by an article devoted to the subject (1929). But his comments on these topics are not elaborate and do not show that he had thought deeply and philosophically about them.

Additional explanations suggest themselves for the larger-scale editing practices that follow the same pattern. It may be that Boas avoided annotating his texts to avoid adding a layer of interpretation to his native fieldworker's primary materials. If so, he apparently did not consider the degree to which his translating and editing in themselves added a layer of interpretation, and the degree to which the texts would remain inaccessible without annotation. Or it may be that Boas' overriding concern was with "interests," rather than "ideas," since, after all, he saw the latter as arising out of the former. Perhaps he presumed that the "interests"—"the passions of the people" (BPC: FB/GH 12/6/26)—shine through in the edited, translated texts, regardless of whether the details of all the "ideas" are visible. Or it may be that, as with names, he was thinking about ease of using the texts; his editorial rearrangements were intended as a reference tool, something like an index or table of contents.

Again, there is probably something to all of these explanations. Fundamentally, however, Boas' editing and translating practices—like his entire profes-

---

7. Unfortunately, most serious readers of the texts have not learned Kwak'wala. Every major reanalysis of Boas' Kwakw'ala material thus far published, with the arguable exception of Goldman's *Mouth of Heaven* (1975), has used Boas' English as the primary source (Locher 1932; Müller 1955; Reid 1974, 1979; Dundes 1979; Walens 1981).

George Hunt waits with megaphone in hand to give stage directions to Kwakwaka'wakw actors on the set of Edward Curtis's motion picture, *In the Land of the Cannibals* (now known as *In the Land of the War Canoes*), near Fort Rupert, British Columbia, in 1914. (Courtesy of the Thomas Burke Memorial Washington State Museum; photograph by Edmund A. Schwinke.)

sional relationship with Hunt—were affected by unresolved tensions in his ideas about native fieldworkers and the role of the professional anthropologist.

The Anthropologist and the Native Point of View

We began this discussion by examining Boas' ideas about primary versus secondary materials, and about the importance of native fieldworkers. While Boas was explicit about the importance of the native point of view, he did not say much about how he conceived the role of the anthropologist in relation to it. Boas' directions to Hunt regarding the Kwakwaka'wakw cookbook may supply a clue:

> When you continue writing for me, I would ask you to write first of all . . . the cooking-book of the Kwakiutl, and then you might ~~study~~ [*sic*] write down all the curious ideas they have about cooking, all the superstitions. (HAR: FB/GH 1/13/99)

It is possible that Boas' deletion of "study" in this passage arose from a worry that Hunt might only study and might never write down—not a completely

unreasonable interpretation given Boas' impatience at Hunt's rate of production during that period of their collaboration. It is also possible, however, that
Boas believed Hunt capable only of recording customs and beliefs and not of
studying them. Hunt, in other words, would not have been able to formulate
the questions that should be asked, analyze the data once collected, or draw
serious, scientific conclusions from that analysis.

Together with Boas' translating and editorial practices, this passage suggests
that he kept, somewhere in the back of his mind, a guide to the division of
labor between the two of them. Hunt could describe customs and beliefs without the bias of an outside observer; Boas could elicit, translate, arrange, and
present those descriptions—without, presumably, adding distortion—according to the accepted canons of science and scholarship.[8] Implicit in Boas' work,
then, is a nascent and still quite hazy distinction between the anthropologist
as a native of his or her own culture, whose perceptions of another culture will
be distorted, and the anthropologist as bearer of a conceptual tool kit that
allows limited bias-free operations on ethnographic data. This distinction, between what later generations would call "emic" and "etic," is an issue with
which North American anthropology still wrestles.

It has already been argued here that Boas' operations on Hunt's data were
by no means free of "distortion." What has not so far been addressed is the
question of whether, starting from Boas' premises, such a feat is even possible.
In fact, within the parameters of his theory of culture, Boas' attempts to present "the culture as it appears to the Indian himself" created a paradox. In a
raw state, pure "manifestations" of "mental life" will, at best, make only partial
sense to outsiders, and are more likely to remain completely incomprehensible.
Further, the mental life of a people is too vast a subject to render in even as
many thousands of pages as Boas published on the Kwakwaka'wakw. Presenting a culture through "manifestations" to an audience of outsiders minimally
requires editorial selection and translation; some amount of annotation and
commentary would seem to be necessary as well. Ethnography through texts,
even for a William Jones or an Ella Deloria, is still parcelling out the native
viewpoint into the categories and meanings of another culture. And then the
product becomes "a presentation of the culture in such a way that it can be
studied or comprehended by an outsider," a rather different kind of object.

It would hardly be fair to Boas to criticize him for failing to resolve a paradox
whose existence could not even have been imagined prior to his intellectual
contribution. There is no guarantee the paradox can be resolved, anyway.
Ethnography itself—indeed, the entire notion of scientific and scholarly in-

8. Boas was an unnamed collaborator, senior investigator, senior author, or editor for many of
his Euro-American students and protégés, but in those cases the issue of relativism does not arise
in the same way.

quiry—is a concept that has meaning and value in our culture, but not necessarily in others. The notion of studying, dissecting, interpreting, and presenting, of acquiring and hoarding knowledge about a people's way of life, is not just a foreign and little-understood concept to some peoples, it can also violate their deeply held values. This goes beyond the kinds of issues that have recently taken center-stage for anthropologists working with North American natives—for example, the issues surrounding cultural representation, disclosure of proprietary knowledge or sensitive religious matters, and treatment of sacred objects—and takes us to the very process of ethnographic inquiry itself. As Toelken discovered, during investigations into how Navajo healers used Coyote stories ritually:

> Since words and narratives have power to heal, they may also be used to injure and kill. Thus, when witches wish to damage the health of others, they use selected parts of the same Coyote stories in *their* rituals; the difference is that instead of integrating the story with a model of order and restoration, their idea of deployment is to use images, symbols, and allusions separately, divisively, analytically, in order to attack certain parts of the victim's body, or family, or livestock. One becomes a witch in order to gain personal fortune and power. . . . Since my questions had been selective and analytical, since I was clearly trying to find out exactly what was powerful about Coyote stories, since I stood to gain [as a folklorist] from this knowledge . . . Navajo informants would assume . . . witchcraft. (1987:396–97)

Granting Boas' premises about the nature of culture, this paradox cannot be eliminated, except when the ethnographer studies "manifestations" from our own culture and then presents them to the same audience. The paradox can, however, be mitigated. It strikes this writer that the divide separating members of two distinct cultures is not different in kind from that separating two members of the same culture. What carries anyone across the divide between his or her own viewpoint and that of another is imagination, empathy, curiosity. Perhaps the practice of ethnography is, at best, something like marriage, an extended good-faith attempt of people with distinct viewpoints to communicate with each other, filled with puzzlement, missed intellectual and emotional rendezvous, and the occasional perfect "That's it! You've got it! You *understand* what I'm saying!" Something not unlike, in other words, the extended collaboration between Boas and Hunt.

It may be that Boas succeeded best not in his own terms, but in a closely related theoretical world where the cultural divide separating anthropologist and native is not just a source of methodological problems, but also a source of opportunity, where the very play of tensions arising from differences in categories, meanings, and values illuminates what each side is trying to understand about the other, and leads both on to further attempts. One could argue that Hunt was the perfect choice as a collaborator in such a venture: a man who had functioned his entire life as an interpreter and cultural middleman, who had a kind of practical understanding of relativity built in to his experience from the very beginning. An absolute judgement would be hard to render on how close the Boas-Hunt texts come to expressing a pure Kwakwaka'wakw viewpoint. From the standpoint of their ethnographic value, it ultimately may not matter, so long as the context of their production is always kept in mind. The texts are a truly extraordinary achievement, and the main problem, since Boas, has always been how to make use of them. It is hoped that the issues discussed here will make the texts more comprehensible and more usable, so that, as Boas intended, scholars will continue to mine them for their riches for generations to come.

Acknowledgments

This paper originated in Berman 1991a, which was revised to become Berman 1991b: 13–57. Portions of the section on translation appeared also in Berman 1992, and part of the section on Hunt's fieldwork methods is a summary of a part of Berman 1994. Along the way the paper has benefited greatly from the insightful comments, suggestions, and information supplied by Dell Hymes, Wayne Suttles, Sally McLendon, Bill Sturtevant, Doug Cole, John Dunn, Jeff Leer, and George Stocking. With regard to the final form of the paper I am particularly indebted to the last-mentioned. Bill Holm kindly made available to me a copy of the Hunt memorandum book. I would also like to thank the staff of the American Philosophical Society, Philadelphia, the Anthropology Archives of the American Museum of Natural History, New York City, and the Archives of the University of Pennsylvania Museum, for their efforts on my behalf. Beth Carroll-Horrocks, Belinda Kaye, and Alessandro Pezzati were particularly helpful.

References Cited

Barbeau, M. 1950. *Totem poles*. National Museum of Canada, Bulletin 119. Ottawa.
Berman, J. 1991a. The production of the Boas-Hunt Kwakw'ala texts. *Working papers for the XXVIth International Conference on Salish and Neighboring Languages*, 1–36. University of British Columbia, August 15–17.
———. 1991b. The seals' sleeping cave: The interpretation of Boas' Kwakw'ala texts. Doct. diss., University of Pennsylvania.
———. 1992. Oolachan-Woman's robe: Fish, blankets, masks and meaning in Boas' Kwakw'ala texts. In Swann 1992:125–62.
———. 1994. George Hunt and the Kwak'wala texts. *Anth. Ling.* 36(4): 482–514.
BLC. See Manuscript Sources.
Boas, F. 1889. On alternating sounds. *Am. Anth.* 2:47–53.
———. 1897. *The social organization and the secret societies of the Kwakiutl*. Report of the U.S. National Museum 1895: 311–738. Washington, D.C.

———. 1900. Editor's note. In Teit 1900:165.

———. 1902. The ethnological significance of esoteric doctrines. In Boas 1940:312–15.

———. 1909a. *The Kwakiutl of Vancouver Island*. The Jesup North Pacific Expedition, Memoir of the American Museum of Natural History V. New York.

———. 1909b. William Jones. *Am. Anth.* 11:137–39.

———. 1910. *Kwakiutl tales*. Columbia University Contributions to Anthropology 2. New York.

———. 1911a. Introduction. In Boas, ed., 1911:I, 5–83.

———. 1911b. Kwakiutl. In Boas, ed., 1911:I, 423–557.

———. 1912. *Tsimshian texts, new series*. Publications of the American Ethnological Society 3:65–284.

———. 1914. Mythology and folk-tales of the North American Indians. In Boas 1940:451–90.

———. 1917a. Introduction to *International Journal of American Linguistics*. In Boas 1940:199–225.

———. 1917b. *Grammatical notes on the language of the Tlingit Indians*. The University Museum Anthropological Publications 8(1). Philadelphia.

———. 1921. *Ethnology of the Kwakiutl*. Bureau of American Ethnology Annual Report 35. Washington, D.C.

———. 1925a. *Contributions to the ethnology of the Kwakiutl*. Columbia University Contributions to Anthropology 3. New York.

———. 1925b. Stylistic aspects of primitive literature. In Boas 1940:491–502.

———. 1929. Metaphorical expressions of the Kwakiutl. In Boas 1940:232–39.

———. 1930. *Religion of the Kwakiutl Indians*. Columbia University Contributions to Anthropology 10 (Part 1, Texts; Part 2, Translations). New York.

———. 1935. *Kwakiutl culture as reflected in mythology*. Memoir of the American Folklore Society 28. New York.

———. 1935–43. *Kwakiutl tales, new series*. Columbia University Contributions to Anthropology 26 (Part 1, Texts [1935]; Part 2, Translations [1943]). New York.

———. 1936. History and science in anthropology: A reply. In Boas 1940:305–11.

———. 1940. *Race, language and culture*. New York.

———. 1947. *Kwakiutl grammar, with a glossary of the suffixes*. New York.

———. 1966. *Kwakiutl ethnography*, ed. H. Codere. Chicago.

Boas, F., ed. 1911. *Handbook of American Indian languages*. Bureau of American Ethnology Bulletin 40. Washington, D.C.

———. 1917. *Folktales of Salishan and Sahaptin tribes, collected by James Teit and others*. Memoirs of the American Folklore Society 11. New York.

Boas, F., & E. Deloria. 1939. *Dakota grammar*. Memoirs of the National Academy of Sciences 23(2). Washington, D.C.

Boas, F., & G. Hunt. 1905. *Kwakiutl texts*. The Jesup North Pacific Expedition, Memoir of the American Museum of Natural History III. New York.

———. 1906. *Kwakiutl texts, second series*. The Jesup North Pacific Expedition, Memoir of the American Museum of Natural History X. New York.

BPC. See Manuscript Sources.

Canizzo, J. 1983. George Hunt and the invention of Kwakiutl culture. *Canad. Rev. Soc. & Anth.* 20(1): 44–58.

Carlson, B., ed. 1977. *Northwest Coast texts*. International Journal of American Linguistics Native American Texts, series 2. Chicago.

Codere, H. 1966. Introduction. In Boas 1966:xi–xxxii.

Curtis, E. S. 1915. *The Kwakiutl: The North American Indian*. Vol. 10. Norwood, Conn.

Deloria, E. 1932. *Dakota texts*. New York.

Dundes, A. 1979. Heads or tails? A psychoanalytic look at potlatch. *J. Psych. Anth.* 2: 395–424.

Fisher, M. W. 1939. Preface. In Jones 1939:vii–ix.

Ford, C. 1941. *Smoke from their fires: The life of a Kwakiutl chief*. New Haven.

Garvin, P., ed. 1970. *Method and theory in linguistics*. The Hague.

Goldman, I. 1975. *The mouth of heaven: An introduction to Kwakiutl religious thought*. New York.

Goldschmidt, W., ed. 1959. *The anthropology of Franz Boas: Essays on the centennial of his birth*. Memoir of the American Anthropological Association 89.

Hall, A. J. 1889. Grammar of the Kwagiutl language. *Transactions of the Royal Society of Canada* 6(2): 59–105. Montreal.

Hallowell, A. I. 1926. Bear ceremonialism in the northern hemisphere. *Am. Anth.* 28(1): 163–275.

Halpin, M. 1978. William Beynon, ethnographer. In Liberty 1978:141–56.

HAR. See Manuscript Sources.

Harris, M. 1968. *The rise of anthropological theory*. New York.

HCF. See Manuscript Sources.

HCU. See Manuscript Sources.

Healey, E. n.d. *History of Alert Bay and district*. Alert Bay, B.C.

Helm, J., ed. 1966. *Pioneers of anthropology*. Seattle.

Hymes, D. 1970. Linguistic method in ethnography: Its development in the United States. In Garvin 1970:249–311.

Jacknis, I. 1991. George Hunt, collector of Indian specimens. In Jonaitis 1991:177–224. Seattle.

Jacobs, M. 1959. Folklore. In Goldschmidt 1959:119–137.

Jonaitis, A., ed. 1991. *Chiefly feasts: The enduring Kwakiutl potlatch*. Seattle.

Jones, W. 1907. *Fox texts*. Publications of the American Ethnological Society 1. Leyden.

———. 1911. Algonquian (Fox). In Boas, ed., 1911:I, 735–874.

———. 1915. *Kickapoo tales*. Trans. T. Michelson. Publications of the American Ethnological Society 9. Leyden.

———. 1917. *Ojibwa texts*. Ed. T. Michelson. Publications of the American Ethnological Society 7. Vol. I, Leyden; Vol. II, New York.

———. 1939. *Ethnography of the Fox Indians*. Ed. M. W. Fisher. Bureau of Ethnology Bulletin 125. Washington, D.C.

Judd, C., B. Simonsen, & K. Scopick. 1989. *Site survey of historic Fort Rupert: Its history, archaeology and architecture*. Victoria, B.C.

Kaplan, S., & K. Barsness. 1986. *Raven's journey: The world of Alaska's native people*. Philadelphia.

KWFN. See Manuscript Sources.

Lévi-Strauss, C. 1963a. The sorceror and his magic. In Lévi-Strauss 1963b:167–85.

———. 1963b. *Structural anthropology*. New York.

Levine, R. 1977. Kwak'wala. In Carson 1977:98–126.

Liberty, M., ed. 1978. *American Indian intellectuals*. St. Paul.

Lincoln, N., & J. Rath. 1980. *North Wakashan comparative root list*. National Museum of Man Mercury Series, Canadian Ethnology Service Paper 68. Ottawa.

Locher, G. W. 1932. *The serpent in Kwakiutl religion*. Leyden.

Lowie, R. H. 1937. *The history of ethnological theory*. New York.

Maud, R. 1982. *A guide to B.C. Indian myth and legend: A short history of myth-collecting and a survey of published texts*. Vancouver, B.C.

———. 1989. The Henry Tate-Franz Boas collaboration on Tsimshian mythology. *American Ethnologist* 16(1): 158–62.

———. 1993. *The Porcupine Hunter and other stories: The original Tsimshian texts of Henry Tate*. Vancouver, B.C.

McFeat, T., ed. 1980. *Indians of the North Pacific Coast*. Seattle.

Milburn, M. 1986. Louis Shotridge and the objects of everlasting esteem. In Kaplan & Barsness 1986:54–77.

Müller, W. 1955. *Weltbild und Kult der Kwakiutl Indianer*. Wiesbaden.

Murdock, G. P. 1960. *Social structure*. New York.

Olson, R. L. 1967. *Social structure and social life of the Tlingit in Alaska*. Berkeley.

Petersen, R. T. 1961. *A field guide to western birds*. Boston.

Phinney, A. 1934. *Nez Perce texts*. Columbia University Contributions to Anthropology 25. New York.

Ray, V. 1955. Boas and the neglect of commoners. In McFeat 1980:159–60.

Reid, S. 1974. Myth as metastructure of the fairytale. In Maranda 1974:151–72.

———. 1979. The Kwakiutl maneater. *Anthropologica* 21:247–75.

Rohner, R. 1966. Franz Boas among the Kwakiutl: Interview with Mrs. Tom Johnson. In Helm 1966:213–45.

Rohner, R., ed. 1969. *The ethnography of Franz Boas*. Chicago.

Rohner, R., & E. Rohner. 1969. Introduction: Franz Boas and the development of North American ethnology and ethnography. In Rohner 1966:xii–xxx.

ROP. See Manuscript Sources.

Shotridge, L. 1917. My northland revisited. *Museum Journal* 8(2): 110–15.

———. 1919a. War helmets and clan hats of the Tlingit Indians. *Museum Journal* 10(1&2): 43–48.

———. 1919b. A visit to the Tsimshian Indians. *Museum Journal* 10(1&2): 49–67.

———. 1919c. A visit to the Tsimshian Indians, continued. *Museum Journal* 10(3): 117–48.

———. 1921. Tlingit woman's root basket. *Museum Journal* 12(3): 162–78.

———. 1928. The emblems of Tlingit culture. *Museum Journal* 19(4): 350–77.

———. 1929. The Kaguanton shark helmet. *Museum Journal* 20(3&4): 339–43.

Shotridge, L., & F. Shotridge. 1913. Indians of the Northwest. *Museum Journal* 4(3): 71–100.

Stocking, G. W., Jr. 1974. The Boas plan for the study of American Indian languages. In Stocking 1992:60–91.

———. 1977. The aims of Boasian anthropology: Creating the materials for traditional humanistic scholarship. *Hist. Anth. Newsl.* 4(1): 4–7.

———. 1992. *The ethnographer's magic and other essays in the history of anthropology*. Madison.

Swann, B., ed. 1992. *On the translation of Native American literature*. Smithsonian essays on Native American literature. Washington, D.C.

Swann, B., & A. Krupat. 1987. *Recovering the word: Essays on Native American literature*. Berkeley.

Teit, J. 1898. *Traditions of the Thompson River Indians of British Columbia*. Memoir of the American Folklore Society VI. Boston.

———. 1900. *The Thompson Indians of British Columbia*. Memoir of the American Museum of Natural History. New York.

———. 1906. *The Lillooet Indians*. Memoir of the American Museum of Natural History. New York.

———. 1909. *The Shuswap*. Memoir of the American Museum of Natural History. New York.

———. 1912. *Mythology of the Thompson Indians*. New York.

Toelken, B. 1987. Life and death in the Navajo Coyote tales. In Swann & Krupat 1987: 388–401.

Tsimshian Chiefs. 1992. Suwilaay'msga na G̲a'niiyatgm: *Teachings of our grandfathers*. 7 vols. Vancouver, B.C.

UPM. See Manuscript Sources.

Walens, S. 1981. *Feasting with cannibals: An essay on Kwakiutl cosmology*. Princeton.

White, L. 1963. *The ethnography and ethnology of Franz Boas*. Texas Memorial Museum Bulletin 6. Austin.

Wilson, P. 1993. Comprehension difficulties with the Boas-Hunt Kwak'wala texts. *Papers for the XXVIIIth International Conference on Salish and Neighboring Languages*, 345–62. University of Washington, Seattle, August 19–21.

Manuscript Sources

BLC   Franz Boas Collection of American Indian Linguistics (*Kwakiutl dictionary* [typescript ed. Helene Boas Yampolsky]), American Philosophical Society, Philadelphia.

BPC   Franz Boas Professional Correspondence, American Philosophical Society, Philadelphia.

HAR   George Hunt Accession Records, Anthropology Archives, American Museum of Natural History, New York.

HCF   George Hunt Correspondence File, Anthropology Archives, American Museum of Natural History, New York.

HCU   George Hunt Manuscript (*Manuscript in the language of the Kwakiutl Indians of Vancouver Island. Preface by Franz Boas, reviser.* [fourteen volumes]), Rare Book and Manuscript Library, Columbia University Libraries, New York.

HMB   George Hunt memorandum book, from a private collection.

KWFN   Kwak'wala Field Notes, in possession of author.

ROP   Ronald Olson Papers (Field Notes), Bancroft Library, University of California, Berkeley.

UPM   Director's Correspondence (G. B. Gordon), Archives of the University of Pennsylvania Museum of Archaeology and Anthropology, Philadelphia.

"THE LITTLE HISTORY OF PITIFUL EVENTS"

The Epistemological and Moral Contexts of Kroeber's Californian Ethnology

THOMAS BUCKLEY

There may be a half a dozen full-blooded Mattole scattered in and near their ancient land. The Government census of 1910 gives 10, with two or three times as many mixed bloods; but these figures may refer in part to Athabascans of other divisions, who here and there have drifted into the district. The Mattole had their share of fighting with the whites, the memory of which is even obscurer than the little history of most such pitiful events. Attempts were also made to herd them onto the reservations of Humboldt and Mendocino Counties. But like most of the endeavors of this sort in the early days of American California, these round-ups were almost as inefficient and unpersisted in as they were totally ill-judged in plan and heartless in intent, and all they accomplished was the violent dispersal, disintegration, and wasting away of the suffering tribes subjected to the process.

(Kroeber 1925:143)

There is a remarkable set of photographs, made in 1915, showing the last known "Yahi Indian," the man called "Ishi," standing with four anthropologists of varying degrees of eminence (in Darnell 1990, following p. 172). The most powerful of these pictures shows Ishi posed between a debonair Paul Radin and an "impulsive" Thomas Talbot Waterman (T. Kroeber 1970:149). To Waterman's left stand Edward Sapir and, finally, Robert Lowie, the tallest of

Thomas Buckley is associate professor in the Department of Anthropology and the American Studies Program, University of Massachusetts, Boston. He has done field work and advocacy anthropology among Native Californians since the early 1970s and is completing a compilation of his writing on Yurok Indian culture and history, which includes chapters on the history of anthropology in northwestern California and on A. L. Kroeber.

the group, leaning in upon it (cf. Golla 1984:195). Looking utterly displaced and almost forgotten among the large and looming anthropologists, Ishi seems to wish to merge with the leafy background, and soon will: he is already ill with tuberculosis and his death is less than a year away. Alfred Louis Kroeber, whom an informed viewer might expect to see in this photograph, is missing.

In 1911, when Ishi emerged as a middle-aged man out of a lifetime of hiding from invading whites, he was taken to the University of California's Museum of Anthropology in San Francisco. There he was made at home as an ethnographic research subject, a living exhibit (a "Stone Age Man"), a janitor, and, as it developed, a friend to several anthropologists and other university personnel. His chief benefactor and one of his three closest friends, of course, was Kroeber, then Chairman of the University's Department of Anthropology and Curator of its Museum (T. Kroeber 1961). In the late spring of 1915 Kroeber had begun a long-planned year's leave from the university that took him first to Zuñi Pueblo, in New Mexico, and then to New York, England, and Germany (1916a & b). He returned to New York and the American Museum of Natural History in November, and he was there when Ishi died on March 25, 1916. Informed by colleagues of his friend's imminent end, Kroeber insisted that Yahi burial practices be observed when the time came:

> I do not . . . see that an autopsy would lead to anything of consequence, but would resolve itself into a general dissection. Please shut down on it. As to disposal of the body, I must ask you as my personal representative to yield nothing at all under any circumstances. If there is any talk about the interests of science, say for me that science can go to hell. I cannot believe that any scientific value is materially involved. We have hundreds of Indian skeletons that nobody ever comes to study. The prime interest in this case would be of a morbid romantic nature. (AK/E. W. Gifford 3/24/15, in T. Kroeber 1961:234)

The letter arrived too late. Ishi's corpse was cut to pieces while it was "still warm" by another of his friends, the surgeon Saxton Pope, its internal organs removed, weighed, and examined, with the skull being found to be "small and rather thick" (Pope 1920:209, 212)

The sources of Kroeber's anguish were complex. His pain was sharpened by the unhappy coincidence of the death of his first wife, Henriette Rothschild, from the same disease in 1913—a loss that had already placed Kroeber in a position where "grief, worry, the agony of living threatened to engulf and overwhelm him" (T. Kroeber 1970:85). Ishi's death cast Kroeber into a deeper, cumulative darkness, intensified by his "[guilt] for being away from California while his friend was dying," by his "helplessness against the legacy of white man's disease" (Darnell 1990:82), and by what, I think, Kroeber understood to be the end of an era, both in the history of civilization and in his own career as an historian of civilization.

Ishi, for all anyone knew, had been "totally wild," "the last aborigine" in California, (AK/Sapir 7/6/11, in Golla 1984:59),[1] the last "illustration" of "the native primitive culture before it went all to pieces" (Kroeber 1912, 1948: 427). By 1914, while Ishi was still alive and apparently well in the University Museum of Anthropology, Kroeber had already begun to view his salvaged ethnographic record of aboriginal Californian cultures, gleaned from the memories of survivors now living in much-changed "bastard" cultures, as complete to the extent possible (1948:427; T. Kroeber 1970:94)—hence his trip to Zuñi in 1915 and the new directions in archeology and ethnology to which it would lead (1916b, 1917b). For Kroeber, Ishi's death must certainly have sealed the case, ending fifteen years of tireless Californian field work and ethnological writing.[2] It must also have been a harsh reminder of the moral miasma surrounding that "little history of . . . pitiful events" which was the cost of the "progress" in which Kroeber firmly "believed" (Steward 1973)—and that had destroyed all of Ishi's original band. The northern California "legacy" of the Gold Rush of 1849 included far more than the "white man's disease" that killed Ishi and so very many other indigenous people. It encompassed outright genocide—at least as defined by the United Nations Convention of 1948 (Norton 1979)—and it was to willful genocide that the Yahis, save Ishi, had been lost (T. Kroeber 1961:40–116).

Kroeber's depression was tinged with anger, and his anguished damnation of science resonates with his feeling that Edward Sapir, who had been doing linguistic work with Ishi, was "partly responsible" for Ishi's death (Darnell 1990: 82). We move from Kroeber's lashing out at science, in response to that death, into an intellectual configuration at once painful and rich. It includes among its components Kroeber's notions of history and of science, and of culture as an integrated fabric "illustrated" by individuals like Ishi, but existing outside of them, "in static balance." Hence it includes Kroeber's debate with his mentor, Franz Boas, over the nature of anthropology—a debate that had been engaged by 1900 and was in full flower at the time of Ishi's death (e.g., Kroeber 1901, 1935; Boas 1936). This configuration (a favorite word of Kroeber's) also encompasses the extraordinary tensions between notions of progress fostered by Victorian liberal positivists and the actual devastation occasioned by Eu-

1. All correspondence between Kroeber and Sapir (hereafter "ES") cited below appears in Golla (1984), where the letters are arranged chronologically.
2. By 1914 Kroeber, who had first come to California in 1900, had gathered most of the information on fifty cultural groups necessary to complete his 995-page *Handbook of the Indians of California* (Kroeber 1925), either through his own fieldwork or through the researches of others that he directed. He began to compose the *Handbook* in 1915 and had completed a draft and submitted it to the Bureau of American Ethnology for publication in 1917, although he continued revising certain chapters into 1918. Because of budgetary constraints due to the world war, the *Handbook* was not published until 1925 (AK/ES 6/14/17, 11/22/18).

ropean peoples' invasion of the American West in the second half of the nineteenth century. Although motivated by grief and frustration, Kroeber's "science can go to hell" sums up, metaphorically, his reaction to a deeply
compounded epistemological and moral dilemma that had much to do with
both his situation in anthropology at the turn of the century and his shaping
of the discipline after that transitional moment. This anthropological dilemma
was later powerfully described by Lévi-Strauss in a paragraph that has particular resonance with Kroeber's life and work:

> Anthropology is not a dispassionate science like astronomy, which springs from
> the contemplation of things at a distance. It is the outcome of a historical process
> which has made the larger part of mankind subservient to the other, and during
> which millions of innocent human beings have had their resources plundered
> and their institutions and beliefs destroyed, whilst they themselves were ruth-
> lessly killed, thrown into bondage, and contaminated by diseases they were un-
> able to resist. Anthropology is the daughter to this era of violence: its capacity
> to assess more objectively the facts pertaining to the human condition reflects,
> on the epistemological level, a state of affairs in which one part of mankind
> treated the other as an object. (1966:126)

Epistemology

1. *The aim of history is to know the relation of social facts to the whole of*
   civilization.
2. *The material studied by history is not man, but his works.*
3. *Civilization, though carried by men and existing through them, is an entity*
   in itself, and of another order of life.

(Kroeber 1915)

Kroeber uttered his "science can go to hell" during a period in his career in
which he was making clear his self-definition as a "humanist," rather than a
natural scientist, and his definition of anthropology as "natural history" rather
than natural science (1952:10). In 1915 he published an emphatic statement
of this identity in a set of "Eighteen Professions" regarding the fundamental
assumptions, aims and methods of ethnology properly understood—that is, as
history—the last of which proclaimed, "In fine, the determination and methods of biological, psychological, or natural science do not exist for history, just
as the results and manner of operation of history are disregarded by consistent
biological practice." In this context, his letter to Gifford takes on a meaning
at once broader and of greater significance to the history of anthropology than
that of a personal reaction of grief.

The case is far from simple. Like most anthropologists, Kroeber did custom-
arily speak of anthropology as "science" in an informal way (e.g., "Universities

want classes, not science, and allot budget and salaries accordingly" [AK/ES 7/17/18]). More to the point are the objectified and synchronic understanding of cultures upon which he built his history of civilization, that history's disregard for individuality, and his lifelong search for fully objective methods by which to quantify degrees of progress—all of which strike some contemporary readers as "natural scientific positivism in anthropology driven to the end" (Wolf 1981:63). Others, however, have found "no clash" between Kroeber's claim to humanism and his positivism, viewing his efforts to formulate a "humanistic statistics" as a coherent extension of Boasian linguistics (Hymes 1961:17). To begin to resolve these seemingly mutually exclusive interpretations, we need a general sense of the nineteenth-century tradition of scientific humanism that was a large part of Kroeber's fin-de-siècle upbringing (T. Kroeber 1970:5–52), and also to review briefly his "rebellion" against Boas' scientific objectives, beginning in 1900 (Thoresen 1971:100–101, citing Darnell 1969).

Scientific Humanism and "Metaphysical Ghosts"

Despite Kroeber's very long and productive career, which spanned two centuries and two world wars, his "basic theoretical thrust was remarkably of one piece, was set very early, and was highly consistent" (Wolf 1981:40–41). Although Kroeber published well over four hundred pieces, including most of his major works, after 1917 (Gibson & Rowe 1961), the essentials of his ethnological thinking were largely formed by the time the United States entered the First World War, when he was forty-one years old; his subsequent thought as well as his personal life followed a "configuration" well set by that time (Thoresen 1975b; T. Kroeber 1970). Thus, while Kroeber's era can hardly be confined to the turn of the century, his thought must be understood in a context dominated by the currents of that transitional moment.

Kroeber's natal society was the bourgeois intellectual and artistic Deutschamerikanish elite of late nineteenth-century Manhattan. German was his first language, and he was nurtured in a rich northern European intellectual tradition that held both the arts (especially literature) and the natural sciences in high esteem. It was a society that celebrated humanistic liberality together with a scientific objectivity that was the natural expression of what Boas called "the ice cold flame of the passion of truth for truth's sake" (1945).[3] Kroeber's

3. It is perhaps noteworthy that three of the men in the 1915 photograph shared this background with Kroeber to some extent, as did Boas (b. Minden 1858, emigrated to New York 1887), mentor to them all. Radin (b. Łódź 1883) and Lowie (b. Vienna 1883, emigrated to New York 1893) were of Kroeber's social class, and Edward Sapir (b. Pomerania 1884, emigrated to New York 1894) aspired to the respectability and stability that the other men enjoyed as birthrights. All five men—including Kroeber—were in Manhattan, either as teachers or as students, in the 1890s—Boas, Kroeber, and Sapir at Columbia, Lowie and Radin at City College. (Waterman was born in Missouri and grew up in Fresno, California.)

first serious intellectual pursuit was entomology. One of his first theoretical works was a youthful manifesto, coauthored with Carl Alsberg around 1892 and presented before the Humboldt Scientific Society, which he and Alsberg founded as teenagers and sustained through their years together at Columbia: "Resolved That Realism Conveys a Greater Moral Lesson than Idealism" (T. Kroeber 1970:22–23). While Alsberg became a physicist, Kroeber went on define himself as a natural historian and humanist, neither a natural nor a social scientist (1936). Taking his models for the practice of anthropology from the natural histories of Linneaus and Alexander von Humboldt (as well as from Franz Boas' linguistics), he accepted the positivism of the natural sciences as appropriate to the study of culture and history, but rejected their goals of causal explanation, prediction, and the formulation of general laws.

In one sense, Kroeber's self-identification as a humanist is rather simple and straightforward. He had an abiding love of literature and history, first fostered in the Manhattan home and schools of his childhood. Entering Columbia as an undergraduate in 1892, Kroeber took both a B.A. and a Master's degree in literature. His first publication, in 1896, was a short story in the *Columbia Literary Monthly*. He defined himself as a "historian" in the early years of his career, and considered all of his own writings literature, rather than science. But his claim to humanism was also a declaration of independence from his mentor, Boas, whom he considered a "spiritual physicist" (1943:25). Kroeber was as much defining what he was not—that is, a natural scientist—as what he was. There are also other, more subtle historical resources in Kroeber's proclaimed humanism that help place him in his moment and milieu.

First of all, the notion of culture that Kroeber was to develop emphasized the primacy of human creativity as the engine of cultural growth and civilization's progress, and it focused on expressive culture—folklore, mythology, religious symbolism, the plastic arts—as revelatory both of the order or "style" of creativity of a given culture and of its people's "psychic nature" (Kroeber 1902:3). It was in some respects closer to nineteenth-century humanistic definitions of culture as artistic and intellectual output than to the emerging anthropological view of culture as a largely unconscious or behavioral phenomenon (cf. Stocking 1968:230). Furthermore, the methods and objectives of Boasian ethnography, as transmitted to Kroeber, reflected the established methods of (humanistic) classical studies and antiquarianism (Stocking 1977). Boas was, of course, singularly important in the transition from humanistic to anthropological constructions of the culture concept, and Kroeber, who underplayed the systematicity of Boas' anthropological culture theory (e.g., Kroeber & Kluckhohn 1952:151), advanced that transition considerably, most signally in his 1917 essay, "The Superorganic." However, with his continuing emphases on creativity and on expressive culture, and on methods originating with classicists, Kroeber never entirely left behind nineteenth-century humanistic understandings of *Kultur*.

Nonetheless, Kroeber found in natural history (as to an extent had Boas) a bridge between humanist notions of culture and a twentieth-century anthropological understanding. In natural history he also found a resolution of the tension between "understanding" the variables in human creativity through Verstehen—the subjective apprehension of order—and the emphasis in the natural sciences on Erklären—on the "explanation" of phenomena through inductive discovery of general laws. The natural history that Kroeber emulated was an empirical, descriptivist enterprise whose goal was the classification of phenomena through Verstehen. In this context, natural history and the secular humanism of the late nineteenth century were complementary applications of Verstehen methodology; both contrasted with the natural sciences, with their commitments to Erklären and to the discovery of general laws (cf. Boas 1887b). All of this seems embedded in Kroeber's much later depiction of linguistics and, by implication, ethnology properly conceived:

> (1) Its data and findings are essentially impersonal and anonymous. (2) Its orientation is spontaneously historical, and potentially historical even for languages whose past is lost. (3) The emphasis is on pattern, or structural interrelation, and away from so-called "functional" interpretations involving need satisfaction, drives, stimulus-response, and other explanations which "decompose" the phenomena dealt with into something ulterior. (4) Explanation is not in terms of genuine scientific cause, that is efficient causes in the Aristotelian sense, but of "formal causes," that is, of other forms as being antecedent, similar, contrasting, or related. (5) indeed, "explanation" in terms of producing cause is largely replaced by "understanding" in terms of historic contexts, relevance, and value significance. (1947, in 1952:107)

While Kroeber's affinity for Humboldtian (and Linnean) natural history is clear in his lifelong fascination with typological classification, he did not share these ancestors' morphological concern nor that of Darwinian natural history with biological evolution. On the other hand, while accepting the irreducible subjectivity of "understanding," he aspired to absolute objectivity (e.g., 1939: Map 28) and thus embraced the positivism of the natural sciences as appropriate to humanistic natural history. He was deeply suspicious of what he termed "sympathy" in the work of other ethnologists, like his early predecessor in California, Stephen Powers (1877). Although Powers was possessed of "an astoundingly quick and vivid sympathy" that allowed him "to seize and fix the salient qualities of the people he described," his ethnology was of the "crudest," with "flimsy texture and slovenly edges" (1925:ix). Kroeber's method, in short, is not easily recognized as "humanistic" today. His work has little concern for experience, individuality, ethnographic circumstantiality, process (as opposed to structure), or meaning, let alone reflexivity, and thus it seems to some today that "there are, in fact, no people" in Kroeber's ethnology (Wolf 1981:57).

However, the turn-of-the-century scientific humanism espoused by Kroeber was not opposed to positivism. It ultimately sprang from a far older, European theological tradition in which the Divine—albeit largely unbeknownst to humanity—was thought to manifest Its will dynamically in the workings of human society, historically understood. This position contrasted with Augustinian Christian radicalism and its emphases on the uniqueness of the privileged individual's revelatory and knowing relationship with God as well as the faithful's alienation from mundane place, time, and society alike (Henry Levinson, personal communications, 1986). Humanists in the former tradition could objectify reality as a phenomenon beyond the individual, in the light of which "individuals . . . shrunk to insignificance" (Kroeber 1952:9). Thus, for Kroeber, "civilization" became the real, an atheistic replacement for an older God which, "though carried by men and existing through them, is an entity in itself, and of another order of life" (1915: Profession 3). This entity expressed itself most clearly not in idiosyncratic, affective human beings but in their "works" as manifest in place and in time. Thus, "The personal or individual has no historical value save as illustration" (Profession 6). So Kroeber resolved the then central problem of sociology: "[A] thousand individuals do not make a society"; a society is "an entity beyond them" (1917a). To glorify the individual as the sole vehicle for the revelation of the real was romantic "idealism."

In taking this position Kroeber differed with Boas, who neither eliminated the individual nor hypostatized society; yet this difference was created through Kroeber's effort to resolve a tension in Boas' own work. Boas had written, "The object of study is the individual, not abstractions from the individual under observation" (1887a:485), but he also advanced the notion that cultural integration was finally psychological, internal to individual actors, and most forceful at the unconscious level, where it was inculcated through enculturation and socialization (cf. Stocking 1974:8). Kroeber took this postulate to its ultimate conclusion: that individual consciousness, affect, and action were culturally determined at the unconscious level, leaving the "personal or individual" with "no historical value." In doing so, Kroeber was joining with many others of the era who were attempting to establish human affairs, cultural and social, as legitimate objects of scientific study, irreducible to individual personality (e.g., Durkheim 1895).

Despite such conflicts inherent in Kroeber's and his mentor's work from early on, however, Kroeber shared many of Boas' deepest convictions: indeed, it has been suggested that Kroeber's "Eighteen professions" of 1915 "in many respects may be regarded as a kind of manifesto of Boasian anthropology" (Stocking 1974:16)—in many respects, it may be added, but not all. Kroeber's belief in the unity of humanity, whereby racial differences were no longer fundamental (Profession 8: "The absolute equality and identity of all human races and strains as carriers of civilization must be assumed by the historian"), was solidly Boasian. Kroeber asserted, for instance, that there were no intrinsic moral differences between the races; specific moralities were acquired, as Boas taught, through enculturation (Kroeber 1910). On the other hand, Kroeber thought that those carrying a specific civilization were nevertheless different from those carrying another. Both men believed that a civilization and its bearers' peculiar "genius" (Boas 1911b) or "psychic nature" (Kroeber 1902)— equivalents of older German romantic ideas of *Volksgeist*—were historically shaped, and that a people's particular morality was a historical accretion and burden, rather than a hereditary trait (e.g., Boas 1896, Kroeber 1910). Here again, however, Kroeber took "one aspect of Boasian assumption and carr[ied] it farther than Boas himself would accept" (Stocking 1974:17). For Kroeber, all men bearing a given culture were, and could, moreover, be treated as, tokens of their cultural type, with the individual once again "shrinking to insignificance" (1952:9), a mere "illustration" (1915) of a historical process of accumulation of traits shared by all carriers of his specific civilization. In this sense, Kroeber's humanism—unlike Boas'—had little need for individual human beings. While Sapir and Radin were to develop Boas' individualism "farther than Boas himself would accept," Kroeber went on the opposite tack. Idealism, routed by "realism" in the humanistic reduction of individuals to the status of "illustrations," reemerged in his work as cultural essentialism.

Like Boas, Kroeber drew strict boundaries between biology and "history," rejecting "heredity" and (natural) "selection" as explanations for "social facts" (1915: Professions 9–11). Eschewing biological evolution as a key to understanding cultural differences, he nonetheless did believe in progress (as did Boas, to some extent) and in evolution more broadly understood. Indeed, according to his friend Carl Alsberg (1936:xvii), Kroeber's turn toward anthropology and away from the natural sciences and literature in 1896 was based in this belief. Results obtained through the natural sciences, Kroeber told Alsberg, were

> not likely to affect men's thinking and to make for progress in the only way that was worth while: to free men intellectually. The confused thinking about religions was perhaps the most important bar to man's progress and freedom. Anthropology was, he thought, capable of bringing some degree of clarity into the confused thought of men, and of freeing them to some degree from hoary tribal taboos. (1936:xvii)

Kroeber had taken up Boas' "crusading attitude that sought to propagate 'the anthropological point of view.'" Yet once again he took a Boasian notion farther than Boas, seeing anthropology, and particularly the culture concept, as both a result of (and thus evidence for) progress, and a means of further progress, while Boas grew increasingly skeptical regarding anthropological reconstructions of history, genetic classification of cultures, and hence, it would seem, of the demonstrability of the truth value of progress (Stocking 1974:15).

Kroeber's understanding of culture history, as it developed between 1896 and 1907, was as a process of linear ("teleological") growth through accumulation (1915). Developing the age-area concept as it had emerged in Germany and been both refined and transmitted by Boas, Kroeber accepted early on that space and time were the proper contexts within which specific cultural phenomena were to be understood (Kroeber 1918; cf. Driver 1962). The similarities among cultures in a given region were thus the results of historical processes of diffusion, not of environmental determination (Profession 7: "Geography, or physical environment, is material made use of by civilization, not a factor shaping or explaining civilization"). History, however, was expressed in the total accumulation of elements within a given area, and the increasing quantity and complexity of a culture's "content" was an index of its progress. Cultures thus could, in fact, be ranked hierarchically, and peoples like Native Californians, whom Kroeber first encountered in 1900, were understood as being culturally impoverished, at the "primitive" extreme of the developmental hierarchy. Kroeber reiterated this—today, much resented—assessment, first laid out in "The Religion of the Indians of California" (1907), in the manuscript for Yurok Myths, left unfinished at his death. Here he spoke of Native Californians' "sense of form" as being "conspicuously rudimentary . . . in all concretely visible phases of Californian civilization," considering the basketry for which these people are often admired "generally overrated." Native Californian "handiwork," Kroeber concluded, "is aesthetically insignificant alongside the products of all other American tribes saving a few of the poorest" (1976:467). Thus while "[t]he so-called savage is no transition between the animal and the scientifically educated man" (Profession 12), human beings themselves progressed through various transitional stages, manifested as material and social cultural "content," from the "savage" and "rudimentary" to the "scientifically educated."

Kroeber's assessments of the quality of cultures—of the "psychic natures" characteristic of each, the relative position of cultures and of these typical "attitudes" or "tendencies" in a hierarchy of cultures, and, finally, the degree of progress each had made in the "race of civilization" (1917a)—were largely based in a humanistic concern for expressive culture, broadened by the nineteenth-century German romantic appreciation of Völkergedanken. Expressive culture was the product of human creativity, which produced not only better, more "realistic-symbolic" plastic art (1901:301), but also more and more intricately interrelated "traits" or "elements." "Poorer" cultures were naturally left behind in that "race" by those with more "massive," "intensely" structured trait inventories (1959:236, 1925:901; cf. 1939:5 ff.)—like those of his own "superior race" (1926:vi). Human creativity, carried by individuals but a product of civilization itself, was thus the engine of history and of progress, and this logical step again underscored the struggle of Kroeber's "realism" against a seemingly inescapable "idealism."

In the intellectual environment of the German-American community in which Kroeber was raised, one "took for granted that one did not believe in religion": "Anthropology," Kroeber declared, "is my religion" (in T. Kroeber 1970:x, 26). It was a religion, however, in which individuals were submerged in the history of civilization, in which all their actions and feelings were culturally determined. "Anthropology" was Kroeber's "religious" practice; the object of his devotions was, as Theodora Kroeber has suggested, "culture" (1970:234).

While it is Kroeber who is most readily identified with the notion of culture (or "civilization") as "superorganic" (1917a), the idea of a "self contained 'super-organic' reality" had long "bewitched the 19th century mind" as a defense against "metaphysical ghosts" (Geertz 1973:11, 1980:135). Despite his avowed "realism," these same "ghosts" haunted Kroeber's cultural determinism.

> When one has acquired the habit of viewing the millennial sweeps and grand contours, and individuals have shrunk to insignificance, it is very easy to deny them consequential influence, even any influence—and therewith one stands in the gateway of belief in unidentified immanent forces; a step more, and the forces have become mysterious. (Kroeber 1952:9)

Kroeber's superorganic "civilization," his cultures succeeding one another in increasing "massiveness," driven forward by "majestic forces or sequences" that acted through the culturally determined agency of human "creativity," constructed as a defense against "metaphysical ghosts," were in fact those very ghosts in material disguise, and may be understood as a secular alternative to God. This enabled Kroeber both to dispense with "man's greatest bar to progress and freedom" and to fend off the nihilism that seemed the necessary consequence of a purely secular historicism. But the "ghost," the Prime Mover, reentered Kroeber's history in the guise of a superorganic culture that determined individual creativity. Sapir spotted the implicit metaphysics of Kroeber's "Superorganic" immediately (1917). And while Kroeber heatedly denied its presence at the time (AK/ES, 7/24/17), late in life he admitted that there were "metaphysically constru[ed] levels of conception or orders of attribute" in his 1917 essay, "The Superorganic" (1952:22).

In reifying "civilization" as a metaphysical force which, "though carried by men and existing through them, is an entity in itself, and of another order of life," Kroeber accepted Kant's radically dualistic separation of phenomena (to be studied through science) and their underlying spirituality (to be apprehended through history). Boas strove to resolve Kant's dualism methodologically by defining history as another way of doing science. Kroeber attempted to resolve this dualism epistemologically, redefining cultural phenomena as epiphenomena to be studied purely as manifestations of "another order of life," thus doing away with the need for science in anthropology, defining himself as a historian of human creativity (cf. Stocking 1974:10).

Since, for Kroeber, civilization itself was finally, if unadmittedly, metaphysical, the lives of individuals and the life of a culture alike were also ultimately metaphysically determined: creativity—the active means of progress—therefore had a metaphysical significance. By abjuring religion, the individual, and sentiment alike, he hoped to achieve a "typological realism" by which the succession of cultures through the "millennial sweep" of history would reveal itself as a progress, yielding a "moral lesson" far more powerful than that of idealism (Thoresen 1975b). Yet Kroeber's understanding of culture evidences the persistence of nineteenth-century German idealism in his thought. Manifested in both cultural essentialism and in a metaphysics which he denied, it, too, had been nurtured in that same erudite and progressive Deutschamerikanisch community that so valued scientific realism.

Boas and Kroeber, Typology and Time
Kroeber was "an anthropologist's anthropologist" (Steward 1961)—neither an epistemologist nor consistently interested in anthropological theory for its own sake (but see, e.g., Kroeber and Kluckhohn 1951). While his ultimate concern was with "majestic forces," these forces could only be apprehended through the phenomenal elements that they produced. Thus Kroeber was, by his own estimation, "a worker in concrete data" (1952:vii): archeological finds, linguistic elements, and culture traits collected as material culture or through ethnographic research. His devotion to particulars was in the service of "pattern recognition," and the classification of cultures in accord with the patterns he deduced was a means of understanding both the historical affiliations of specific cultures and the "growth" of civilization (e.g., 1944). Whether he was a humanist, positivist, realist, or idealist is, to an extent, beside the point. He was all of these and more, by turn and sometimes simultaneously. He had to be in order to negotiate the conflict between his emergent definition of culture as a general (albeit, metaphysical) object and his emphasis on particular subjects of study (cf. Geertz 1973:10). His concern with civilization and with cultures as generalized objects, however, did not imply an interest in formulation of the general laws governing the emergence of these objects.

By 1915 Kroeber was ready to profess that "[t]he causality of history is teleological" (Profession 17). But this is a statement of how cultures "grow" and
history works—by accumulation, in a linear fashion and in the direction of
superior civilizational massiveness and intensity. Profession 17 presents a further specification of what civilization is; it is not an expression of interest in
the cause of civilization itself, in why civilization arises (cf. Thoresen 1971:
62). This concern with the what rather than the why of history was to distinguish Kroeber's work, at least in his own mind, from that of Boas, even before
Kroeber had completed his doctorate in anthropology under Boas in 1901.

Kroeber joined Boas' seminar in linguistics in 1896, while Boas was curator
at the American Museum of Natural History. In 1897, when Kroeber was an
assistant in literature and rhetoric at Columbia and Boas had been appointed
lecturer in anthropology, Kroeber changed his field to anthropology. By 1898
Kroeber was an assistant in anthropology and on his way to completing the
first Columbia doctorate in that discipline. His doctoral research and collecting was carried out among Arapahoe Indians in Wyoming in the fieldwork
seasons of 1899, 1900, and 1901, and he completed his dissertation, published
as "Decorative Symbolism of the Arapaho," later in 1901 (1901; T. Kroeber
1970:46–52).

Kroeber had been "enormously stimulated" by Boas' assignment of his 1896
seminar students to the task of extrapolating the grammar from Chinook, Inuit, Klamath, and Salish texts—a task that Boas himself went about like "a
zoologist who starts a student with an etherized frog or worm and a dissecting
table" (in T. Kroeber 1970:47). However, he did not find so compelling Boas'
"inductive" method or his interest in discovering general laws governing the
creation of grammars that might illustrate the psychic unity of humanity.
Rather, said Kroeber, it was the process of "recognizing patterns" in the texts
that resonated with his already "strong bent" and "proclivity" (AK/D. Hymes,
in T. Kroeber 1970:46). Years later Kroeber was to write, of the study of "cultural and historical phenomena," that "recognition of pattern is the suitable
and fruitful goal of nearer understanding" (1952:9)—nearer, that is, than the
explanation of cultural and historical (or grammatical) causality. Kroeber's appreciation of the significance of cultural patterns was manifest in his 1901
dissertation, where he based an analysis of a people's "type" on the "style" that
emerged as a pattern in their art taken as a whole. By 1901, then, a dispute
was already developing between Kroeber and Boas that hinged upon Kroeber's
insistence that "recognition of pattern" was indeed what anthropologists
should be up to, rather than a search for general laws and causal explanation.

Kroeber's approach to linguistic and cultural phenomena was partially a reflection of an inherited "'object' orientation of 19th century anthropology."
Boas trained his students to do fieldwork "intended to produce a body of material that had an objective character in the particular sense that it consisted

of material and non-material artifacts created by a people themselves" (Stocking 1977:5). In 1903, when questioned about his expectations of his students,
Boas responded,

> I have instructed my students to collect certain things and to collect with every-
> thing they get information in the native language and to obtain grammatical
> information that is necessary to explain their texts. Consequently the results of
> their journeys are the following: they get specimens; they get explanations of the
> specimens; they get connected texts that partly refer to the specimens and partly
> simply to abstract things concerning the people; and they get grammatical infor-
> mation." (in Stocking 1977:4)

Kroeber's doctoral fieldwork was intended not simply to compile an ethnographic profile of Arapahoe people, but equally as a collecting trip to add
Arapahoe artifacts to the holdings of the American Museum of Natural History. Similarly, his initial employment in California in 1900, for which he was
recommended by Boas, was as a curator of the Californian Indian artifact collection at the San Francisco Academy of Sciences Museum (T. Kroeber 1970:
53 ff.). His "object orientation" was further encouraged by the "salvage" nature of his early ethnographic inquiries in California, where his primary data
were the memory-artifacts of his Native Californian informants, rather than
observational records compiled through participation in social action. Yet
there are important differences between Kroeber's responses to this orientation
and those of Boas.

Boas' purpose in amassing objectified data, as well as physical objects, was
to painstakingly build up a cumulative understanding of a culture through understanding the interrelationships of the objects he collected within their own
cultural contexts (see Stocking 1968:225). Like Boas, Kroeber objectified cultural "content" as a considered methodological step rather than as an inheritance unreflected upon. "I don't give a red cent," Kroeber wrote to Sapir in
1917, "whether cultural phenomena have a reality of their own, as long as we
treat them as if they had" (AK/ES 11/17). Both men accepted as a matter of
course that cultural and linguistic traits formed integrated wholes (which
Kroeber was to further reify as "fabrics," "substances," or "bodies"). Kroeber's
interest was not so much with understanding the interrelationships among
these objectified traits within their own cultural contexts, however, as with
the typological classifications that the accumulation of data on traits made
possible.

Thus, Kroeber's effort was toward gathering "information, ordering and clas-
sifying it meaningfully, and integrating it into the existing stock of knowledge
as a context, which thereby would be given gradually increasing significance"
(1952:3). Kroeber held that Boas, by contrast, "was fundamentally impatient
with classification, especially where it tended to become an end in itself"

(1943:24). Kroeber's emergent method, once he began working in California in 1900, was to survey as many languages and cultures as possible, as fast as possible, both salvaging rapidly disappearing cultural and linguistic knowledge and building up inventories of elements from which classifications of languages and of culture types—and thus the histories of each—might be deduced.[4] Boas found this wrong-headed (while admitting that he had once done much the same in British Columbia) and in 1902 wrote Kroeber to that effect: "I am of the opinion that you ought not to do much more miscellaneous work among the various tribes, but that you should take up one group by itself and work it out thoroughly" (in Darnell 1969:305). Kroeber did not agree. In the next few years the rift widened as Kroeber "rebelled" by procrastinating in meeting Boas' request for a contribution on the Yokuts language for Boas' *Handbook of American Indian Languages* (Boas 1911a). Kroeber most specifically resisted, by this means, Boas' goal of investigating the underlying universal "psychology" manifested in human languages, to reveal the general laws governing their forms (Thoresen 1971:100–104).

Kroeber's interest in typological classification as providing the proper context for understanding the significance of cultural phenomena entailed a disinterest, not only in both Boasian cultural context and causal explanation, but also in Native Californian "explanations" and textual testimony through which that context might be more fully apprehended. Defining culture as manifested most clearly, not in "mental action" but in a "body or stream of products of mental exercise" (1917a), Kroeber was not much interested in native testimony regarding what Boas called "abstract things concerning the people." Indigenous exegesis was of concern primarily for the "items" that it revealed: otherwise it was largely "ethnographically irrelevant" (Kroeber & Gifford 1949:82).

> Kroeber had no interest in meaning. His . . . interest [was] in the externality of form. . . . What comes to mind is a discussion of Yurok narrative and poetry, which is a splendid wording of the quality of the Yurok style of delivery. It talks about how the Yurok recite and talk, but it never touches on what they're talking about. (Wolf 1981:56)

For Kroeber, meaning was individual, affective, a matter of "aesthetic sense," graspable only through "sympathy" and not subject to positive reduction. One could not make "a single exact and intelligible remark" about the meaning of Yurok Indian music, for instance, because that meaning was em-

---

4. Kroeber's speed and tenacity in acquiring ethnographic and linguistic data were to become legendary. He was known to gather a vocabulary in an unknown language from a chance informant while waiting for a train (Hymes 1961:5) and, in 1913, berated L. L. Loud for heel-dragging in gathering information for a complete Wiyot ethnogeography when, "With a proper informant this is an affair of only a couple of hours" (Heizer 1970:16).

bedded in the singers' "profoundest feelings" (Kroeber 1925:96). While Boas, in principle, entered into dialogue with his objects, Kroeber's discourse on culture content was purely monological.

Kroeber saw the original contextualization of cultural content in Native Californian circumstantiality as jeopardizing the entire project of a natural history of culture. Ethnography posed important risks and challenges since, "from the point of view of culture, archaeological data come ready to hand as the purest there are, with language probably second. In archaeology facts are certainly less mixed, not only than in history, but in ethnography" (1952:8). The significance of a given element of cultural content was to be established in terms of its relationships to other elements within a fixed spatial (rather than social) conjunction, in which it could be apprehended by the analyst as a constituent of a pattern, established by "natural argument" (that is, by deduction) rather than by indigenous exegesis (e.g., 1907, 1908; cf. Kroeber & Gifford 1949:3). Thus Kroeber objectified culture as its content and simultaneously abstracted this content from its social context, relocating its significance in analytic contexts where it could be examined and grasped undefiled (or "mixed") by indigenous individuality and affect. His anthropology, as classificatory natural history, could only gain significance by denying significance to native experience.

The idea that the vast diversity of the world's cultures revealed to Europeans through colonialism might be analytically simplified by organizing them according to geographical areas of similar cultures was a popular one in the late nineteenth century, especially among German scholars. In the United States, Boas first formally propounded, not just this simple understanding of culture areas, but also the idea that these areas were historical as well as geographical units: the spatial coefficients of processes of cultural growth by diffusion, through time (e.g., 1896). In Boasian culture area theory, space *became* time, regions that were at once geographical and comparable to European historical eras (Kroeber 1939:264).

By 1918 Kroeber was able to state that "At least half of the anthropologists of this country have been reared in an atmosphere over which the concept of the culture area hovered insistently" (1918:209). As Kroeber developed the Boasian culture area concept in his early work (e.g., 1907), he took for granted that, absorbed in action and process, the indigenous individual could have no awareness of his or her existence within an historical period: could have no sense of being in *a* time, but only an experience of existing *through* time. By the same token, his or her (but, in Kroeber's work, largely his) awareness of the areal coefficients of his experience had to be dimmed by his experience, not of "*a* place," or a region, but simply of "the world." Only through abstracting content from Native Californians' experience of it and reordering it in terms

A. L. Kroeber and Ishi reconstructing pre-contact material cultural practice at their camp on Deer Creek, in the summer of 1914. (Courtesy of the P. A. Hearst Museum, University of California, Berkeley.)

of deduced patterns could the integration of a culture as a historical entity be made known and, with it, the belongingness of each culture in its place.

In order for this areal context to lend significance to cultural content, content itself needed to be rigidly specifiable, held "in static balance" (Kroeber 1959): Kroeber "lacked dialectics" (Stanley Diamond, in Silverman 1981:63). Thus Kroeber's ethnology stressed both the areal autonomy of pre-contact cultures in, for example, California (Kroeber 1907, 1908, 1920), and a historical reconstruction that recreated a synchronic moment before "the native primitive culture . . . went all to pieces" under extra-areal contacts (Kroeber 1948: 427)—to wit, the Euro-American invasion of the Western Hemisphere. Kroeber's reconstructed aboriginal cultures, as areally bounded, synchronic entities, could not be historically transformed through acculturation (however traumatic), but by definition perished upon contact with "more massive" cultures (cf. Steward 1973)—another reflection of Kroeber's underlying essentialism. On the other hand, they could be compared, area with area, time with time. It was in such comparison that "the race of civilization" became apparent and progress was revealed. In all, Kroeber's culture history is a highly abstract and odd sort of history indeed—one that is essentially static, like a series of museum tableaux constructed to display the artifactual results of several coordinated collecting expeditions, much as Boas had organized the North Pacific Hall at the American Museum of Natural History in New York (e.g., Jonaitis 1988).

Morality

> *After some hesitation I have omitted all directly historical treatment in the ordinary sense; that is, accounts of the relations of the natives with the whites and of the events befalling them after such contact was established. It is not that this subject is unimportant or uninteresting, but that I am not in a position to treat it adequately. It is also a matter that has comparatively slight relation to aboriginal civilization.*
>
> *(Kroeber 1925:vi)*

In 1900, on Boas' recommendation, Kroeber came from Columbia to the Academy of Sciences in San Francisco by way of Wyoming and his continuing Arapahoe research. Finding his museum responsibilities light, he undertook his first California fieldwork, travelling roughly 350 miles north from San Francisco to the mouth of the Klamath River, about 30 miles south of the Oregon border. There he encountered Yurok Indians—people who were to provide him with a lifelong research interest (1904a & b, 1976). In 1901, after concluding his work in Wyoming, Kroeber took up a probationary position as an instructor under Frederic Ward Putnam in the new Department of Anthropology at the University of California, the first such department west of Chicago (T. Kroeber 1970:53–62). In 1903, Kroeber and Putnam initiated the Ethnographic and Archaeological Survey of California. Kroeber's mission, originally financed directly by Phoebe Apperson Hearst, the department's sponsor (Thoresen 1975a), was to collect, through a massive and well-organized ethnographic effort throughout the state, all of the aboriginal cultural and linguistic materials that he possibly could before the last of those Native Californians who recalled them died. This enormous, even heroic effort in salvage ethnography eventually involved a dozen or more collaborating fieldworkers, including T. T. Waterman, Llwellyn L. Loud, and Edward Sapir, all of whom played important roles in Ishi's last years.

The "Little History"

Ishi's death, while certainly the best known, was but one among hundreds of thousands by disease or violence that had reduced the indigenous population of California from something like 300,000 to less than 20,000 between 1769, when the first Spanish mission was founded, and Ishi's capitulation in

1911. The extent and rate of Native Californian mortality specifically by violence had been particularly grim in northern California between the Gold Rush of 1849 and the end of the Modoc War in 1873, less than thirty years before Kroeber's arrival in San Francisco. Overall population decline among the Yurok Indians, whom Kroeber visited at the mouth of the Klamath in 1900, was not to level off until 1910—a year after Kroeber had become chairman of his department. His entrée into California, then, came at the end (barely) of a time of terrible human tragedy and demographic collapse: it was a "little history of pitiful events" that included the extermination of Ishi's Mill Creek band by white vigilantes, against the protests of other more liberal and humanitarian non-Indians (Kroeber 1925:880–91; Cook 1976; but cf. Thornton 1987; Hurtado 1988).

As the nineteenth century turned into the twentieth, similar protests arose most immediately in response to the American invasion of the Philippines. Intellectuals and activists, such as William James at Harvard, cried out against American imperialist designs on the islands and the destruction of "the soul of a people who never did us an atom of harm in their lives" (*Boston Evening Transcript*, 3/1/99). At the same time, other voices sang another tune: "We do not want the Filipinos. We want the Philippines. The islands are enormously rich, but, unfortunately, they are infested with Filipinos. There are many millions there and it is to be feared their extermination will be slow" (*The Argonaut*, 9/30/99). These voices were most effectively—if somewhat less bluntly—represented by newspapers controlled by Phoebe Apperson Hearst's son, William Randolph Hearst (O'Toole 1984:285–86). Such opinions were entirely familiar, especially in northern California, where three decades earlier a common sentiment had dictated that, "The Indian must be exterminated or removed . . . this may not be the most christianlike attitude but it is the most practical" (*Humboldt Times* 5/23/63). Kroeber was aware of these voices and knew that they had helped to precipitate a 90 percent decline in the indigenous population during the years between the Gold Rush and his own arrival in California (1925:880–91).

Kroeber's lasting reputation is that of a liberal-thinking academic who avoided political commitment. He chided Sapir for suggesting that the United States should give up the Philippines once they had been secured (AK/ES 11/27/17) and later strenuously opposed applied anthropology as unnecessary meddling (Steward 1973). Although he served on the San Francisco Commonwealth Club's Committee on Indian welfare in the 1920s (*The Commonwealth* 21[3], 1926) and testified in Indian land claims cases in the 1950s, there is little evidence that he was professionally committed to California Indian welfare, beyond a personal concern for Indian friends like Ishi. As to the morality of the white invasion of northern California and the Indian genocide in which it culminated, he was largely silent. Despite his recognition that the whites' intentions were often "heartless" and that Native Californians had "suffered" grievously, he decided, "after some hesitation," to omit most of the history of the California tribes' "violent dispersal, disintegration, and wasting away" from the *Handbook*. Several considerations contribute to an understanding of his silence.

As previously noted, Kroeber held a firm faith in progress, which he defined as a teleological growth in numbers of culture traits, in the complexity of their structural interrelationships (or "pattern") in forming a cultural fabric, and in the creative "intensity" generating these traits and radiating them outwards, through diffusion (Buckley 1989). He also was explicit in his belief that there was "a direct relation between culture attitudes and culture elements" (Thoresen 1971:257); thus, for example, the "civilization" of Shasta Indians in northeastern California was "a pallid, simplified copy of the Yurok and Karok, as befits a poorer people of more easily contented aspirations" (1925:288). Progress was driven by more intense "attitudes" or "tendencies" that led people like the Yuroks to the development of monetary systems, an interest in personal property, and an "elaborate and precise code of rights" (1925:2–3). If the appreciation of "rights," which is to say ethics, would seem thus to have been a mark of progress, then the perpetration of genocide in northern California should have seemed an anomaly in the "race of civilization." It is not clear, however, that Kroeber avoided the topic because it compromised his progressivist assumptions; rather, he deemed himself "not in a position to treat . . . adequately" the recent history of Native Californians, and limited his task to "understanding" their pre-contact cultures as his sole task (1925:vi and above).

Kroeber's not being "in a position" to treat recent Californian history adequately must also have reflected the micro-political realities of his own institutional situation. Establishing a foothold at the University of California, where he was directly dependent on the good graces of the Hearst family until 1908, and indirectly so until 1919, Kroeber was indeed in a poor position to investigate the nature of Indian/white relations in the state (T. Kroeber 1970:73–74). Publicizing recent California history "in the ordinary sense" would have been profoundly awkward in view of the Hearsts' political power, their journalistic postures, and their role in the Spanish War.

While acknowledging that history included the "billions of woes and gratifications, of peaceful citizen lives or bloody deaths that have been the fate of men" (1917a), Kroeber saw this history, "in the ordinary sense," as but a "little history" when viewed against "the millennial sweep and grand contours" of the growth of civilization—the big History that was his ultimate concern. His various works on the Philippines, the fruits of documentary research rather than fieldwork, further demonstrate his dedication to salvaging knowledge of indigenous cultures imperiled by American expansion but do not much reflect upon the "woes and . . . bloody deaths" of Philippinos during his own lifetime (e.g., Kroeber 1919). When he later formally discussed racism in the United States he referred to the debate on Japanese ownership of land in California and to the disenfranchisement of Negroes in the Deep South as "practical problems" that had to be solved "morally and emotionally," rather than scientifically (1948:205 ff.). He did not, however, mention the virulent anti-Indian sentiment in California which had led to the quasi-legal enslavement of Indians well into the 1880s and which had certainly not abated during Kroeber's early years in the state (Heizer & Almquist 1971; Rawls 1984). Kroeber was aware of the effects of the white invasion on Native Californians but for him this invasion was most pertinent, not as a moral problem, but as a force that disrupted the integrity of cultures. Thus, for example, Kroeber sought to recapture the reality of Yurok Indian culture "before the white man came and irreparably tore the fabric of native life to pieces" (in Spott & Kroeber 1942:v). That the white man also tore a considerable number of Yurok men, women, and children to pieces may have been personally disturbing, but it was not a matter of professional concern.

Kroeber was not indifferent to the "suffering" of tribes subjected to "heartless" forces. Rather, he had an "unusual personal resistance" to "vehement" emotions in the contexts of "scientific and business relationships" (AK/ES 11/20/21). When once asked why he did not delve into his Yurok informants' experiences of the contact era, for instance, he replied that he "could not stand all of the tears" (A. R. Pilling, personal communication, 1988); he reputedly "could not bring himself to write" Ishi's story in full because of the pain it caused him (T. Kroeber, in Buzjalko 1988:80; but see Kroeber 1912). One can also speculate that he, like so many anthropologists, may have felt that a full examination of the conduct of whites in northern California after the Gold Rush would breach the Boasian canon of objectivity. To speak of "pitiful events" and "heartless intentions" was perhaps going quite far enough, rhetorically. Apolitical irony was more Kroeber's style:

> Statistics as to the number of Modoc in the past 50 years are somewhat vitiated by the inaccuracy that pervades most official figures for reservations on which several tribes are joined. This is perhaps not a grave fault for the Indian Office, whose avowed purpose has been the breaking down of national particularity as part of what it denominates tribal life in distinction from American citizenship; but it is unfortunate for the historian. (Kroeber 1925:320)

Finally, however, Kroeber's neglect of modern California history was most decisively determined by his own theories of culture and of history, and by the

Members of a group of vigilantes who, funded by settlers, had by 1868 largely exterminated Ishi's Mill Creek band of Yahi Indians: left to right, Sandy Young, Hi Good, Jay Salisbury, and Ned, an Indian. Ned eventually killed Good, and Young killed Ned. (Courtesy of the Native Daughters Museum, Oroville, California.)

ethnographic methods through which he both developed and explored these in California, particularly between 1900 and 1907, the years of his most intensive Yurok fieldwork.

Yurok National Character

In 1849, prospectors found gold on the Trinity River, the major southern tributary of the Klamath. By 1850, the peoples of the greater Klamath and Trinity drainages saw the beginning of what some would come to call "the end of the world." The first six months of 1850 brought an influx of about 10,000 whites into the country and many more soon followed (Bledsoe 1885). Salmon spawning beds in the many smaller streams that fed the lower Klamath were already silting in by 1851 due to hydraulic mining, and Indians lost streamside house sites as well in the white search for gold. The Indians resisted and the whites revenged their losses, sometimes to horrible extremes. Murder, rape, and kidnapping of Indian children by whites became commonplaces. Villages were burned. The inhabitants of whole towns were removed to U.S. Army forts that were, more plainly, concentration camps, or were taken into protective custody in refugee resettlement centers later called reservations. Fostered by malnutrition, diseases beyond the ken of "Indian doctors" proliferated and killed: smallpox, measles, influenza, venereal diseases, and various forms of tuberculosis all took their tolls. As the white population continued to grow, Indian death and dispossession increased. Yurok warriors joined the regional resistance (and sometimes joined white militias as mercenaries and scouts, settling old regional scores). Fighting was sporadic but continuous until 1865 when, subdued by flood, disease, and hunger, outgunned and outmanned, perhaps daunted by the defeat of the neighboring Chilula people, armed resistance largely ceased. But the population decline precipitated by the invasion did not. Between 1850 and 1910 the Yuroks' numbers declined from an estimated 2500 to 668 reported individuals (Cook 1976:237).

Although repopulation slowly began after 1910, the lot of the indigenous people did not improve either rapidly or markedly. In 1926, twenty-six years after Kroeber's first visit and ten years after Ishi's death, Robert Spott, an influential speaker from Requa, at the mouth of the Klamath, described his own Yurok people's situation to a newly sympathetic white audience at San Francisco's Commonwealth Club:[5]

> We are California Indians from the Klamath River, and I am here to tell you that we are almost at the end of the road. My English is broken, but I will explain to you as near as I can. In the old time, away back, we had a place where we used to go and pick berries for our winter supply. Then again, we had a hunting ground where we killed the game for our winter supply. And again, we had a place where we used to go to gather acorns for our winter supply. Then again, we could go up along the river to where a fishing place was left to us. But today, when we go back to where we used to find our berries, there is the sign "Keep out." What are we going to do?
>
> Then again we go to where we used to go to hunt. You see the sign again, "Keep out. No shooting allowed." All right. We go away. Then again, we go down to where we used to fish. That is taken up by white men. What are we going to do? We cannot do anything.
>
> There is a strip along the Klamath River which you have heard is an Indian reservation. It is a mile on each side of the river. Yes, it is. There are some good lands. Do you think that we own it? No. It is homesteaded by white men. Then

5. The address was arranged by Ruth Kellett Roberts, a socialite from Piedmont, across the Bay from San Francisco. Mrs. Roberts was "Chairman of Indian Welfare of the Women's Federation for the district embracing the lower Klamath" (Graves 1929:101). She was a strong and practical worker. At the time she was living for much of each year in Requa, at the mouth of the river, where the Spott family lived and where her husband, Harry C. Roberts, was an accountant at a salmon cannery (see Valory 1968). While Spott apologizes for his "broken" English in his 1926 address, the transcription of it hardly merits this description. The late Arnold R. Pilling suggested that Mrs. Roberts herself made the transcription, bringing Spott's "Indian English" into closer alignment with what she perceived to be standard English.

again, there is the Indian reservation at Upper Klamath that they have allotted to us. The Indians are stationed in an Indian village. The surveyor comes and he says, "There is land for you. You locate over there." Well, that land is no good. We want this land where we used to pick berries. But "No. That is homesteaded already. You have to take this."

You hear that Indians will not work on their homes. But they will work if the land is good. We cannot raise anything upon rocks or in gravel.

Are we not native sons of these United States? I did make up my mind in the war that I am American and I went across overseas to fight for this country. Then the officers came to me while I was overseas and they told me, "You are alright. You fought for your country." I just gave them a smile and I thought to myself, "Where is my country when I get home?"

There are many Indian women who are almost blind, and they only have one meal a day, because there is no one to look after them. Most of these people used to live on fish which they cannot get, and on acorns, and they are starving. They hardly have any clothing to cover them. Many children up along the Klamath River have passed away with disease. Most of them from tuberculosis. There is no road into here where the Indians are. The only road they have got is the Klamath River.

To reach doctors they have to take their children down the Klamath River, to the mouth of the Klamath. It is 24 miles to Crescent City, where we have to go for doctors. It costs us $25.00. Where are the poor Indians to get this money from to get a doctor for their children? They go from place to place to borrow money. If they cannot get it, the poor child dies without aid. Inside of four or five years more there will be hardly any Indians left upon the Klamath River. . . .

So I am here to tell you how we are standing up along the Klamath River. Often we see a car go past. It is the Indian Service. Do you suppose the man driving that car would stop? Always he has no time for the Indians, and the car with some one from the U.S.A. Indian Service goes past just like a tourist. When he does come to his office . . . just the minute he sees an Indian coming in he meets him by the door, and he says "I got business to do. I have not got any time for you. I will be back in two days." When he comes back the Indians will be sitting outside of that house waiting for him, and he just goes right through the Indians, and into the house, and comes right out again. But if he sees a white man there, he will stop in front of the white man and whisper to him. . . . And just the minute the Indians are waiting in front of the Government building there will be two or three white men in there talking with him. (Spott 1926: 133–35)

Twelve years Kroeber's junior, Robert Spott first met the anthropologist in 1900; their relationship was an important one in the annals of American ethnology. As lifelong informant, Spott was also Kroeber's colleague, collaborating on at least two publications, one of monograph length (Spott & Kroeber 1942; Kroeber 1960). He was also a personal friend and an occasional house guest of the Kroebers (T. Kroeber 1959:161, 1970:158–60). Kroeber noted in his obituary of Spott his friend's role as Chairman of the Yurok Tribal or-

Robert Spott, dressed for the Deerskin Dance, flanked by Harry K. Roberts (left) and Harry C. Roberts, about 1920. (Collection of the author.)

ganization and mentioned Spott's battle service in World War I—duties Spott undertook "without serious impairment of [his] feeling" for the remote Yurok past (1954). But in Kroeber's portraits of Spott it is his importance and reliability as a traditionalist, as a bearer of pre-contact Yurok cultural knowledge and values, that is overwhelmingly stressed (Spott & Kroeber 1942:v; Kroeber 1954). The Robert Spott who spoke before the Commonwealth Club, who himself suffered from tuberculosis, who negotiated with the Department of the

Interior, sportsman's lobbies, and salmon cannery owners for Indian rights and wages, whose sister was—among very much else—a famous cook at the white-owned tourist hotel in Requa, barely appears in Kroeber's accounts of him. Rather, the Robert Spott made public by Kroeber provides a reliable window into an authentic Native Californian past, not unlike Ishi: "Much knowledge of his people died with [Spott]" (1954:282). This Robert Spott was not an important witness to a troubled and oppressed Yurok present.

Kroeber's published relegation of Robert Spott to a Yurok cultural past was consistent with the anthropologist's general approach to Yurok culture:

> In 1900, those Yurok who were 70 years old had been adults when the native culture was first impinged on. Their knowledge of that culture was therefore first hand. In fact, at many points the cultural practices were still unchanged, which is why it was selected for study. At the same time, transformation of the Yurok into disadvantaged and second-class Americans was going on as a result of contact with our infinitely more massive society—a transformation that has been accelerated since 1900. This process proved traumatic for many Yurok. It is not gone into here. (1959:236)

The anthropologist held that he could reconstruct pre-contact Yurok culture without attending to a post-contact Yurok history, as though it had not happened, and had no bearing on the understanding of "[un-]impinged on" Yurok culture.

In the *Handbook*, Kroeber placed the (aboriginal) Yuroks at the top of the cultural hierarchy in California: their culture "attains on the whole to a higher level, as it is customary to estimate such averaged values, than any other that flourished in what is now the state of California" (1925:1). Later in his life, however, Kroeber held that, despite their cultural eminence in California (which, after all, did not place them very high in the general scheme of things, even in Native North America), the Yuroks' "psychic nature" had taken a mysterious turn for the worse:

> For some unknown reason the culture had simply gone hypochondriac, and all members of the society, whatever their congenital individual positions, had fear and pessimism pounded into them from childhood on. They were taught by all their elders that the world simply reeked with evils and dangers, against which one sought protection by an endless series of preventive taboos and magical practices. (1948:309)

Kroeber was not, however, speaking here about the effects of white colonization. In all of his ethnographic writing on the Yuroks, "The present tense must be construed as a narrative one, referring to a century or more ago" when "[t]he undisturbed, pre-1850 native culture seems to have been largely in static balance" (1959:236). Returning to the Boasian concern for "the genius of a people," Kroeber described the "character" of Yuroks who lived twenty years before he was born in a hundred-year-old, immemorial ethnographic present:

> The Yurok are an inwardly fearful people, cautious and placatory. Before other persons, pride often covers up their fear, but in the face of nature, taboo or fate, they are timorous and propitiating. Moreover, they are suspicious of motives, quick to become jealous, and, by their own accounts, given to envy.
>
> They are touchy to slight, sensitive to shaming, quickly angered. Their restraints of prudence break with a jerk, and they are then likely to explode into reckless violence of speech and anger. They hate wholeheartedly, persistently, often irreconcilably. They scarcely know forgiveness; their pride is too great. . . .
>
> I might add that among the only slightly acculturated aged Yurok I knew or met in the first decade of this century, the men often seemed to me bitter and withdrawn, and some were of terrifying mien, but the old women made an impression rather of serenity. (1959:236–40)

In this essay, Kroeber was belatedly responding to an article by his friend and colleague, Erik H. Erikson, on Yurok "Childhood and world image" (1943; cf. Elrod 1992). Until very late in his career, Kroeber had largely resisted direct involvement in the culture and personality studies that at one time or another had occupied so many of Boas' other most notable students (e.g., Kroeber 1952:263). When he did come to psychology *per se* it was as pathology, rather than from a relativist perspective. But in writing that the Yuroks "had simply gone hypochondriac," he left unaddressed the degree to which this hypochondria was a result of contact. Implying that it was an artifact of the frozen past, he did not even hint that the fearful, suspicious, touchy, bitter, and withdrawn people he described might be the traumatized survivors of invasion and genocide. Neither did he suggest that the Yuroks he had met might have responded directly to *him*, a white man—for among the human individuals absent from Kroeber's ethnography was, of course, Kroeber himself.

It is difficult to know what Kroeber's experience of Yurok responses to his presence among them was, for he seldom mentioned any such personal experience in his published work. This followed from his rhetorical objectivity, from his methodological neglect of individual personalities (including his own), as well as from his goal of reconstructing a past Yurok ethnographic "present" from which he himself had indeed been absent. Thus we know very little about critical Yurok reactions to him and to his research efforts when he was on the Klamath. We do know that some Yuroks were "bitter and withdrawn" in his presence, greeted him with "terrifying mien," and no doubt refused to cooperate with him (1959:240); and in his posthumously published *Yurok Myths* he wrote in passing of the types of stories that a "Yurok of the time [1900–1907] was likely to tell a strange white man" (1976:420). Nevertheless, the very existence of this book testifies to Kroeber's success in over-

coming Yurok hesitations as, indeed, his cumulative Yurok ethnography testifies to his ability to elicit the cooperation of many Yurok cultural experts
who entered into (often long-lasting) collaboration with him. Although Alfred Kroeber seldom mentions anything as personal as friendship, Theodora
Kroeber did, and we know through her that her husband had warm, reciprocal
friendships with several Yurok Indians including, of course, Robert Spott (T.
Kroeber 1970:157 ff.).

However, Kroeber reconstructed the culture of these pre-contact people as
though he had never come among their survivors. It is probable that his portrayal of their "national character" contains considerable insight, or hindsight,
into certain aspects of the dynamics of their former lives; he was expert in his
vocation, and the old-time Yuroks were indeed exacting, as far as we may dis-
cern them. It is more than probable that there were other, rather different
dynamics in those lives as well. There seems no room for humor among Kroeber's Yuroks, for instance, though Yurok social relations are now and seem
always to have been full of it. Nor do the Yurok Indians described by Kroeber
seem capable of gentleness, let alone love. Kroeber's "interpretation" takes no
account, for instance, of the tenderness—and humor—evident in the nicknames that Waterman (1920:215) noted as being given to little girls by their
parents: "Married-into-Snail's-house," "Married-to-Rabbit," ". . . to Pigeon,"
". . . to Chipmunk." (The nicknames gently parody traditional public adult
names based on marital statuses.)

Again, it is undeniable that Kroeber *was* present among his immemorial
Yurok survivors, and it is difficult to imagine today that his interpretation was
not influenced by the "character[s]" of the Yuroks that he knew. Nor can we
assume that his interactions with them were not influenced by their thirty-
five-year experience of white domination before his arrival, as yet another
strange white man on the river. Kroeber's own avoidance of this possibility
helped to support his effort to place the Yuroks and others within the cultural-
typological framework of a highly abstract history. Eventually he graded the
"massiveness" (estimated in terms of social complexity and elaboration in
material culture, among other more ineffable things) in Yurok "civilization" at
3+ on a scale of 1 to 7, slightly more advanced than the Navajos (3), for
instance, yet slightly more "retarded" than the Cherokees (4−) (Kroeber
1939: Table 18; Hurtado 1988:2).

Kroeber's version of "Yurok national character" is subtly coherent with his
view of history. Once again, Kroeber shared Boas' concern for value systems in
cultures, including ethics (1952:5–6; Kroeber & Kluckhohn 1952:96), holding that there was no evolutionary development of moral instinct in human
beings and that all people were, potentially, equally moral—the "uncivilized"
and winners in the "race of civilization" alike (1910, 1917a). A particular morality or an apparent lack thereof were both acquired cultural traits. Yet Kroe-

ber's invocation of "nature, taboo, or fate," in 1959 serves to primitivize "the"—or his—"Yurok" and to contradict his previously proclaimed relativism (cf. Alsberg, above). It places them as types, not so much in a hundred-year-old ethnographic present as in an ahistorical, primitive developmental stage. Their hatred, their inability to forgive, is attributed to an intransigent pride that marks a primitiveness both psychological and moral; Kroeber goes on to say that the Yuroks are—that is, were—"puerile," "infantile" (1959: 240). The proof is in the oldest men, the least "acculturated," whose bitterness and petulance are most palpable, their character most indicative of an authentic "national character" present before contact, before "the native primitive culture . . . went all to pieces" (1948:427). He did not attend to a seemingly more obvious conclusion: that these were the men who had witnessed the longest suffering. Nor did he consider the possibility that the Yurok people he met hated understandably, as full adults, fully in history, because unforgivable things were being done to them by Kroeber's own people.

Kroeber acknowledged that contact "proved traumatic for many Yurok" (1959:236)—as though the invasion had not proven "traumatic" for all, eventually, and as though, like children at the primal scene, the Yuroks had not the inner resources to withstand the rough-and-tumble of millennial History. It is as if it were no fault of "the superior race" that had transformed the Yuroks into "disadvantaged and second class Americans," but rather some inner Yurok weakness, an immaturity all their own—the price of a life before time: the price of being "retarded."

Alternative visions were possible. In 1903, Pliny E. Goddard, Kroeber's colleague at the University of California until 1909, deplored the violence and immorality of the white invaders and acknowledged its disastrous consequences for the Hupas, eastern neighbors of the Yuroks. Kroeber's student, Llwellyn L. Loud, later wrote of the massacre of between forty and seventy Wiyot Indians, the Yuroks' southern neighbors, on an island in Humboldt Bay in 1860 as a "climactic act of barbarity and inhumanity on the part of . . . vicious whites" (1918:329). While Kroeber replaced Goddard in his department with the scientifically "tame" T. T. Waterman (AK/ES 7/17/18), whom he perceived as less threatening to his own academic hegemony, Waterman, too, understood the recent history of California, and of the Yurok Indians specifically, rather differently than did Kroeber.

T. T. Waterman: An Alternative Moral Vision

Thomas Talbot Waterman had started out to study for the ministry but was drawn to anthropology, via linguistics, by Goddard. He next worked as Kroeber's assistant at the University [of California] Museum in San Francisco and, under Kroeber's direction, went to the Klamath River to study the Yurok language in 1909. Kroeber sent him to finish a doctorate in linguistics under Boas at Columbia, but Boas found him underprepared and, in 1913, Waterman completed an ethnographic dissertation. He had returned to California in 1910, when Kroeber appointed him instructor in the Department of Anthropology at Berkeley and assistant curator at the museum. Waterman's unusual success as a teacher of undergraduate anthropology helped free Kroeber from teaching, enabling him to attend to his own "scientific" work.

While Kroeber seldom, in his professional writing, mentioned his personal relationships, good or bad, with Yurok individuals, Waterman did. Thus his Yurok work in all likelihood gives us a better sense of probable negative Yurok responses to Kroeber, as well as to Waterman himself, than does Kroeber's work or that of Theodora Kroeber, with its protective loyalty to her husband. Although "Yurok Geography," Waterman's major publication in Yurok ethnography (1920), was written with Kroeber's cooperation, it is a non-Kroeberian work in many subtle ways. Its very existence, like the existence of Kroeber's Yurok oeuvre, testifies to the cooperation Waterman was able to elicit from Yurok informants. He noted, however, that he was occasionally unable to obtain such cooperation:

> the sketches represent observations made with a tapeline and compass on the spot. In some cases, where the Indians were ill-tempered about it, the work was done hastily or surreptitiously. At times their opposition made work of any sort impossible. (1920:227)
>
> I was able to get no direct information about [the town of] tu'rip on account of the hostility of the Indians toward my efforts at investigation. (235)
>
> The people [of sre'gon] were unwilling to tell me anything about house-names or geography, and I think they passed the word along that I was not to be told by anybody else. (244)
>
> The people [at wa'ase] gave me, rather unwillingly, a few house-names, most of which turned out later to be apocryphal. They objected to my making a map. (249)

Like Kroeber, Waterman understood the—to him—shadowed aspect of Yuroks' personalities: "Prominent among their traits is a certain sinful pride, a love of squabbling, and readiness to take offense" (1920:201; see also Waterman 1925). But he was also aware that Yurok resistance to his research did not arise out of some timeless, "hypochondriac" cultural defect in Yurok "national character," but from the fact that he was white. What Kroeber called a "little history of pitiful events" Waterman called "the white invasion" (1920:255), long before the term and the concept became common in scholarly discourse (e.g., Jennings 1975). Waterman also acknowledged how recent this event was, in 1909, and its continuing vividness in Yurok consciousness.

Dave Durban, the brother of Weitchpec Frank, had been a sort of paid scout for the government during this period [ca. 1865], so he was held partly to blame for the fact that a Hupa was killed by the soldiers. Since that time old Spencer has not "liked" Frank because he is the brother of Dave Durban, the ex-scout. He does not speak to Frank when the two meet. (1920:202)

Waterman was forthright about white depredations against the Yuroks, including the burning of the village of Weitchpec in the 1850s and the displacement of other villages by white placer mining. Unlike Kroeber, then, he wrote quite frankly of the ongoing "friction between the races" and its implications for his own research (1920:256). These latter he occasionally noted:

When I visited the town of tur'ip I found myself involved in an involuntary quarrel with a certain old man because I was a white man. The old Indian's nephew had once been jailed for making fast his gill-net at the bank of the river, in aboriginal fashion, but in defiance of the federal statute governing methods of fishing and disregarding the pains and penalties therein made and provided. The old man held me partly to blame for the action of the Federal Grand Jury, though I defended myself as best I could. He refused, with some politeness, to talk to me or to take my money. (203)

Waterman acknowledged, then, that the Yuroks he depicted were, unlike Kroeber's immemorial tokens, caught in a "static balance," shaped by "the white invasion." And he made clear, in "Yurok Geography," that his ethnography was what we would now call the "dialogical" result of his own presence on the Klamath. It is not, however, that Waterman's reflexivity and historical sensitivity were "ahead of" or otherwise uncharacteristic of "his time"—any more than were Llwellyn Loud's nascent ethnoarcheology (Loud 1918), J. P. Harrington's polyphony and thick description (1932), Jaime de Angulo's pragmatic understanding of language use (J. de Angulo & Freeland 1931), or Angulo's appreciation of intersubjectivity, or ironic celebration of cultural survival (J. de Angulo 1950) somehow "ahead of their time" in the ethnology of indigenous northern California. These interests only seem anticipatory, rather than characteristic of the period, because they came at a time in Californian ethnology that was dominated by Kroeber's professional voice, sometimes rather emphatically (G. de Angulo 1985:7, 9).

Ethnography as Mythology

Kroeber, for his part, had his own good reasons for chastising Loud (who seemed to be wasting scarce research funds among the Wiyots of Humboldt Bay), for supporting the "tame" Waterman over Paul Radin, a brilliant but unreliable anthropologist, and for being angry at Jaime de Angulo for failing to show up for a job that Kroeber had gone to some trouble to secure for him in Mexico (G. de Angulo 1985; Heizer 1970). Kroeber had the many real problems of a great and ambitious scholar-administrator, managing as best he could a disparate lot of assistants together with his own career, including its academic politics ("institutions . . . want certain institutional goods and my institution holds me responsible . . . for deliveries" [AK/ES 7/17/18]). My point, however, is that Kroeber's Native Californians were dialectically constructed along with a particular epistemology, and that the construction of both incorporated a considered response to the moral situation of white America at the turn of the century—a response (or unresponsiveness) that was distinctly Kroeberian.

To some large extent, Kroeber's "overriding progressivism" (Diamond, in Silverman 1981:58), with its assumption of the ultimate disappearance of the integrated, putatively "real" cultures of Native Americans, was a sophisticated, intellectualized expression of a belief in "the vanishing Indian" then wide-spread among historians and thoughtful laypeople alike. For example, A. J. Bledsoe, the first comprehensive (if erroneous) historian of the "Indian wars" of northwestern California in the 1850s and 1860s, suggested the following in 1881:

> A few years to come will see the last of these Indians, who once roamed the forests and mountains of Del Norte in large numbers, and who could then truly boast that they were the "monarches of all they surveyed." Flying before the march of civilization like chaff before the wind, they have rapidly been reduced in numbers, until at the present time, a mere remnant of the earlier tribes are left to go down with the setting sun of their declining strength. (1881:109)

Like Kroeber and many others, Bledsoe's conviction in the ultimate replacement of this "mere remnant" (which included Yuroks) by whites had a metaphysical foundation. While Kroeber believed that "civilization" itself, expressed through human "creativity," culturally determined, assured the ascendance of "the superior race," Bledsoe held that "the mighty arm of capital" was the instrument of progress (1881:6).

Although Kroeber was avowedly apolitical in his ethnology, his reconstruction of a Yurok culture caught in static balance and free of the contaminating influences of traumatizing contact with whites was profoundly political—not unlike Bledsoe's history. The Yuroks that Kroeber constructed were a people outside of—or before—time, and most especially before genocide. His ethnographic present tense is an element in a speech register suitable for a mythic actor's soliloquy, as when Yurok ritualists prayed in a speech register attributed to their own creator-heroes, bringing those creators back into being by the beauty and power of their language (Buckley 1984). In this sense, Kroeber's ethnographic portrait of the Yuroks is indeed humanist "literature," as he claimed all of his writing was. Kroeber's language, rather than summoning forth the ancient ones, projected the Yuroks back as depersonalized actors in an all-time before history "in the ordinary sense," distinct from the teleological, millennial History of civilization. Thus he protected the "static" culture that he inscribed from historic contamination or "mixing," quite as myths relate an all-time unconditioned by a limited present or immediate past—indeed, a time by which the experienced past and present are themselves conditioned. Kroeber's discipline and rigor hid within its seeming objectivity a nostalgia and romanticism as much a part of the legacy of Goethe and Humboldt as other aspects of the natural history that, for Kroeber, defined the appropriate discourse to which anthropology should contribute.

Ishi Between Two Moral Worlds

> On that day a surveyor, H. H. Hume happened to notice a bundle hanging high in a live oak tree. On examination it proved to be several old barley sacks and pieces of canvas wrapped around a collection of curious objects. The cache, for so it was, contained tanned deerhides with the hair left on, a pair of much worn moccasins, little bundles of pine pitch, and pine needles whose sheathed ends all pointed neatly in one direction. There was also a bar of unused soap, a cylinder of "sweetened" charcoal about an inch wide and three inches in length, a few nails and screws tied separately in a rag, and a sharp piece of steel with an eyehole at the large end. The cache was probably Ishi's. It was found four months before Ishi turned up at the slaughter house. (T. Kroeber 1961 : 113)

Theodora Kracaw enrolled as an undergraduate at the University of California in 1915, but never met Ishi. She did meet Kroeber, who was to be her second husband, when, newly widowed, she returned to Berkeley for doctoral study in anthropology in 1924 (Buzaljko 1988). Although she did not finish the degree she was perhaps Kroeber's most loyal protégé, and also among the first to move the study of California Indians firmly into the twentieth century through her biography of Ishi, "The Last Wild Indian in North America" (1961). In *Ishi*, Theodora Kroeber at once promulgated her husband's vision of Native Californian culture history and expanded it to include, at last, genocide in northern California, confronting a history that did not fit into his work, as he had defined its objectives.

By 1960, the year of Kroeber's death, a half century of cataclysm suggested that his faith in progress had been misplaced. Theodora Kroeber was twenty-one years younger—a writer fully in and of the twentieth century—and she seems to have written *Ishi in Two Worlds* in part in response to what the mid-twentieth century had revealed about Western Civilization. The Nazi holocaust in Eastern Europe, the bombing of Dresden, Hiroshima, and Nagasaki, Stalin's mass murders, the collapse of empire and the end of classic colonialism

Ishi, shortly after he emerged from hiding in northern California on August 29, 1911. (Courtesy of the P. A. Hearst Museum, University of California, Berkeley.)

after the Second World War, the Negro civil rights movement in the United States of the mid-fifties, all helped to place the history of Indian-white relations in late nineteenth-century California in a harsh new light. In the late 1950s, the evidence that a profound potential for genocide, racism, and oppression lay darkly in the very heart of Western civilization seemed irrefutable.

One must read *Ishi* within this context, so vastly changed over that within which Kroeber formulated his anthropology between 1900 and 1915. While the luster of "The Biography of the Last Wild Indian in North America" seems a bit tarnished today, a bit dated—like its subtitle—one does well not to neglect the crucially important fact that it confronted a wide, twentieth-century audience for the first time with some of the bare facts of Indian-white relations in nineteenth-century northern California. Even after numerous other accounts have appeared, Chapter 3, "A Dying People," is still crushing in its open, factual confrontation of the details and results of the Anglo-American invasion of Yana territory that began in 1844. The continuing power of the chapter, its undiminished capacity to make us feel deeply sorrowful and outraged, is a tribute to Theodora Kroeber's integrity and courage, as well as to her skillfully exercised literary restraint. Next to her account of the fate of Ishi's Mill Creek band, Sherburne Cook's earlier scientific reports on the native Californian demographic collapse, intended for a professional audience, seems heartlessly objectivist (1976). If Cook permitted a scholarly audience to assess the human cost of the development of Euro-American society in California, Theodora Kroeber led her non-Indian audience to confront the evil that determined that cost, giving many readers a first chance to grapple with a truth with which many among her Native American readers had long been well acquainted.

Nonetheless, as grounded in its own present and as influential as it was, *Ishi* is also deeply rooted in Alfred Kroeber's anthropology. It is thus something of a mixed bag, a transitional and pivotal work that at once promulgates a now anachronistic anthropology and that fully encounters the awful events of late nineteenth-century California Indian history, as anthropology seldom did.

In *Ishi*, Theodora accepted her husband's commitment to the concept of culture as distinct and discrete, static and integrated—the pure token of a specific synchronic type that should be understood in the typological context of other, comparable, static cultural wholes (Thoresen 1971:23–27). Her Yana-Yahi culture, for instance, could not be transformed into a new version of itself. It could only disappear or be polluted beyond recognition by acculturation, becoming what Alfred Kroeber had called a "bastard" culture. Thus, Theodora Kroeber's painful disdain, in *Ishi*, for Sapir's first Yana linguistic consultant, the acculturated, English-speaking Sam Batwi, who is implicitly presented as, not only a failed Yana, but as not a *real* Indian at all (1961:149–

50). Theodora Kroeber neglected the fact that Ishi, "the last wild Indian," had spent his entire life adapting to the white presence in his ancestral lands, as the cache discovered shortly before his emergence makes so vividly clear.

Quarantined in the "Stone Age," denied a history of adaptation to invasive Euro-American society, Ishi became a "last-of." He is not succeeded by the likes of "the damned old crank" Sam Batwi, a Maidu-Yana, who in fact could be seen as simply carrying the Yana's acculturation, signified by Ishi's cache, several steps farther (Waterman/ES 11/18/11, in Darnell 1990:80). Rhetorically, in *Ishi in Two Worlds*, Ishi the individual became "the Yahi," and the Yahis became the last wild Indians, and all passed away with Ishi himself, absorbed into the romance, however tragic, of the Kroebers' non-Indian past. Alfred Kroeber, an anthropologist-as-hero, not Batwi, was to be Ishi's true cultural and historical heir. He alone "*understood*" (T. Kroeber 1961:151 [italics in original]). Ishi, finally, was inscribed as a tragic hero in emergent Euro-American creation mythology. As Theodora Kroeber wrote, Alfred Kroeber "had found, as have others, his own equivalent of that old Indian life" (1970:157).

Thus *Ishi* contains both the reductive and romantic flaws inherent in its own literary and anthropological past and the painful historical awareness that characterizes more recent works about Native California. To some degree *Ishi* enabled these works, not only in its genuinely historical approach, which focused on "the little history," but in its intersubjectivity as well. Theodora Kroeber humanized Ishi (and through him, the victims of genocide), in part by portraying his relationships with those he lived among at the Museum of Anthropology in San Francisco—Kroeber, Pope, Waterman, Loud, the others—in ways more common in 1961 to novels than to anthropological writing. Her humanism is far more recognizable as such today than was that earlier variety espoused by her husband. Like her husband, Theodora Kroeber treated Ishi's individuality as a manifestation of a culturally determined personality type, for example; but while Alfred Kroeber turned his informants into types, she turned these types into vividly imagined, fully dimensional characters. Both were romantic idealists, dealing with fictive essences. But while her husband's romanticisms were scientized and reduced, Theodora Kroeber's were fictionalized and individuated (in an entirely European, not Native American, way—see also T. Kroeber 1959). She identified with her subjects, thus enabling her reader to do the same, while Kroeber's subjects became his objects.

Both Alfred and Theodora Kroeber were humanistic mythologists of sorts: he hoped to create timeless types, hiding his passions as he did so; she made a hero of Ishi, whom she never met, and she made heroic those men whom she did know and love—like Robert Spott and, above all, her husband. But their methods were in a sense inverse. To construct his progressivist creation myth of the vanishing race supplanted by the "superior," more "massive" Europeans,

Kroeber reduced individuals he knew well, like Ishi, Robert Spott, and so many others, to tokens of past cultural types. Theodora Kroeber inscribed her mythos by constructing individuals she never met, like Ishi, like most of the people whose photographed faces appear in *Almost Ancestors,* as sharply and lovingly defined characters (T. Kroeber & Heizer 1968). Both revealed certain truths and obscured other truths.

Some of the truths that the Kroebers obscured are heard today in Native California, where readers tend to object to the message embedded in the *Handbook of the Indians of California:* that real California Indians were as they are described in this book and that they no longer exist in a true sense. A new Yurok Indian tribal roll has recently been compiled listing approximately 3520 individuals, and, since their new tribal organization and constitution were accepted by the federal government in 1993, the Yurok Indians have comprised the largest recognized tribe in California. Again, while it is probably true that Ishi was the last representative of "the Yahi"—a tribal designation invented by Alfred Kroeber (AK/ES 5/29/15)—not all "Yana"-speaking peoples perished with this southern group. After 1900, surviving Yanas were largely absorbed by the refugee Indian population of the Pitt River country in northeastern California, originally the territory of the Achumawis, aboriginal neighbors and allies of the Yanas. The descendants of nineteenth-century Yanas continue to live there today. Some of them come to the Phoebe Apperson Hearst Museum of Anthropology at the University of California, Berkeley, to learn traditional songs from recordings made of Ishi on Edison cylinders, between 1911 and 1915 (Lowie Museum 1990:4). And here we encounter a truth perhaps missed by both Alfred Kroeber and many of his contemporary critics alike.

Kroeber reduced his ethnographic subjects to objects, and his objectified "pre-contact" cultures implied the absence of valid Indian cultures in California in the twentieth century. Resent this though they may, Native Californians have long accepted the non-Indian idea of a real "native . . . culture," often defined in the Boasian terms most tellingly introduced, in California, by Kroeber: language and music, traditional narratives, religious rituals, and material culture. Yuroks, for instance, have long used an objectified understanding of "culture" both in constructing their own accounts of the Yurok past (e.g., Thompson 1916) and in the continuing struggle for cultural survival that has, so far, been successful to a degree that would perhaps surprise Kroeber himself. Two kinds of "salvage" have emerged. Kroeber would probably reject contemporary traditionalists' version of Yurok culture, salvaged from the wreckage of modern history, as a "bastard" culture, unlike "the native primitive culture before it went all to pieces" that he arrested in his "salvage ethnography." Yet this cumulative salvage ethnography today provides those most actively engaged in "saving" their own Yurok culture with a virtual textbook, however selectively it is consulted. Thus, as a Yurok elder dissenting from the majority Yurok opinion of "anthros" once said to me:

> Thank God for that good Doctor Kroeber and Doctor Waterman and Gifford and those other good white doctors from Berkeley who came up here to study us. If they hadn't taken an interest in us and come up here and written it all down we wouldn't know a thing today about who we really are.

Acknowledgments

I especially want to thank Henry Levinson, University of North Carolina at Greensboro, who urged me on at the beginning of this research, in 1985, although it is only now that I begin to understand my debt to him. And I wish to remember, here, the late Florence Shaughnessy (Yurok) and the late Harry K. Roberts, and to thank Julian Lang (Karuk). Each helped me to recognize that "the natives' point[s] of view" regarding anthropology can open important perspectives too often overlooked. Finally, I thank Peter Nabokov for a crucial quotation, Dell Hymes, and George Stocking.

References Cited

Alsberg, C. 1936. Alfred Kroeber, I: Personal reminiscences. In *Essays in anthropology presented to A. L. Kroeber in celebration of his sixtieth birthday, June 11, 1936*, ed. R. Lowie, xiii–xviii. Berkeley.

Angulo, G. de, ed. 1985. *Jaime in Taos: The Taos papers of Jaime de Angulo.* San Francisco.

Angulo, J. de. 1950. Indians in overalls. *The Hudson Review* 3(3): 237–77.

Angulo, J. de & L. S. Freeland. 1931. Karok texts. *Int. J. Am. Ling.* 6:194–226.

Bledsoe, A. 1881. *History: Del Norte County, California, with a business directory and travelers guide.* Eureka, Calif. (1971).

———. 1885. *Indian wars of the northwest: A California sketch.* San Francisco.

Boas, F. 1887a. The occurrence of similar inventions in areas widely apart. *Science* 9: 485–86.

———. 1887b. The study of geography. *Science* 9:137–41.

———. 1896. The limitations of the comparative method in anthropology. *Science* 4: 901–8.

———, ed. 1911a. *Handbook of American Indian languages.* Bureau of American Ethnology Bulletin 40. Washington, D.C.

———. 1911b. *The mind of primitive man.* New York.

———. 1936. History and science in anthropology: A reply. *Am. Anth.* 38:137–41.

———. 1945. *Race and democratic society.* New York.

Buckley, Thomas. 1984. Yurok speech registers and ontology. *Lang. in Soc.* 13:467–88.

———. 1989. Kroeber's theory of culture areas and the ethnology of northwestern California. *Anth. Quart.* 62:15–26.

Buzaljko, G. 1988. Theodora Krakaw Kroeber. In *Women anthropologists: A biographical dictionary*, ed. U. Gacs, A. Kahn, J. McIntyre, and R. Weinberg, 187–93. New York.

Cook, S. 1976. *The conflict between the California Indian and white civilization.* Berkeley.

Darnell, R. 1969. The development of American anthropology 1879–1920: From the Bureau of American Ethnology to Franz Boas. Doct. diss., University of Pennsylvania.

———. 1990. *Edward Sapir: Linguist, anthropologist, humanist.* Berkeley.

Driver, H. 1962. The contribution of A. L. Kroeber to culture area theory and practice. *Indiana Univ. Pub. Anth. Ling.*, Memoir 18:1–28.

Durkheim, E. 1895. The rules of the sociological method. Trans. S. Solovay & J. Mueller. Ed. G. Catlin. New York (1938).

Elrod, N. 1992. *500 years of deception, a classic case in the twentieth century: Erik H. Erikson's portrayal of the Native Americans.* Trans. C. Brooks. Zurich.

Erikson, E. 1943. Observations on the Yurok: Childhood and world image. *Univ. Cal. Pub. Am. Arch. Eth.* 35:257–302.

Geertz, C. 1973. *The interpretation of cultures.* New York.

———. 1980. *Negara: The theater state in nineteenth century Bali.* Princeton.

Gibson, A., & J. Rowe. 1961. A bibliography of the publications of Alfred Louis Kroeber. *Am. Anth.* 63:1060–87.

Goddard, P. 1903–4. Life and culture of the Hupa. *Univ. Cal. Pub. Am. Arch. Eth.* 1:1–88.

Golla, V., ed. 1984. *The Sapir-Kroeber correspondence.* Survey of California and Other Indian Languages, University of California, Berkeley. Report 6.

Graves, C. 1929. *Lore and legends of the Klamath River Indians.* Yreka, Calif.

Harrington, J. 1932. *Tobacco among the Karuk Indians of California.* Bureau of American Ethnology Bulletin 94. Washington, D.C.

Heizer, R., ed. 1970. *An anthropological expedition of 1913, or, get it through your head, or, yours for the revolution: Correspondence between A. L. Kroeber and L. L. Loud, July 12, 1913–October 31, 1913.* University of California at Berkeley, Archaeological Research Faculty (duplicated).

Heizer, R. & A. Almquist. 1971. *The other Californians: Prejudice and discrimination under Spain, Mexico and the United States.* Berkeley.

Hurtado, A. 1988. *Indian survival on the California frontier.* New Haven.

Hymes, D. 1961. Alfred Louis Kroeber. *Language* 27:1–28.

Jennings, F. 1975. *The invasion of America: Indians, colonialism, and the cant of conquest.* Chapel Hill.

Jonaitis, A. 1988. *From the land of the totem poles: The Northwest Coast Indians art collection at the American Museum of Natural History.* New York.

Kroeber, A. 1896. Mademoiselle's dowry. *Columbia Literary Monthly* 4:229–36.

———. 1901. Decorative symbolism of the Arapaho. *Am. Anth.* 3:308–36.

———. 1902. *The Arapaho, Part I.* Bureau of American Ethnology Bulletin 18. Washington, D.C.

———. 1904a. A ghost dance in California. *J. Am. Folklore* 17:32–37.

———. 1904b. Types of Indian culture in California. *Univ. Cal. Pub. Am. Arch. Eth.* 2:81–103.

———. 1907. The religion of the Indians of California. *Univ. Cal. Pub. Am. Arch. Eth.* 4:319–56.

———. 1908. The anthropology of California. *Science* 27:281–90.

———. 1910. The morals of uncivilized people. *Am. Anth.* 12:437–47.

———. 1912. Ishi, the last aborigine. *World's Work Magazine* 24:304–8.

———. 1915. Eighteen professions. *Am. Anth.* 17:283–88.

———. 1916a. What an American saw in Germany. *The Outlook* 12:92–95.

———. 1916b. Zuñi potsherds. *Anth. Pap. Am. Mus. Nat. Hist.* 18:i–37.

———. 1917a. The superorganic. *Am. Anth.* 19:163–213.

———. 1917b. Zuñi kin and clan. *Anth. Pap. Am. Mus. Nat. Hist.* 18:i–204.

———. 1918. Review of C. Wissler, *The American Indian. Am. Anth.* 20:203–9.

———. 1919. *Peoples of the Philippines.* American Museum of Natural History Handbook, series 8. *New York.*

———. 1920. *California culture provinces. Univ. Cal. Pub. Am. Arch. Eth.* 17:151–69.

———. 1923. *Anthropology.* New York (revised 1948).

———. 1925. *Handbook of the Indians of California.* Bureau of American Ethnology Bulletin 78. Washington, D.C.

———. 1935. History and science in anthropology. *Am. Anth.* 37:539–64.

———. 1936. So-called social science. *J. Soc. Phil.* 1:317–40.

———. 1937. Thomas Talbot Waterman. *Am. Anth.* 39:527–29.

———. 1939. Cultural and natural areas of native North America. *Univ. Cal. Pub. Am. Arch. Eth.* 38:i–242.

———. 1943. Franz Boas: The man. *Mem. Am. Anth. Assn.* 61:5–26.

———. 1944. *Configurations of culture growth.* Berkeley.

———. 1952. *The nature of culture.* Chicago.

———. 1954. Robert Spott 1888–1953. *Am. Anth.* 54:282.

———. 1959. Yurok national character, in ethnographic interpretations, 7–11. *Univ. Cal. Pub. Am. Arch. Eth.* 47(3): 236–40.

———. 1960. Yurok speech uses. In *Culture in history,* ed. S. Diamond, 993–99. New York.

———. 1976. *Yurok myths.* Berkeley.

Kroeber, A. & E. Gifford. 1949. World renewal: A cult system of native northwest California. *Anth. Rec.* 13:1–155.

Kroeber, A. & C. Kluckhohn. 1952. *Culture: A critical review of concepts and definitions.* Papers of the Peabody Museum of Archaeology and Ethnology, Harvard University 47. Cambridge, Mass.

Kroeber, T. 1959. *The inland whale: Nine stories retold from California Indian legends.* Bloomington.

———. 1961. *Ishi in two worlds: A biography of the last wild Indian in North America.* Berkeley.

———. 1970. *Alfred Kroeber: A personal configuration.* Berkeley.

Kroeber, T. & R. Heizer. 1968. *Almost ancestors: The first Californians.* San Francisco.

Lévi-Strauss, C. 1966. Anthropology: Its achievement and its future. *Cur. Anth.* 7:124–27.

Loud, L. 1918. Ethnogeography and archaeology of the Wiyot territory. *Univ. Cal. Pub. Am. Arch. Eth.* 14:221–437.

Lowie Museum. 1990. Ishi. (Duplicated brochure.)

Norton, J. 1979. *Genocide in Northwestern California: When our worlds cried*. San Francisco.

O'Toole, G. 1984. *The Spanish War: An American epic 1898*. New York.

Pope, S. 1920. The medical history of Ishi. *Univ. Cal. Pub. Am. Arch. Eth.* 13:175–213.

Powers, S. 1877. *Tribes of California*. Berkeley (1976).

Rawls, J. 1984. *Indians of California: The changing image*. Norman, Okla.

Sapir, E. 1917. Do we need a superorganic? *Am. Anth.* 19:441–47.

Silverman, S., ed. 1981. *Totems and teachers: Perspectives on the history of anthropology*. New York.

Spott, R. 1926. Address. *The Commonwealth* 21(3):133–35.

Spott, R. & A. Kroeber. 1942. Yurok Narratives. *Univ. Cal. Pub. Am. Arch. Eth.* 35:143–256.

Steward, J. 1961. Alfred Louis Kroeber 1876–1960. *Am. Anth.* 63:1038–59.

———. 1973. *Alfred Kroeber*. New York: Columbia University Press.

Stocking, G. W., Jr. 1968. *Race, culture, and evolution: Essays in the history of anthropology*. New York.

———. 1974. The basic assumptions of Boasian anthropology. In *The shaping of American anthropology, 1883–1911: A Franz Boas reader*, ed. Stocking, 1–20. New York.

———. 1977. The aims of Boasian ethnography: Creating the materials for traditional humanistic scholarship. *Hist. Anth. Newsl.* 4(2):4–5.

Thompson, L. 1916. *To the American Indian* Berkeley. (1991).

Thoresen, T. 1971. A. L. Kroeber's theory of culture: The early years. Doct. diss., University of Iowa.

———. 1975a. Paying the piper and calling the tune: The beginnings of academic anthropology in California. *J. Hist. Beh. Scis.* 11:257–75.

———. 1975b. Typological realism in A. L. Kroeber's theory of culture. In *Toward a science of man: Essays in the history of anthropology*, ed. T. Thoresen, 205–12. The Hague.

Thornton, R. 1987. *American Indian holocaust and survival: A population history since 1492*. Norman, Okla.

Valory, D. 1968. Ruth Kellet Roberts 1885–1967. *Kroeber Anth. Soc. Pap.* 38:1–9.

Waterman, T. T. 1918. The Yana Indians. *Univ. Calif. Pub. Am. Arch. Eth.* 13:35–102.

———. 1920. Yurok geography. *Univ. Calif. Pub. Am. Arch. Eth.* 16:174–314.

———. 1925. All is trouble along the Klamath: A Yurok Idyll. In *The California Indians: A source book*, compiled and ed. R. Heizer & M. A. Whipple, 475–80. Berkeley (1951).

Wolf, E. 1981. A. L. Kroeber. In Silverman 1981:34–55.

ORIENTALISM AS *KULTURPOLITIK*

German Archeology and Cultural Imperialism in Asia Minor

SUZANNE MARCHAND

Despite his deft evisceration of the constitution promulgated at the time of his accession in 1876, Sultan Abdul Hamid II was not destined to enjoy his autocratic reign in peace. In the 1870s and 1880s, a series of humiliating financial and diplomatic setbacks debilitated the Ottoman ruler, who had hoped to centralize and consolidate his power. A breach in Franco-Ottoman relations was followed by a disastrous war with Russia in 1877, the economically paralyzing creation of a European-led committee to administer the Ottoman public debt in 1881, and the humbling extension of British colonial control in Egypt in 1882. Increasingly under attack from nationalist groups on the Ottoman peripheries, by 1890 Abdul Hamid faced the doubly disagreeable prospect of external dismemberment and internal disintegration.

The new Sultan, not surprisingly, listened eagerly to overtures from the newly founded German empire, the one great power without any obvious interest in the wholesale or partial dismemberment of the Ottoman state. In 1883 General Colmar Freiherr von der Goltz led a military mission to Turkey, and began to reorganize the Ottoman officer corps on German lines; in 1888, two prominent German bankers were awarded the concession to build a railway from Ankara to Constantinople, with a view to extending the line to Baghdad. In 1889, Kaiser Wilhelm II made his first visit to the Ottoman capi-

Suzanne Marchand is assistant professor of European Intellectual History at Princeton University. She received her Ph.D. from the University of Chicago in 1992. Her book *Down from Olympus: Archaeology and Philhellenism in Germany, 1750–1970*, will be published this year (1996) by Princeton University Press.

tal, and in the following year the two imperial powers signed a mutually bene-ficial trade agreement, multiplying German entrepreneurial contact with the southeast and giving new currency to mid-century fantasies about Germany's destiny in *Mitteleuropa* (Schöllgen 1984; Trumpener 1968).

This seeming abandonment of German neutrality in the East took place against the fervent opposition of Reich Chancellor Otto von Bismarck, who hoped to play Austrian, Russian, and British interests off against one another without entangling the Reich in Ottoman affairs. Even after the chancellor's departure from office in 1890, the Foreign Ministry retained the Bismarckian conviction that Germany should preserve its posture as neutral spectator in Asia Minor, and this despite increased German investment in Asia Minor, the new Kaiser's sympathy for his Turkish counterparts, and the pro-colonialist agitation of pan-Germans. Even with the further strengthening of German-Turkish economic and diplomatic ties after 1898, the Foreign Ministry was careful to preserve the fiction of equal partnership, and to cloak colonial am-bitions in high-minded rhetoric about German's civilizing mission abroad—even as it exploited raw materials and developed markets for German goods inside the Ottoman state. Disinterestedness, or at least the illusion of disinter-estedness, was believed to be in the state's best interest.

An oft-voiced motive underpinning German intervention in Asia was the notion that Germany had been entrusted with a special mission to bring *Kultur* to the unenlightened Turks. The intellectual counterpart of the economic modernizing mission of the *Bagdadbahn* (the train line to Bagdad), German cultural activity in the East aimed at the creation of a spiritual bond between the two nations as well as the cultivation of a consumer market for German products (Schöllgen 1981:142–44). This idea was neither new nor specifi-cally German; since the Reformation, Protestant and Catholic missionaries had ventured forth to teach their faiths and German language to heathens the world over, and the French and the British, of course, had long since shoul-dered their own variants of the "white man's burden." But the Germans, as usual, were late in taking up as a national pursuit what had been the preserve of local or confessional groups—so late, in fact, that the state bureaucracy felt obliged to intervene in order to speed and streamline the construction of German-Turkish "friendships." Germany's "*pénétration pacifique*" (Schöllgen 1984:xiv) required state management; even cultural philanthropy, at this stage of imperialist hostilities, was too important to be left to private groups and amateur activists.

Scholars, however, did have a role to play. The later nineteenth-century German scientific community had studiously cultivated a disinterested, anti-utilitarian reputation, and this aura of apolitical neutrality ideally suited it for launching the practice that was later termed *Kulturpolitik*. The fundamental assumption of this practice was that disinterested philanthropy or scholarship could increase national prestige abroad. As a coupling of Reformation (as well as Enlightenment) missionary zeal with imperialist diplomatic designs and imperious nationalist pride, *Kulturpolitik* in theory aimed at conversion without force, friendship without binding ties, and benevolence without short-term reward. An exclusively scientific *Kulturpolitik* thus complemented the diplomatic strategy of preserving the outward sovereignty and territorial integrity of the Ottoman regime, offering irreproachable evidence that Germany wished only to assist in Turkish modernization and international scientific progress. *Kulturpolitik* also performed domestic functions, centralizing and standardizing cultural patronage by giving state bureaucrats national funds to distribute among appropriately credentialed individuals and agencies. Thus, as the Reich bureaucracy began subsidizing professorial exchanges, conferences, exhibits at international fairs, and institutes devoted to linguistic and cultural training of bureaucrats and businessmen, the Wilhelmine Empire entered an era characterized by a new interdependence of cultural and political spheres.

German scholars had their own reasons for wishing to expand their activities abroad, not least among which was a desire to give material embodiment to the preeminence Prussia had achieved in the intellectual sphere. The confluence of their aims and the ambitions of the German state was particularly apparent in the relatively new discipline of classical archeology, a profession steeped in the tradition of Humboldtian humanism but deeply indebted to the nationalist exhibitionism that accompanied the founding of the Second Reich. The discipline's slow divergence from classical philology had been hastened as Germany's rise to world-power status introduced a desperate desire to bring the collections of the Royal Museums in Berlin up to the level of those of the Louvre and the British Museum. For classical archeologists of this era, invoking the lofty aura of pure science provided reassurance that this acquisition orientation represented neither a threat to the cultural property of other states nor an abandonment of conventional academic pursuits and practices; indeed science, as well as national loyalty, compelled scholars to press on. As Alexander Conze, director of the German Archeological Institute (Deutsches Archäologisches Institut), suggested to Reich Chancellor Hohenlohe in 1900, new archeological forays into the East represented for the Reich not only "a scientific duty of the first order," but also "a German duty" (P 37815: Conze/Hohenlohe 5/3/00). Conze insisted that digs be performed by the Archeological Institute, not by the Royal Museums, in order to insure preservation of the artifacts for future generations and to evade reputation-damaging charges of unscientific methods and pure acquisitiveness. The museum administration did not object to this arrangement, as long as its right to commandeer half the finds was not impaired (P 37815: KMim/AA 7/31/00). In general, after about 1880, Institute scholars and museum administrators worked closely together, with the Institute providing the expert personnel and

Excavations at Pergamon, 1906. Alexander Conze appears at the lower left, wearing a straw boater and a white coat. (Courtesy of the Bildarchiv preussischer Kulturbesitz, Berlin.)

the museum administration providing large portions of the necessary funds. Bound by overlapping memberships, social ties, and cultural interests, both groups recognized the virtues of indirect acquisition and scientific procedure, and were generally backed by an overseas diplomatic corps anxious to further German interests without overstepping the bounds of official neutrality.

Nineteenth-century German archeologists frequently blamed the subordinate status of their discipline within the general field of classical studies (*Altertumswissenschaft*) on the public's lack of familiarity with ancient objects, as opposed to its intimate knowledge of ancient texts, ingrained as this was in the cultured middle classes (*Bildungsbürgertum*) by means of the *Gymnasium* (e.g., Brunn 1885). There is clearly truth in this, for as German museums began to fill with stately monuments of the ancient past, new social groups coalesced to back the advance of the science of excavation, rather than that of textual criticism. The German Orientalist Society (Deutsche Morgenländische Gesellschaft), founded in 1844 as an association of aristocratic amateurs and philologists from several nations, was superseded with the formation of fund-raising societies like the Orient Committee (Deutsche Orient-Comité) in 1887 and the appearance of politically influential organizations such as the German Orient Society (Deutsche Orient-Gesellschaft), founded in 1898. Ironically, however, archeology's newfound social prominence, especially after

SUZANNE MARCHAND

its triumphs in Asia Minor in the 1890s, created the conditions for the demise both of its paramount international scientific standing and its central role in the rhetoric of nationalist cultural conquest. The rush of self-righteous classical archeologists, aggressive "orientalists," loose-cannon pioneers, amateurish politicians, greedy museum bureaucrats, and wily diplomats to organize German archeological colonization in the relatively unexplored and unregulated Ottoman state finished in a chaotic free-for-all. This lack of coordination between cultural interest groups not only betokens a complete lack of consensus about legitimate authority in matters of *Kulturpolitik*, but also underscores the variety of motives operating behind scientific exploitation of the Orient. Finally, such a tale of disciplinary disintegration indicates the extent to which German classical studies, in proceeding from words to things, and from German lecture halls to far-flung eastern locales, took up into itself the contradictions and covert designs of the *pénétration pacifique*.

The telling of this sort of tale will compel us to examine in careful detail the domestic social, political, and institutional contexts which shaped nineteenth-century German scholarship. This approach contrasts sharply with that adopted by Edward Said's *Orientalism* and Martin Bernal's *Black Athena*, both of which treat issues closely related to the subject at hand. Although these books have spurred important debates, Said's elision of nineteenth-century German *Orientalistik* and Bernal's inability to explain the genesis of K. O. Müller's Egyptophobia are indicative of both authors' difficulty in working out the complex relationships between politics and intellectual production. Partly this is the product of the difficulties of construing Germany's political and economic intentions with respect to the Ottoman Empire; where Said and others can draw straight lines from the articulation of the "Orient" by British and French scholars and literary figures as an imaginative space to its subjugation under imperial rule, this is not the case with Germany. Here, the absence of overt colonial aspirations and the undeniable modernizing role played by German business has rendered discussion of her "orientalist" imagination rather problematic. In effect, German cultural engagement in the Orient was insufficiently "orientalizing"—that is, deficient in the distancing tactics Said so carefully analyzes in French, British, and American literature—to suit his argument. German operators in the East dealt in raw materials and in artifacts—that is, in things, which, owing to the peculiar nature of German-Ottoman relations, had to be traded or negotiated—and relationships built on such conditions must necessarily take on a different character and give rise to very different "discursive formations" than those established on the basis of direct imperial rule. This example makes one wonder whether the downplaying of significant political, cultural, social, and scholarly differences between *European* nations (perhaps in a deliberate and not wholly unjustified attempt to identify the communal mentalité of the Occidental aggressor) does

not obscure more than it reveals of the actual process of the formation and
dissemination of discriminatory ideas. In any event, Said and Bernal have
shown us that humanistic scholarship creates as well as imbibes the prejudices
of its time; it is now our job to show how and with what cultural consequences
this occurs.

Orientforschung from Exegesis to Expropriation

Of vital importance to the understanding of the sacred history of Adam's heirs
as well as to the profane history of the progress of nations, European study of
Asia Minor and the Orient can claim a long and venerable legacy (see Rossi
1984; Grafton 1991). Until the late eighteenth century, "oriental studies"
(*Orientalistik*) generally meant the study of Semitic texts; here too, the study
of *Realien*[1] played a very minor, auxiliary role. Even more so than in the case
of the classics, *Orientalistik* was limited to language training and to either the
training of travellers (missionaries, doctors, entrepreneurs, officials) or to theological pursuits. Until the eighteenth century, students wishing to pursue Ara-
bic, Persian, or Hebrew left the Holy Roman Empire to do so, journeying to
England, Holland, Switzerland, or Constantinople, or had to hire private tutors, as did the Reformation-era cabalist Johannes Reuchlin (Schwab 1984:
21). The Enlightenment and the decline of the Turkish threat in the West
opened a period of new historical consideration (as opposed to theological
vilification) of Islamic culture; oriental *Realien* were drawn into the purview
of scholars with the publication of Barthélemy d'Herbelot's *Bibliothèque orien-
tale* in 1697 (Fück 1955:103; Said 1978:63–67). Göttingen developed an important school of "oriental" philology and biblical criticism under J. Michaelis
and J. G. Eichhorn in the later eighteenth century (Shaffer 1975:17–33). An
Imperial-Royal Academy of Oriental Languages was opened in Vienna in
1753, primarily to provide insightful diplomats and reliable translators for the
Austrian state (Roider 1980). During the Romantic era, interest in and knowledge of India and the East surged, opening an era rightly characterized as an
"oriental Renaissance." Herder celebrated the Orient as the cradle of man-

---

1. *Realien* is extremely difficult to translate. In nineteenth-century usage, it indicated scholarly
subject matter which was not strictly grammatical, linguistic, or philosophical; thus, a *Realphilolog*
(also called *Sachphilolog*) might study geographical, historical, ethnographic, archeological, religious, or biographical details of ancient culture. In general, until very late in the nineteenth
century, those who studied *Realien* held much less prestigious positions in academia and in society
at large than their linguistically absorbed colleagues, probably owing to their descent from, and
still-existing connections to, the antiquarian tradition. For more on this tradition, see Momigliano
1990.

kind; the Schlegel brothers learned Sanskrit; the aging philhellenist Wilhelm von Humboldt thanked God he had lived to see the translation of the *Bhagavad Gita* (Schwab 1984:59). Inspired by the prospect of using the new study of comparative philology to comprehend man's nature and history, the Romantic generation ransacked the oriental mind in search of itself.

Curiously, however, the period after 1830, which saw the passing of the Romantic generation, marked the advent of a new Mediterranean-centeredness and the decline of universal histories which juxtaposed oriental and occidental cultures. The result of a number of profound changes in educational organization and humanistic scholarship, this parting of philosophical and theological faculties would have enormous influence on the fledgling discipline of archeology, which derived its method and mindset almost exclusively from the classical philologists. With the deaths of scholars like Wilhelm von Humboldt, Karl Lachmann, Moritz Haupt, and Friedrich Creuzer, men who had held together the study of oriental and classical languages and cultures by sheer force of erudition, academic standing, and venerable old age, the way was opened to younger generation engaged in more specialized pursuits. The classicists of this generation, particularly those ensconced in the Prussian universities, combined a highly skeptical and meticulous method of source criticism with a keen desire to rid higher education of clerical influence, contributing to a profound secularization of classical studies. By virtue of its subject matter and its long heritage, oriental studies could not imitate this change of perspective, but it did attempt to shore up the declining social prominence of the field by borrowing ideas and material from the emerging science of comparative philology to address quasi-"anthropological" questions involving the genesis of language and languages and the movements of pre- or non-classical peoples. Even as artifacts began to play a greater role in debates on these politically resonant issues, classical archeologists left these discussions largely to orientalists, prehistorians, or German philologists (*Germanisten*), most of whom remained outside of or on the fringes of the academy.[2] Thus classical archeologists, especially those who would fill the museums with "oriental" artifacts, increasingly came to define themselves as suppliers of the matériale for

2. In 1864, there were 43 full professors of classical philology at German universities, and only 14 *Germanisten* and 3 *Orientalisten* (classified by Ferber as "Indologists"), with several more orientalists probably categorized as Old Testament exegetes in the theological faculty; in 1890, there were still 56 classicists to 24 Germanists and 7 orientalists; in 1910, the numbers were 62, 30, and 10, respectively (Ferber 1956:206). This sociological and intellectual divergence of classical studies and comparative linguistics should go some way to explaining the over-representation of German and orientalist philologists (Paul de Lagarde, Max Müller, the Grimms, Karl Müllenhoff), as compared to their classicist colleagues, in genealogies of Nazi ideology. The latter group, though equally nationalist and more influential, at least in elite circles, simply defined "primitive" or "anthropological" subjects as belonging to someone else's area of expertise.

the science of the future, rather than as interpreters of meaning in the present, while orientalists continued the search for origins and meanings.

In addition to this generational reorientation and disciplinary divergence, the underdevelopment of the academic study of oriental artifacts was also partly the product of technical constraints: the slowness and subjectivity of pre-photographic representations; the difficulty of travel and transport before the arrival of railroads; the expense and danger of voyages into the exotic (or enemy-colonized) *Morgenland*. But partly, too, the European eye—trained in Rome, Paris, London, and even backwater Berlin to appreciate Renaissance paintings and classical sculpture—could assimilate only with difficulty the repertoire of the Orient. "Oriental" art, characterized by Hegel as bizarre, grandiose, and purely symbolic, was held in low esteem. This was especially true of Indian art, but Islamic and even Byzantine styles were also late to acquire museum space and the attentions of art historians and connoisseurs (Marchand 1994). Nineteenth- and even early twentieth-century archeologists of all nationalities blithely destroyed all post-classical settlements during excavations in the East in order to burrow down to the Greek or Roman remains below.

In Germany, for several reasons, oriental *Realien* received a particularly hostile and halting reception. First, by the time the objects of the East began to arrive in the mid-nineteenth century, a distinctive bias in favor of philological understanding, ascetic aesthetics, and classical pedagogy had settled on the *Gymnasien* and universities, and, by extension, on the educated middle class. Second, without a colonial toehold in Asia, Prussia was just sending its first archeological expedition to Egypt (1842–45) when the Louvre and the British Museum opened their sensational displays of Assyrian and Persian art. With the exception of classical artifacts found on Turkish soil, very few of the antiquities excavated in the East were presented to the general public before the First World War; the artifacts needed to dislocate philhellenist habits were simply not there (cf. Schwab 1984:113–17). It was not until the commencement of excavations at Pergamon in the late 1870s that funds became available and diplomatic conditions favorable for the Reich to enter the competition for acquisitions in the East. Thereafter, however, by banking on personal connections to well-placed Turks and the declining influence of the French and British at the Sublime Porte, German scholars, diplomats, and museum bureaucrats began to press for new investment in oriental *Kulturpolitik*.

Efforts to organize expeditions in the early 1880s were undertaken by several bodies, with varying amounts of public funding and differing relationships to the academy and the state. In 1881, the Cultural Ministry approved 3000 marks for an expedition to Palestine by the German Association for Research on Palestine (Deutsche Verein zur Erforschung Palästinas, or DVzEP); in 1883, the state devoted 35,000 marks to the Prussian Academy of Sciences plan

(backed by Helmut von Moltke) to explore Kurdistan (P 37745: DVzEP/Gos-
sler 10/28/82; M 20772: Gossler/Kaiser 3/27/83). Because the state bureaucracy, especially the chancellor, was still not wholly convinced of the virtues
of excavation overseas, the Archeological Institute could not depend on state
subsidies until after the ascension of Wilhelm II, who took a personal interest
in archeological research. Various other efforts were made to raise funds for
digs in the Orient, culminating in 1887 with the creation of the Committee
for the Study of the Ruins of the Ancient Orient (Comité behufs Erforschung
der Trümmerstätten des Alten Orients), or Orient Committee. Described by
one archeologist as an organization of "scholars and money bags" (DAI/CH
Box 2: Adolf Erman/Humann 12/5/87), the Orient Committee did indeed
fund several expeditions to Sendschirli in northern Syria between 1888 and
1902. But from the standpoint of the museum administration, this arrangement had a major flaw: the acquisitions made during these expeditions belonged to the Orient Committee, and had to be purchased individually by the
museums at great cost (Pallat 1959:187, 189; P 37692: Bosse/Kaiser 10/7/98).

By the late 1880s, however, archeologists had discovered powerful advocates for their plans in the Cultural Ministry and the museum administration.
Gustav von Gossler, the national liberal who held the post of Prussian Cultural
Minister from 1879 to 1891, and Richard Schöne, the powerful General Director of the Royal Museums (himself an archeologist by training), both looked
to excavation in the East as a means to enhance the nation's collections—and
prestige—at bargain prices. With their assistance, German archeological excavation in Asia Minor expanded rapidly during the 1890s, owing much to
new state funds as well as Orient Committee monies now flowing into overseas
projects. In addition to expeditions organized by the academy of sciences, the
Archeological Institute directed digs (funded by the museums, the Kaiser, and
the Foreign Ministry) at Priene (1895–98), Magnesia (1891–93), and Thera
(1895–1902). The Orient Committee sent five parties to Sendschirli between
1888 and 1902, and excavations at Troy were recommenced with funds allocated by the Kaiser in 1893. The yearly budgets of the Archeological Institute
and museums increased by leaps and bounds, even though actual excavation
costs were often funded separately through bequests from the Kaiser's personal
disposition fund. Institute officials, museum bureaucrats, academy of science
members, politicians, and diplomats in far-flung places descended on the Kaiser with excavation plans, petitions for funding, and earnest assurances of swift
museological triumph. Count Radolin (ambassador in Constantinople, 1892–
97) warned the Foreign Ministry that were the Reich not forthcoming with
sufficient funds (he estimated 300,000 marks) to show their capability of finishing a grand dig at Miletus, the French would surely receive the necessary
excavation permit (firmen). An attached "Vermerk" explained that a dig at
Miletus was of vital importance "because this is perhaps the last place where

sizeable art treasures in the area in question [Greek settlements on the Turkish coast] are to be found" (P 37718: Radolin/AA 7/17/94). Even the liberal politician, prehistorian, and pathologist Rudolf Virchow denounced the Reich for its laxity in procuring oriental originals; in a speech to the Prussian Landtag, Virchow angrily contrasted the "extraordinary treasures" collected by the British and the French in the East to the paltry cast collections displayed in German museums (Renger 1979:159).

From Bagdad, Consul Richarz, clearly uncomfortable in an area of French and British predominance, applied regularly to the Foreign Ministry to send archeologists to Mesopotamia. In 1896, he proposed a German dig on the site of the ancient city of Uruk (Warka). "Frenchmen, Englishmen, and North Americans have overlooked it," Richarz enthused, "just as if by fate's decree, the act of unearthing these cultural centers, these schools which produced thousands of years of ancient wisdom, were reserved for the nation of poets and thinkers, the docta Germania" (P 37690: Richarz/Hohenlohe 8/25/96). Their interests moving ever eastward, the German scholars and businessmen of the Orient Committee evinced great enthusiasm for Richarz's cause (P 37690: Orient-Comité/Hohenlohe 2/2/97), and soon the academy of sciences took up the plan, adducing its importance to "the cultural significance of the German Empire." Dispelling fears that the nation might receive no concrete recompense, the academy claimed "that treasures . . . like those that fill the halls of the British Museum and the Louvre, are still there . . . in great quantity." An Uruk expedition, the academy concluded, would be of great profit "for science in general and for German science in particular, as well as for the sake of our public collections" (P 37691: Akademie der Wissenschaften/Bosse 2/13/97).

In matters archeological as in matters naval and imperial, blame for Germany's backwardness fell squarely on the central state; whereas in other countries individuals, private groups, and universities took on much of the burden of keeping up with Emile Botta or Flinders Petrie, in Germany, "keeping up" scientifically became an official imperative, an indispensable aspect of national self-esteem. In 1900, Archeological Institute Director Conze informed Chancellor Hohenlohe that new funding for German digs was an urgent requirement, "for the sake of our standing among nations" (P 37815: Conze/Hohenlohe 5/31/00). Invocations of nationalist pride and concern for international scientific standing were of course not uniquely German, but part of a larger decosmopolitanizing of the study of antiquity, illustrated by the founding of separate archeological "schools" in Rome and Athens by the major European powers in the 1870s and 1880s. Nor can the German archeologists' appeal to patriotic sentiments to obtain funds for *Kulturpolitik* abroad be equated with the frenzied nationalism of a Pan-German League or a Navy League. But once archeology was established as a realm for the representation of national triumphs, in an era of ever-increasing agitation for colonial conquests and other demonstrations of Germany's newfound international prestige, this rhetorical logic could hardly be undone.

In the last two years of the century, three essential events consolidated this coincidence of state and scientific goals in Asia Minor: the founding of the German Orient Society in 1898, the Kaiser's second friendship visit to Constantinople and the Levant, and the negotiation of a secret exportation treaty between the Sublime Porte and the Kaiserreich. In the wake of these developments, German archeological work in the East underwent vast expansion, funded by numerous state-affiliated agencies (the Archeological Institute, the Prussian Landtag, the Academy of Sciences, the museums, the Orient Society, and the Kaiser himself). A partial list of the major efforts would include the following digs: Miletus, Baalbek, Pergamon (recommenced in 1901), Kos, Boghazkoi (ancient Hattusa), Didyma, Samos, Borsippa, Far and Abu-Hatab, Kalat Schergat (ancient Assur), Babylon, Axum, Abusir, Jericho, Tel El Amarna, and Warka (ancient Uruk). While it is impossible to reckon the total costs to the German state, a rough idea can be garnered from Wiegand's (conservative) estimate that between about 1899 and 1913, more than 4 million marks in public and private funds had been devoted to digs in Asia Minor (DAI/TW Box 23: "Prememoria" in diary 11/13/13). Ushering in this era of enormous scientific, economic, political, and psychological investment in archeology, each of these three facilitating events was intimately intertwined with the progress of Germany's *pénétration pacifique*.

Founded in January 1898, the German Orient Society was officially made a subsidiary of the museum administration in order that its finds would automatically be considered state property. Its presidium included two well-connected princes, the director of the Deutsche Bank and president of the *Bagdadbahn*, Georg von Siemens, the undersecretary of the Foreign Ministry and director of the Colonial Office, Freiherr Friedrich von Richthofen, and Admiral F. Hollmann (a close personal friend of the Kaiser), two powerful Cultural Ministry bureaucrats, Friedrich Althoff and Richard Schöne, and two scholars skilled in the organization of academic-political joint ventures, Eduard Sachau and Alexander Conze. Regular members included well-established professors, diplomats, trade representatives, churchmen of both cloths, members of the Reichstag, and important businessmen (F. A. Krupp pledged a yearly subsidy of 3000 marks; see M FS/A–39: DOG membership list). In 1901, the Kaiser himself took over the official protection of the body. Yet despite the wealth and prominence of its backers, after a few years of heavy private investment, the Orient Society became more and more a funnel through which funds granted by the Kaiser and the Prussian state poured into the museums' coffers. After reaching a peak of 307,397 marks in 1903 (including 50,000 from the Kaiser and 88,600 from Prussia), total income began to drop, even though state contributions increased. By 1909, the Reich was paying a total of 150,000 marks of a 215,905 mark budget (see M FS/A–39: "Jahresberichte"). What had begun as an association of private patrons had quickly become a holding company for the Reich's cultural investment in the Ottoman Empire.

In the announcements and minutes of the Orient Society, the invocation to realize Germany's long-overdue cultural mission in the Orient played a major role. The organization attested to the great service to historical understanding performed by "the Anglo-Saxon countries" in taking up Assyrian and Babylonian studies with such vigor, and registered its discontent with Germany's passivity in the realm of archeological expropriation: "[F]or us Germans the time has come to take our part in the great work of opening up and recovering the most ancient Orient by means of systematic excavation, thereby to supply German science . . . as well as our public collections [with] monuments of ancient Asiatic art" (M FS/A–39: untitled announcement, p. 17; see also Delitzsch 1898). Similarly, an announcement in the *National-Zeitung* saw the need for excavation and collection as the logical end of German literary study of the Orient:

> Germany's inferior position with respect to excavations in Asia Minor, especially in Babylon and Assyria, in no way equivalent [to that of other European nations], stands in the sharpest contrast to the intensive and successful research in philology, general history, and cultural history that we have conducted precisely in this area. This inferior position affects not only our museum collections, but also is reflected in the public's prevailing view of oriental history and artifacts. Outside of professional and scholarly circles, many regard [the remains of] Babylonian-Assyrian history and culture as curiosities and have frequently made fun of them. (M FS/A–39 "Eine Deutsche-Orient Gesellschaft," *National-Zeitung* 1/19/98:21–22)

Scientific advancement, for this society of scholars, bankers, politicians, and churchmen, had become a less belligerent realm in which to pursue international rivalries and to express their resentment for Germany's late leap into colonial activity.

On October 18, 1898, Wilhelm II arrived in Constantinople to commence his tour of the Levant. His trip followed the German negotiation of peace between Greece and the Ottoman Empire, ending a brief war between the two long-time enemies. Taking the part of the Turks against France and Russia, which defended Greece, and England, which tried to snatch Crete for itself, the Germans had reasserted their commitment to the preservation of the Ottoman state. Wilhelm's journey also followed four years of Turkish massacres in Christian Macedonia and Armenia, and his friendly bearing toward the Sultan was widely viewed as an anti-European affront. Before his departure, Wilhelm had been drawn into the campaign to wrest new permits from the

Theodor Wiegand, who directed German monument protection efforts in the Ottoman Empire during World War I, prepares to survey a new site. (Reprinted from Carl Watzinger, *Theodor Wiegand*, 1944.)

Turks by Reinhold Kekulé von Stradonitz, whose lectures on antiquity had impressed the young Kaiser and who (chiefly as a consequence of his friendship with Wilhelm) had recently been appointed director of the Berlin antiquities museum (Watzinger 1944:85). In Constantinople, the young and enterprising excavator Theodor Wiegand took up the museums' cause, pleading for the Kaiser's intercession to gain a profitable agreement from the Turks on the distribution of finds from projected digs at Miletus, Baalbek, and Babylon (DAI/ TW Box 22: diary, copies of Kekulé/Wiegand 10/11/98; Wiegand/Kekulé 10/24/98). At a second encounter during the imperial *Orientreise*, Wiegand urged Wilhelm to support a general expansion of German archeological work in Asia Minor (P 37693: Marschall/Hohenlohe 12/7/98). On the Kaiser's return to the Reich, Chancellor Bernhard von Bülow spoke before the Reichstag on the subject of Germany's right to extend its protection over its citizens abroad, opening a new campaign to spread German *Kultur* overseas, and Wilhelm faithfully took up Wiegand's cause as part of this cultural calling. He undoubtedly broached the matter of permits for German digs in Mesopotamia with the Sultan, as Cultural Minister Bosse had requested (P 37718: Bosse/

Kaiser 10/7/98), employing his "friendship" with his Turkish counterpart to extract concessions above and beyond those agreed to by the Turkish antiquities administration, a tactic he would repeat in future years.

A major concession won by just such imperial intervention was the secret antiquities accord of 1899. Though the Turkish antiquity law of 1884 specified that all finds became the property of the Ottoman government, due to the close personal relationship between Carl Humann (the excavator of Pergamon and Magnesia) and Hamdi Edhem Bey (the Turkish Museums Director), the Germans had always been able to negotiate a better settlement. By 1897, however, Museums Director Schöne had grown fearful that this personal tie would be too expensive and/or unstable to last forever. Pointing jealously to the Austrian excavation at Ephesos, where the Sultan's personal decree had allowed excavators to retain all of their finds, Schöne suggested that an official agreement, giving Germany half of all finds, should be negotiated between the Sultan and the Kaiser (P 37718: Schöne/Bosse 4/27/97). Months later, the new ambassador in Constantinople, Adolf Freiherr Marschall von Bieberstein, told Chancellor Hohenlohe that as soon as the Priene excavations were complete, the arrangement proposed by the Schöne should be recommended to the Sultan as the personal wish of the Kaiser (P 37718: Marschall/Hohenlohe 1/25/98). Joining the call for an overall treaty, Wiegand reported to the Foreign Ministry that the French and Russians, as well as the Austrians, had made special deals with the Sultan to split their finds in half (DAI/TW Box 13: Wiegand/AA 3/2/98). A year later, Wiegand reiterated his request for Wilhelm's personal intervention, now especially to be recommended given "the excellent relations between Turkey and the German Empire and the great personal veneration of the Sultan for His Majesty, our most gracious Kaiser . . ." (P 37718: "Prememoria" 5/99). The young excavator even made a special trip to Berlin to breakfast with the sovereign, solidifying with photographs of the Greek monuments of Priene and Baalbek the Kaiser's determination to bring home material commemorations of German scientific prowess (Watzinger 1944:89–90).

Finally, in November 1899, the Sublime Porte issued a "Note verbale" announcing: "The [Turkish] Foreign Ministry has the honor of informing the Ambassador of his Majesty the German Emperor that an Irade of his Imperial Majesty the Sultan now authorizes the Berlin Royal Museums to keep for themselves half the antiquities that they discover in the course of authorized investigations . . ." (reprinted in PA/AA, 27-468a2: Bernstorff [EP]/Reichkanzler Hertling 5/11/18). From this time forward until the advent of World War I, museum bureaucrats, archeologists, and diplomats would continue to invoke this secret accord. It is testimony both to Germany's ultimate designs on the Ottoman Empire and to the manifold frustrations entailed in the Reich's "informal" approach, that in 1917 Royal Museums Director Wilhelm von Bode would press for the forced passage of an explicit exportation law, based on that of colonized Egypt, yet offering precisely the same provisions as had the secret accord (PA/AA 27–468a: Bode/KMin 3/28/17).

Archeological Diplomacy and Cultural Imperialism, 1900–1905

If the founding of the elite Orient Society, the newfound friendship between the Sultan and the Kaiser, and the negotiation of a secret acquisitions accord infused German archeological work in Asia Minor with new funds, force, and political significance, this entanglement of scholarly and quasi-imperialist ambitions posed new problems for the *Altertumswissenschaftler*. A new generation of more assertive mien had joined the campaign in the East, eager to apply imperial pressure on reluctant or simply inefficient Turks. As some archeologists on the ground quickly realized, however, diplomatic or political pressures brought to bear on Turkish officials could often be counterproductive, jeopardizing the negotiation of additional permissions or lucrative acquisition treaties. The expansion of German ambitions and undertakings after the turn of the century, inciting a corresponding rise in Turkish circumspection and internal dissension, would require an archeological diplomacy of greater and greater finesse—and produce a cultural "friendship" characterized by increasing levels of suspicion and mutual distrust.

Due to the constraints imposed by "informal imperialism," the extension of German archeological work in the East was at every step bound up with changes in international, as well as Turkish and German domestic political affairs. The Reich depended heavily on the preservation of the personal relationship Humann had established with Hamdi Edhem Bey, sometime Turkish Cultural Minister and long-time Director of the Ottoman Museums (from the 1880s until his death in 1910). Hamdi was the son of Edhem Pasha, an influential former Grand Vizier and ambassador to Paris. He and his younger brother Halil, who succeeded him as Museums Director (holding the post until 1931), were educated in Europe and absorbed to a considerable degree European tastes and the nineteenth-century (German) scientific ethos. Ironically, part of Hamdi's European experience included training in oil painting under France's foremost "orientalist" painter, Jean-Léon Gérôme; this artistic training apparently suited him in the Sultan's eyes to take over the directorship of the museums, a position vacant after the death of the German classical philologist Anton Déthier in 1881 (Watzinger 1944:179, 79). Halil had attended *Gymnasium* in Germany and studied chemistry at the universities of Vienna and Zurich. The brothers came of age in an era of double-pronged Ottoman policy, in which the Sultan sought to emphasize the Moslem, non-Western aspects of his regime while simultaneously attempting to modernize the civil service, transportation network, and educational system along European lines (see Lewis 1961). The same dualism was embodied, in different form, in the reformist but deeply nationalist Young Turk movement, to which Hamdi and Halil belonged, and it is precisely this contradictory relationship to Europe that underlay much of their—and by extension, much of the Ottoman state's—archeological diplomacy.

The passage of the first Ottoman antiquities protection code in the early 1880s, which was engineered by Hamdi and Halil, followed closely on the heels of several major European expropriations, including that of the Pergamon altar. Seeking to impose on excavators conditions comparable to those outlined in the Greek antiquities law, the Ottoman statute gave the first signal that the investigation and preservation of monuments of the non-Moslem past might be of sufficient value to deserve the state's attention. Even after the flurry of European interest in "oriental" excavations, however, few native Turks showed great interest in art and archeology, whether Western or Islamic, though some higher Turkish officials did begin to recognize the tourist value of classical antiquities (PA/AA 27–468: ET/Hohenlohe 8/24/99). As Wiegand had astutely noted, the Porte, if not the antiquities administration, was quite willing to dispense with Greek artifacts in order to acquire much-needed Western goodwill (P 37718: Wiegand "Prememoria" 5/99). Abdul Hamid's inconstancy, suspicious nature, and low regard for art and artifacts posed endless political dilemmas for those Western-educated individuals who sought to retain Ottoman dominion over cultural treasurers—particularly the classical remains coveted by Europeans—found on Turkish soil. Hamdi, for example, though responsible for overseeing the excavation and export of antiquities, was forbidden to pass beyond the walls of Istanbul for more than a decade because Abdul Hamid suspected him (rightly) of sympathizing with the Young Turks (see Wiegand 1970:36, 142). Furthermore, the tiny number of trained officials and the frequent hostility of local populations to excavators' appropriations of land, labor, and building materials made the operation of the antiquities administration a difficult social, as well as political, endeavor. Thus Hamdi was required to force European scholars to comply with their own ethos of disinterested research, using the underdeveloped administrative apparatus of a thoroughly unmodern state and in the absence of any well-defined social support for his protective maneuvers. Only the advent of Attatürk would provide the political climate and social basis for an active and effective campaign against European exploitation.

Ironically, however, the dictates of German-Turkish "friendship" actually allowed Hamdi both to command the deference of German scholars and to profit personally from their transgressions of his decrees. To "compensate" Hamdi for the division of finds at Miletus in 1902, the German museums purchased one of the Turkish official's paintings for the lucrative price of 6,000 francs (about 5,000 marks) and arranged for Hamdi to receive a decoration from the Kaiser (StMB: IM7 Wiegand/Schöne 5/23/03). Under these conditions, it was clear that the delicate negotiations necessary for the extension of archeological excavation could not be accomplished by Berlin-based scholars and bureaucrats; daily negotiations with men like Hamdi, whom Humann described as "working himself into a rage over something trivial and ten minutes later dancing the can-can" (in Pallat 1959:188) required a savvy, adventurous, and well-connected man on the scene, qualities possessed in abundance by Theodor Wiegand.

A poor *Gymnasium* student who came to archeology by way of modern art rather than through the normal channels of academic classical studies, Wiegand would never hold a university post (Watzinger 1944:25–33); he was no philologist, in either the narrowly professional or the broader social definition of the term. He was instead a prodigious fund-raiser for archeological projects and an invaluable cultural liaison, due in part to his contacts with big industrialists, mediated through his in-laws, the Siemens family. As successor to Humann (head of museum operations in Smyrna) beginning in 1897, and as scientific attaché to the German embassy in Constantinople, Wiegand shouldered most of the burden of mediating between Turkish officials and German museum bureaucrats, diplomats, scholars, and political figures in the crucial years 1897 to 1918. His task was to balance the acquisition-lust of the museum administration with the pride and political positions of Germanophile Turkish officials.

Wiegand made his debut as scholar-diplomat in the midst of discussions on the establishment of the secret German-Turkish accord. In 1898, he advised the German embassy in Constantinople that though Hamdi was devoted in principle to the promotion of German scientific projects, the powerful Turk could easily make good on his threats to sabotage the Sultan's infringements on the 1884 antiquities law (P 37692: Marschall/Hohenlohe 6/11/98). Wiegand was convinced that, secret accord or no, Hamdi's connivance was vital to the successful execution of digs, and especially to the export of artifacts. Although he relocated to Berlin in 1908 to become director of the Royal Museums' Antiquities Collections, Wiegand continued to play a major role in negotiations and to base his archeological diplomacy on the twin principles of apolitical scientism and solicitude for the Turkish museum director.

Owing to Wiegand's careful diplomacy, relations between the Archeological Institute, the Berlin museums, the Sublime Porte, and the Turkish cultural minister seem to have been reasonably pacific until 1902. The division of finds was accomplished at the digging sites, and Wiegand, to avoid future Turkish recriminations, had even returned to Priene material surreptitiously shipped to Berlin by Humann. He had taken this unprecedented step, Wiegand explained in his diary, ". . . first of all because I can't reconcile with my scientific conscience the idea that because of their stealthy importation we would conceal good discoveries for years and not include them in the forthcoming Priene report, and secondly because for the sake of the future I must make myself in every way unobjectionable [*einwandfrei*] in the eyes of the Turks" (DAI/TW Box 22: diary 6/20/99). When the Kaiser dictated a gracious thank-you to the Sultan for granting the Orient Society permission to excavate the sacred site of Kalat Schergat (Assur), he echoed precisely Wiegand's "disinterested" rhetoric: "Far from wanting to excavate the earth in order to extract treasures or profit, the German Society pursues only purely scientific ends and will find the greatest recompense for its labors in succeeding in the discovery of authentic documents which shed light on the foundations and roots of that ancient oriental culture, upon which rests the greater part of modern culture in the Orient as in the Occident" (P 37699: Kaiser/Sultan 7/20/02).

This brief period of genteel archeological diplomacy did not, however, last long. According to Wilhelm von Bode, in early 1902 he was approached by the young Byzantinist Josef Strzygowski, who showed him photographs of an elaborate Sassanid castle ruin, languishing in the deserts of Syria, known as Mschatta. Convinced that with the completion of the Mekka railway, the monument would be plundered, Bode appealed to the Kaiser for assistance in acquiring the castle's monumental gateway. Wilhelm was impressed by the photos and Bode's pleas: "We must have that, cost what it will!" he averred, and promised to write the Sultan directly about the matter. Chancellor Bernhard von Bülow, Bode reported, was delighted that the Kaiser was taking an interest in such things, and sped off to inform the Embassy in Constantinople (Bode 1930: 155–56). Others in the Reich bureaucracy, however, were less enthusiastic. Schöne feared newspaper reports detailing the Kaiser's interest in the ruin would generate American competition for its acquisition (StMB: IM6 Schöne/Puchstein 5/23/02). In May 1902, the Cultural Ministry and the archeologist Karl Schumacher warned the Kaiser not to intercede in the negotiation between the Institute and the Constantinople embassy over the site (M 20775: Studt [KMin]/Kaiser 5/26/02). A year later, arrangements for Mschatta's acquisition had not been resolved, and Wiegand was becoming concerned that the Kaiser's personal participation in archeological affairs would produce a Turkish reaction against German high-handedness (DAI/TW Box 13: Wiegand/[Schöne] 2/26/03). Negotiations on Mschatta collapsed when Hamdi, upon seeing photographs of the huge, monumental gateway, refused to consent to this violation of his antiquities law (P 37702: Wangenheim/AA 5/20/03). Despite Hamdi's obstruction, Baron von Wangenheim, second-in-command at the Constantinople embassy, promised his superiors at the Foreign Ministry that he would see if the Sultan might hand over the Mschatta gate as a personal gift to the Kaiser; Hamdi, he wrote, might be won over later with a "compensation" (P 37702: Wangenheim/

AA 5/16/03). By June, Wangenheim reported that this "gift" had been arranged, though only over the protests of Turkish officials, and conveyed his hopes that the German press would not celebrate the victory over the export law too loudly (P 37703: Wangenheim/Bülow 6/15/03). Finally, Wangenheim recommended that the Kaiser should not, as proposed, give the Sultan an ornate book of illustrations; since the Sultan actually preferred guns, horses, and dogs to books, pictures, and sculptures, he should receive instead a team of black thoroughbreds to complement the white horses given by Franz Josef of Austria (P 37703: Wangenheim/AA 6/20/03). The horses arrived at Constantinople in November 1903; several weeks later, the Mschatta Gate arrived in Berlin, packed in 442 cases.

Even before the Gate arrived, the proud new possessors began to worry about the diplomatic costs of its acquisition. Museums Director Schöne informed the head of the Kaiser's Civil Cabinet that the Sultan's gift had ". . . awakened much envy abroad and [had] especially received quite uncharitable treatment from the British press." "Under these conditions," Schöne recommended, "public discussion of the acquisition of the facade and its artistic and art-historical significance should be, if possible, avoided." He decided to "withhold all information about the sculptures from the press" (M 20776: Schöne/von Lucanus 12/23/03). Stifling the art historians and the Berlin press, however, was to no avail; in Turkey, the damage had been done. The Sultan himself suffered no pangs of conscience; indeed he is said to have boasted to a retainer of the painless diplomatic gains made by the Mschatta gift. "Look at these stupid foreigners; I pacify them with broken stones" (Watzinger 1944:170). Hamdi, however, was so outraged that he tendered his resignation. It was refused, but the museum director returned to his post considerably less enthusiastic about foreign excavators and increasingly attuned to the dangers of an "inondation scientifique allemande." Under these conditions, warned embassy attaché Wangenheim, pressure should not be applied to gain new permits in eastern Jordan, "For apart from the complete hopelessness of any prospect of taking steps in this direction after the completion of the negotiations over Mschatta, the Turks could see in this a proof of the real existence of the territorial aspirations in Turkey ascribed to us by our foes and an attempt to make this operative in the inauguration of a kind of *Kolonialpolitik*. To create this sort of impression," Wangenheim concluded laconically, "would be politically unwise" (P 37704: Wangenheim/Bülow 8/10/03). In short, the extraction of archeological concessions was beginning to be seen as an incipient form of colonial rule.

His pride hurt and his suspicions aroused, Hamdi imposed new strictures on German excavators. Continuance permits given without hesitation in the past were increasingly refused, pending Hamdi's issuance of a new antiquities law to which all excavators would be subject. Finds were now required to be reported immediately to the government, rather than awaiting the post-excavation division into halves. The Prussian museum administration, of course, was highly distressed at this turn of events, and Schöne appealed to the Cultural Ministry to pressure the Foreign Ministry and the Constantinople embassy to do something about Hamdi's new measures, which contradicted the provisions of the secret accord (P 37705: Schöne/KMin 2/6/04). Several weeks later, Ambassador Marschall reported that in the division of the finds at Kalat Schergat, the secret agreement had not been honored and the Germans would receive nothing; a widely publicized imperial Irade decreed that everything would remain in the Ottoman museums. "There can be no doubt," Marschall explained, "that Hamdi Bey's schemes are to be seen first of all as an act of revenge for the Mschatta affair, from which he still has not recovered." Anxious to elevate his own museum to the level of the great European institutions, Hamdi had begun to petition the Sultan for state funds for Turkish-run excavations; according to the ambassador, he was apparently employing a most effective appeal to the Sultan's vanity, arguing "that today most of the European sovereigns, including our most gracious Kaiser and the ruler of Austrian-Hungary, patronize archeological undertakings" (P 37705: Marschall/Bülow 3/27/04). Hurting Hamdi's pride had unleashed his nationalist ambitions, and hereafter negotiations would have to come to grips with both factors—or overcome the museum director's considerable powers of resistance with greater and greater shows of force.

Hamdi Edhem, however, was not the sole object of German archeological diplomacy. Both professional archeologists and diplomats made concerted efforts to exclude amateur excavators and explorers from participation in the cultural colonization of the Ottoman Empire. As the "Orient" began to attract the attention of scores of local "scientific" societies and "friendship" associations, plans for expeditions to the East multiplied with great rapidity. Recognizing the diplomatic advantages of scientific disinterestedness, however, established scholars feared the extension of privileges to the uninitiated. As Reich imperialist designs grew larger, attempts were made by the Institute, the museum administration, and the diplomatic corps to restrict cultural expropriation in the Ottoman hinterlands to licensed members of the classicist establishment.

A good example of this crusade against outsiders was the 1902 campaign waged by Wiegand, Schöne, and Wangenheim against the excavation plans of one Dr. Waldemar Belck, a chemist who had travelled widely in Asia Minor while employed by the Siemenswerke in Turkey (Renger 1979:173–74). Known in archeological circles as, according to Wiegand, "a rather arrogant dilettante," Belck was objectionable for having had a natural-scientific education and for having accepted the patronage of Rudolf Virchow, a recently defeated Institute opponent in the matter of the founding of the Römisch-

Germanische Kommission (see Marchand 1992:ch. 4). Diplomatically, too, Belck was a risk; following an attempt on his life, he had induced the Kaiser to demand a large indemnity from the penurious Sultan (Renger 1979:174). Wiegand opened his attack on Belck by underlining the diplomatic complications caused by the chemist's previous trips to the East: "There is present danger that the Turkish government's mistrust of Mr. Belck will gradually be transferred to the great, established scientific enterprises of Germany, which have previously known how to keep themselves free from the suspicion of [participating in] political or religious propaganda." Wiegand added that the leadership of Belck's organization, the newly formed German Society for the Scientific Study of Anatolia (Deutsche Gesellschaft für Wissenschaftliche Erforschung Anatoliens), included several prominent "friends of the Armenians," a feature sure to excite Turkish distrust and animosity (P 37700: Wiegand/ET 8/18/02). Schöne, drawing on the testimony of Conze and a museum assistant, confirmed Wiegand's negative assessment of Belck and cautioned against allowing more than one organization to receive digging permits from the Turkish government. "German, especially Prussian, archeological interests in Turkey," he warned, "would be seriously threatened in all sorts of ways through [the establishment of] a second, competing center of operations" (P 37701: Schöne/KMin 9/30/02).

Seconding the dark intimations of Wiegand and Schöne about Turkish discomfiture at the prospect of the founding of the Anatolian Society, Wangenheim turned the minor issue of Belck's incompetence into a straightforward disquisition on the clandestine means indispensable to the *pénétration pacifique*:

> The idea of Germany's gradual spiritual conquest [*geistige Eroberung*] of Asia Minor is thoroughly sound and capable of development. The interim intellectual goals already pursued, or to be pursued, by our schools, our doctors, and our archeologists could very well become, in the course of time, the crystallization point onto which German economic and colonizing undertakings are grafted. The economic will follow the intellectual conquest as a natural result, and then these two diffused phases will naturally be followed by the third stage, that of political exploitation [*Verwerthung*] and consolidation of the cultural values we have created. But for the execution of such a farsighted policy, it is above all necessary that we know when to hold our tongues, that neither at home nor anywhere abroad, to say nothing of among the Turks, do we allow it to be thought that our cultural efforts in Turkey aim at anything else than the satisfaction of German scholarly ambitions and the friendly intention to bring new vitality to the penniless Turkish state coffers. . . . Nothing is more disruptive to the careful and continuing development of our operations than the deportment of German agitators who urge the cultural conquest of the Orient, [and] who are perpetually discussing the subject of Germany's putative future plans in Turkey in public meetings and in the press, and have recently manifested a tendency to

come together in associations [like the Anatolian Society]. . . . If our *Altertums-forschung* has been increasingly successful, this is above all to be credited to the tactful and modest behavior of the scholars sent here who have extracted the most precious treasures from the Turkish soil for us, and also who know how to gradually put to rest the Turks' initial mistrust of their activity. (P 37700: Wangenheim/Bülow 8/24/02)

Belck's interference endangered the scientific and economic exploitation of the East, but, even more seriously, his tactless behavior threatened to expose the hypocritical foundations of German *Kulturpolitik* in the Ottoman Empire.

Wangenheim's dictum captures in full the fretful megalomania driving cultural policy in the Orient. Strategically and ideologically, "friendship" with the Ottoman state still suited the Wilhelmine Empire; as a window on Egypt and India, a barrier to Russian expansionist ambitions, and a pacific neighbor on Austria-Hungary's weak eastern border, the Sultanate served important defensive purposes, while Wilhelm could not help but approve Abdul Hamid's deeply anti-democratic system of rule. But, craving material enrichment and imperial stature, citizens of the Kaiserreich could not be content with mere "friendship," and began to press—with increasing numbers and rising voices—for concessions, and, finally, conquest. As German entrepreneurs, explorers, and excavators ventured deeper and deeper into the Ottoman hinterlands, this diplomatic contradiction would appear in sharper focus, forcing officials of the Bismarckian school—generally established, older diplomats, businessmen, and scholars—back on assurances of disinterested neutrality, and driving the equally self-interested proponents of *Weltpolitik* to acts of expropriative impudence. In the archeological realm, the culmination of this generational and ideological clash would come at the edge of the text-historical world: Mesopotamia.

Babylon, Assur, and the Collapse of Disciplinary Solidarity

By the mid-1890s, numerous voices had been raised in support of commencing German excavation in Mesopotamia, widely thought to be the next great region for archeological exploration. In 1897, following a call from Schöne, the Commission for the Archeological Study of the Lands of the Tigris and Euphrates was formed to sell the state on the idea; its members included Schöne (president), Archeological Institute Director Conze, the director of the Oriental Seminar at the University of Berlin, Eduard Sachau, the Greek philologist Hermann Diels, the Egyptologist Adolf Erman, and Cultural Ministry representative Friedrich Schmidt-Ott. The Commission recommended that an "informational" expedition be sent to the area right away and demanded that diplomatic intervention be used to circumvent the antiquities law once more, giving the Germans a wide "Spielraum" (embracing all of Vilajet Mossul, containing the palaces of the Assyrian kings), a long tenure (fifty years), and a large share of the finds. The French had paid the Persians 50,000 francs for such an all-inclusive arrangement in that region and had benefitted greatly from this; now that Germany was in a favorable political position to extract similar concessions from the Sultan, the Commission argued, why not seize the opportunity? The Commission concluded its appeal with a warning that failure to act would consign Germany to a place in the shade, shut out of yet another carving up of the globe (P 37691: Kommission/Bosse 12/21/97).

Despite the Commission's failure to secure a fifty-year excavation permit, an archeological reconnaissance team did survey the Tigris-Euphrates basin during the winter of 1897–98, funded by the Orient Committee member and cofounder of the Orient Society, Dr. James Simon (P 37692; Bosse/Kaiser 10/7/98). The expedition was headed by Sachau and Robert Koldewey, a quarrelsome architect who had excavated minor sites in the East under foreign patronage. Enthusiastic at the prospects for monumental acquisitions, Schöne transmitted the party's findings to the Cultural Ministry. For the modest price of 500,000 marks, the Museums Director argued, a grand-scale excavation at Babylon might be organized, a plan promising abundant and diverse treasures (P 37692: Schöne/Bosse 8/13/98). Cultural Minister Bosse passed Schöne's advice to the Kaiser, adding an elaborate appeal to take up the subject of the Babylon permit personally with the Sultan during his upcoming *Orientreise*. The Minister described in glowing terms the prospects of a dig in "the venerable, holy, mother-city of Mesopotamia," striking a now common competitive tone and suggesting, perhaps for the first time, that Germany's obsessive interest in philology might have contributed to its archeological and museological backwardness (P 37692: Bosse/Kaiser 10/7/98).

On December 30, 1898, a small party of excavators appointed by the Orient Society left Damascus for Babylon, following a route that hardly differed from that travelled by Alexander the Great. Since the *Bagdadbahn* was not yet complete, the means of transportation were also the same: all equipment and personnel arrived at the site via camel caravan (Andrae 1961 : 29). Despite their remote location and harsh desert conditions, German archeologists had by 1902 succeeded in excavating large sections of the monumental city walls, and had filled six hundred crates with fragments of the tiled Ishtar Gate facade. Koldewey and Assyriologist Friedrich Delitzsch explained to the Foreign Ministry that the relief was to be sent directly to Berlin to prevent damage to the fragments and to facilitate swift reconstruction of the facade by German scientists, allegedly with the view to returning the rebuilt gate to the Ottoman museums (P 37700: Delitzsch & Koldewey/AA 6/8/02; KMin/AA 8/11/02).

Aside from the Ishtar Gate and numerous seals, however, Babylon did not

The excavations at Babylon, about 1910, showing a side view of the Ishtar gate in the left center. (Reprinted from Robert Koldeway, *Das wiedererstehende Babylon*, 1913.)

divulge the rich cache of tablets and sculpture sought by the museum, the Academy of Sciences, and the Orient Society, and by 1902 German attention was straying to other nearby Mesopotamian sites. Delitzsch, whose "Babel und Bibel" lectures had made him a national celebrity (see below), in late 1902 submitted a memorandum to the Kaiser and the Reich bureaucracy urging the sovereign to arrange with the Sultan a dig at the most important of these sites, Kalat Schergat (ancient Assur). Delitzsch recommended speedy action, before the British recovered from the Boer War or the French made a deal with the Ottoman museums. Wilhelm's marginalia confirmed the effectiveness of Delitzsch's nationalistic appeal: "That cannot be!" and, "We must do it!" he wrote beside Delitzsch's descriptions of the threat posed by British and French acquisition of digging rights. And the Assyriologist's final plea that German scholars be accorded exclusive rights to publish all found materials received the Kaiser's proud endorsement: "Yes! We will carry the light of German genius there too!" (P 37700: Delitzsch's *Denkschrift* titled "Kalat Schirgat" 2/26/02). By early 1903, the Orient Society had begun excavations at Assur under the direction of Walter Andrae. The dig continued for eleven long years, employing an average of 180 to 200 workers (Andrae 1961:143).

Notwithstanding their remote locations, German digs in Mesopotamia, like those on the Turkish coast, were hampered by failures in archeological diplomacy. Exacerbated by the haughty behavior of Koldewey and Andrae, the Mschatta episode had its impact here as well. The first manifestation of

Hamdi's crackdown on antiquities exports occurred in early 1905, when his proxy Bedri Bey attempted to confiscate the numerous carefully packed cases of Assur finds. Andrae refused to hand over the boxes, and the Constantinople diplomatic corps, regretting the Reich's failure to instruct scholars on proper behavior overseas, prepared itself for "another Mschatta" (P 37708: Marschall/ Bülow 2/1/05). A second apocalyptic missive from Marschall to the Foreign Ministry complained that Andrae was behaving as if Assur were "a con-quered country" rather than the Sultan's personal property, and he conveyed Wiegand's worries that this conflict would produce a final rupture with Hamdi, just when the Reich "has so many archeological irons in the fire" (P 37708: Marschall/AA 2/24/05). The Foreign Ministry did its best to prevent news of the controversy from reaching the Kaiser; Wilhelm's close friend (and Orient Society president) Admiral Hollmann was sworn to secrecy, and Delitzsch was instructed to avoid the subject in his upcoming Orient Society lecture. As the Ministry explained to Chancellor von Bülow, the Kaiser had to be restrained from soliciting the Sultan's personal intervention; after Mschatta, this could only further alienate Hamdi and damage German interests (P 37708: AA/ Bülow 2/25/05).

Wiegand's personal negotiations with Hamdi resulted in an agreement to send sixty-two cases to Constantinople for study and division of the finds. It appears, however, that the Kaiser not only learned of the dispute, but credited a rumor conveyed by Hollmann that Turkish local officials were selling Ger-man Mesopotamian finds to the British and French. Wilhelm immediately telegraphed Marschall, demanding that Bedri Bey be fired and all finds be sent directly to the Imperial palace in Berlin (P 37708: Marschall/AA 2/24/05; DAI/TW: Wiegand/Koldewey 3/4/05; Pallat 1959: 316). The Turks responded by taking away Andrae's permit and ordering the transport of all the finds to Constantinople (P 37708: EC/AA 3/5/05). Wiegand wrote to Koldewey, pleading for the Mesopotamian crew to refrain from inciting Turkish animos-ity and to show Hamdi greater respect: numerous German digs and acquisi-tions were at stake (DAI/TW Box 6: Wiegand/Koldewey 3/4/05).

By mid-1905, German-Turkish cultural relations had reached a nadir; the digs at Babylon, Assur, and Pergamon had been suspended and the status of finds from these sites, plus negotiations over those of Baalbek, Miletus, and Didyma, were in daily flux. Ambassador Marschall was asked by the Foreign Ministry to use the opportunity of his presentation of a book on Persian poetry to the Sultan to discuss permit renewals and to apply for permission to use a motorboat given to Koldewey by the Orient Society to transport equipment and finds to and from the Mesopotamian sites on the Tigris (P 37709: AA/ Marschall 3/18/05). The ambassador was successful in the first of these aims; approval for the boat, however, was denied after Koldewey's secret machina-tions aroused Turkish suspicion that the Germans either wished to evade the antiquities law or to demand trading privileges in the area equivalent to those held by the British (P 37709: EC/AA 6/9/05 and ET/Bülow 5/11/05; DAI/ TW Box 6: Wiegand/Koldewey 8/2/05).

Events in Mesopotamia after 1905 revealed an important schism developing in the archeological world. The Archeological Institute and its parent institution, the Foreign Ministry, had pioneered archeological excavation in the East, and had bombarded the state with requests for patronage and appeals to nationalist pride and prestige. Their commitment to discreet diplomacy and gradual "cultural conquest," however, increasingly vexed the more pugnacious Orient Society, under the leadership of members of the Kaiser's entourage and backed by the aggressive new museums director, Wilhelm von Bode. Created in 1829 as an aristocratic society of dilettantes and diplomats, the Institute had become an exclusive organization of professional classical archeologists, while the Orient Society encompassed a much wider and less academic public in its membership. The Orient Society dedicated itself to the ancient Orient as a whole, including biblical and prehistoric pursuits, while the Archeological Institute, digging mostly in Ionian and Roman settlements, maintained much of the philhellenic spirit even in its forays into Asia Minor. Oriental Society excavators tended to be younger than those of the Institute, and to have more technical (architectural or engineering) backgrounds than philological ones. Both Andrae and Koldewey, as well as Ernst Herzfeld and Julius Jordan (who assisted in Assur and executed numerous other Society digs and surveys), were architects by training; with the exception of Koldewey, the dig leaders in Mesopotamia were all born after 1870, and like Koldewey (an eccentric by any measure) were closer to prehistorians like Carl Schuchhardt and Felix von Luschan than to any of the Institute classical archeologists (Andrae 1952:242, 212). Andrae was young enough to have read *Rembrandt als Erzieher* as an impressionable young student bored by lifeless Greek and Latin studies at the Technische Hochschule in Dresden (Andrae 1961:3–12). Touched by *fin-de-siècle Lebensphilosophie*, and later an avid theosophist, Andrae's interests in nature, religion, and art harkened back to a more romantic strain in *Orientforschung*, one that now had little to do with the professional, increasingly specialized pursuits of the Archeological Institute.

The clash of the two bodies can be seen as a classic translation to the cultural sphere of the confrontation between an older generation of National Liberals and a rising corps of new nationalists, with the difference that in the realm of *Wissenschaft*, the older generation long succeeded in using its semi-meritocratic credentials to block the access of outsiders. But soon after the new century commenced, the resentment and the politico-acquisitive truculence of newer groups like the Orient Society began to express itself here too, provoking last-ditch efforts by the classicists and the diplomatic corps to save the Reich's position and German archeology's scientific reputation. Koldewey,

Andrae, and other Society excavators, backed by the Imperial court, German
industrialists, and high members of the clergy, and underwritten by a now established tradition of German scientific prowess, resented what they perceived
to be onerous Turkish restrictions and pusillanimous German diplomacy.
Vexed by the dictates of Wiegand and the diplomats that he modify his behavior toward the "stupid and greedy" members of the Turkish Antiquities Commission, Koldewey vented his frustration to Orient Society secretary Bruno
Güterbock. He had to obey the Turks, Koldewey complained, "Because I have
the strict order to do everything that the commission, in the name of its big
boss [Hamdi], desires, and if I take the communications from Constantinople
seriously, we would do well here, when His Excellence Hamdi Bey slaps us on
the left cheek, not only to offer him the right cheek, but to thank him most
politely" (P 37709: Koldewey/Güterbock 4/11/05). When Wiegand re-
proached Koldewey for his critical statements about the embassy, which had
been leaked to the Kaiser by Güterbock, Koldewey apologized to Wiegand
personally, but maintained that the diplomats had done nothing to prevent
the Turks from treating the Mesopotamian excavators "like mangy dogs, to
the general amusement of all the other nations and to our own deepest embarrassment" (DAI/TW Box 6: Wiegand/Koldewey 6/18/05 and Koldewey/
Wiegand 7/18/05).

  The stubbornness and arrogance of the Orient Society excavators was the
subject of Marschall's communication to Bülow in late May 1905. Marschall
contrasted the behavior of two unnamed younger archeologists (clearly Koldewey and Andrae) to that of Wiegand, who had just succeeded in wresting
the digging permit for Didyma from the French, and that of Institute veterans
Conze and Humann, who had been respectful of Turkish customs (including
petty bribery) for the sake of Germany's long-term archeological interests. "Every official who needs money is certainly not a half-addicted scoundrel, but is
rather a poor devil who is not paid by the state and therefore hopes to find the
foreign Effendi's pocketbook open to cover his modest needs," wrote the ambassador, demonstrating the ethnographic sensitivity that had endeared older
excavators to Turkish officialdom. The ambassador continued:

> If he finds this and also a few friendly words, he makes a favorable report to
> Constantinople, and all goes swimmingly. If his hopes are disappointed and he
> is insulted to boot, the opposite occurs. This is from the European standpoint
> morally reprehensible, but it corresponds to the morals of the country. The im-
> provement of the latter lies beyond the realm of archeological inquiry. (P 37709:
> Marschall/Bülow 5/26/05)

It was easy enough to obtain the Sultan's connivance, the ambassador continued, but the important thing was to break Hamdi's resistance, and, for that,
high-handed and rude behavior, like that of the Society's excavators, could
not be tolerated.

In the years before the World War, Orient Society members continued to vex the embassy and the Archeological Institute by interfering in what the classicist-diplomatic circle believed to be their bailiwick. In 1907, the issue of the motorboat resurfaced, and, to Marschall's horror, the Orient Society insisted that the boat be German-owned and -operated, and that it display the German flag. The Society, the diplomat told the chancellor, mistakenly considered the flying of the flag to be a "Machtfrage" (power issue), and was unwilling to compromise with the very patient Turks (P 37714: Marschall/Bülow 5/1/07). A constant source of embarrassment, the Kaiser in 1908 ordered the performance in Berlin of the pantomime-play "Sardanapal" (Assurbanipal), for which he recruited Andrae, Delitzsch, and other Orient Society scholars to ensure that props, costumes, and hairdos were stylistically accurate. Wilhelm invited dignitaries foreign and domestic to the play's opening night and proceeded to offend the British and French (as well as German Reichstag members) by adding to the archeological spectacle a speech praising Assyria's lack of parliaments (Andrae 1961:180–82).

The Young Turk revolution of 1908 introduced additional complexities into archeological diplomacy. The rebellion rode in on a wave of pro-British sentiment and anti-German rhetoric; in addition to forcing the Sultan to restore the 1876 constitution and parliament, rebels insisted that pro-German higher officials be removed from their posts (Lindow 1934:103–6). Anglophile enthusiasm proved short-lived, however, as the British refused a large loan for the Young Turks and then backed a brief counter-revolution in April 1909. Germany emerged from the debacle again the most-favored nation among Turks in high political (and cultural) circles. In the midst of the rebellion's confusion, Wiegand managed to ship home to Berlin another enormous relic of the Greek past: the market gate of Miletus. Of 533 crates of finds, only 33 went to Constantinople, the remainder to Berlin. In May 1908 Wiegand confided to his diary: "We have succeeded in packing up the entire market gate of Miletus, of which three-quarters of all the ancient dressed stones were found, with the designation 'architectural fragments,' without the Turkish officials having the least idea that they have ceded to us a whole monument the size of Constantine's Arch in Rome" (DAI/TW Box 22: diary 5/15–21/08). With the disintegration of German *Kulturpolitik* and the onset of Ottoman diplomatic chaos, the intrepid excavator's commitment to preserving the appearance of disinterestedness had clearly waned.

Even more clearly than the appropriation of the Miletus Gate, the death of Hamdi in February 1910 marks the end of an era of German-Turkish cultural relations. Hamdi was succeeded by his younger and more nationalist brother Halil Edhem Bey, who proved to be more difficult to manipulate and more susceptible to internal political pressure than his predecessor. Although Halil remained sympathetic to German interests until his retirement in 1931, the governments he served were deeply divided, and domestic political tensions prevented any overt Germanophilic behavior on his part. In 1910, the new director of the Ottoman museums was denounced by the Turkish parliament for having given a key to the artifacts storehouse at Babylon to Koldewey, and was threatened with big cuts in the museum budget if he did not act immediately. Although Wiegand and the embassy insisted that Koldewey relinquish the key (P 37716: Miquel [ET]/Bethmann 6/15/10), negotiations on finds thereafter seem to have broken down completely. By 1913, with the finds from Didyma, Babylon, and Assur hanging in the balance, even Wiegand was anxious to invoke the secret accord to save "the enormous scientific harvest [lying] in German excavation sites in Turkey," though he fully realized that the antiquities question had become a highly sensitive matter of international as well as domestic Turkish politics (DAI/TW Box 23: diary, "Prememoria" 11/13/13 sent to the EC, Bode, and Helfferich).

In Germany, *Kulturpolitik* had become a free-for-all; the embassies and Wiegand could no longer control the actions of the more aggressive Orient Society, Wilhelm II, and Museums Director Bode. In 1912, Wiegand had to force his way onto the presidium of the Orient Society, he reported, "since the members didn't want to elect me." "Still and yet . . . the one-sided mistrust of classical archeology as the rival of oriental studies persists" (in Wenk 1985: 19). The Finance Ministry, which had failed to strike big archeological expenditures from the Kaiser's personal budget, sent him into a rage in attempting to block Prussia's allocation of 20 million marks to outbid an American offer to buy artifacts from the Ottoman museums (Wenk 1985:19–20; DAI/TW Box 23: diary 2/20/14). The Orient Society, Bode, Reich Chancellor Bethmann-Hollweg, and Rudolf von Valentini, head of the Kaiser's civil cabinet, all resented Wiegand's direct missives to the Kaiser, which circumvented their authority; outraged Society members, Wiegand said, now considered him "the blackest intriguer on God's earth" (DAI/TW Box 23: diary 2/18/14). In return, Wiegand berated the elite association for allowing news of the six hundred cases of finds at Assur to leak to the public (DAI/TW Box 23: diary 3/15–18/14, 3/22/14). Wiegand's decision to involve the Kaiser in negotiations also produced a break with Wangenheim, and with Wiegand's friend Karl Helfferich, who resented this new disturbance in German-Turkish relations just as he was negotiating an important new agreement on the *Bagdadbahn*. Wangenheim, Wiegand wrote, was so angry with the excavator as to swear that "all the strychnine in the world would not be enough to poison me and my archeological colleagues" (DAI/TW Box 23: diary 6/19/14). The combination of inter-ministerial backbiting, archeological infighting, and belligerent nationalist agitation was fast unravelling the diplomat's carefully constructed plans for future conquest.

The status of the Assur finds was still being debated in 1914, when the dig was declared complete. Six hundred crates of artifacts were packed and awaiting shipment to Berlin by early January; but in February, the Constantinople embassy reported that an audience with the Grand Vizier had failed to release them (PA/AA 27–468a1: ZK/AA 1/13/14; M 21355: EC/AA 2/3/14). On March 13, the Kaiser telegraphed the Foreign Ministry, commanding the dip-lomatic corps to tell the Grand Vizier that the Kaiser himself wanted the Assur finds; Wangenheim conveyed the message and also promised to discover how the French and the British had evaded the 1907 antiquities law (PA/AA 27–468a1: Wangenheim/AA 3/14/14). The ambassador put heavy pressure on the Turks to comply with the secret accord, but warned the Foreign Ministry that an ultimatum could cause the pro-German Grand Vizier to fall, and perhaps result in a diplomatic break between the empires (PA/AA 27–468a1: Wangenheim/AA 3/27/14). Several days later, the Turkish Foreign Minister Said Halim promised Wangenheim that the government would allow the six hundred crates to be sent to Germany, but that this would be concealed from the Ottoman parliament; hereafter, too the 1899 secret accord would be in-valid (PA/AA 27–468a1: Said Halim/Wangenheim 3/30/14). Wangenheim expressed gratitude for the concession of the crates, but remained cagey about the future of the accord; he reminded the Berlin bureaucrats, however, that taking advantage of the situation to extract further booty would not be ulti-mately to Germany's benefit. "Our political perception in Turkey rests on our absolute loyalty [to the Ottoman state]," wrote the ever-calculating Wangen-heim. "Therefore we must also remain irreproachable in archeological mat-ters" (PA/AA 27–468a1: Wangenheim/Said Halim 4/1/14).

The final irony of the Mesopotamian campaign lies in the fact that the Assur and Babylon finds, the cause of great expenditure and the source of fac-tional rivalries and diplomatic snarls, reached the Reich only after the sun had set on Wilhelmine *Weltpolitik*. The Assur negotiations represented a case of Mschatta redux, for Halil had no intention of allowing the Grand Vizier to preside over his terrain. In April, Halil informed Bode that he could not stand idly by as the antiquities administration and codes constructed by his brother and himself were destroyed, and refused renewal of all digging permits (DAI/ TW Box 23: copy of Halil/Bode (undated) in diary 4/23/14; M 21355: Wiegand/ZK 5/22/14). On June 7, a telegraph arrived in Berlin, confirming that Halil had closed down the Babylon dig; the Kaiser's marginalia on the missive asked "Have these mad devils gone berserk?" provoking the earnest query from Schmidt, "Whom does the Kaiser really mean in this note? The Turks or the Foreign Ministry?" (DAI/TW Box 23: diary 6/11/14). At last, the Grand Vizier intervened to arrange the shipment of finds and approve new permits for Babylon and Pergamon—but not until July 1914 was the German share of the Assur finds put aboard a steamer in Basra (PA/AA 27–468a31: Wangenheim/AA 6/22/14; Andrae 1927a:1). On August 1, the Assur crates arrived in Lisbon, where they were first impounded and then confiscated when

Portrait of Walter Andrae. (Courtesy of the Deutsches Archäologisches Institut, Abteilung Baghdad.)

the Portuguese entered the war on the Allied side in 1915. All efforts to return the finds to Germany (including a half-hearted one conducted by the British Museum in 1923) foundered on Berlin's unwillingness to compromise; Wilhelm, in exile, recommended sending a warship to Porto to bombard the city until the finds were released (Andrae 1961:258). At last in 1926, Andrae and the Foreign Ministry worked out an agreement to share some of the finds with the University of Porto, and the Assur material, together with 536 crates of Babylon finds, impounded by the British in Babylon in 1917 (and secured for the Germans by the English adventurer and diplomatic attaché Gertrude Bell under a new Iraqi antiquities code), finally flowed into the Berlin Royal Museums (see Andrae 1927a & b, 1961:257; Renger 1979:188). By this time, both the scientific and museological competition that had inspired the excavations and the German-Ottoman "friendship" that had underwritten the concessions were no longer the prevailing forces in cultural politics. And yet, the exhibition and explication of Mesopotamian artifacts, lagging far behind their excavation, continued to be bound to the idiosyncrasies of the Kaiserreich's chaotic *Orientpolitik* and German archeology's internal rivalries long after the *pénétration pacifique* had failed.

Informal Imperialism, Archeological Positivism, and the Persistence of Philhellenism

The sensation created by the excavation and acquisition of the Pergamon altar in the early years of the Kaiserreich was the product not only of the altar's monumentality, but also, in large part, of its (admittedly hellenistic) Greekness. The desire to procure grand Greek monuments had driven excavators of the 1890s to investigate Baalbek, Priene, and Miletus, all sites of Ionian settlement on the Turkish coast. But as archeologists penetrated deeper and deeper into the "Orient," leaving behind the Greek colonies on the western coast, German ambitions had settled on outstripping other nations in number, scale, and "scientificness" of their digs, and their celebration of their finds had come more and more to rest on the historical, rather than aesthetic, importance of the objects they uncovered. Digs in Assyria, Egypt, and Abyssinia (at Axum, 1906) led excavators far beyond Winckelmann's horizons, even beyond Schliemann's "new world," into cultural epochs increasingly less amenable to the philologically based pedagogy institutionalized in German higher education than the caricatured classicism of the Romantics. The progress of German archeological penetration into Asia Minor confirms the extent to which this nineteenth-century aestheticism, philological bias, and credo of non-utilitarian cultivation—the heritage and catechism of German archeologists before the 1880s—could be set aside in the rush to acquire more objects, more sites, more national glory. If the rise of *Orientforschung* and excavation in Asia Minor did not completely divert scholarly attention from the Mediterranean world, or eradicate the neohumanist proclivity for words over things, it did, like the school reform movement, indicate the extent to which the "tyranny of Greece" no longer held the German nation in its thrall.

After Schliemann's excavations at Troy and Mycenae, it had become increasingly evident that the quest for the foundations of European civilization would take scholars deep into the preliterate past. Yet most scholarly historians of antiquity did not yet take the testimony provided by objects seriously and found archeological reports interesting only insofar as they illuminated textual evidence. This was particularly the case in "oriental" studies, so long bound up with the study of Christian theology. In 1902, Friedrich Delitzsch opened the first of his three extremely popular lectures on the topic "Babel und Bibel" (which the Kaiser ordered him to repeat in private) with the following explication of Germany's investments in archeology in the Near East: "Why expend such energy in this far away, inhospitable, dangerous land? Why this costly ransacking of this millennia-old rubbish heap, all the way down to water level, when there is no gold or silver to be found? Why this international competition to secure as many as possible of these desolate mounds for excavation? . . . To these questions, there is but one answer, if not an exhaustive one; the major motivation and goal [of these endeavors] is *the Bible*" (Delitzsch 1902:1).

Delitzsch's interest in the new discoveries was clearly structured by his philological training; the importance of the objects described in his lectures depended on their ability to corroborate or correct literary accounts. Delitzsch's archeological evidence served primarily to buttress what proved to be an anti-Semitic attack on the integrity and sanctity of the Old Testament (see Delitzsch 1921); neither he nor the many antagonists his lectures called forth believed Babylonian artifacts to be worthy of consideration beyond the confines of this theological debate (Delitzsch 1904:57; Lehmann 1994). If the archeologists had demonstrated their ability to delve beneath the textual testimony of the ancient Near East, the frame into which the orientalists placed this material was recognizably the legacy of nineteenth-century critical philology.

Curiously too, improvements in archeology's social and scientific status were not accompanied by any major attempts to reconceive the secular culture of the ancient world. By the 1890s, both prevailing modes of "archeological" analysis bequeathed by Winckelmann to his nineteenth-century followers— the aesthetic appraisal and the iconographic/style-historical analysis of the individual artifact—had given way to "scientific" descriptions of sites and finds, at least in the accounts rendered by on-site excavators. Now that an increasing number of excavators were trained architects, rather than historians (as was Ernst Curtius) or philologists (as were Richard Lepsius and Alexander Conze), excavation reports included many more measurements and discussions of building materials than interpretations of objects or rhapsodies on the splendors of ancient form. Wilhelm Dörpfeld, the architect who secured "scientifically" Schliemann's claim to Hissarlik's Trojan authenticity, was much to blame for this shift in style, as was also Conze, who demanded thorough-going "physiognomic" investigations of building complexes (see Conze 1897). In imitation of these two anti-aesthetic, architecturally oriented excavators, on-site archeologists took to carefully recording details and dimension, postponing historical or cultural generalizations until full, exacting description was complete.

If painstaking archeological reporting was heavily influenced by the work of Conze and Dörpfeld, however, so too did several practical aspects of the post-1870 digs contribute to the maturation of this late-arriving archeological positivism. First, with a few obvious exceptions like the Pergamon altar, Reich excavators turned up little in the way of monumental sculpture, the bread and butter of nineteenth-century iconological analysis. This would prove particularly true in Mesopotamia, where centuries of grave-robbing and recent British and French treasure-trawling had left the Germans little in the way of moveable museum pieces. Second, iconographic analysis like that of Winckelmann or Otto Jahn (or, for that matter, like Erwin Panofsky's "iconology"), depends on the situation of the artifact in a universe of other contemporary texts and artifacts; in contrast, the objects issuing from relatively unstudied cultures, whose literary remains were fragmentary at best, and whose chronology and contacts with other cultures were the subject of wide speculation and dispute, resisted the sort of contextualization necessary for such discussion. Third, the very specialized technical skills and willingness to relocate to "uncivilized" sites in the East that made excavators valuable to the museums and the academic community also made them unsuitable as interpreters of meaning. Far from the Reich's libraries and lacking in the strict philological training demanded of the professoriate, the site archeologist himself was expected to make his reports as accurate, succinct, and theory-free as possible.[3] Finally, as the Kaiserreich succeeded in acquiring permit after permit in the East, on-site archeologists had little time to consider artifacts individually. Duty to science and to the state called them to proceed with excavation as rapidly as possible and to delay analysis of meaning for the future, a practice which the art critic Karl Scheffler later identified as *Anhäufungspolitik*, or the policy of heaping things up (Wenk 1985:25–26). Stuffing museum basements with easily attainable artifacts of unknown value in order to preserve them for later "scientific" inquiry, *Anhäufungspolitik* was the perfect museological expression of the *pénétration pacifique*.

In the case of the excavations in the Orient, all of these practical factors mitigating against interpretations of meaning were exacerbated by the mutual

3. The discrepancy in the styles of excavators and interpreters is clearly reflected in the *Jahrbuch des DAI*, in which the main articles down to World War I were still largely iconological investigations of Greek and Roman sculpture, vases, and mosaics, while site reports, stressing street plans, water channels, and measurements, were printed in the *Archäologischer Anzeiger*, an information sheet attached to the *Jahrbuch*. The sudden increase of new digs, acquisitions, and archeological activity is witnessed by the fact that, by 1906, the *Anzeiger* had overtaken the *Jahrbuch* article section in length; in 1912, the ratio was 706 pages in the *Anzeiger* to just 344 pages of *Jahrbuch* articles.

hostility between Orient Society excavators and many members of the academy, as well as by the precarious political position of the Reich in Ottoman cultural affairs. In Babylon, Koldewey dug winter and summer, with between 200 and 250 workers, leaving himself little time to appraise individual pieces. The eccentric architect was anxious to finish this dig, central to his plan for the systematic excavation of all of Mesopotamia, before German-Turkish relations degenerated and permits were apportioned to rival nations. The Berliners remained unimpressed by Koldewey's discovery of colored tile reliefs and enjoined the excavator to look for inscriptions (Andrae 1952:145), and a quarrel with Delitzsch further accelerated digging rather than deliberation. As Andrae later recalled, the excavators of Babylon (at the time) possessed no particular sensitivity to or interest in religious matters, and none could "read" the art objects uncovered,

> . . . because no one understood their language. Images of gods, images of kinds, the largest and the smallest, down to terra cottas the size of your hand—[these] might have borne witness to the hierarchies of the spiritual world, which cannot be expressed in words and writing. How many thousands of naked figures of women, figures of armed men, groups of gods and groups of animals have passed through the hands of excavators, been registered, and put aside. Have they received any evaluation of their true content, of their image-language [*Bildsprache*]? (Andrae 1952:217)

Koldewey and Andrae themselves had had little chance to evaluate the religio-cultural meaning of excavated pieces; while the penury and diplomatic isolation of the 1920s had furnished some archeologists time for interpretation and reflection, the rich remains of Mesopotamian culture remained in Lisbon, inaccessible to the excavators. Koldewey did not live to see his finds returned to the Reich, and could participate neither in the publication of the project's results nor in the reconstruction of the Ishtar gate, finished only in 1930 (Andrae 1952:172, 246).

The Ishtar gate is not the sole example of the slow progress of oriental objects from the excavation site to the Berlin museums. In fact, it remained the *only* object in the Asia Minor section of the Pergamon museum until 1934, when exhibits were at last mounted of oriental materials that had languished thirty years and longer in museum basements (Oppeln-Bronikowski 1934:18). Despite the museums' avid participation in the *acquisition* of oriental *Realien*, considerably less ardor, it seems, was put into their exhibition. Artifacts of eastern, non-classical provenance had been combined with Egyptian objects until Delitzsch's appointment as head of a separate Asia Minor Department in 1899. Limitations of space in existing museum buildings and internal strife complicated an already difficult process of assimilating new antiquities into the existing collections of casts, coins, and *Kleinkunst*, and orientalia did not have first priority in reorganizations. Of course, material from classical sites in Asia

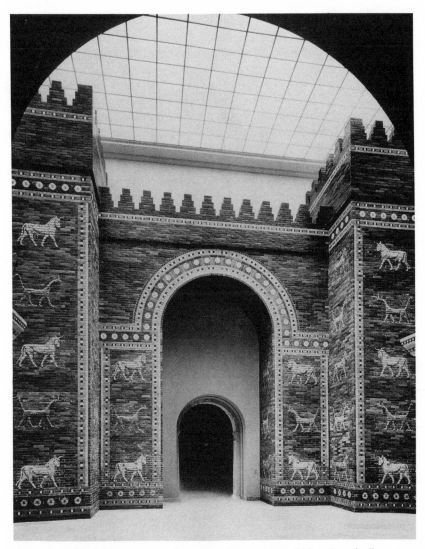

After years of languishing in museum basements, the reconstructed Ishtar Gate finally went on display at the Pergamon museum in 1930. (Courtesy of the Bildarchiv preussischer Kulturbesitz, Berlin.)

Minor such as Miletus, Baalbek, Priene, and Pergamon came not to the Asia Minor Department but fell under the sculpture or antiquities departments. Mschatta posed a categorization dilemma, which, to Bode's considerable vexation, was solved by placing the monumental gateway in the basement of the new Kaiser Friedrich Museum (largely for German artifacts) (Schmidt-Ott

1952:80). East Asian art (mostly porcelains) was sent to the Arts and Crafts Museum, while Islamic pieces were generally consigned to the overcrowded ethnography museum until they received their own museum section in 1932 (1952:79).

The preoccupation with classical antiquity characteristic of nineteenth-century German universities, *Gymnasien,* and the state bureaucracy cast long shadows over the interpretation of artifacts uncovered in excavations in the Orient, as did philhellenism's diplomatic complement, the "intellectual conquest" of Asia Minor. Not only did pre- and especially post-classical oriental artifacts remain largely hidden from the view of the general public, but interpretation of these items fell largely to the lot of university philologists or theologians, steeped in the classical and Biblical traditions of the West. The predictable result was not only the eschewal of questions involving cross-cultural comparisons, but also the underappreciation of the originality and "otherness" of the Orient. The combination of occidental biases and the *Anhäufungspolitik* practiced by cultural imperialists had resulted in very limited intellectual gains, despite the enormous scholarly, political, and social energies invested in "oriental" endeavors.

Acknowledgments

I would like to thank Victor Stater, Margot Browning, and George Stocking for their helpful comments on and criticisms of this essay. Versions of the paper were presented to the History of Human Sciences Workshop at the University of Chicago and at a symposium on "German History from Perspective of Art Collectors, Donors, Museums" at the Institute for Advanced Study; another version of the essay will appear in my forthcoming book on German philhellenism (Princeton University Press, 1996). Research on this topic was made possible by a grant from the Social Sciences Research Council (1989/90), and a summer research grant from Princeton University (1993).

References Cited

Andrae, W. 1927a. Der Rückerwerb der Assur-Funde aus Portugal. *Mitteilungen der Deutschen Orient-Gesellschaft* 65:1–6.
———. 1927b. Reise nach Babylon zur Teilung der Babylon-Funde. *Mitteilungen der Deutschen Orient-Gesellschaft* 65:7–27.
———. 1952. *Babylon: Die versunkene Weltstadt und ihr Ausgräber Robert Koldewey.* Berlin.
———. 1961. *Lebenserinnerungen eines Ausgräbers.* Berlin.
Bernal, 1987. *Black Athena: The Afroasiatic roots of classical civilization.* Vol. 1: *The fabrication of ancient Greece, 1785–1985.* New Brunswick.
Bode, W. von. 1930. *Mein Leben.* Vol. 2. Berlin.

Brunn, H. 1885. *Archäologie und Anschauung* (Rektorrede). Munich.

Conze, 1897. Pro Pergamon. In *Entdeckungen in Hellas*, ed. Heinrich A. Stoll 475–92. Berlin (1979).

Delitzsch, F. 1898. *Ex Oriente Lux! Ein Wort zur Förderung der deutschen Orient-Gesellschaft.* Leipzig.

———. 1902. *Babel und Bibel.* Stuttgart.

———. 1904. *Babel und Bibel: Ein Rückblick und Ausblick.* Stuttgart.

———. 1921. *Die grosse Täuschung.* 2d edition. Stuttgart.

Ferber, C. von. 1956. *Die Entwicklung des Lehrkörpers der deutsche Universitäten und Hochschulen, 1864–1954.* Vol. 3. Göttingen.

Fück, J. 1955. *Die arabischen Studien in Europa bis in den Anfang des 20. Jahrhunderts.* Leipzig.

Grafton, A. 1991. *Defenders of the text: The tradition of scholarship in an age of science, 1450–1800.* Cambridge, Mass.

Lehmann, R. G. 1994. *Friedrich Delitzsch und der Babel-Bibel Streit.* Freiburg, Switzerland.

Lewis, B. 1961. *The Emergence of modern Turkey.* London.

Marchand, S. 1992. Archaeology and cultural politics in Germany, 1800–1965: The rise and fall of German philhellenism. Doct. diss., University of Chicago.

———. 1994. The rhetoric of artifacts and the decline of classical neohumanism: The case of Joseph Strzygowski. *History and Theory* Beiheft (December): 106–130.

Momigliano, A. 1990. The rise of antiquarian research. In *The classical foundations of modern historiography*, 54–79. Berkeley.

Oppeln-Bronikowski, F. von. 1934. Kulturelle Höchleistung. *Deutsche Zukunft* 5/27/34, p. 18 (in BSB/WA, Kasten 5).

Pallat, L. 1959. *Richard Schöne.* Berlin.

Renger, J. 1979. Die Geschichte der Altorientalistik und der vorderasiatischen Archäologie in Berlin von 1875 bis 1945. In *Berlin und die Antike*, ed. W. Arenhövel & C. Schreiber, I:151–92. Berlin.

Roider, K. 1980. The Oriental Academy in the *Theresienzeit. Topic: A Journal of the Liberal Arts* 34:19–28.

Rossi, P. 1984. *The dark abyss of time: The history of the earth and the history of nations from Hooke to Vico.* Trans. Lydia G. Cochrane. Chicago.

Said, E. 1978. *Orientalism.* New York.

Schmidt-Ott, F. 1952. *Erlebtes und Erstrebtes, 1860–1950.* Wiesbaden.

Schöllgen, G. 1981. "Dann müssen wir uns aber Mesopotamien sichern!" *Saeculum* 32(2): 130–45.

———. 1984. *Imperialismus und Gleichgewicht: Deutschland, England und die orientalische Frage, 1871–1914.* Munich.

Schwab, R. 1984. *The Oriental Renaissance: Europe's rediscovery of India and the East, 1680–1880.* Trans. G. Patterson-Black & V. Reiking. New York.

Shaffer, E. S. 1975. *"Kubla Khan" and the fall of Jerusalem.* Cambridge, Eng.

Trumpener, U. 1968. *Germany and the Ottoman empire, 1914–1918.* Princeton.

Watzinger, C. 1944. *Theodor Wiegard.* Munich.

Wenk, S. 1985. *Auf den Spuren der Antike: Theodor Wiegand, ein deutscher Archäologe.* Bendorf am Rhein.

Wiegand, G., ed. 1970. *Halbmond im letzten Viertel: Briefe und Reiseberichte aus der alten Türkei von Theodor und Marie Wiegand 1895 bis 1918*. Munich.

Manuscript Sources

Abbreviations

BSB   Berlin, Staatsbibliotek. "WA" indicates the papers (Nachlaß) of Walter Andrae.

DAI   Deutsches Archäologisches Institut Archiv. "TW" indicates the papers (Nachlaß) of Theodor Wiegand. "CH" indicates the papers (Nachlaß) of Carl Humann.

M   Merseberg, Zentrales Staatsarchiv. Documents subtitled 2.2.1 belong to the files of the Kaiser's Civil Cabinet (Zivil Kabinet). The sub-heading "FS" refers to the papers (Nachlaß) of Friedrich Schmidt-Ott.

P   Potsdam, Zentrales Staatsarchiv. All files cited above come from the Foreign Ministry, Legal Affairs Section (Auswärtiges Amt, Rechtsabteilung). "DVzEP" indicates Deutsche Verein zur Erforschung Palästinas.

PA/AA   Politisches Archiv, Auswärtiges Amt (Bonn). All citations in this paper come from the Cultural Section (Kulturabteilung) of the Foreign Ministry.

StMB   Staatliche Museen zu Berlin, Zentralarchiv. "IM" indicates Islamisches Museum.

Abbreviations

AA   Auswärtiges Amt (Foreign Ministry)
EC   (German) Embassy Constantinople
EP   (German) Embassy Pera
ET   (German) Embassy Therapia
ZK   Zivil Kabinet (Civil Cabinet)

INDEX